GENEALOGICAL

PERIODICAL

ANNUAL

INDEX

KEY TO THE
GENEALOGICAL LITERATURE

CATHERINE M. MAYHEW, COMPILER
LAIRD C. TOWLE, PH.D., EDITOR

VOL. 18   1979

HERITAGE BOOKS, INC.

3602 MAUREEN LANE, BOWIE, MD 20715

ISBN 0-917890-24-8

INTRODUCTION

GPAI is the only comprehensive surname, locality, topical, and book review index to the genealogical periodical literature. As such it strives to encompass all English-language genealogical periodicals. The current edition covers 147 genealogical periodicals with about 7700 index citations.

In preparing the index entries each article is scanned to identify its true content which is often not revealed adequately by its title. In this manner the depth of coverage is made much greater than could be attained by merely combining tables of contents. In addition, coverage includes all the book reviews appearing in all the genealogical periodicals covered. Thus most of the genealogical books published in the 1978-1979 period are cited here under the appropriate surname, locality, or topical heading. This feature should add greatly to the researchers ability to locate recently published genealogical material. Heraldry and related subjects are also included. Surname periodicals are noted under the principal spelling of the name, but are not indexed in detail.

All the periodicals indexed in GPAI are contributed by their publishers for that purpose. If there is a periodical you wish to see included in future issues of the index, please contact the editor of that periodical suggesting that his periodical would be well served by being included in GPAI, and also notify GPAI of the existence of the new periodical.

GPAI is protected by copyright law. No part of GPAI may be reproduced by any means without the express permission of the editor, except that brief excerpts may be quoted for book review purposes.

HOW TO USE GPAI

The GPAI index is based primarily on surname, locality, and topical categories. Look for the desired references under these classifications bearing in mind variant spellings of surnames, and the various names by which a locality may have been known during successive historical periods.

Articles dealing with compiled genealogical data, family records, etc., are indexed under the name of the male head of the household or family in most cases. This is followed by his date of birth, marriage, or death when given, or by the approximate date when he flourished. The names of his spouse(s) are also included in the citation followed by the geographic areas where he and/or his descendants are known to have lived as revealed in the article. In those cases where a woman is the principal subject of the article, it is indexed under her name using an analogous format.

Some description of the type and scope of the article is also furnished using abbreviations such as "geneal", "fam rec", etc. For indexing purposes "geneal" means a compiled genealogical record usually covering three or more generations; "fam rec" means a brief description covering one or two generations; "lineage" usually refers to a multi-generation account of one line of descent.

Articles dealing with source records are indexed under the appropriate geographic heading. For the most part United States locations are arranged by states, while foreign locations are indexed first by country, then by state or province as appropriate. The citations include a description of the type of records appearing in the article and the time period covered. Unfortunately, the latter is often not adequately specified in the articles.

Book reviews are indexed under surname, locality, or topic just as are regular articles, except that the citation identifies it as a book review using the abbreviation "bk rev". Authors names and dates of publication have been omitted in the interest of brevity. In a few cases where books by different authors fall into exactly the same index category the author's names have been added in parenthesis.

GPAI does not index queries, society news, reprinted material, or items of transient interest, but does index all material of archival value. Since many articles could be indexed under several different headings, but normally are not, the reader would be well advised to look for possible alternative headings and spend some time browsing through the index.

The reference citation to the periodical is given at the end of each index entry using code letters identifying the periodical and the notation - volume:number:beginning page. A table lists the code letters for each periodical indexed along with the address of the publisher and the specific issues indexed.

Extensive use of abbreviations is made in the interest of brevity in the citations. In most cases these are self-evident, but a table of abbreviations is included for reference. The states of the United States are abbreviated by the well-known official two-letter postal designations which are not included in the table.

The periodicals covered by this index will be found in most large genealogical libraries, and in many smaller libraries as well, depending on their areas of interest. If your local library does not have the periodicals you need, try to obtain them by inter-library loan, or purchase the individual back numbers needed. If you choose the latter approach, direct a paid-reply postcard to the publisher requesting current information on availability and cost for the specific issues of interest to you.

ABBREVIATIONS

abstr-abstract   admin-administration
acc-account   affdt-affidavit
add-addition   Am-American

anc ch-ancestor chart
Angl-Anglican
anniv-anniversary
appl-application
apprent-apprentiship
Arg-Argentina
assoc-association
Aust-Austria
Austral-Australia
auto-autobiography
avail-available

b-born
B C-British Columbia
bapt-baptism
Bapt-Baptist
Bar-Baron, Baroness
Barb-Barbados
bibl-bibliography
biog-biography
bk-book
BLWT-bounty land warrant
bp-baptized
bro-brother
bus-business

c-circa
C Z-Canal Zone
Can-Canada
cat-catalog
Cath-Catholic
cem-cemetery
cert-certificate
ch-church
child-children
Co-County
Col-Colonial
collect-collection
Cong-Congregational
cont-continued
Cont-Continental
corr-correction
Czech-Czechoslovakia

d-died
dau-daughter
delinq-delinquent
Den-Denmark
depos-deposition
desc-descendant
descr-description
dict-dictionary
direct-directory

ed-edition
elem-elementary
emig-emigrant
encyc-encyclopedia
Eng-English, England
Epis-Episcopal
Eur-Europe
Evang- Evangelical

f-flourished
fam-family
Fed-Federal
Fin-Finland
Fr-France

gen-generation
geneal-genealogy, genealogical
geog-geographical
Ger-Germany
grad-graduate
guard-guardianship

h-husband
hist-historical, history
Hol-Holland
Hung-Hungary

illust-illustrated
incl-including
inscr-inscription
intro-intorduction
imm-immigration, immigrant
inv-inventory
Ir-Ireland
It-Italy
LDS-Latter Day Saint
lib-library
lic-license
Luth-Lutheran

m-married
marr-marriage
memb-member
Menn-Mennonite
Meth-Methodist
mil-military
misc-miscellaneous
mort-mortality
mss-manuscripts

N B-New Brunswick
N E-New England
N S-Nova Scotia

Neth-Netherlands
news-newspaper
Nor-Norway
soc-society
O-Ontario
obit-obituary
orig-original

pass-passenger
period-periodical
pet-petition
Pol-Poland
poss-possible
prep-prepare
Pres-Presbyterian
prof-professional
Prov-Provincial
Prus-Prussia
publ-published, publication

rec-record
recoll-recollections
ref-reference
reg-register, regiment
Repub-Republican
req-requirement
res-research
rev-review
Rev-Revolutionary
RR-railroad
Rus-Russia

sched-schedule
Scot-Scotland
sis-sister
soc-society
Sp-Spain, Spanish
superint-superintendents
supp-supplement
Sw-Swedeb
Switz-Switzerland

tech-technique
Terr-Territory
territ-territorial
trans-transcription
twp-township

Univ-University

v-volume
vr-vital records
vet-veteran
vol-volunteer

w-wife
W-Wales
wid-widow
WW-World War

x-extra issue

PERIODICALS INDEXED

AB The Appleland Bulletin - The Genealogical Society of North Central Washington, POB 613, Wenatchee, WA 98801 7:3-4 8:1-2

ACL Allen County Lines - Allen County Genealaogical Society, POB 12003, Ft. Wayne, IN 46862 4:1-4

AG The American Genealogist - Dr George E McCracken, 1232 39th Street, Des Moines, IA 50311 55:1-2

AGE Acadian Genealogy Exchange, 863 Wayman Branch Road, Covington, KY 41015 8:1-4

AGS Austin Genealogical Society Quarterly - Austin Genealogical Society, Box 774, Austin, TX 78767 20:1-4

AH Ancestor Hunt - Ashtabula County Genealogical Society, c/o Henderson Library, 54 E. Jefferson St., Jefferson, OH 44047 1:2-3 2:2-4 3:1-4 4:1-4 5:2-4 6:1,4

ANC Ancestry - Palm Beach County Genealogical Society, POB 1746, West Palm Beach, FL 33402 14:1-4

AW Ancestors West - Santa Barbara County Genealogical Society, POB 1174, Goleta, CA 93017 5:1-4

BB Beaver Briefs - Willamette Valley Genealogical Society, POB 2083, Salem, OR 97308 11:1-4

BCG The British Columbia Genealogist - The British Columbia Genealogical Society, 100 West 49th Avenue, Vancouver, British Columbia, Canada 5:1-4 6:1-4 7:1-4 8:1-4

BGS Boulder Genealogical Society Quarterly, Boulder Genealogical Society, POB 3246, Boulder, CO 80307 1:1,2 2:1-3 3:1-4 4:1-4 5:1-4 6:1-4 7:1-4 8:1-4 9:1-4 10:1-4 11:1-4

BR Bluegrass Roots - Kentucky Genealogical Society, POB 153, Frankfort, KY 40601 6:1-4

BWG Bulletin of the Watauga Assoc of Genealogists - Watauga Assoc of Genealogists, Sherrod Library, East Tennessee State Univ, Johnson City, TN 37601 8:1-2

CDS Car-Del Scribe, Box 716, Middleboro, MA 02346 16:1-6

CHG Chicago Genealogist - Chicago Genealogical Society, POB 1160, Chicago, IL 60690 11:1

CHI Concordia Historical Institute Quarterly - Concordia Historical Institute, 801 De Mun Avenue, St Louis, MO 63105 52:1-4

CI Central Illinois Genealogical Quarterly - Decatur Genealogical Society, POB 2205, Decatur, IL 62526 11:1-4 12:1-4 13:1,3,4 14:1-4 15:1-4

CLG The Colonial Genealogist - The Hartwell Company, 1617 West 261st Street, Harbor City, CA 90710 10:1,3

CO Colorado Genealogist - Colorado Genealogical Society, POB 9671, Denver, CO 80209 40:1-4

CPY The Certified Copy - Greater Cleveland Genealogical Society, POB 9639, Cleveland, OH 44140 8:1-4

CSB Copper State Bulletin- Arizona State Genealogical Society, POB 42075, Tucson, AZ 85733 14:1-4

CTA Connecticut Ancestry - The Stamford Genealogical Society, Inc, c/o Ferguson Library, 96 Broad Street, Stamford, CT 06904 21:3,4 22:1,2

CTB The Connecticut Historical Society Bulletin - The Connecticut Historical Society, 1 Elizabeth Street, Hartford, CT 06105 44:1-4

CTN The Connecticut Nutmegger - Connecticut Society of Genealogists Inc, POB 435, Glastonbury, CT 06033 7:1-4 8:1-4 9:1-4 10:1-4 11:1-4 12:1-4

DAR Daughters of American Revolution Magazine - N.S.D.A.R., 1776 D Street, Washington, DC 20006 113:1-10

DC The Dutchess - Dutchess County Genealogical Society, POB 708, Poughkeepsie, NY 12602 7:1-2

DCG Douglas County, Georgia Genealogy, 8823 Rose Avenue, Douglasville, GA 30134 2:10

DE Downeast Ancestry - Rosemary E Bachelor & Mary H Dormer, POB 398, Machias, ME 04654 2:5-6 3:1-4

DG Dallas Genealogical Society Quarterly - Dallas Genealogical Society, POB 12648, Dallas, TX 75225 25:1-4

DM Detroit Society for Genealogical Research Magazine - Detroit Society for Genealogical Research, 5201 Woodward Avenue, Detroit, MI 48202 42:3-5 43:1-2

DWC De Witt County Genealogical Society Quarterly - De Witt County Genealogical Society, Box 329, Clinton, IL 61727 5:1-4

EG   The English Genealogist - The Hartwell Company, 1617 West
     261st Street, Harbor City, CA 90710 #12

EWA Eastern Washington Genealogical Society Bulletin - Eastern
     Washington Genealogical Society, POB 1826, Spokane, WA 99210
     16:1-4

FAM Families - Ontario Genealogical Society, Box 66 Station Q,
     Toronto, Ontario, Canada M4T 2L7 18:1-4

FF   Fayette Facts - Fayette County Genealogical Society, POB 177,
     Vandalia, IL 62471 8:1-4

FG   Flint Genealogical Quarterly - Flint Genealogical Society, c/o
     Mrs Ransom L Richardson, 1150 Woodside Drive, Flint, MI 48503
     21:1-4

FH   Family Heritage, 26 Third Place, Brooklyn, NY 11231 2:1-4

FLG The Florida Genealogist - Florida Genealogical Society Inc,
     POB 10249, Tallahassee, FL 32302 2:1-4

FP   Footprints - Fort Wayne Genealogical Society, POB 9767, Fort
     Wayne, TX 76107 22:1-4

FTR The Family Tree - Howard County Maryland Genealogical Society,
     7373 Hickory Log Circle, Columbia, MD 21045 #20

GCB Grant County Beacon, 24 Herbel Drive, Marion, IN 46952 19:1-4

GE   Genealogy - Indiana Historical Society, 140 N Senate Avenue,
     Indianapolis, IN 46204 #42-49

GER Germanic Genealogist - The Hartwell Company, 1617 West 261st
     Street, Harbor City, CA 90710 #16,17,18

GFP Genealogical Forum of Portland, Oregon, Bulletin - Genealogi-
     cal Forum of Portland, Oregon, 1410 S W Morrison, Room 812,
     Portland, OR 97204 28:5-10 29:1-4

GGM Georgia Genealogical Magazine - Rev. Silas Emmett Lucas, Jr,
     POB 229, Easley, SC 29640 #71-74

GH   Genealogical Helper - Everton Publishers Inc, POB 368, Logan,
     UT 84321 33:1-6

GJ   Genealogical Journal - Utah Genealogical Assoc, POB 1144, Salt
     Lake City, UT 84110 8:1-4

GL   Gleanings From the Heart of the Cornbelt - The Bloomington-
     Normal Genealogical Society, POB B, Normal, IL 61761 13:1-4

GN   Genealogical Newsletter of the Nova Scotia Historical Society
     - c/o Terrence Punch, 30 Melwood Avenue, Armdale, Halifax,
     Nova Scotia #26,27,28,29

GNJ The Genealogical Magazine of New Jersey - Genealogical Society
     of New Jersey, POB 1291, New Brunswick, NJ 08903 54:1-3

GP   Georgia Pioneers Genealogical Magazine - Mary Carter, POB
     1028, Albany, GA 31702 16:1-4

GR   The Genealogical Record - The Houston Genealogical Forum, 7130
     Evans Street, Houston, TX 77061 21:1-4

HG   Hoosier Genealogist - Indiana Historical Society, 315 W Ohio
     Streetm Indianapolis, IN 46202 19:1-4

HH   Hawkeye Heritage - Iowa Genealogical Society, POB 3815, Des
     Moines, IA 50322 14:1-4

HJA Hoosier Journal of Ancestry, POB 33, Little York, IN 47139
     6:1-4

HTR Heart of Texas Records - Central Texas Genealogical Society
     Inc, 1717 Austin Avenue, Waco, TX 76701 22:1-4

IA   Irish Ancestor - Pirton House, Sydenham Villas, Dundrum, Dublin 14, Ireland 11:1-2

IG Illiana Genealogist - Illiana Genealogical and Historical Society, Box 207, Danville, IL 61832 15:1-4

IL Illinois State Genealogical Society Quarterly - Illinois State Genealogical Society, POB 2225, Springfield, IL 62705 11:1-4

IRA Irish American Genealogist - The Hartwell Company, 1617 West 261st Street, Harbor City, CA 90710 #13-16

ITG Italian Genealogist - The Hartwell Company, 1617 West 261st Street, Harbor City, CA 90710 #2

JCG Johnson Count Genealogist - Johnson County Genealogical Society & Library Inc, Box 8057, Shawnee Mission, KS 66208 7:1-4

JG Journal of Genealogy - Robert D Anderson, Box 31097, Omaha, NE 68131 4:1-4

JJG Toledot: Journal of Jewish Genealogy, 808 West End Avenue #1006, New York, NY 10025-7978 3:1-4

JMS Je Me Souviens - American-French Genealogical Society, POB 2113, Pawtucket, RI 02861 2:2

KA Kentucky Ancestors - Kentucky Historical Society, POB H, Frankfort, KY 40601 14:3,4, 15:1,2

KCG The Kansas City Genealogist - Heart of America Genealogical Society & Library, Kansas City Public Library, 311 East 12th Street, Kansas City, MO 64106 20:1-4

KFR Kentucky Family Records, POB 1465, Owensboro, KY 42301 7:81-100

KG Kern Gen - Kern County Genealogical Society, POB 2214, Bakersfield, CA 93303 16:1-2,4

KIL Knox County Genealogical Society Quarterly - Knox County Genealogical Society, POB 13, Galesburg, IL 61401 7:1-4

KK Kansas Kin - Riley County Genealogical Society, 2005 Claflin Road, Manhattan, KS 66502 17:1-4

KN Kinships - The South Bay Cities Genealogical Society, Suite 2, 1510 Cravens Avenue, Torrance, CA 90501 2:1-4

KY The Kentucky Genealogist, 118 W Breckenridge, Louisville, KY 40203 21:1-4

LL Lifeliner - Genealogical Society of Riverside, POB 2664, Riverside, CA 92506 14:1-4 15:1-4

LM Laurel Messenger - Somerset County Historical Society, Box 533, Somerset, PA 15501 20:1-4

MCH Moultrie County Heritage - Mountrie County Historical & Genealogical Society, POB MM, Sullivan, IL 61951 7:1-4

MCR Milwaukee County Genealogical Society Reporter - Milwaukee County Genealogical Society, 916 E Lyon Street, Milwaukee, WI 53202 10:1-6

MD Maryland Genealogical Society Bulletin - Maryland Genealogical Society, 201 W Monument Street, Baltimore, MD 21201 20:1-4

MGR Midwest Genealogical Register, Midwest Genealogical Society, Box 1121, Wichita, KS 67201 14:1-4

MH Menonite Heritage - Illinois Mennonite Historical & Genealogical Society, 918 S University, Normal, IL 61761 6:1-4

MHM Maryland Historical Magazine - Maryland Historical Society, 201 W Monument Street, Baltimore, MD 21201 74:3,4

MI Michigana - Western Michigan Genealogical Society, Library Plaza N E, Grand Rapids, MI 49502 24:1-4

MIS Michiana Searcher - Elkhart County Genealogical Society, 1812 Jeanwood Avenue, Elkhart, IN 46514 11:1-4

MKT The Marin Kin Tracer, Marin County Genealogical Society, POB 1511, Novato, CA 94947 2:1-4

MMG Maryland Magazine of Genealogy - Maryland Historical Society, 201 W Monument Street, Baltimore, MD 21201 2:2

MN Minnesota Genealogist - The Minnesota Genealogical Society, Box 16069, St Paul, MN 55116 10:1-4

MQ Mayflower Quarterly - General Society of Mayflower Descendants, POB 297, Plymouth, MA 02361 45:1-4

NA Nebraska Ancestree, 1420 East 32nd Street, Kearney, NE 68847 2:1,2

NAS Northeast Alabama Settlers, Northeast Alabama Genealogical Society, POB 674, Gadsden, AL 35902 17:3,4 18:1,2

NCJ The North Carolina Genealogical Society Journal - North Carolina Genealogical Society, POB 1492, Raleigh, NC 27602 5:1-4

NER New England Historical & Genealogical Register - New England Historic Genealaogical Society, 101 Newbury Street, Boston, MA 02116 133:1-4

NGI National Genealogical Inquirer - Janlen Enterprises, 2236 South 77th Street, West Allis, WI 53219 3:1-4

NGS National Genealogical Society Quarterly - National Genealogical Society, 1921 Sunderland Place N W, Washington, DC 20036 67:1-4

NMG New Mexico Genealogist - New Mexicoa Genealogical Society, Box 8734, Albuquerque, NM 87198 18:1-4

NSN North Suburban Genealogical Society Newsletter - North Suburban Genealogical Society, Winnetka Public Library, 768 Oak Street, Winnetka, IL 60093 4:1-6

NW Northwest Genealogical Society Quarterly - Northwest Genealogical Society, POB 6, Alliance, NE 69301 2:1-4

NYR New York Genealogical & Biographical Record, 122 East 58th Street, New York, NY 10022 110:1-4

OC Orange County Genealogical Society Quarterly - Orange County Genealogical Society, POB 1587, Orange, CA 92668 16:1-4

OG Olympia Genealogical Society Quarterly - Olympia Genealogical Society, c/o Olympia Public Library, 8th & Franklin, Olympia, WA 98501 1:1-4 2:1-4 3:1-3 4:2-4 5:1-4

OHR Ohio Records & Pioneer Families - Ohio Genealogical Society, 454 Park Avenue West, Mansfield, OH 44906 20:2-4

OK Oklahoma Genealogical Society Quarterly - Oklahoma Genealogical Society, POB 314, Oklahoma City, OK 73101 24:1-4

ORB Oregon Genealogical Society Bulletin - Oregon Genealogical Society, POB 1214, Eugene, OR 97400 17:5-10 18:1-4

PF The Pastfinder - Genealogical Assoc of S W Michigan, POB 573, St Joseph, MI 49085 8:3,4 9:1,2

PGB Prince George's County Genealogical Society Bulletin - Prince George's County Genealogical Society, POB 819, Bowie, MD 20715 11:1-10

PM Pennsylvania Mennonite Heritage - Lancaster Mennonite Conference Historical Society, 2215 Millstream Road, Lancaster, PA 17602 2:1-4

PN Polish Genealogical Society Newsletter, 984 Milwaukee Avenue,

Chicago, IL 60622 1:1-2

PR The Prairieland Register - Prairieland Genealogical Society, Southwest Historical Center, 703 North 6th Street, Marshall, MN 56258 3:1-4

PT Pioneer Trails - The Birmingham Genealogical Society Inc, POB 2432, Birmingham, AL 35201 21:1-4

QBC Connections - Quebec Family Historical Society, POB 1026, Postal Station Pointe Claire, Pointe Clarie, Quebec, Canada H9S 4H9 2:1

QY The Quaker Yeomen - James E Bellarts, POB 1791, Portland, OR 97207 6:1-4

RED Redwood Researcher - The Redwood Genealogical Society Inc, Box 645, Fortuna, CA 95540 11:3,4 12:1,2

REF The Reflector - Amarillo Genealogical Society, POB 2171, Amarillo, TX 79105 21:1-4

REG The Register - Kentucky Historical Society, Old State House, Frankfort, KY 40602 77:4

REP The Report - Ohio Genealogical Society, POB 2625, Mansfield, OH 44906 19:1-4

RES The Researcher - Tacoma Genealogical Society, POB 1952, Tacoma, WA 98401 11:1-4

RIR Rhode Island Roots - Rhode Island Genealogical Society, Box 207, Mapleville, RI 02839 5:1-4

RRS The Ridge Runners - William A Yates, POB 274 Ozark, MO 65721 12:1,2,X

SCC Santa Clara County Historical & Genealogical Society Quarterly - Santa Clara County Historical & Genealogical Society, 2635 Homestead Road, Santa Clara, CA 95051 15:3,4 16:1,2

SCG Scottish-American Genealogist - The Hartwell Company, 1617 West 261st Street, Harbor City, CA 90710 #13-16

SCR The Genealogical Record of Strafford County - Straffird County Chapter NHSOG, POB 322, Dover, NH 03820 2:3-6 3:1-2

SCS The Searcher - Southern California Genealogical Society Inc, The Sons of the Revolution Building, 600 S Central Avenue, Glendale, CA 91204 14:1-4 15:1-4 16:1-4

SGS Seattle Genealogical Society Quarterly Bulletin - Seattle Genealogical Society, POB 549, Seattle, WA 98111 29:1-4

SMV Santa Maria Valley Genealogical Society Quarterly - Santa Maria Valley Genealogical Society, POB 1215, Santa Maria, CA 93454 11:1

SN The Sequoia Genealogical Society Newsletter - The Sequoia Genealogical Society, POB 3473, Visalia, CA 93277 5:1-8

SPG Spanish-American Genealogist - The Hartwell Company, 1617 West 261st Street, Harbor City, CA 90710 #31-34

STC St Clair County Genealogical Society Quarterly - St Clair County Genealogical Society, POB 431, Belleville, IL 62222 2:1,2

STK Stalkin´ Kin - San Angelo Genealogical & Historical Society, POB 3453, San Angelo, TX 76901 7:1-4

TA Tulsa Annals - Tulsa Genealogical Society, POB 585, Tulsa, OK 74101 14:1-3

TAK The-A-Ki-Ki - Kankakee Valley Genealogical Society, 304 S Indiana Avenue, Kankakee, IL 60901 8:3-4 9:1-2

TB   Trail Breakers - Clark County Genealogical Society, 801 S E
     119th Avenue, Vancouver, WA 98664 6:1-4
THT The Thorny Trail - Midland Genealogical Society, POB 1191,
     Midland, TX 79701 1:1-2 2:1-2 3:1-2 4:1-4 5:1-4 6:1-4 7:1-2
TOP The Topeka Genealogical Society Quarterly - Topeka Genealogi-
     cal Society, POB 4048, Topeka, KS 66604 9:1-4
TRI Tri-City Genealogical Society Bulletin - Tri-City Genealogical
     Society, Rt 1 Box 191, Richland, WA 99352 17:1-4 19:1-4
TS   Treesearcher - Kansas Genealogical Society, Box 103, Dodge
     City, KS 67801 21:1-4
TSP The Tri-State Packet - Tri-State Genealogical Society, 21
     First Avenue, Evansville, IN 47710 2:3-4 3:1-2
TST Tri-State Trader - Genealogical Department, POB 90, Knights-
     town, IN 46148 11:39-52 12:1-37
TT   Tree Talks - Central New York Genealogical Society, Box 104,
     Colvin Station, Syracuse, NY 13205 19:1-4
TTL Timbertown Log - Saginaw Genealogical Society, 505 James Ave-
     nue, Saginaw, MI 48607 7:1-4
VA   Virginia Genealogical Society Quarterly - Virginia Genealogi-
     cal Society, POB 1397, Richmond, VA 23221 17:1-4
VAG The Virginia Genealogist - John Frederick Dorman, Box 4883,
     Washington, DC 20008 23:1-4
VL   Valley Leaves - Tennessee Valley Genealogical Society, POB
     1512, Huntsville, AL 35807 13:3,4 14:1,2
VQ   Valley Quarterly - San Bernadino Valley Genealogical Society,
     POB 2505, San Bernadino, CA 92406 16:1-4
WB   Whatcom Genealogical Society Bulletin - Whatcom Genealogical
     Society, POB 1493, Bellingham, WA 98225 9:3-4 10:1-2
WCK West-Central Kentucky Research Assoc Bulletin - West-Central
     Kentucky Family Research Assoc, POB 1465, Owensboro, KY 42301
     12:1-4
WI   Wisconsin State Genealogical Society Newsletter - Wisconsin
     State Genealogical Society, POB 207, Mequon, WI 53092 25:3,4
     26:1,2
WPA Western Pennsylvania Genealogical Quarterly - Western Pennsyl-
     vania Genealogical Society, 4338 Bigelow Blvd, Pittsburgh, PA
     15213 5:1-4
YP   Yellowed Pages - Southeast Texas Genealogical & Historical
     Society, POB 3827, Beaumont, TX 77704 9:1-4
YV   Yakima Valley Genealogical Society Bulletin - Yakima Valley
     Genealogical Society, POB 445, Yakima, WA 98907 11:1-4

ERRATA

It is unreasonable to expect that a publication of this type can
be flawless. Occasional human errors in the preparation of the
citations, as well as in the typing of the copy, are to be expect-
ed and must be excused. Since the citations to most periodicals
involve numerous references in any given issue of GPAI, and each
reference involves redundancy in that the volume, issue, and page
number are all given, these minor errors are easily overcome by
any capable researcher. The more serious errors are the

systematic ones that the reader may not be so able to spot and circumvent. Please make the following corrections to previous editions of GPAI:

Volume 14 - Add the periodical code: SWG The Southwestern Genealogist, 5301 Hanawalt, El Paso, TX 79903 13:1

Volume 17 - Three systematic errors have been detected: all references to "The North Carolina Genealogical Society Journal," code NCJ, were erroneously cited as NCR, a presently unused code; likewise, all references to the "Genealogical Newsletter of the Nova Scotia Historical Society," code GN, were erroneously cited as NS, another unused code; finally, the code DC was erroneously omitted from the table of periodicals indexed. This code is correctly identified above; the issues covered in Vol. 17 were 5:1-4 and 6:1-4.

We regret these errors and hope that they did not lead too many researchers astray.

ATTENTION GENEALOGICAL PERIODICAL EDITORS

If your periodical was not indexed in this issue of GPAI, you can assure its inclusion in future editions by contributing a complete file of back issues (beginning with 1974 if possible) and a current subscription to:

Genealogical Periodical Annual Index
Laird C Towle, Ph.D., Editor
3602 Maureen Lane
Bowie, MD 20715

The periodicals thus received will be indexed and included in the next issue of GPAI.

ABBOT, fam recs in Eng ch recs 1813-1861 BCG 7:1:16

Theodore d1864 w Hannah Blake Loring, MA, Bible rec CTN 10:3:418

ABBOTT, Daniel b1796 w Sally Sherman, CT, Bible rec CTN 12:2:234

Elijah Trial d1856 m Margaret Sarah Abbott, CT, Bible rec CTN 12:2:234

ABELL, Robert James b1867 w Mary Eliza Hatheway, MO, TX, CO, anc ch THT 7:2:78

ABRAMS, Hardin Taylor b1847 w Mary Knuce, Lucy Beard, IL, Bible rec CI 11:4:151

ADAM, Jacob Abraham f1823 w Maria Fecher, geneal, bk rev REP 19:2:91

ADAMS, Abigail b1712 h Samuel Adams, Richard Hale, CT, Bible recs BGS 10:4:27

Abigail (Smith) b1744 h John Adams-US Pres, MA, biog notes DAR 113:5:494

Claude Monroe b1905 w Gladys Pearl Haggart, WA, MO, anc ch FF 8:3:60

fam of IL, letters c1862 CI 11:2:45

Francis b1813 w Eleanor Green, OH, anc ch REP 19:1:26

Geoffrey William b1895 w Ethel Gray Vaughan, IL, KY, anc ch FF 8:2:26

Hannah Ann (White) b1838 h John Adams, IN, obit CI 15:1:12

Hiram b1805 w Elizabeth Staats, NY, MI, anc ch REP 19:1:31

Jeremiah b1794, CT, geneal, bk rec DM 42:3:136

Jesse J b1908 w Mary Rose Tuljus, PA, MI, anc ch OC 16:4:121

John b1711 w Mercy Sanderson, Abigail Faulkner, MA, Bible rec NGS 67:4:252

Nathan b1748 w Phebe Ensworth, CT, MA, Bible rec BGS 10:4:26

Nimrod b1790 w Nancy Etchison, NC, IN, anc ch REP 19:4:160

geneal, bl rev GH 33:2:82 IL

11:1:55 GE 42:10 KA 15:1:63 CDS 16:1:33

William Samuel b1848 w Julia Ellen Hammond, IL, geneal FF 8:3:71

ADAMSON, Jesse b1777 w Mart, TN, geneal CI 15:4:125

Thomas b1834, Bible rec CI 13:4:129

ADCOCK, John cf1812 w Nancy Ellender Hicks, NC, TN, IL, geneal FF 8:2:89

Ross Oswell b1912 w Ethel M Wallis, TX, OK, CA, anc ch NGI 3:3:177

ADDINGTON, Rebecca Ann (Leffler) b1855, OH, obit MCH 7:2:51

ADDISON, Anthony b1803 w Mary Juliet Thompson, MD, Bible rec MD 20:4:340

Henry m1751 w Rachel (Dulany) Knight, MD, Bible rec MD 20:4:337

ADLER, Theodore C b1832 w Henrietta Phillip, Ger, NY, Wi, auto & geneal BGS 9:1:19

ADOPTEES, adoption & name changes OR 1905-1907 BB 11:1:5

hist of adoption laws GE 42:1

notes on NGI 3:1:3 3:2:73 3:3:145

orphan trains from NY 1882 AH 1:2:17

personal searches KCG 20:1:24 SCS 16:2:36

search book for adult adoptees, bl rev GH 33:4:109

solving adoption problems in geneal GJ 8:2:72

ADY, Jonathan f1743 w Rebeckah, Bible rec MD 20:3:237

Jonathan m1807 w Elizabeth Mcatee, Bible rec MD 20:3:239

AHERN, P d1868, IR, WA, OBIT TB 6:2:9

AIKINS, William James b1837 w Phebe Jane Ebner, OH, IL, NE, UT, anc ch REP 19:3:128

AKINS, Arshall Richmond b1890 w Ida Myrtle Davis, MO, IL, anc ch FF 8:4:43

Thomas A b1808 w Margaret S

Rofs, MD, OH, MO, CO, Bible rec BGS 6:4:27

ALABAMA, Benton co, census 1850 NAS 17:3:87 17:4:107 18:1:13 18:2:43

Bibb Co, Bapt Ch hist, bk rev GH 33:6:77

Haysop Creek, Haysop Bapt Ch hist & cem inscr, bk rev GH 33:5:71 TST 12:36:23 OK 24:3:138 KCG 20:4:208

Birmingham, hist notes PT 21:1:9

Relay House guest reg 1881-1882 PT 21:1:3 21:2:43 21:3:83 21:4:123

Blount Co, hist, bk rev YP 9:1:37

Butler Co, hist, bk rev YP 9:2:104

Cherokee Co, census 1850 NAS 17:3:89 17:4:111 18:1:19 18:2:49

Cleburne Co, Ross fam cem inscr NAS 17:4:105

Colbert Co, census 1855 VL 13:3:109

Robert Morley White cem inscr VL 13:3:101

Shaw cem inscr VL13:4:151 14:1:5 14:2:55

Coldwater, hist & map VL 14:2:51

Confederate soldiers living 1907 NAS 17:3:85 17:4:98

DeKalb Co, geneal & hist notes v3, bk rev YP 9:4:230

geneal & hist notes v4, bk rev YP 9:4:230

McNaron cem inscr NAS 18:2:39

Newman cem inscr NAS 18:2:39

Nicholson fam cem inscr THT 2:2:32

tax recs 1852, 1855 NAS 18:2:40

Franklin Co, census 1855 VL 13:3:109

Ezzell fam cem VL 13:4:153

Frankfort, old Frankfort cem inscr VL 13:3:103

mort sched 1870 VL 13:3:105

Russellville, Mt Pleasant Meth Ch, notes on VL 14:1:7

hist 1800-1860, bk rev MHM 74:4:374

Jackson Co, Chancery Court Rec bk "O" 1846-1847 VL 14:2:60

mort sched 1870 VL 13:3:114 13:4:162 14:1:12

old Bostick Hill cem inscr VL 14:1:14

probate recs 1856-1857 VL 13:3:111 13:4:159 14:1:9 14:2:59

Jefferson Co, census 1880 PT 21:1:31 21:2:69 21:3:109 21:4:143

census 1880 index PT 21:4:151

Concord Bapt Ch cem inscr PT 21:1:11 21:2:51 21:3:91

marr recs 1855-1859 PT 21:1:15 21:2:55 21:3:95 21:4:131

orphans court recs 1837-1844 PT 21:1:28 21:2:61 21:3:103 21:4:137

orphans recs bk 2 1830-1837 PT 21:1:25

Lamar Co, Bethabara cem inscr PT 21:3:94

Lauderdale Co, Civil War Bushwackers hist, bk rev GH 33:5:72

North Carolina cem inscr VL 13:3:117 13:4:165 14:1:15 14:2:63

Lawrence Co, misc news abstr VL 13:3:126

tract bk VL 14:1:19 14:2:70

Limestone Co, deed rec I 1819-1825 VL 13:4:177 14:1:29 14:2:77

marrs 1854-1858 VL 13:3:127 13:4:173 14:1:25 14:2:73

Lowndes Co, Braggs, New Bethel Bapt Ch minutes 1828-1868, bk rev GH 33:5:71 KCG 20:4:211

Collirene, hist, bk rev NYR 110:2:122

Madison Co, Big Voce Mt Pleasant Soc session bk VL 13:3:133 13:4:183 14:1:35 14:2:85

births reg 1886-1902 VL 13:3:133 13:4:181 14:1:33 14:2:83

Helion Lodge #1 VL 13:3:135

Huntsville PO unclaimed letters 1833 VL 13:4:179 14:1:31

land recs, bk rev VL 14:2:95

natural recs VL 14:2:79

Marathon, hist & map VL 14:1:1

Marshall Co, orphan's court 1836-1837 VL 13:3:140 14:2:90

probate minutes 1836-1839 VL 13:3:137 13:4:185 14:1:37 14:2:87

misc abstr court cases 1898 MCR 10:3:74

misc biogs to 1870, bk rev CTN 9:3:474

misc fams geneal, bk rev YP 9:1:37

misc geneal notes v1,2, bk rev NYR 110:1:56

misc recs v3-4, bk rev NGS 67:1:73

Mobile, arrival on ship "Pelican" 1704 of Pelican girls AGE 8:2:58

Morgan Co, deed bk A 1826-1827 VL 13:3:143 13:4:194 14:1:43 14:2:91

Rock Creek cem inscr VL 13:3:141 13:4:191 14:1:41

mort sched 1850 NAS 17:4:100

mort sched 1860 NAS 17:4:101

Muscle Shoals, hist v5, bk rev GH 33:1:82

hist v6, bk rev GH 33:1:82

muster roll 1836 Capt Shockleford's Co of Army of Repub of TX VL 14:1:58

Natchitoches, hist, bk rev GH 33:1:82

US Post Office clerks 1889 PT 21:2:92 21:4:125

ALBER,Marvin Elmer b1919 w Dorothy Lucille Davis, NE, CO, anc ch BGS 10:3:43

ALBERTSON, fam of NY, geneal NYR 110:1:10 110:1:88

ALBRECHT, fam geneal, bk rev KCG 20:4:204

ALBRITTON, Francis bc1609, VA, geneal, bk rev STK 7:2:58

ALDERMAN, William Sr bc1640 w Mary Case, CT, geneal, bk rev BB 11:3:47

ALDRICH, Amasa b1786 w Eleanor Clarke, Bible rec CTN 12:2:232

Nelson Wilmarth b1841 w Abby P Chapman/Greene, RI, biog RIR 5:3:1

Seymour f1846, letter KN 2:3:34

ALDRIDGE, Joshua f1804, KY, Bible rec THT 6:1:13

ALEXANDER,Guy Ernest b1895 w Marion Gertrude Grant, MA, ME, anc ch BGS 11:2:83

Lyman Terry b1864 w Emma Stell Winney, TX, geneal THT 5:3:11

ALFORD, Russell b1824 w Martha Jane Rodgers, MO, OR, biog notes ORB 17:5:47

ALFRED, William, geneal (1970), bk rev LL 15:2:82

ALFSON, John J b1845 w Groe Gunufsdotter, Norway, W, Bible rec PR 3:1:7

ALGYER, David b1812 w Elizabeth Selmer, NY, IL, Bible rec PR 3:2:45

ALLAN, fam of Scot & VA, geneal NGS 67:2:98

ALLEN, Sarah Sylvine b1867 to D A Reardon, Bible rec CTN 12:3:415

Timothy b1691 w Rebecca Cary Rachel Bushnel, CT, geneal CTN 7:2:30

Timothy b1712, CT, notes on CTN 7:2:301

Timothy b1715 w Dorothy (Gallup) Read, CT, biog notes CTN 7:2:300

Timothy b1748 w Mary Allan, Lois Silsby, CT, biog notes CTN 7:2:300

Timothy Jr b1715 w Sarah Parmalee, Jerusha, CT, geneal CTN 7:2:301

ALLENBACH, George Robert b1910 w Irene Isabel Richardson, MO, CO, anc ch BGS 9:3:41

ALLERTON, & related fams, geneal, bk rev SGS 29:1:68

Isaac f1653 w Elizabeth, geneal notes MQ 45:1:23

ALLING, Roger f1640, Eng, CT, geneal 1899, bk rev CTN

10:2:346

ALLISON, fam of NC, geneal, bk rev GH 33:6:85

AMBROOK, Mary (Lilley) b1849 h Charles Ambrook, MA, CO, biog notes BGS 5:4:12

AMERICAN INDIAN, Algonquin legends of New England: folk lore of Micinac, Passamaquoddy & Penobscot tribes (1884), bk rev CDS 16:3:4

Cherokee, emig rolls 1817-1835, bk rev GH 33:4:110 KCG 20:4:209

hist & legends (1921), bk rev CSB 14:1:23

hist in GA, bk rev CDS 16:5:47

Cherokee Nation, fam of Fox Taylor, GA GP 16:1:41

reservees 1817-1819 & 1846-1847, bk rev KCG 20:4:210

Saline Co cem inscr TA 14:2:37

Chickasaw Nation, census 1847 THT 4:3:17

"Chickasaw Express" marrs & obits 1892-1903 OK 24:3:135

traders 1899 TA 14:3:91

Chief Crazy Horse biog NGI 3:3:136

Chippewa geneal guide MN 10:3:103

Choctaw Nation, Friendship Bapt Ch OK recs OK 24:3:131

Goodwater School pupils 1858 TA 14:1:20

Comanche cem inscr OK TA 14:2:31

Creek Indian, census 1832, bk rev YP 9:2:103

research guide prior to removal OK 24:1:36

geneal ethnic res guide, bk rev GH 33:5:69

geneal res guide GH 33:3:6 33:5:5 OG 3:2:37 SCS 14:3:76 14:4:102

hist notes in photos TST 12:15:1

Idaho Indians, bk rev CDS 16:1:6

Indian photographs, bk rev CDS 16:5:47

Miami tribe list 1871 TOP 9:1:15

misc references GR 21:2:58

misc sources for research AW 5:2:45 5:3:76

New England Indians, bk rev CDS 16:3:3

Nez Perces, missionaries' view, bk rev CDS 16:3:5

Pottawatomie tribe hist & tribal roll 1863 KK 17:3:49

Shawnee, hist, bk rev REG 77:4:295

muster roll from OH to KS 1832 JCG 7:2:38

Tlingit Indian design hist, bk rev CDS 16:5:46

Tunxis, legends & hist of CT Tunxis Indians, bk rev CTN 11:4:698 CDS 16:1:4

AMES, Adelbert w Blanche Butler, geneal, bk rev CDS 16:1:5

Frances Herbert b1900 w Carrie Lucille Carpenter, TX, anc ch RRS 12:1:95

Norman Burton b1872 w Laura Bell Burant, KS anc ch KK 17:2:25

AMOS, Walter f1794 w Ann Roberts, MI, biog notes MI 24:4:131

AMYETT, Jesse L b1899 w Sophia Katherine Dietz, TX, anc ch THT 7:2:72

ANDERSON, Soren b1834 w Marie Hansen, Denmark, NY, KS, geneal BGS 11:2:68

Allen Charles b1921 w Rosa Lee May Trambly, NE, CO, anc ch BGS 10:4:37

Bible rec PR 3:3:51

Daniel b1771 w Jane Dinsmore, DE, VA, OH, anc ch REP 19:3:129

fam of NJ, geneal, bk rev LL 15:2:82

Frank Clinton b1892 w Ada May Flower, PA, TX, CA, anc ch TRI 17:1:7

George b1785 w Nancy Law, anc ch REP 19:2:83

John b1770, NJ, geneal, bk rev CTN 10:3:522

John b1848, Bible rec PR 3:3:51

Peter d1907, Civil War pension claim MKT 2:1:14

Stoddard Moore bc1768, PA, geneal LM 2:3:3

William C m1820 w Mary Key Witcher, TX, Bible rec HTR 22:3:85

ANDREW, Philip Sr bc1805 w Jane, Eng,Can, IA, Geneal, bk rev KCG 20:4:206

ANDREWS, fam of IL, geneal FF 8:3:72

Ichabod b1767 w Lola Tuttle, Bible rec CTN 11:4:593

John J b1850 w Rovilla Reeves, MO, anc ch FF 8:2:25

Sherlock f1821 w Pamela Thomas, Bible rec CTN 10:3:420

ANGELL, William, geneal, bk rev TB 6:3:20

ANGEVINE, fam of Fr & NY, geneal, bk rev CTN 11:2:337

ANGLE, Abel Riley b1834 w Cora Louise Douty, MD, NY, Bible rec NYR 110:1:29

ANGLING, Adren b1790, TX cem inscr THT 7:2:104

ANKETELL, fam geneal, bk rev REP 19:3:134

ANSLEY, John b1814 w Lucy Ann Sharp Hayden, ME, Bible rec WB 9::152

ANTHONY, Earl Elwood Sr b1884 w Mary Bessie Adaline Fowler, TX, anc ch THT 6:3:77

Susan Brownell b1820, MA, biog notes DAR 113:6:656

ANTONIDES, John b1798 w Rebecca Lillie, OH, anc ch REP 19:1:36

APPLEGATE, Clari, KY letters 1863 CI 12:2:55

ARCENEAUX, Joseph Amedee b1910 w Elizabeth M Grambo, LA, anc ch AGE 8:4:126

ARCHER, name index to 1919 geneal, bk rev REP 19:3:136

ARDOUREL, Jean Francois Baptiste b1843 w Rosine Manen, Fr, CO, geneal BGS 8:4:17

ARIZONA, biog sketches in Archives CSB 14:1:11

Clark Co, Gurdon, Davis cem inscr THT 5:1:11

death recs index v1,2, bk rev GH 33:1:83

death recs supp I CSB 14:2:35

Pima Co, marrs 1906-1908 CSB 14:1:3

Tombstone, Boothill Graveyard, hist notes on misc burials REF 21:1:12 21:2:26 21:3:8

ARKANSAS, Arkansas Co, census 1850 & 1860, bk rev KCG 20:1:46

census 1870, bk rev GH 33:1:82 KCG 20:1:47

marrs 1786-1875 v1, bk rev KCG 20:4:210

Carroll Co, Mountain Meadows Massacre, notes on REF 21:3:4

Clark Co, Gurdon, Bethel Spring cem inscr THT 3:2:23

Franklin Co, marr recs 1850-1861, bk rev GH 33:1:82

Greene Co, geneal sketches, bk rev OC 16:4:135

Luxora, Rosa cem inscr SCS 14:3:85

Miller Co, Jonesboro, bk of lost recs 1835-1838 FP 22:1:23

misc wills & admin FP 22:1:23

Saline Co, marr bks A & B 1836-1860, bk rev KCG 20:4:211

Sebastian Co, census 1860, bk rev GH 33:2:74

hist of physicians, bk rev GGM 71:8

Sharp Co, census 1870, bk rev GH 33:1:83

ARMACOST, William Elijah b1880 w Rosabella Tracey, MD, anc ch MD 20:2:122

ARMIJO, Piedad m1866 h Horace Butler Smith, NM, biog notes NMG 18:2:53

ARMIT, William m1757 w Agnes Lees, Ir, geneal, bk rev NGS 67:1:71

ARMSTRONG, Dennis William b1944 w Georgette Mae Vanarsdall, OR, WA, anc ch ORB 18:3:65

Earl Wyatt b1875 w Della Thankful Fish, KS, CO, anc ch

BGS 9:4:48

Mary b1757 h John Armstrong, KY, notes on TSP 3:1:42

ARNETT, Anthony b1819 w Mary Rose Graham, Fr, Ir, IL, CO, biog notes BGS 2:2:8

John Alexander b1874 w Ella Kincaid, TX, anc ch STK 7:4:188

ARNETTE, John Quern f1837 w Frances Elam Eliza Coleman, Bible rec GGM 74:296

ARNOLD, Benedict b1741, biog, bk rev CTN 12:3:536

John f1630, Eng, MA, geneal CTN 7:2:307

ARONHALT, William Sanson b1823 w Rebecca Rodruck, OH, anc ch REP 19:2:82

ARTER, fam of OH, geneal, bk rev REP 19:3:133

ASHBY, Robert, VA, geneal v2, bk rev YP 9:2:109

ASHLEY, Ashleys of Am Quarterly, 165 Elm St, South Dartmouth MA 02748

geneal, bk rev CDS 16:1:3

ASHTON, John Leonard, IL indenture 1847 CI 15:3:106

ASKEW, "Brother" m 1798 w F Smith, VA, marr rec NCJ 5:4:263

ATCHLEY, Joshua b1791 w Mary Ann Mason, OH, anc ch REP 19:4:163

ATER, George f1790, MD, OH, biog notes OHR 20:2:60

ATKINS, Cornelia, IL letter 1855 TRI 17:4:73

Thomas Hamilton b1883 w Berta Lou Tatum, TX, anc ch NAS 17:4:95

ATKINSON, Frances Martha b1857 h David Allen Martin, TX, CA, biog notes FH 2:3:82

George Earl b1901 w Dorothy Greenhalgh, WA, NE, anc ch EWA 16:2:75

ATWELL, James b1787 w Fanny Frink, CT, NY, anc ch REP 19:3:132

ATWOOD, John b1819 w Sarah Shaldrick, Eng, IL, geneal FF

8:2:93

AVE, Jacob b1790 w Susan Traxler, PA, OH, anc ch REP 19:3:117

AUGENSTEIN, fam of Ger, geneal FF 8:1:55

AULP, Samuel f1787 w Catherine Dickey, Scot, Ir, PA, OH, geneal, bk rev SCC 16:1:9 REP 19:2:91 HH 14:2:103

AUSTERMILLER, Conrad A b1818 w Catherine Wagner, Ger, OH, anc ch REP 19:1:36

AUSTIN, William b1750 w Martha Rogers, Lucy Closson, RI, NY, OH, Bible rec CTN 12:2:235

AUSTRALIA, New South Wales, free settlers 1828 IR 11:2:95

AUSTRIA, geneal res guide GH 33:6:9

guide to geneal recs, bk rev ITG 2:55

AVERY, James b1620 w Joanna Greenslade, Eng, MA, geneal BGS 9:2:16

AYERS, John d1675 w Susannah Symonds, MA, geneal, bk rev GH 33:6:85

William Marion b1852 w Frances Emma Snyder, IN, OK, Bible rec GR 21:4:153

BABSON, Joseph b1731 w Martha Somes, ME. fam rec DE 5:2:20

BACON, Bacon Families Association Newsletter, 1424 Lark Ln, Naperville, IL 60565

BADOUGH, Louis b1909 w Eleanora Wilhelmia Vollmar, TX, anc ch GR 21:3:93

BAGGETT, Joe Byron b1906 w Robbie Adrian, TX, anc ch AGS 20:2:46

BAILEY, Andrew b1904 w Lucille Watson, VA, anc ch OC 16:2:62

Edmund b1779 w Rebecah Clanton, VA, Bible rec VA 17:2:47

George M D b1845 w Sallie L Davis, Bible rec HG 19:3:58

William bc1819 w Nancy Ryan, VT, OH, anc ch REP 19:1:27

William Ball b1824 w Ann

Elizabeth Murphy, VA, Bible rec VA 17:2:46

BAIRD, fam of TX, letters 1876-1882 DG 25:4:204

John, TX, medical recs 1868-1880 DG 25:4:213

William Homer b1920 w Lillian Juanita Guger, AL, anc ch NAS 18:1:1

Wyllys Warner d1828 w Olivia Pomeroy Green, geneal, bk rev BGS 8:4:33 CTN 9:3:471

BAKER, Abraham b1841 w Louisa Cline, OH, anc ch REP 19:3:124

Andrew Jackson b1861 w Mary Hannah Mayhew, IA, NE, anc ch BGS 10:4:43

Charles, GA, geneal, bk rev GGM 71:6

Daniel b1842 w Sarah Asenith Young, WI, Bible rec ORB 17:8:67

David b1786 w Rebecca Morris, RI, Bible rec VA 17:3:94

Elijah d1829 w Olive Carson, CT, Rev War pens appl TT 19:1:19

Elisha b1756, RI, NY, Rev War pens appl TT 19:1:19

Elisha d1821 w Polly Stone, RI, NY, Rev War pens appl TT 19:1:20

fam of KY, geneal KA 14:3:157

Francis f1830 w Nancy Ann Davis, Mary Brandenburg, MD, MO, IL, biog notes KA 15:2:102

James Cox b1799 w Priscilla Ann Ridenauer Gould, Eng, PA, OH, KS, anc ch REP 19:3:127

James F Jr b1806 w Honor B Hull, WV, OH, anc ch REP 19:2:88

Jerman d1792 w Martha Murray/Ward, Bible rec VA 17:2:49

Joel f1776, MA, geneal, bk rev CTN 7:4:521

Joseph b1781 w Miss Mcwherter, NC, IL, geneal, bk rev MCH 7:1:28

Moses b1708, NC, KY descs BR 6:3:98

Thomas Jefferson b1857 w Mary Melana Moore, KS, anc ch RRS 12:1:119

William f1800, NC, IN, geneal, bk rev KY 21:1:34

William D w Marilla (Martin), IL, letter 1843 CI 15:3:96

William Hiram Christianberry b1825 w Elizabeth Davis, IN, biog & fam notes HJA 6:3:1

BALDRIDGE, Henry bc1870, IL, diaries extracts CI 14:4:147 15:1:15 15:2:13 15:3:111 15:4:139

BALDWIN, fam of NC, fam recs DAR 113:5:547

Israel f1775 w Elizabeth, Bible rec CTN 12:3:414

Joseph III b1742 w Mary Pettit, PA, VA, anc ch REP 19:3:132

Martillus b1844 w Rachel J Gammon, Rebecca E Darrow, Bible rec FP 22:2:67

BALE, Robert Ezra Lee b1894 w Velma Pauline Raybell, KS, WA, anc ch OG 5:1:37

BALES, John b1650 w Mary Clayton, Eng, PA, MD, geneal, bk rev GH 33:2:82

BALL, Gehazi Ranson b1815 w Mary Buckner, NC, Bible rec THT 5:1:27

John bc1585, geneal, bk rev CTN 9:4:605

William b1784 w Marcy Harvey, Can, OH, geneal (1937), bk rev AH 5:3:70

BALLARD, James m1859 w Esther Birchard, Can, biog notes FAM 18:3:98

Nelson m1829 w Rachel Caldwell, NY, WI, geneal, bk rev GH 33:2:82 CTN 12:2:364

Thomas b1762 w Abigail Richardson, fam rec CTN 11:3:387

BALLINGER, William b1781 w Violet Craig, VA, KY, anc ch AGS 20:3:80

BANGEN, Hans H b1838 w Eline Thompson, Norway, MN, geneal, bk rev TB 6:4:27

BANKS, William d1853 w Margaret

W Martin, MD, VA, Bible rec VA 17:3:91

BANNIONG, Jeremiah b1789 w Elizabeth Ann Brooks, NC, IL, geneal CI 15:2:17

BARAEKMAN, Milam J w Frances W Goodyear, Alice Tetlow, MO, IL, Bible rec HJA 6:2:37

BARBADOS, recs, wills & adm vl 1639-1680, bk rev GJ 8:3:171

wills & admin recs vl 1639-1680, bk rev NGS 67:4:311

BARBEE, fam of NC, geneal supp, bk rev BGS 9:1:37

BARBER, Jesse Lee Jr b1919 w Bessie Louise Flournoy, TX, anc ch THT 7:1:19

BARDWELL, Duane Ray b1878 w Emma Mae Caryl, MI, anc ch NGI 3:3:175

BARECKMAN, James b1817 w Margret Ellener, IL, Bible rec HJA 6:3:43

BAREKMAN, Lambert Thomas b1852 w Alice Belle Hess, IN, Bible rec HJA 6:4:39

BARGAMIAN, Akabe (Hekimian) b1885 h Avedis Bargamian, Armenia, RI, biog notes FH 2:1:12

BARHAM, Ana C (Mrs) b1808, VA, Bible rec VA 17:3:96

BARICKMAN, Benjamin b1824 w Mary Agusta Latham, CT, Bible rec HJA 6:3:42

Daniel b1790 w Mary, Bible rec HJA 6:2:37

Daniel b1821 w Rachel Cramer, Emma Caroline Swarthout, IL, Bible rec HJA 6:2:37

Willis b1865 w Eliza Lemans, IL, Bible rec HJA 6:3:42

BARKER, David b1760 w Mary Jamison, NH, MA, fam rec CTN 7:2:318

Ephraim m1752 w Hannah Cove, CT, geneal 1897, bk rev TB 6:3:21

Leonard b1867 w Mary Elizabeth Benn, Eng, CT, Bible rec CTN 7:2:316

Wilbur Jay m1893 w Caroline L Mileham, MO, Bible rec BCG 6:3:19

BARKMAN, John b1785, PA, Bible rec HJA 6:4:39

BARNES, Edmund b1853 w Charlotte Campbell, IN, biog notes THT 2:1:23

George b1796 w Mary Montross, NY, Can, biog notes FAM 18:1:6

John b1791 w Anna Jones, NC, Bible rec HG 19:3:59

Robert Henry b1826 w Keturah, Bible rec CPY 8:4:89

William b1793 w Ruth Ann Wheeler, Eng, OH, anc ch REP 19:1:32

BARNET, Ann Walker b1805 h Grover Stout Deats, Curtis Hooks, AL, Bible recs VL 14:2:65

BARNEY, fam of OH, geneal, bk rev REP 19:4:166

BARNHILL, Arnold Beaton b1917 w Mary Ethel Hatch, Can, anc ch WB 10:2:66

BARNS, Leoi b1803 w Orpha Barker, MA, Bible rec MD 20:3:241

BARR, John b1799 w Comfort Marvel, SC, IL, biog & fam recs SWC 5:3:61

BARNUM, Abram f1854, IA, fam letters BGS 6:3:11

BARRON, Hollis Roscoe b1904 w Vivian Lenore Bell, AR, anc ch TOP 9:2:47

Thomas Mason b1818 w Penelope McFarland, DC, KY, Bible rec KY 21:1:66

BARTLETT, Henry b1847 w Ann Melissa Deitz, OH, Bible rec KK 17:2:28

Hugh b1799 w Leah Wilborn, KY NC, anc ch AGS 20:2:57

Isaiah b1793 w Miriam Mason, Bible rec REP 19:1:12

BARTON, Alphonso m1874 w Fannie Easterwood, AR, IS, OR, Bible rec & biog notes ORB 17:7:61

Charles King b1886 w Elizabeth Connell Currie, Scot, NJ, anc ch AG 55:2:118

Thomas bc1794 w Rebecca

Holland, KY, MO, IL, biog & fam notes IL 11:1:34

BASHORE, Riley A m1902 w Ora Trimble, OH, marr cert WA 9:4:154

BASKIN, fam recs, bk rev TS 21:1:28

BASTEDO, William b1781 w Upame (Euphemia) Longstreet, NJ, Bible rec GNJ 54:2:63

BATEMAN, William f1630, Eng, MA, geneal, bk rev GH 33:4:116 NYR 110:4:248 CLG 10:1:58

BATES, John f1864 w Ann Jennings, VT, anc ch REP 19:3:128

Martin L b1804 w Emily Cannon, MA, Bible rec IL 11:3:129

Morgan, letters from trip aroung the horn 1849, bk rev SCS 16:4:122

Sarah Jane (Lindsey) Preston b1843 h John Preston, Miller Preston, Mr. Bates, IN, IA, CA, biog RED 11:4:13

BATTERSON, James dc1730, geneal CTN 7:3:462

James Jr f1776 w Rachel Oysterbanks, geneal CTN 7:4:629 8:1:159

William f1775 w Grissel Jeacock, CT, biog notes CTN 7:3:463

BATTEY, Phebe (Mrs) b1804, RI, biog notes RIR 5:2:1

BATTOE, John d1833 w Annis, IL land recs CI 12:3:104

Sally m1818 h Meridith Outhouse, Zachariah Cudd, KY, IL, biog CI 12:2:51

BAUERLE, William Fredrick b1887 w Lillie Jane Craig, anc ch FF 8:3:57

BAUMGARDNER, Charles William Carl b1906 w Vivian Gaynells Carroll, VA, anc ch CPY 8:3:70

Jacob f1790, PA, OH, IL, fam rec FF 8:2:43

BAUMHARDT, Adam b1856 w Anna Margeretha Stockel, NY, Bible rec WB 10:2:62

Robert M b1889 w Ella C

Fuessner, OH, anc ch ACL 4:4:83

BAUER, George Leonard f1860 w Babette Guckenberger, Ger, WI, letters from Ger MCR 10:2:43

BAUMANN, fam of NY, geneal, bk rev YP 9:1:40

BAXTER, Richard Rufus b1928 w Luanne Doreen Harpune, MT, anc ch NW 2:4:128

BAYER, Ernest Henry b1866 w Nellie Catherine Wolking, NY, MO, AR, anc ch OC 16:2:62

BAYLES, Max Sr b1892 w Ruby Caroline Brunk, WA, CA, anc ch cont KG 16:1:15

BEADLES, Milt mc1880 w Anna Caley, IL, notes on MGR 14:1:21

BEAL, John Sr b1781 w Mary Magdalena Korns, PA, anc ch REP 19:1:36

Shadrach d1815, VA, geneal, bk rev VAG 23:2:143

BEALL, Minian b1625 w Ruth Moore, Scot, MD, geneal MD 20:3:214 20:4:325

BEALS, John m1844 w Sarah Ann Kelsay, Bible rec BWG 8:1:33,34

BEAM, David f1767, NC, geneal, bk rev CDS 16:4:13

Henry w Barbara, will 1802 TRI 17:1:9

BEAMAN, fam of IN, geneal, bk rev KY 21:1:34

BEANS, Thomas Allen b1881 w Winnifred Harlan, IL, anc ch NW 2:2:57

BEARD, Andrew bc1670 w Mary Williams, MA, geneal, bk rev VQ 16:2:27

BEARDSLEY, Barna b1797 w Mary Boylan, NY, OH, biog VQ 16:1:10

BEASLEY, James Samuel Jr b1908 w Emma Weaver Glass, AL, LA, anc ch GR 21:1:8

Leonard Fletcher b1907 w Lillian Mae Bowen, OH, TX, anc ch BGS 11:4:175

BECK, Anton b1844 w Rosina

Koenig, Ger, TX, geneal, bk rev GH 33:6:86 KCG 20:4:205

BECKWITH, fam of CT & MA, biog notes ANC 14:1:17

Gurden b1791 w Eunice Bush, OH, geneal AH 6:1:6

BEESE, Walter Theodore b1888 w Jessie Louraine Tucker, WI, anc ch GR 21:2:53

BELDEN, Daniel b1648 w Elizabeth Foote, Mrs Hepzibah Welles, Mrs Sarah Mattoon, CT, MA, biog notes BGS 11:4:165

Richard bc1591, Eng, CT, biog notes BGS 10:3:22

BELDING, Job Kelsy b1795 w Rebecca Ferris, CT, NY, geneal NYR 110:4:208

BELL, Thomas b1803 w Rebecka Cristy, PA, Bible rec AH 5:2:49

BELLEVILLE, Jean f1670 w Hester Casier, NY, geneal, bk rev HH 14:2:104

BELTON, Frank S m1860 w Susannah, NH, KS, marr notice TOP 9:3:87

BENJAMIN, fam in Am, geneal, bk rev CTN 10:3:523

Herbert m1902 w Nellis William, IL marr cert GL 13:3:71

BENNETT, Ebenezer b1743, Scot, NY, geneal, bk rev TOP 9:1:17

Thomas b1685 w Elizabeth, Eng, NC, geneal, bk rev GH 33:3:82

Thomas d1792 w Sarah, geneal FF 8:3:76

BENSON, John b1782 w Mary Burch, NY, IN, Bible rec CTN 10:2:365

BENTLEY, William w Mary, KY will 1817 BR 6:3:99

William Jr w Nancy, KY will 1833 BR 6:3:99

BENTLEY-JEFFRIES, Bible rec KA 15:1:40

BENTON, Moses Henry b1816 w Adelphia Ann Henry, Permelia Ann (Leatherman) Blair, IA, Bible rec HH 14:3:152

William A b1906, CT, geneal, bk rev NYR 110:1:57 GH 33:2:83 CTN 11:3:517 KCG 20:2:92

BENTZ, Edward m1898 w Mattie B. Wiswell, OH, marr cert CPY 8:2:41

BERK, Ernest b1837 w Anna Martha Fisher, Ger, MI, anc ch REP 19:3:117

BERNARD, John Peter m1759 w Mary Abney, VA, geneal, bk rev CTN 9:4:605

Peter f1700, Eng, Am, geneal, bk rev BGS 10:2:31

BERNER, Karl Amandus f1833 w Kristine Karoline Knodler, Ger, IA, IL, geneal, bk rev CI 11:4:125

BERRIAN, George Washington b1838 w Lucinda S, IL, KS, Bible rec BGS 8:2:6

BERRIER, Jacob, GA, fam letters 1846-1864 DG 25:3:169

BERRY, Barnabas b1759, Bible rec CHG 11:1:22

fam of MD, geneal, bk rev REP 19:4:173

BERRYMAN, William b1794 w Mary Landers, KY, Bible rec KA 14:3:163

BERTHOUD, Charles Henry Lewis b1787 w Louisa Houst, Amanda Nellis, Switz, NY, biog notes BGS 11:2:67

BERTRAM, Adda, letter 1883 BGS 4:2:8

Russell T b1924 w Gloria E Werker, IN, anc ch ACL 4:1:13

BERTRAND, Joseph E J b1879 w Katherine Louise Kruse, Can, MI, WI, anc ch NGI 3:3:178

BESLY, Oliver bc1687, SC, birth cert NYR 110:4:239

BETHARD, James Wesley b1885 w Nettie Mae Freeman, IL, anc ch FF 8:3:58

BETTES, Jeremiah bc1753 w Sarah Smith, ME, biog notes DE 3:2:26

BETTS, John Michael b1878 w Augusta Carolina Swanson (Svensdaughter), Sweden, MN, CA, anc ch OC 16:4:120

BETTY, Robert Carroll b1815 w Dorcas Lois Warren, TN, TX, letters & biog notes THT

2:2:43

BETZ, Philip b1826 w Elizabeth St Clair, PA, Bible rec PF 9:2:33

William Chalmers b1854 w Rosa S (Olmsted) Markward, PA, MI, Bible rec PF 9:2:30

BETZNER, Samuel b1738 w Maria Detweiler, Ger, PA, biog notes BGS 8:3:15

BEYER, John Philip d1753, PA, geneal, bk rev CTN 8:4:539

BIBLIOGRAPHY, almanacs, early Am almanacs, bl rev NER 133:2:142

Am ch rec v1,2 (Kirkham), bk rev OG 1:4:118

Am geneal period & period indexes 1978, bk rev TST 11:43:29 GE 42:11

Am genealogies to 1900 (Munsell), bk rev CDS 16:3:6

biog dict 1978 supp 2, bk rev GE 42:10 NYR 110:1:54

commonly missed sources in geneal PF 8:3:55

dictionary catalog of research libraries of NY public lib, bk rev TS 21:2:75

geneal & local hist bks in print v2, bk rev YP 9:1:41

geneal research & resource books, bl rev TB 6:2:21

misc geneal publ TST 12:9:45

BICKLE, Charles b1850 w Fanny Eliza Bacon, WI, IA, NE, KS, CA, OR, biog notes YV 11:3:114

BIDWELL, Horace b1812 w Susan Mc Collum, Mary Jane Comstock, MA, NY, MI, geneal DM 42:4:151

Isaac b1755 w Rhoda Beckwith, CT, geneal, bk rev REP 19:4:175

BIGELOW, Daniel Richardson b1824 w Ann Elizabeth White, WI, WA, Bible rec OG 3:1:9

BIGGERSTAFF, Robert b1786 w Margaret Gibbs, Eng, Bible rec MGR 14:4:160

BIGGS, William b1755 w Nancy Munday, Nancy (Judy) Lunce-

ford, WV, biog IL 11:2:88

BILDERBACK, Gabriel b1805 w Nancy Bruce, PA, anc ch REP 19:3:125

BILL, fam geneal supp, bk rev AG 55:1:64

Roswell Mason b1810 w Merinda Nelson, VT, geneal, bk rev RES 11:4:148

BILLINGS, Eugene Richard b1943 w Linda Kay Beaver, CA, anc ch THT 7:2:80

Heman A b1823 w Mary E Cleghorn, IA, letter & Bible rec OC 16:4:125

Warren b1807 w Emiline McGregory, MA, Bible rec CTN 10:2:365

BILLS, Benjamin m1825 w Harriet Woodbury, OH, marr rec AH 2:4:108

BINGHAM, Daniel Edward b1874 w Cora Rasella Etcheson, IL, anc ch FF 8:3:59

James b1748 w Susanna (Scheimer) Bingham von Steuben, PA, geneal AG 55:1:42

BIRCHARD, Samuel m1824 w Ruth Pearson, Can, VT, biog notes FAM 18:3:98

Thomas f1635 w Mary Robinson, CT, MA, notes on CTN 9:3:476

BIRGE, David b1753 w Abigail Howland, CT, MA, VT, geneal, bk rev CTN 8:4:540

BIRKEY, Silas f1887 w Phoebe Good, IL, biog notes MH 6:2:22

BIRNIE, John b1784, Scot, SC, geneal, bk rev CTN 7:3:363

BISBEE, Reuben b1804 w Mary Armstrong, VT, CT, Can, KS, biog notes FAM 18:1:6

BISHOP, fam of CT, geneal, bk rev KY 21:3:115

Gardner f1817, RI, OH, geneal 1957, bk rev REP 19:4:168

Ira E b1905 w Matilda Stefanik, WI, IL, biog notes TST 11:49:36

John b1845 w Caroline Auger, Eng, Bible rec AH 4:4:136 5:3:96

BISSELL, Austin bc1790 w Clarissa Stacy, Bible rec NER 133:4:300

Israel f1775 w Lucy Handcock, MA SCS 16:1:17

BITTERMAN, August Jr b1883 w Justina Neiman, Russ, SD, WA, anc ch OG 3:3:66

BIVENS, fam of IL, notes on CI 11:4:151

BIXBY, fam of MA, notes on LL 14:2:81

BLACHOWICZ, Jon b1871 w Honorata Zolatynska, anc ch PN 1:2:27

BLACK, Adam b1779 w Elizabeth, Bible rec SCS 14:3:67

Herbert Guy b1889 w Clarissa E Babson, ME, geneal DE 3:4:16

Ross Wilson b1917 w Ethel Geraldine Laurence, AR, anc ch NAS 18:1:2

William Clair b1885 w Avice C Molera, NV, CA, anc ch RED 11:4:17

BLACK GENEALOGY, African Meth Epis Ch (CO) hist & recs BGS 11:4:142

births DE 1810-1853 NGS 67:4:264

black genesis, geneal guide, bk rev GE 46:4 TST 11:49:36 GH 33:2:71 NYR 110:2:119 WCK 12:1:17 DM 43:1:47 CDS 16:3:6

black Luth Ch (AL) hist CHI 52:3:129

"entitled-free papers" VA 1823-1863 VA 17:4:133

geneal ethnic res guide, bk rev GH 33:5:69

geneal res guide SGS 29:2:109 29:3:219

hist of Muhlenberg KY, bk rev WCK 12:2:24

misc sources HTR 22:1:1

NJ slave births 1804-1833 GNJ 54:2:83

notes on NGI 3:2:75 3:3:148

pioneers in OH, bk rev REP 19:4:169

res guide, bk rev OG 4:2:58

res in OH recs JG 4:5:19

BLACKBURN, Martin d1897 UT, obit LL 15:4:173

fam of CO, Bible rec BGS 4:3:10

James f1770 w Jane Rankin, geneal, bk rev GH 33:1:90

BLACKMORE, Arthur Jr mc1628 w Susan Burnett, fam notes NGS 67:3:215

BLACKWELL, Blackwell Newsletter, RR 2, Hensall, Ontario NOM 1X0 Canada

John b1800 w Elizabeth Biggs Murphy, Ir, Can, geneal & biog notes IRA 13:247 FAM 18:1:7

BLACKWOOD, Hampton Craig b1831 w Eliza Kirkpatrick, SC, IL, fam rec TB 6:2:11

BLAKE, John Harney b1831 w Frances Mahon, Prus, IA, OR, biog notes ORB 17:9:83

BLALOCK, fam of TX, geneal, bk rev GH 33:4:116

Wyatt Conklin b1908 w Cleo Mae Beel, NE, TX, anc ch GR 21:2:54

BLANCHARD, Augustin Silvain b1815, LA, bapt cert AGE 8:2:49

fams of NY, NC, VA, CO, fam recs BGS 11:1:12

Joseph m1803 w Maria Angelica Picoue, LA, marr cert AGE 8:2:50

Wlter Louis b1921 w Mary Christine Clay, TX, anc ch GR 21:4:136

BLANKENSHIP, Isham bc1738 w Sarah, VA, TN, geneal FF 8:2:95

BLANKENSHIP-POWERS, Bible rec PGB 11:8:89

BLAZER, Henry f1860 w Rebecca A, OH, fam rec KN 2:2:35

William b1816 w Elizabeth Rouse, OH, Bible rec HH 14:1:38

BLESS, Marshall Robert b1906 w Verneena Mildred Hughes, IL, AR, anc ch BGS 11:3:134

BLINN, Theodore b1779 w Sarah Wright, MA, fam rec AH 3:2:46

BLODGET, Abner b1774 w Zeruiah Rice, Bible rec NEW 133:4:299

Joseph b1696, Bible rec NER

133:4:299

BLUNDELL, William A b1889 w Hazel Pearce, CO, WA, biog notes EWA 16:2:48

BLYTHE, A M b1859 w Telva Kelso, IL, obits MCH 7:2:57

BOCOOK, George Washington b1837 w Martha Scott, KY, Bible rec TOP 9:3:64

BODDY, John Cowen m1860 w Elizabeth Daniels, Bible rec TRI 17:2:37

BOESE, Benjamin G, geneal supp, bk rev BGS 10:3:35

BOGER, Daniel b1821 w Margaret Engle Deal, PA, geneal LM 20:1:1

MATHIAS B1809 W ANNA METZGER, OH, BIBLE REC ACL 4:2:28

BOHNENSTIEHL, Jacob b1801 w Margaretha Voise, Ger, MS, IL, geneal, bk rev GH 33:5:81

BOISAUBIN, Vincent Paul b1910 w Helen Matthews, MO, anc ch BGS 11:4:184

BOLDT, William F b1901 w Verna Theodora Fairbanks, WA, MN, anc ch MN 10:3:109

BOLTER, Richard f1653, MA, geneal NER 133:4:255

BOLTON, Richard bc1800 w Frances, Ir, Can, biog notes FAM 18:1:7

Timothy b1759 w Sybil Bennett, MA, biog LL 15:2:68

BONALOE, Pedro Pablo w Maria Hernandez, marr notice AH 5:3:71

BONE, William f1692 w Jane McWilliams, Ir, PA, NC, geneal FF 8:4:45

BONNEY, Herbert Hamilton b1865 w Eugenia Benecia Norment, MS, LA, anc ch GR 21:3:97

BOONE, Daniel b1734 w Rebecca Bryan, PA, KY, VA, biog, bk rev REG 77:4:294

James D bc1800 w Catherine Smith, MO, OH, anc ch REP 19:3:115

BOOTH, Charles H b1856 w Alma Flint, IA, OH, fam recs AH 5:3:86

fam of OH, notes on AH 5:3:86

BORDEN, Samuel d1812, NH, Bible rec CTN 11:2:215

BORING, Thomas bc1780 w Ruth Mann, MD, OH, anc ch REP 19:4:165

BORNER, Jonas b1781 w Sarah Artz, VA, Bible rec VA 17:1:5

BOSLEY, Hannah, MD, notes on MD 20:3:188

BOTKIN, George b1783 w Sarah Hester, Bible rec IG 15:2:56

BOTSFORD, Samuel, CT, geneal, bk rev CTN 10:3:522

BOTTERON, Frederick b1815 w Marion Goodier, Switz, IN, anc ch REP 19:4:162

BOTTORF, Daniel Hall b1868 w Nina Winona Hess, PA, anc ch ANC 14:1:10

BOUIE, Robert f1830 w Rebecca Lakin, MD, OH, geneal, bk rev REP 19:1:45

BOURG, Antoine b1609, Fr, Can, geneal, bk rev GN 2:5:141

BOURGEOIS, George J Sr b1900 w Mabel Julie Ford, LA, anc ch AGE 8:1:31

BOURLAND, geneal, bk rev KA 14:3:189

John w Catherine Randolph, Ir, VA, geneal, bk rev CTN 11:4:701

BOUTON, Gould b1731 w Elizabeth Gilbert, MA, biog notes BGS 2:1:7

BOWEN, Griffith b1600 w Margaret, Fleming, Wales, MA, geneal NGS 67:3:163

W L L b1838 w Mary E Jewell, TN, GA, biog notes GP 16:3:1

BOWER, Walter Wesley m1883 w Sylva S Thomas, KS, Bible rec OC 16:1:22

BOWERS, Clarence Harvey b1919 w Joy Arlene Addleman, OR, anc ch TB 6:3:16

fam of PA, Bible rec TA 14:1:6

Ira John b1902 w Bessie Ellen Eads, IL obit MCH 7:1:9

BOWERSOX, Harold Franklin Nuss b1907 w Joyce Kathryn Arnold, PA, anc ch PGB 11:5:48

BOWES-LYON, Elizabeth h HRH
George VI of Eng, biog, bk
rev AG 55:2:127

BOWIE, Mary b1789 h Abraham Bird
II, GA, biog notes PGB 11:5:52

BOWLES, fam of IL, geneal FF
8:3:79

Jonathan b1776 w Phebe Parker,
NH, Bible rec CTN 11:3:407

BOWMAN, Eugene Fowler b1917 w
Rosemary Tallent, MO, anc ch
BGS 11:2:79

Ezra Alva w Jane Margaret
Belknap, PA, geneal, bk rev
CTN 10:3:525

fam of NY, geneal, bk rev YP
9:1:40

fam of VA & KY, geneal, bk
rev CDS 16:1:4

fam of OH, geneal, bk rev REP
19:4:167

fam of PA, fam recs, bk rev GE
42:11

George m1731 w Mary Hite, VA,
geneal, bk rev TS 21:2:75

BOYD, James f1774 w Jane
MacMaster, Scot, geneal, bk
rev SCS 15:3:89

James b1817 w Susanna Barr,
Bible rec NGS 67:3:228

Samuel b1840 w Angeline
Simpson, OH, MO, anc ch REP
19:3:126

BOYER, Lewis b1755 w Rosanna
Kerns, MD, OH, geneal, bk rev
REP 19:2:90

Maria b1778 h Augustine Boyer,
MD, NY, cem inscr MMG 22:54

BOX, Robert Sr bc1734 w Mary
Williams, SC, fam rec STK
7:1:4

BRACHA, John Sr b1844 w Marie
Cernie, SD, anc ch HJA 6:3:49

BRACKEEN, fam of AL, bk rev CI
13:3:115

BRACY, Daniel N m1891 w Ella
Hunter, CO, marr cert THT
7:2:97

BRADBURY, Thomas bc1610 w Mary
Perkins, Eng, ME, MA, geneal
AG 55:1:1,5

BRADDOCK, Alfred Arthur b1868 w
Flora I Campbell, MI, WI, CO,
anc ch BGS 10:4:38

BRADEEN, fams of N E, geneal,
bk rev CTN 10:1:157

BRADEN, Samuel b1811 w Margaret
Gates, Mary Bennett, Hettie
Bennett, IA, OH, fam rec CI
15:1:17

BRADFORD, Wesley b1821 w Sarah
Ebersole, Bible recs OK
24:3:134

BRADLEY, Francis M b1834 w
Tennie Lee Thaxton, AL, anc
ch RRS 12:1:112,113

Thomas bc1790 w Catharine
Ridley, Eng, Can, geneal EG
12:288

BRADY, Henry William bc1827 w
Elizabeth Ann Culler, PA, OH,
IN, anc ch REP 19:2:83

BRAGG, George Thomas b1885 w
Mary Evangeline Francis, MN,
IL, CO, anc ch BGS 11:4:176

BRAINERD, David m1812 w Hannah
Dodge, fam rec AH 3:3:75

BRAMHALL, Sarah b1779 h Israel
Richmond, William Worcester,
MA, ME, biog notes DE 3:4:4

BRANCH, Christopher d1681, VA,
geneal, bk rev CTN 9:2:308

BRANDENBURG, fam geneal, bk rev
KK 17:3:70

BRANDON, Allen W m1887 w Mrs
Martha E Wade, Bible rec CI
14:4:126

BRANSFORD, John, VA, geneal, bl
rev KA 15:1:63

BRANT, Joseph b1742, NY, at
battle of Minisink DAR
113:7:784

Molly b1736, Can, loyalist,
biog, bk rev GN 2:6:172

BRASHEAR, Samuel Sr b1673 w Ann
Johns, MD, biog notes PGB
11:5:53

BRATTON, William H b1836 w Nancy
A Evans, Bible rec HH 14:2:88

BRAY, Sidney Crockett b1899 w
Allene Patterson, TN, TX, anc
ch RRS 12:1:100

Summer G d1884 w Hattie G, ME,
fam cem inscr DE 3:2:20

BRAYTON, Charles R b1840 w
Nettie Beldon, RI, obit RIR

5:4:10

BRAZIL, Sao Paolo State, Campo Cem Santa Barbara D'Oeste cem inscr, bk rev GH 33:2:72

BREED, Hiram Nichols b1809 w Nancy Stone, NH, Bible rec LL 14:1:29

BRENDT, Elmer Elstow b1908 w Anice Alice McGraw,a Can, KS, anc ch OG 4:2:39

BRENNAN, Patrick bc1808 w Mary, Ir, Can, biog notes FAM 18:1:7

BRETT, Mathew D w Mrs Annie M Olsted, CO marr 1871 BGS 4:2:25

William, Ir, geneal, bk rev IR 11:1:69

BREWSTER, Dewitt C b1809 w Elsey Ann Roberts, Clarinda Jane Burdick, OH, biog notes REP 19:1:11

William b1566, Eng, MA, geneal & biog notes MQ 45:4:219 BGS 1:1:4 1:2:2 2:1:10

William J Sr b1843 w Alice A Huntley, Bible rec RES 11:3:83

BRIDGES, Thompson d1921 w Sarah M Keith, IN, Bible rec HJA 6:4:39

Wilmer b1861 w Rozella Morrison, Rozetta Mayfield, Bible rec HJA 6:4:38

BRIDWELL, fam of VA, geneal, bk rev YP 9:1:41

Noah f1815 w Nancy Cuppy, KY, pens appl KY 21:1:52

BRIEN, James d1875 w Margaret (Hartley) Franklin, KY, pens appl KY 21:1:53

BRIERLY, John b1834 w Emma, Eng, CO, biog notes BGS 5:3:11

Thomas f1815 w Margaret Cooper, KY, pens appl KY 21:1:53

BRIGGS, Clement, MA, geneal, bk rev CSB 14:1:22

George Isaac b1872 w Elizabeth Welch, IL, anc ch GL 13:3:67

Joseph b1794 w Mary, Bible rec IG 15:4:105

Joseph b1858 w Hannah Mary West, Can, biog notes FAM

18:1:7

William G f1812 w Rhods Wright, KY, pens appl & fam rec KY 21:1:54

BRIGHAM, Winsor b1788 w Marinda Cone, MA, NY, Bible rec AH 3:3:94

BRIGHT, fam Bible rec NAS 17:4:106

John f1813 w Elizabeth Morrison, KY, pens appl KY 21:1:56

William f1813, KY, pens appl KY 21:1:56

BRIGMAN, Joshua b1781 w Temperance Quick, NC, GA, Bible rec GGM 74:301

BRIGNAC, fam of LA, geneal, bk rev YP 9:2:105

BRINEY, fams of PA, OH, KY, bk rev VAG 23:4:311

BRINK, Harry S f1835 w Mary Goldsmith, OH, Bible rec TB 6:1:21

Harry Sherman b1873 w Bessie Eulolia McFarland, OR, WA, anc ch TB 6:2:29

BRINSON, Lewis b1817 w Lucinda O'Neel, Bible rec TS 21:3:83

BRISBINE, James P b1836, OH, biog notes AH 1:3:26

BRISCOE, geneal, bk rev YP 9:3:164

BRISTOW, Jane b1736 h Thomas Greenwood, VA, geneal CLG 10:3:136

BRITTAIN, William Lee b1893 w Luetta Weeks, TX, anc ch NAS 18:2:33

BRITTINGHAM, William f1659 w Elizabeth Williams, Eng, MD, geneal DG 25:1:40

BRITTON, fam of IL, misc recs FF 8:1:57

Laurence Walter b1896 w Myrtle Bell Short, TN, anc ch NAS 17:3:65

BRIXNER, Adam b1871 w Lula Emerson, NM, obit NMG 18:4:124

BROADDUS, Mordecai Redd f1834 w Sarah Ann Miller, VA, Bible rec VA 17:4:118

BROCK, Isaac b1787 w ____, ____,
Sarah Sparks, NC, TX, biog
notes THT 1:2:12

Lucy Hannah Garvin, SC letter
1862 THT 2:2:27

BROCKWAY, Hiel b1775 w Phebe
Merrill, CT, NY, biog, bk rev
CTN 9:3:469

BROOKE, John P d1829 w Mary
Prescott, Ir, SC, fam rec FP
22:4:194

William Crawford b1813 w Mary
Timmons, GA, Bible rec FP
22:4:195

BROOKS, George b1754 w Mary
Atwood, ME, MA, anc ch OC
16:3:96

Robert b1780 w Rachel, VA, KY,
IN, biog notes IG 14:3:69

Thomas dc1695 w Mrs Joanah
Owen, VA, biog notes VAG
23:3:163

BROTHERS, Joseph Israel b1871 w
Elizabeth Cooper Webb, AL,
OK, anc ch NAS 17:3:67

BROTHERSON, Peter Porter f1860 w
Caroline Henrietta Kauffman,
PA, TX, geneal, bk rev GH
33:6:87

BROUSE, George m1813 w Betsy
Shaver, Can, Bible rec FAM
18:3:120

BROWN, Alexander Hamilton b1831
w Sarah J Stephenson, VA, IL,
Bible rec CI 15:3:97

Charles Arthur b1876 w Missouri
Pearl Fitzwater, OR, CA, WA,
anc ch ORB 18:2:31

fam of NY, Bible rec TT 19:2:83

fams of NC, SC, TN & MD,
geneal, bk rev WCK 12:2:34

Hait b1822 w Abigail Arnold,
MA, MI, anc ch REP 19:3:121

Henry F b1845 w Mary K Rice,
OH, IA, NE, Bible rec NA
2:2:42

Joel H b1791 w Mariah M, Maria
Burt, VA, KY, Bible rec CI
15:3:96

Mary L b1865 h Edwin M
Crandall, IN, IL, obit CI
15:1:13

Michael b1802 w Jane Walls, PA,

OH, anc ch REP 19:1:38

Nancy (Beeman) h James H Brown,
IL 1851 letter BGS 4:4:27
5:2:15

Nathan Jr b1790 w Mary Kimball,
ME, Bible rec DE 3:1:12

Nathaniel d1867 w Jane, TN, IL,
geneal & will CI 11:1:22

Oliver b1811 w Margaret P
Robertson, PA, Bible rec TOP
9:3:88

Orrin b1814 w Abigail Brewster,
ME, NH, Bible rec NER
133:4:300

Peter f1667, MA, CT, notes on
NGS 67:4:253

Thomas A b1839 w Eliza, Bible
rec SMV 11:1:14

William bc1725 w Christiana
Thompson, Scot, PA, revised
geneal, bk rev HH 14:2:104

William b1815 w Sarah Elizabeth
Coleman, TN, TX, biog notes
AGS 20:3:122

William b1905 w Virginia May
Harris, KS, MO, anc ch TOP
9:2:43

Z Taylor b1850 w Sarah
Mulholland, IL, TX, notes &
cem inscr THT 5:2:1

BROWNE, Thomas b1605, Eng, MA,
geneal, bk rev TS 21:4:173

BRUCE, George b1650, VA, geneal,
bk rev NGS 67:2:148

Henry b1777 w Eleanor, KY,
diary KA 15:1:26

Roosevelt b1904 w Beulah
Jarmon, AL, GA, anc ch NAS
18:1:3

Timothy b1752 w Matilda
Wheeler, MA, Bible rec CTN
10:3:366

William b1804 w Elizabeth A
Hayes, IL, Bible rec GL
13:2:44

BRUCKER, Johann Adam b1787 w
Rosalie Reitzi, Ger, Aus, MI,
geneal, bk rev GH 33:3:104

BRUNK, George R b1871, PA, biog,
bk rev PM 2:4:32

Jacob I, geneal, bk rev PM
2:2:24

BRUNKA, Jacob b1817 w Johanna

Marheine, geneal, bk rev CDS
16:3:3

BRUNNER, Henry b1739 w Rosina
Hartmann, Fr, PA, anc ch OC
16:4:121

Roy Samuel b1881 w Mary Duff,
PA, IN, CA, anc ch OC
16:4:120

BRYAN, Jerry, diary 1876, bk rev
CI 15:3:116

Thomas f1677, Eng, NJ, geneal,
bk rev IL 11:3:182

BRYANT, George Edward m1863 w
Sarah Jane Smith, MO, IL,
Bible rec CI 14:3:88

Thomas f1724 w Mary Shaw, Eng,
PA, geneal, bk rev DM 43:2:89
NGS 67:1:70

William Cullen, geneal, bk rev
ANC 14:4:122

BUCHANAN, David f1784, NY, notes
on NGS 67:3:214

James w Susan, Scot, MD,
letters 1798 MHM 74:4:344

BUCKBEE, Richard b1764 w Phebe
Boice, NY, Bible rec CTN
11:3:405

BUCKINGHAM, Charles G b1846, OH,
CO, biog notes BGS 2:1:4

BUCKNER, William m1773 w
Elizabeth Smith, VA, Bible
rec VA 17:1:3

BUELL, Samuel f1687, children AG
55:1:54

BUELTEL, Mary (Juenemann) b1872
h Henry Bueltel, IA, KS, obit
MGR 14:4:177

BUFFO, William Donald b1931 w
Betty Lou Schreiter, CO, anc
ch BGS 11:3:129

BUHRMASTER, John W w Gertrude M
Oglesby, IL, anc ch FF 8:3:62

BUIS, Marcellus b1878 w Florence
Hockman, IN, IL, anc ch GL
13:3:68

BULLA, Daniel, IN, NC, diary
1834 BGS 7:2:20

BULLER, Henry b1740, fam tree,
bk rev TB 6:1:33

BULLINGTON, fam of AL, geneal,
bk rev CI 13:3:115

BUMPUS, fam of MA, geneal, bk
rev MQ 45:3:161

BUNK, Jacob d1787 w Anna
Stouffer, Ger, PA, MD, geneal
bk rev GH 33:2:83

BUNN, Joseph b1836 w Mary Jane
Guest, Can, biog notes FAM
18:1:8

BUNNELL, Augustus Loretto b1838
w Mary Elizabeth Stanley, MI,
Bible rec CTN 12:2:236

Havilah b1772 w Dorcas Gale,
Bible rec CTN 11:4:592

William w Margaret, PA, will
1840 LL 15:1:34

BUNYARD, Roy Richard b1897 w
Blanche Elmore, IL, anc ch FF
8:4:42

Samuel b1819 w Mary Miles, Mary
Thompson, IL, geneal FF
8:3:81

BURCH, Frank Henry b1872 w
Nellie Mariah Cochran, CO,
anc ch BGS 9:3:43

Harry Irving b1892 w Ida
Virginia Montgomery, Can, VA,
MI, anc ch BGS 9:4:45

John f1820, Eng, Can, biog
notes FAM 18:1:8

BURGEE, Joab Waters f1800,
geneal, bk rev GH 33:1:90

BURGESS, Benjamin, AL, justice
of peace cert 1829 VL
10:4:160 14:1:57

BURGIN, Henry Newton b1866 w
Catherine E Saathoff, AL, TX,
anc ch GR 21:4:135

BURKE, Byron Ray b1855 w Blanche
Bovard, IL, Bible rec & biog
notes GL 13:1:18

BURKEPILE, John George b1788 w
Barbara Mersmore, PA, MD, anc
ch REP 19:3:118

BURKHOLDER, fam of PA & OH part
2 (1927), bk rev TB 6:4:28

Henry bc1805 w Anna Marie
Scaburn, OH, anc ch REP
19:1:30

BURKS, Amanda Nite f1871, TX,
auto BGS 9:2:21

BURNETT, Henry Cornelius b1825,
VA, KY, biog REG 77:4:266

James Cunningham b1766, geneal,
bk rev KY 21:1:34

John bc1825, CT, biog notes GFP

29:3:51

BURNHAM, Francis b1779 w Anna Hare, NH, Can, Bible rec KCG 20:2:68

Horace, TX, fam letter 1835 DG 25:1:38

John Bird b1869, DE, AK, biog, bk rev GH 33:5:81

BURNS, Frederick John b1875 w Florence Isabelle Pursell (Tilley), OH, IL, MI, notes on FG 21:3:55

Nicholas b1803 w Jane, Ir, Can, biog notes FAM 18:1:8

William Thomas b1916 w Joan Crawford, CA, anc ch THT 7:1:9

BURRIS, fam geneal vl, bk rev GH 33:2:83

BURROUGHS, Peleg, MA journal 1781, geneal ref CLG 10:3:147

BURTON, Charles d1863, IL cem inscr CI 15:3:110

Solomon, geneal, bk rev BGS 10:1:31

BURWELL, John b1602 w Alice Heath, Eng, CT, geneal CTN 12:3:539

BUSCH, Herman Henry b1799 w Anna Maria Lupker, Ger, OH, anc ch REP 19:4:163

BUSH, Isaac m1843 w Temperance Roberts, GA, biog notes GP 16:4:1

Marcus Eddie b1868 w Emma Pearson, OH, IA, NE, Bible rec NA 2:2:41

Owen, WA, biog notes OG 3:1:6

William Hamilton b1822 w Ann Scofield, OH, anc ch REP 19:3:130

BUSHUE, fam of IL, geneal, bk rev CI 15:2:12

Michael, geneal, bk rev CI 13:3:115

BUSSARD, Nicholas Andre b1931 w Nancy Louise Owen, IL, WA, anc ch WB 9:4:148

BUSSEY, George f1635 w Lydia, VA, MD, geneal PGB 11:9:97

BUTCHER, Fred A m1925 w G LaVerne Towner, geneal, bk rev OC 16:1:34

BUTLER, Albina Leslie Conger, diary 1892 LL 15:3:124

Alvin DeMel b1912 w Ada Marie Huelsman, TX, IL, anc ch THT 7:1:23

Ann (Ronth) bc1755, Eng, VA, fam notes NGS 67:4:290

Daniel b1735 w Barbara Austin, Bible rec CTN 11:2:216

fam geneal, bk rev GH 33:5:82

Joseph N b1879 w Mertie B Lord, ME, anc ch OG 3:3:67

Oscar Allen b1914 w Ruth Idella Calvert, TX, anc ch GR 21:2:52

Polly f1854, Shawnee Indian, OH, biog notes QY 6:2:7

BUTT, John b1826 w Margaret E Williamson, OH, anc ch REP 19:4:161

BUTTOLPH, Benoni b1772 w Mary Gibb, CT, OH, IA, biog notes CTB 44:2:64

BUTTON, Earl Sheffield b1806 w Celena Jane (Fisher) Burlingham, CT, KS, IA, fam rec MGR 14:1:25

BRYAN, Thomas b1663 w Elizabeth Scattergood, Rebecca Collins, Eng, NJ, geneal, bk rev GH 33:5:83

BYAM, George d1680, MA, geneal, bk rev CTN 9:1:126

BYBEE, Halbert Pleasant b1888 w Ruth Woolery, IN, TX, anc ch GR 21:4:139

BYRD, Henry b1764 w Nancy Baldwin, VA, geneal, bk rev GH 33:4:119

BYRNE, J J d1880 w Lillie Loring, NY, TX, letter THT 3:1:20

CABELL, geneal (1895), bk rev CDS 16:1:4

CADY, John F b1841 w Sarah C, IN, KY, Bible rec TS 21:3:106

CAIN, James m1855 w Elizabeth Kean, Bible rec MD 20:3:238

CALAWAY, fam of CT, geneal, bk rev CTN 10:2:347

CALDER, John, donation land

claim WA, bi rev TB 6:4:28

CALDWELL, William E m1868 w Mary J McCreery, PA, marr cert THT 2:2:43

CALIFORNIA, Agua Mansa, census 1856 VQ 16:3:37

Pioneer Memorial Park cem inscr VQ 16:1:5

Arqonauts index 1849, bk rev CTN 8:2:319

assn of 144th field artillery roster 1924 OC 16:2:40

Blue Lake, hist RED 12:2:15

BLWT grantees 1847-1855 NGS 67:2:143 67:4:313

Corona, telephone direct 1909 LL 14:3:108

Ferndale, fire dept 1898 RED 12:2:16

Masonic Lodge hist RED 11:3:16

geneal res guide MKT 2:2:34 KN 2:2:5 2:3:4

geneal res guide to UCLA lib KN 2:1:27

geneal ties with British Columbia, Can GE 49:1

Hijar-Padres Colony memb 1834 SCS 14:1:6

Humboldt Co, census 1880 RED 11:3:3 11:4:3 12:1:3 12:2:3

Eureka, bus direct 1877 RED 11:3:9

misc bk B RED 11:4:9 12:1:14 12:2:11

misc news abstr RED 11:3:12 11:4:15

misc place names RED 12:1:17 12:2:18

Rohnerville, Eel River Jockey Club hist RED 11:3:7

Hydesville, public school reg & visitor rec 1894-1895 RED 11:3:13

imms from CT 1849-1860, guide to CTN 7:3:353

index, biographees in 19th century county hists, bk rev GH 33:5:72 33:6:77 IL 11:4:233 GE 47:14 VAG 23:3:236 NYR 110:4:246 WCK 12:3:48 DM 43:2:89 CSB 14:4:164 NGI 3:3:167

Orton's recs of Civil War

vols, bk rev GH 33:1:83 GE 42:11 GJ 8:3:174 VAG 23:1:71 NYR 110:2:120 CDS 16:1:4 SPG 31:587 WCK 12:2:35

sixty-one county hists 1855-1898, bk rev SPG 31:589

Kern Co, map 1892, bk rev GH 33:1:83

notes on early settlers KG 16:1:1 16:2:36 16:4:81

LaVilla de Sinaloa, mil lists 1748 SPG 31:556

Los Angeles, founders LL 14:4:153

misc abstr court cases 1898 MCR 10:6:139,141

private land claim recs SPG 31:544

Rio Vista, hist notes, bk rev CDS 16:1:33

Riverside, index to city reg 1910 LL 14:1:2 14:2:51 14:3:112 14:4:154

news extracts 1906 LL 14:4:176

Sherman Indian school registration recs LL 14:1:18 15:2:88

Riverside Co, deed recs index 1893-1895 LL 14:1:43 14:2:87 14:3:143 14:4:182 15:1:17 15:2:83 15:3:139 15:4:167

marrs 1908 LL 15:2:49

natural recs 1914-1917 LL 14:1:39 14:2:77

natural recs 1918 LL 15:4:175

probate recs 1901 LL 15:1:2

probate recs 1902 LL 15:2:79

probate recs 1903 LL 15:3:118

probate recs 1904 LL 15:4:169

San Bernardino, Campo Santo Memorial Park (Old Cath Cem) cem inscr LL 14:2:71 14:4:184 15:3:147

San Bernardino Co, births 1890-1899 VQ 16:1:3 16:2:18 16:3:35

marrs 1871-1877 VQ 16:4:52

San Buenaventura, mission rec 1811-1812, bk rev SPG 31:590

San Diego Co, Pala Mission cem inscr OC 16:4:144

San Jose, autograph album 1892-1895 of Minnie Senn SCC

16:4:98

Santa Ana, Old Santa Ana cem inscr OC 16:2:43 16:3:101 16:4:131

Santa Barbara Co, census 1852 AW 5:1:10

census 1870 mort sched AW 5:1:25

marrs 1876 AW 5:1:20

marrs 1877 AW 5:2:42

migration patterns 1850 AW 5:1:9

misc pioneers AW 5:1:19 5:2:70 5:4:102

news abstr SMV 11:1:7,14,17

Santa Clara Co, geneal libs, notes on SCC 16:2:29

marr licenses 1876-1880 SCC 16:2:32

pioneers biog notes SCC 16:1:1 16:2:19 16:3:72

voter rolls 1900 SCC 16:1:5 16:2:16 16:3:63 16:4:88

Santa Clara Valley, obits 1977 SCC 16:3:79 16:4:106

shipwrecks, bk rev CDS 16:2:3

Southern CA, coast counties, early settlers KG 16:1:7 16:2:28 16:4:87

transportation hist, bk rev SPG 31:590

USC class 1915 KN 2:1:14

SP-Mexican fams, bk rev SCS 14:2:53

Stockton, news abstr 1850-1855, bk rev CTN 11:4:699 CDS 16:1:33

news death notices v2 1856-1862, bk rev TB 6:3:23

Torrance, Roosevelt Memorial Park cem inscr KN 2:2:7 2:3:21

Tulare Co, marr rec index 1853-1892, bk rev DWC 5:4:112 WB 10:2:69

Visalia, cem recs to 1920 SN 5:1:3 5:2:3 5:3:3 5:4:3 5:5:4 5:6:4 5:7:3 5:8:3

CALKINS, Calvin Chase b1841 w Catherine R Boyce, Lilla (Davis) Katz, NY, IL, CO, geneal BGS 9:3:14

CAMERON, Ina Cecelia, auto, bk

rev TB 6:1:33

CAMP, Edward d1659, CT, geneal, bk rev CTN 10:4:705

Frederick Tracy b1850 w Marion Fee, PA, WA, geneal, bk rev TB 6:3:20

geneal, bk rev OC 16:1:33

Samuel f1775, CT, VA & GA, geneal, bk rev GGM 71:6

CAMPBELL, Aaron Isaac b1904 w Mittie Thompson, TX, anc ch THT 6:3:89

Arthur Lee f1812 w Sarah Thompson, VA, TN, KY, biog notes BGS 8:1:20

James M b1813 w Maria Jane Moor, Bible rec HTR 22:4:128

Jesse b1883 w Amy Inez Dayton, IA, anc ch GR 21:4:142

Journal of Clan Campbell Soc, 636 Chesopeian Tr, Virginia Beach VA 23452

Lewis b1836 w Philena Pein Argo, IL, acct bk 1852 & biog notes DWC 5:1:16,20

Richard b1776 w Martha Reed, Ir, OH, anc ch REP 19:4:160

Robert d1725 w Janet Stuart, Scot, Ir, MA, CT, geneal, bk rev GH 33:3:104 NYR 110:3:183 CTN 12:2:363 KCG 20:4:207

CANADA, Acadia, Acadian hist & geneal, corrections AGE 8:2:52 8:3:81 *;4:112

censuses AGE 8:4:118

Acadians in NE JM 2:2:10

Alberta, sources of geneal at Prov archives, bk rev ACL 4:2:25

British Columbia, Alberni, Riverbend cem inscr BCG 6:3:7

Alert Bay, residents 1934 BCG 7:3:82

Blind Bay cem inscr BCG 7:3:77

Camp McKinney cem inscr BCG 8:1:3

Chilliwack, news vr 1891 BCG 8:1:6

clock & watchmakers 1700-1900 BCG 7:1:35

Courtenay, biog hist, bk rev BCG 6:2:21

Cowichan Bay, Dougan fam cem

inscr BCG 6:1:19

Delta, map & hist BCG 8:3:50, 52

Delta, museum & archives BCG 8:4:76

Denman Island, biog hist, bk rev BCG 6:2:20

Denman Island, orig Crown grants BCG 6:2:9 6:3:1

Denman Island, pioneers in local direct BCG 7:3:60

geneal ties with CA GE 49:1

Hedley, cem inscr BCG 5:1:22

Hedley, hist BCG 5:1:21

Hornby Island, biog hist, bk rev BCG 6:2:20

Hornby Island, orig Crown grants BCG 6:2:9 6:3:1

Lone Butte cem inscr BCG 5:3:13

Midway, Cemetary on the Range cem inscr BCG 8:2:25

Nakusp, hist BCG 5:3:2

Oliver cem inscr BCG 6:2:18

Pender Harbour, Forest View cem inscr BCG 6:4:5 7:3:55

Pender Harbour, Kleindale cem inscr BCG 6:4:7

registration of births, deaths, marrs act 1872 BCG 5:4:28

removals to Revelstoke cemeteries BCG 8:1:15

Richmond, hist & map BCG 8:3:50

Rocky Mountain Rangers 1902 BCG 8:4:90

Shawnigan Lake, cem inscr BCG 5:4:31

Smithers, hist BCG 6:2:16

Sorrento, St. Mary's Anglican-United Ch cem inscr BCG 7:3:48

Surrey, map & hist BCG 8:3:50,53

telephone direct 1890 BCG 5:3:15

Vancouver, Eleventh Reg of Royal Irish Fusileers of Can 1912-1913 BCG 7:3:47

Vancouver Island, Union City 1889 BCG 7:3:73

Vernon, Pioneer Park cem inscr

BCG 7:1:2

Victoria, direct 1860 BCG 5:4:2

Victoria, news extracts 1862 BCG 6:1:17

Victoria, WWI 13th Field Ambulance BCG 6:4:9

Canada Company Settlers hist, bk rev FAM 18:3:137

Canadian geneal handbk, bk rev BCG 7:1:9

direct of Can recs & mss repositories, bk rev BCG 6:1:9 8:2:34

gazeteer 1846, bk rev OG 3:2:58

geneal guide to Public Archives TT 19:3:129

geneal handbook, bk rev NGS 67:4:310 OG 5:2:58

geneal res guide TST 12:34:37 OG 3:2:39 FTR 20:1 SGS 29:2:129 29:3:231

guide for Canadians, bk rev OG 5:4:116

imms from Channel Islands hist, bk rev GH 33:4:109 DE 3:3:28 KCG 20:3:146

Manitoba, dog lic 1847-1945 BCG 8:1:24

geneal res guide GJ 8:2:91

news extracts BCG 7:3:54

New Brunswick, St John, Irish imm 1847, bk rev BCG 8:4:83

New Westminster, May queens 1870-1955 BCG 6:4:12

Newfoundland, fam names, bk rev GN 2:7:215

hist demography, bk rev IR 11:1:69

news in microform BCG 5:1:13

Nova Scotia, Annapolis Co, Clements Twp, misc deeds 1784-1803 AG 55:1:32

biblio of publ geneals, bk rev GN 2:8:250

Cape Breton Island, Inverness Co, Mabou pioneers hist v2, bk rev GN 2:7:213

Cape Breton Island, Presb Ch hist 1920-1975, bk rev GN 2:8:249

Cape Breton Island, Victoria Co, hist 1885 (Patterson), bk

rev CDS 16:2:4

clansmen biogs, bk rev GN 2:8:246

Cumberland Twp, settlers c1770 NGS 67:3:182 67:4:267

Digby Co, St Mary's Bay area hist vl,2, bk rev GN 2:6:172

Dowling's Co, Royal N S vols 1780 NGS 67:1:59

Eastern Shore Dist census 1871 GN 2:8:252

Eastern Shore Dist census 1871, index GN 2:5:151

geneal res guide GJ 8:2:59

geneal res guide, bk rev GN 2:6:175 CTN 12:1:179 BCG 8:4:78 CDS 16:2:5 SCS 16:2:58

Halifax Co, hist & geneal, bk rev GN 2:8:246

news abstr vr 1813-1822, bk rev CTN 12:1:179 CDS 16:2:4

Passamaguoddy geneal hist 1975, bk rev TB 6:4:21

Scots empire hist, bk rev GN 2:7:216

marr lic bonds 1800-1805 GN 2:6:182 2:7:219 2:8:256

Queens Co settlers 1759-1764 TT 19:2:73

Ontario, Baldoon, hist FAM 18:4:161

Borough of Etobicoke, Stonehouse Primitive Meth Chapel hist & cem inscr FAM 18:3:127

Duncombe Rebellion 1837 & arrest list FAM 18:4:151

Durham Co, marrs 1805-1817 FAM 18:4:223

emig to MI FAM 18:4:169

Gainsborough Pres Ch rec FAM 18:2:75

geneal res guide BCG 5:4:29 NGS 67:1:14 PGB 11:X:11

Glengarry Co, Charlottenburgh Twp, Williamstown, St Andrew's Ch reg 1799-1914 BCG 7:1:4

guide to archival resources vl Peterborough region, bk rev ACL 4:2:25

guide to geography FAM 18:1:29

guide to hist county atlases

FAM 18:1:31

Hastings Co, land owners 1878, notes on WB 10:2:60

London, geneal res guide FAM 18:4:214

London, Liparian Italian Colony 1874-1905 FAM 18:4:197

London, misc cem inscr FAM 18:4:184

loyalists' descendants, bk rev GJ 8:4:219

Middlesex Co, pioneers biogs 1904, bk rev GN 2:7:212

Middlesex Co, South Yarmouth Twp, early hist FAM 18:4:191

Perth Co, archives res guide FAM 18:4:220

Saltfleet, hist, bk rev BCG 7:3:53

western Ontario geneal & hist resources FAM 18:4:209

Williamstown cem inscr vl,2, bk rev BCG 6:1:9

Ottawa, hist of early news FAM 18:3:117

Public Archives guide QBC 2:1:7

passports 1681-1752, bk rev DM 43:2:87

Port Royal, census 1678 AGE 8:2:41 8:3:83

ship pass list, "Empress of Ireland" 1911 BCG 5:3:24

"Lake Manitoba" 1911 BCG 6:1:10

"Missanabie" 1915 BCG 5:2:29

"Scandinavian" 1919 BCG 6:2:1

"Sierra Nevada", "Oregon", "Devastation" & Pacific 1862 BCG 8:3:67

ship pass lists TRI 19:4:67

Quebec, geneal res guide TST 12:25:47 12:26:46 NGS 67:1:34 JMS 2:2:4

Megantic Co, Inverness Twp, hist, bk rev GH 33:6:76

news extracts BCG 6:4:16

parishes, villages & townships BCG 6:4:11

state & Prov archives guide (1977), bk rev TB 6:4:32

United Church of anada, central archives, geneal res

guide BCG 6:4:1

Upper Canada, migration from Scot 1823, bk rev GN 2:7:212

natural recs 1828-1850, nominal index 1828-1830 FAM 18:3:103

Scot emig to new settlements 1821, bk rev GN 2:7:212

Vancouver, news extracts BCG 6:2:15

WWI, Canadian Expeditionary Force to France BCG 7:1:10

letters from the front, bk rev BCG 8:3:64

Yukon, geneal res guide BCG 8:4:81

CANADY, Julia d1873, WI cem inscr WI 25:3:166

CANN,Isaac f1868 w Elizabeth, Can, Bible rec GN 2:7:208

CANNON, John Rutler b1796 w Patience Lowry Smith, TN, anc ch YP 9:1:5

Newton b1761 w Betsey Juett, DE, KY, geneal, bk rev GH 33:4:116 TST 12:16:40 KCG 20:2:94

CAPPUCCIO, Leo b1910 w Alice Maybelle Sewell, PA, NY, anc ch BGS 11:3:136

CARD, John Winship Stinson b1821 w Isabella B White, ME, Bible rec DE 3:4:14

CARLETON, John bc1637 w Hannah Jewett, Eng, MA, geneal, bk rev REP 19:1:46

CARLIN, Emma H h William, WI, biog notes TST 12:3:38

Squire b1801 w Sarah Wolcott, NY, OH, biog VQ 16:1:11

CARLTON, Archibald, VA, GA, AL, geneal, bk rev CTN 9:2:309

CARMICHAEL, Andrew d1841 w Margaret Mansfield, KY, OH, IN, anc ch REP 19:2:83

fams of Scot, NC & SC, geneal, bk rev GH 33:1:91

LeRoy b1905 w Ethel Liston, IL, NB, anc ch BGS 11:2:80

CARNAHAN, John, PA will 1882 KK 17:1:7

Samuel w Susan, KS will 1869 KK 17:1:7

CARNES, Joseph A b1821 w Elizabeth Acker, OH, anc ch REP 19:1:26

CARON, Pierre Auguste (Beaumarchais) f1775, Fr, biog notes DAR 113:5:469

CARPENTER, fam of Britain, bk rev TB 6:2:17

Nathen b1759 w Catherine Mathews, NY, geneal, bk rev CTN 11:1:46

Philo 1911 w Hanah, NY, WI, Bible rec KG 16:4:93

Walter Corwin b1906 w Anna Harriett Dulin, OH, anc ch BGS 9:3:50

CARR, Franklin P b1852 w Alice Jane Carr, IN, Bible rec HJA 6:3:42

Jehiel b1824 w Mary Jane Crowe, Can, Bible rec BCG 6:2:6

Samuel b1827 w Elizabeth McCaslin, IN, Bible rec HJA 6:2:36

CARRICK, James b1856 w Alice Orline Lamb, KY, KS, obit MGR 14:4:155

CARRINGTON, Dane b1787 w Nancy Manross, CT, NY, Bible rec WI 25:3:128

CARROLL, Daniel II b1730, MD, geneal, bk rev KN 2:4:27

Raford b1808 w Sarah Jernigan, NC, IL, geneal FF 8:4:64

CARSON, Paul Iglehart b1894 w Edith Marion Holmes, IL, anc ch BGS 9:4:47

Wesley b1792, VA, KY, geneal, bk rev KY 21:3:115

CARTER, Allan Loraine b1890 w Olga May Meloy, MS, PA, TX, anc ch THT 6:3:72

Gilbert b1811 w Mary Ann Hodgins, Ir,Can, biog notes FAM 18:1:8

Hattie M (Brown) d1932 h L O Carter, IL, fam recs & obit CI 15:3:98

Henry, names listed in estate inv 1829 MD 20:4:294

Hugh d1891, AL, obit VL 14:1:13

John Elam b1856 w Emily Samantha Parker, IN, IL, KS,

anc ch BGS 11:2:81

Milton Harry b1904 w Lorraine Florence Tabbitt, IL, anc ch MD 20:4:331

Theodrick b1840, TN, biog, bk rev GH 33:3:104

William b1781 w Margaret Updike, VA, OH, anc ch REP 19:3:117

William m1828 w Rebecca Sylvester, TN, MO, Bible rec ORB 18:4:93

William J b1844 w Lucy E. Wheeler, OH, obit AH 4:3:95

CARTMELL, fam of VA, OH, IL & KY, geneal, bk rev GFP 29:1:5 KCG 20:3:147

CARVER, Timothy f1750 w Rebecca Washburn, MA, NY, Bible rec CTN 12:2:234

CASE, A M, MI, letter 1837 MI 24:2:63

Abel Jr b1786 w Miriam Squires, Bible rec CTN 11:2:219

Allen b1814 w Nancy, Bible rec AH 3:4:113

Halbert B b1838,OH, biog notes AH 3:2:57

James m1872 w Ella S Farrar, Bible rec CTN 10:2:267

CASEY, Abner bc1700 w Harriet Green, Ir, Am, geneal, bk rev GH 33:6:86

CASKEY, George Washington bc1829 w Martha Ann Tisdale, OH, IA, anc ch REP 19:3:130

CASSO, Lorenzo f1859 w Mathilda Reine Ramagosse, LA, geneal, bk rev YP 9:2:105

CASTLE, Polly Curtis b1841 h Henry Fuquary, James Fuquay, James Henry Robinson, George Boyden, Samuel R Weed, Robert E Edwards, William Baker, Harrison Strodes, IN, biog notes TSP 3:1:14

Richard f1728, Ir, notes on IR 11:2:119

CATALANO, Casimir f1854 w Concetta Palomisano, It, anc ch ITG 2:42

CATHCART, John f1776, PA, IN, biog notes MIS 11:4:52

CATHERWOOD, Mary Hartwell, local sketches IL, bk rev VAG 23:4:312

CATLIN, James Edwin f1865 w Eliza Mills, PA, Civil War diary begun at Caonfederate prison YV 11:4:183

CATTELL, Mary (Ogborne) Engle b1688 h John Engle, Jonas Cattell, Thomas French, biog notes GNJ 54:2:49

CAUDILL, Jeremiah b1824 w Jane Holbrooks, KY, anc ch REP 19:3:122

CAUSEY, Thomas bc1774 w Mary Swift, MD, NC, IL, geneal FF 8:4:70

CAVILEER, John d1831, biog notes GNJ 54:2:132

CESTER, Orville Ray b1920 w Beatrice Lena Hurtle, SD, CA, anc ch CPY 8:3:71

CHADBOURN, Joseph S f1862, TX, Civil War discharge LL 15:3:146

CHALFANT, James Madison, PA, NE, acct bk 1858 BGS 7:3:12

John d1725, PA, geneal, bk rev BGS 5:2:20

John Mac b1886 w Minnie Elma Shoemaker, NE, CO, anc ch BGS 9:4:41

CHAMBERLAN, Jonathan b1774 w Hannah Culver, IN, geneal FF 8:2:68

CHAMBERLAIN, Philo Haines b1893 w Marian Louise Dow, IL, WI, anc ch FF 8:2:28

CHAMBERLIN, Joseph Fitch b1905 w Blanche O Buckingham, IA, anc ch ACL 4:2:34

CHAMBERS, Maxwell d1816, NC, cem inscr NCJ 5:1:60

CHANDLER, Abram f1776 w Sarah, NY, geneal AB 7:4:75

Albert b1841 w Lizzie Englehart, ME, MO, KS, Bible rec YV 11:1:41

Ann Dugan (McCall) Oldham b1822, KY, TX, fam rec THT 1:2:12

Jacob b1793 w Elizabeth Reeder, AR, Bible rec TA 14:3:69

Preslon b1820 w B A Bartlett, Bible rec TA 14:3:67

Robert Grissom b1898 w Edith Bernice Roxburgh, IL, CA, anc ch FF 8:3:58

CHAPLIN, Reuben b1817 w Mary Barr, Bible rec HH 14:2:81

CHAPMAN, George Henry m1842 w Nancy Maria Currier, OH, CT, diary BGS 3:3:9

Joseph d1898, ME, CA, biog notes DE 2:5:7

Orrin b1787 w Penelope Gates, CT, fam rec THT 1:2:36

Robert b616 w Ann Blith, Eng, CT, biog notes BGS 10:4:18

CHAPPELL, Eleanor (DeWolf) b1832 h Chauncey C Chappell, OH, obit AH 1:3:11

CHARLEMAGNE, lineage bk 2, bk rev CTN 7:2:296

misc pedigrees of Emperor Charlemagne's descendants v 3, bk rev VAG 23:3:233

CHARLES, fam, Bible rec NW 2:4:118

Jonathan b1813 w Rowena Bannister, ME, NY, auto MGR 14:2:74

CHARLTON, David b1831 w Lydia Barnes, Can, biog notes FAM 18:1:9

CHASE, George Franklin d1918 w Augusta A Staples, MA, ME, CO, Bible rec BGS 7:4:19

John Henry b1806 w Olive Skinner, OH, anc ch REP 19:4:159

Philander m1796 w Mary Fay, Sophia May Ingraham, VT, NY, OH, biog notes OHR 20:2:65

William d1684, MA, geneal 1968, bk rev REP 19:1:42

William b1787, NY, MI, geneal, bk rev TS 21:1:26

William Bradford b1886 w Jesse Emma Telke, WI, CA, anc ch PGB 11:7:74

CHATARD, fam recs 1794-1892, film rev GH 33:6:91

CHAUVIN, fam of Can, misc notes AGE 8:2:46

Louis b1702 w Marguerite

Mallet, Angelique Perthuit, Can, anc ch AGE 8:2:48

CHEESMAN, Edward b1810 w Sarah Chandler, Eng, OH, anc ch REP 19:3:123

CHENAULT, Anderson b1788 w Emily Cameron, Bible rec KA 15:1:40

CHENEY, Brothers of CT, silk merchants hist CTB 44:3:65 44:4:106

Claudius Franklin, MA, geneal, bk rev CSB 14:1:21

CHENOT, Jean Josepah b1788 w Marie Barbe Mathiew, Marie Barbe Fisteur, Fr, PA, OH, biog STC 2:2:69

CHERRY, James H m1897 w Mary Jane Call, IL, Bible rec CI 14:4:149

CHEYNEY, fam of MD, geneal MD 20:1:33

CHILDERS, E P, OK, letter 1890 BGS 9:3:29

CHILDS, fam of RI, letters c1836 THT 7:1:30

CHILTON, James, "Mayflower" descs, bk rev GH 33:4:112 GE 47:13 VAG 23:3:232 NYR 110:4:249 DM 43:144 GN 2:7:216 CTN 12:2:365 NGS 67:4:303 TB 6:4:31

CHINESE AMERICAN GENEALOGY, geneal res guide, bk rev GH 33:5:69

CHIPMAN, Benjamin b1752 w Abigail Milliken, ME, geneal MQ 45:4:194

CHITTENDEN, Giles b1769 w Mary Hawley, CT, VT, Bible rec CTN 10:2:363

CHOAT, Isham b1802 w Rebecca Vorhis, TX, fam rec FP 22:1:9

CHOUTEAU, Marie Terese Bourgeois b1733 h Rene Chouteau, Pierre Laclede, LA, geneal, bk rev GH 33:1:91 IL 11:1:53 OC 16:2:70 TS 21:1:26 SCS 16:1:20

CHRISTIAN, John Hunt b1774 w Mary (Heath) Bates, VA, Bible rec VAG 23:3:191 MD 20:4:335

Philip f1778 w Barbara DeVault, PA, fam notes EWA 16:4:151

CHRISTIANSEN, Olar Theodore b1907 w Gustava Sophia Anderson, NE, IL, IA, anc ch OC 16:4:122

CHRISTIAN-SKELTON, index to 1965 geneal, bk rev GH 33:3:104

CHURCH, Benjamin diary of King Philip's War 1675-1676, bk rev CTN 8:2:318

CHYNOWETH, William m1818 w Biddy, Eng, MD, NC, OH, IA, Bible rec HH 14:3:151

CISLER, fam geneal, bk rev CI 15:4:155

CLACK, Sterlaing b1759 w Mary Wood, VA, NC, KY, biog notes KFR 7:89

CLARDY, James b1782 w Frances Richardson, VA, SC, TN, Bible rec CPY 8:3:72

CLARK, Amos b1847 w Sarah L Elston, OH, anc ch REP 19:2:88

Elijah f1773, GAa, biog notes GP 16:2:1

Elizabeth f1661 h William Furber, NH, biog notes AG 55:2:120

fams of Springfield MA land recs 1690-1800 DM 42:3:129

Harry Waite b1877 w Ada Blanche Jones, IN, IL, anc ch HJA 6:4:37

Henry Fish b1809 w Mary Roberts, NY, Bible rec CTN 11:3:408

Henry Harrison b1880 w Sophia Rae Douglas, WI, MN, IL, anc ch NGI 3:1:37

John bc1640, MA, CT, geneal DM 43:2:61

John Alexander dc1928, KY, IL, biog notes MCH 7:3:87

M J b1924 w Hazel Lucille Helton, MN, TX, anc ch THT 6:3:85

Marshall b1874 w Lillian V Peabody, IN, KS, Bible rec TS 21:4:170

Peter F, OR, biog notes, bk rev BB 11:3:48

Samuel Sr, geneal, bk rev OG 2:2:58

fam of AL, notes on VL 13:4:164

CLAY, Harry, KY, letter 1851 REG 77:4:263

CLAYPOOL, Perry R bc1815 w Mary Ann Burnett, Bible rec GFP 28:10:189

CLAYTON, Jesse b1816, NC, biog notes NCJ 5:1:23

John bc1638 w Mary, Eng, NJ, geneal QY 6:2:3

CLAYTOR, William b1805 w Esther, VA, PA, IL, fam rec FF 8:2:36

CLEAVER, Stephen b1766 w Rebecca Smith, Elenor Tapley, Mary Hays, VA, WV, KY, MO, biog KA 14:4:223

CLELAND, Robert b1805 w Lilley Wylie, Ir, Can, biog notes FAM 18:1:9

CLEM, John C m1778 w Susannah, Neth, MD, OH, geneal IG 15:2:49

CLEMENT, Leonard b1677 w Marie Jeanne Morissette, Fr, Can, geneal, bk rev GH 33:1:91

CLEMMER, Abraham G b1828 w Anna Elizabeth Dimmig, Emmaline Buchart, PA, WA, Bible rec YV 11:1:40

CLEMONS, Eli P b1775 w Ruth Hanscum, ME, Bible rec DE 2:5:14

fam of ME, geneal, bk rev REP 19:1:44

CLEPPER, James Duncan b1901 w Lela Myrtle Briers, TX, anc ch GR 21:3:94

CLERGY, Col clergy descendants supp 1978, bk rev NGS 67:3:223

Col clergy in N E, bk rev CTN 10:4:704

Col clergy of CT, bk rev OC 14:1:32

Col clergy of VA, NC, SC, bk rev TST 12:5:37

CLEVENGER-STILTNER, geneal, bk rev OG 2:1:28

CLEVELAND, Mary Jane b1839 h William Camp, Clinton Little, Philip Dayhuff, PA, IL, Bible rec CI 14:4:128

CLIMO, fam of Cornwall, Eng,

geneal, bk rev BCG 8:1:14

CLINE, Reuben H f1841 w Sarah Elvina Taulbee, geneal FF 8:1:47

William b1747 w Jane Woten, NJ, OH, IN, anc ch REP 19:3:123

CLORE, Michael f1717, geneal, bk rev KY 21:3:115

CLUXTON, George Alton b1890 w Alma Jane Haggenmacher, OH, IL, anc ch FF 8:3:58

COALE, fam of Eng & Am, geneal v1-2, bk rev NGS 67:4:302

COBB, John Fb1825 w Mary A Millett, ME, Bible rec DE 3:4:22

Joseph f1588, geneal, bk rev HTR 22:1:5

COBURN, Otis R b1816 w Emma A Barstow, NY, OH, anc ch REP 19:4:156

William B b1825 w Virona Forbes, CT, Bible rec CTN 7:2:318

COCHRAN, George b1793 w Rebecca Barkley, Bible rec BWG 8:1:38

James A b1840 w Lucy W Rannelds, Bible rec BGS 6:4:3

James Allen b1843 w Grace Maria Rannells, MO, CO, geneal BGS 9:1:8

Robert f1784 w Agnus (Nancy), KY, geneal KY 21:3:83

COCHRUN, William C b1814 w Diannah Peel, OH, anc ch REP 19:3:120

COCKERHAM, Carlton Ray b1925 w Mattie Zula Ray, WV, anc ch RRS 12:2:209

COE, Robert d1856, VA will MGR 14:4:157

COFFIN, George H, ME, Civil War diary DE 3:1:30

COHEN, Jerome b1919 w Evelyn Marie Powers, CA, anc ch NGI 3:2:111

COKE, William Walter b1905 w Beulah Ethel Hayes, MO, anc ch TB 6:4:25

COLBERT, Benjamin Franklin f1846, OK, notes on THT 5:1:33

COLBURN, Theodore b1830, Can, geneal, bk rev CI 14:1:29

COLE, Adolphus E w Marina, VA, letter 1863 THT 3:1:14

Andrew P w Acenith A Bishop, geneal, bk rev CTN 11:1:41

James Jr bc1762 w Jemima Curtis, VA, SC, TX, anc ch YP 9:1:2

John b1725 w Sarah Page, Sarah Chapman, CT, notes on AG 55:1:39

Joseph R m1827 w Harriet S Pilcher, Bible rec HJA 6:3:43

Lloyd F b1919 w Ella Mae Rhodes, an, ID, WA, anc ch DG 4:3:70

Oviatt, OH, notes on TT 19:1:23

Scott Matthew b1886 w Hettie Mae Moon, TX, anc ch FF 8:3:59

COLEMAN, George b1790 w Isabella Clarke, Bible rec KN 2:2:35

COLLADAY, Jacob Woodward b1811, PA, geneal, bk rev NGS 67:2:148

COLLAR, Walter W f1882, CT diary excerpts LL 14:3:137

COLLARD, Elijah Simmons b1778 w Mary Stark, VA, TX, geneal THT 6:3:99

John N b1817, w Rachel D Turnbough, Mary Ann Moore, MO Bible rec THT 5:3:5

COLLES, Christopher b1739, Ir, NY, biog notes BGS 8:3:31

COLLESON, William w Mary Townsend, NC marr license 1722 NCJ 5:3:149

COLLETTE, Antoine b1859 w Domithilde LeBlanc, Can, anc ch AGE 8:2:66

COLLIN, John b1732 w Sarah Collin, Bible rec NYR 110:2:75

COLLINS, Edward Miller b1900 w Glacie Merle Cox, MO, anc ch OC 16:3:99

Robert Fred b1924 w Sarah Josephine Taylor, OK, anc ch ORB 17:9:85

William, Wales, geneal, bk rev NYR 110:3:180

COLORADO, Arkansas Valley, hist 1881, bk rev TB 6:3:23

Boulder, burials of misc foreign born BGS 11:4:158

census 1860 BGS 3:1:5

census 1870 BGS 7:3:7

Central School reg 1885 BGS 5:3:32

city direct 1896 BGS 8:1:23 8:4:5

Columbia cem, bodies removed to Green Mountain cem 1916 BGS 4:1:15

Columbia cem, cem inscr BGS 4:4:28

Cong Ch members (cont) BGS 6:1:19

Cong Ch recs 1864-1889 BGS 4:3:3

Cong Ch recs cont BGS 8:2:9 8:3:21 8:4:22 9:1:30 9:2:26

direct 1896 BGS 9:3:8 9:4:5 10:1:6 10:2:3 10:3:2 10:4:4

First Cong Ch bapt recs BGS 4:2:9

First Meth Ch recs 1894 BGS 5:4:17

hist notes BGS 3:1:16,17 3:3:1,4,19 3:4:1,5,10 4:1:1, 12,14,21,28 4:2:17,20 4:3:8, 11,22,25 5:2:18 5:3:29 5:4: 18,26 6:2:4 6:3:3,6 6:4:16 7: 1:12 7:2:1,12,25 7:3:17 7:4: 5,14

hotels hist, bk rev BGS 3:1:7

marrs to 1880 BGS 3:1:8 3:3:12 3:4:12 4:1:6 4:2:12

Meth Ch hist BGS 7:3:13

military burials BGS 3:1:11 3:3:16

Sacred Heart of Jesus Cath Ch hist & recs BGS 5:2:2 5:3:5 5:4:3 6:2:10 6:3:14 6:4:18 7:1:5 7:2:6

St John's Epis Ch recs BGS 5:1:2

school teachers 1890 BGS 5:3:33

soldiers in Spanish-Am War BGS 5:1:16

Trinity Evang English Luth Ch recs BGS 4:4:2 6:4:29

Trinity Luth Ch, hist & recs BGS 9:L3:10 9:4:11 10:1:3

Boulder Co, Altoona City,

census 1860 BGS 6:3:8

Burlington cem inscr BGS 4:3:12

Caribou, hist notes BGS 5:2:1

court house recs BGS 10:1:1

court houses BGS 7:4:3

deaths 1869-1870 BGS 6:2:17

deaths 1879-1880 BGS 6:2:17

Eldora, hist notes BGS 6:1:1

Eldora, poll bk 1901 BGS 8:1:2

Erie, hist notes BGS 6:3:1

farmers direct 1892 BGS 6:3:19 6:4:5

geneal res guide BGS 7:3:24

Gold Hill, census 1860 BGS 6:1:10

Hygiene, Church of the Brethren (Ger Bapt), hist & recs BGS 11:1:20

Hygiene, direct 1896 BGS 11:1:25

Hygene, St Vrain (Dunkard) Ch cem/Pella cem inscr BGS 4:4:9

Jamestown, hist notes BGS 5:4:1

Lafayette, direct 1896 BGS 11:2:58

land claims 1859 BGS 5:3:33

Longmont, hist notes BGS 4:2:10

Lyons, hist notes BGS 5:3:1

Lyons Tollhouse, hist notes BGS 7:4:1

map BGS 5:2:29a

Masonic Lodges BGS 11:4:153

marrs 1866-1910 BGS 1:1:7

mort sched 1884-1885 BGS 5:4:21

mort recs 1902-1904 BGS 5:1:9 5:2:10 5:3:13

Nederland, hist notes BGS 4:4:1

news abstr BGS 6:1:26

pioneer cem locations BGS 5:3:18

school dist #2 1888-1891 BGS 10:2:9 10:3:13 10:4:13 11:1:6

school dist #2 census 1902 BGS 11:1:10

school teachers 1893-1894 BGS 5:2:17

Sugar Loaf Dist, hist notes BGS 7:1:1

Sunshine, hist notes BGS 5:1:1

Sunshine, Sunshine cem inscr BGS 5:4:12

Superior, Superior cem inscr BGS 5:3:20

Superior, Superior (old Louisville) cem inscr BGS 9:3:34

townships 1872 BGS 6:2:25

Valmont, direct 1896 BGS 11:3:102

Valmont, Valmont Community United Pres Ch, hist & recs BGS 11:3:99

Ward, hist notes BGS 6:2:1

Boulder Valley, old school districts BGS 11:1:5

Cath bapt in northern CO BGS 7:1:5 7:2:6

Colorado militia, Tyler's Rangers 1864 hist BGS 5:3:22

communities 1885, 1911 CO 40:4:165

Cripple Creek, First Cong Ch, misc members 1912 SGS 29:3:226

Fort Logan hist CO 40:3:101

geneal res guide BGS 8:1:11 8:2:2

geneal res guide, bk rev TB 6:3:22

Golden cem inscr CO 40:1:33 40:2:42 40:3:136 40:4:188

hist, bk rev CTN 9:1:125

homestead entries index CO 40:2:49 40:3:107 40:4:155

imms from Czech, notes on FH 2:2:46

index to fam recs at geneal soc CO 40:4:181

Louisville, Louisville cem inscr BGS 8:3:27 8:4:25 9:1:33 9:2:29 9:3:30

Loveland, hist BGS 8:3:31

maps 1860, 1861 CO 40:2:45

mining laws index CO 40:1:14

misc marrs 1859-1862 BGS 9:1:24 9:2:12

naturalizations CO 40:1:19

newspapers CO 40:3:104

placenames CO 40:3:104

Primos, mining camp school reg 1907 BGS 5:3:32

public recs of CO CO 40:2:43

Pueblo, misc news abstr 1876 THT 5:1:30

RR builders 1879-1880 CO 40:4:153

Ryssby, Swedish Luth Ch hist & recs BGS 7:3:1

St Vrain Dist (Burlaington), census 1870 BGS 7:4:9

Salina cem inscr BGS 5:1:5

Sunset cem inscr BGS 5:1:4

territ laws abstr 1861-1876 BGS 4:2:1

Weld Co, Pleasant View cem inscr BGS 5:1:6

COLVER, Amos b1813 w ____, Mary Jane Fry, Margaret Hackleman Jackson, OH, OR, biog notes ORB 17:7:64

COMBS, Charles b1793 w Abigail Revis Brassfield, NC, IN, anc ch HJA 6:3:48

COMPUTER, National geneal computer bank JG 4:5:20

CONANT, George m1718 w Mary Howland, MA, noltes on MQ 45:3:138

COND, Charles W b1826 w Jane Frances Driggs, Bible rec CTN 11:4:596

CONDITT, Fielding b1771 w Sally Cheeves, VA, NC, TN, geneal v9, bk sev GH 33:4:117

CONDER, E P N b1860 w M Ann Harkness, NC, Bible recOTHT 3:1:11

CONGER, Albina Leslie b1837 h Seymour Stevens Butler, OH, IN, diary extracts LL 14:4:195

CONNECTICUT, Barkhamsted, hist, bk rev CTN 9:1:126

beginner;s geneal res guide, bk rev CTN 9:3:468

Bethlehem, hist, bk rev CTN 9:3:474

births before 1730 (Barbour) CTN 7:1:11 7:2:168 7:3:328 7:4:486 8:1:9 8:2:173 8:3:329 8:4:634 9:1:6 9:2:162 9:3:335 9:4:504 10:1:13 10:2:212 10:3:387 10:4:567 11:1:13 11:2:198 11:3:380 11:4:565 12:1:7 12:2:194 12:3:386

12:4:564

Bridgewater, hist 1703-1833 (1882), bk rev CTN 10:2:348

Bristol, St Ann Parish marrs 1908-1977, bk rev AGE 8:4:109

Tunxis Indian legends, bk rev CTN 11:4:698 CDS 16:1:4

cem inscr before 1800 CTN 7:1:36 7:2:200 7:3:347 7:4:508 8:1:29 8:2:201 8:3:355 8:4:544 9:1:119 9:2:175 9:3:371 9:4:530 10:1:38 10:2:228 10:3:409 10:4:592 11:1:26 11:2:220 11:3:398 11:4:586 12:1:32 12:2:222 12:3:408 12:4:594

census 1762, descr CTB 44:2:33

census 1850 (part) CTN 10:2:355 10:4:588 11:1:35 11:2:228

Col justice CTN 11:3:371

Col town officials CTN 12:4:585

East Haddam, hist 1871, bk rev CTN 9:2:307

Eastford, hist, bk rec CTN 10:4:701

Fairfield, hist & geneal 1930, bk rev CTN 9:2:310

geneal notes of first settlers (1856), bk rev CTN 11:4:698

geneal res guide OK 24:4:190 CTN 12:3:371

geographic dict 1894, bk rev NYR 110:3:184 CTN 11:4:700 NGS 67:1:73

Glastonbury, hist, bk rev CTN 9:2:308

hist 1853, bk rev CTN 9:2:316

Greenwich, loyalists hist, bk rev CTN 10:2:351

Griswold, Brewster fam cem NSN 4:2:19

guide to vr published in CTN MN 10:4:171

Guilford, births & deaths 1690-1715 CTN 10:1:160

marr recs 1690-1715 CTN 8:3:347

Hartford, Col hist, bk rev CDS 16:3:4

vr 1645-1825 (Barbour), bk rev CTN 10:2:343 DM 42:3:137

hist, bk rev CTN 9:4:608

hist notes DAR 113:5:502

hist series v1-5, bk rev CTN 8:4:542

Killingworth, land recs errors in Barbour collect CTN 11:2:226

land recs guide CTN 7:2:174

Lebanon, Goshen Cong Ch recs CTN 12:3:392

Ledyard, Gales Ferry Village, hist, bk rev 9:3:470

Litchfield Co, reg of Rev War burials, bk rev CTN 9:2:309

Lyme, hist, bk rev CTN 10:2:350

hist (1876), bk rev CTN 10:2:348

vr 1665-1850, bk rev CTN 10:3:525

Mansfield, hist 1702-1972, bk rev CTN 8:2:319

marrs before 1750 CTN 7:1:25 7:2:178 7:3:338 7:4:499 8:1:19 8:2:185 8:3:341 8:4:527 9:2:168 9:3:346 9:4:518 10:1:27 10:2:199 10:3:410 10:4:584 11:2:208 11:3:388 11:4:576 12:1:22 12:2:210 12:3:400 12:4:579

marrs to 1800 (1896), bk rev CTN 9:2:306

Middlesex Co, Deep River, old Winthrop cem hist & misc, bk rev CTN 10:2:345

Middletown, early settlers CTN 7:1:17

Milford, fams geneal, bk rev NYR 110:4:245 GH 33:3:98 MQ 45:2:91 NGS 67:3:224

misc names from 1850 census CTN 10:3:421

misc vr missing CTN 9:4:524

Morris, Morris Academy hist, bk rev CTN 9:2:313

survey of early houses, bk rev CTN 9:2:314

New Hartford, hist notes 1775 & 1852, bk rev CTN 9:4:607

New Haven, Col news abstr 1755-1775, bk rev TST 12:25:48 GH 33:5:72 NYR 110:4:245 DM 43:2:88 CTN 12:3:535

fams v1-9 (Jacobus), bk rev CTN 7:1:128

New London, public lib holdings

CTN 8:2:316

New London Co, Stonington, hist, bk rev TB 6:2:21

New Milford, fams geneal, bk rev CTN 12:1:175

hist 1703-1833 (1882), bk rev CTN 10:2:348

Newington, hist 1833-1836 (1937), bk rev CTN 10:2:341

Newtown, Tory hist 1774-1783 CTB 44:3:88

Norwalk, loyalists hist, bk rev CTN 10:2:351

Norwich, hist 1866, bk rev CTN 10:3:525

Rev War hist, bk rev CTN 8:4:541

Old Lyme, early settlers CTN 7:1:3

place names, bk rev CTN 9:3:467

Plymouth, First Cong Ch hist 1739-1939, bk rev CTN 9:3:472

probate recs CTN 7:3:334

Redding, Tory hist 1774-1783 CTB 44:3:88

Rev War, Anglicans hist, bk rev CTN 12:3:537

cavalry commanded by Elisha Sheldon, CT Bicentennial series XIII, bk rev CTN 9:1:128

hist of art & architecture, bk rev CTN 11:3:522

hist of Cong Ch, bk rev CTN 11:3:519

hist of industry, bk rev CTN 12:3:537

hist of science, technology & medicine, bk rev CTN 12:3:536

hist of society, bk rev CTN 11:3:518

New Haven battle CTN 9:4:510

newspapers hist, bk rev CTN 9:1:129

women's hist, bk rev CTN 9:1:129

Ridgefield, Tory hist 1774-1783 CTB 44:3:88

Scot imm 1828 CTB 44:4:97

Simsbury, hist 1931, bi rev CTN 7:2:297

Somers, hist, bk rev CTN 10:2:349

pictorial hist, bk rev CTN

12:1:177

Stamford, Ferguson lib geneal materials CTN 12:2:187

land recs abstr 1666-1767 cont CTA 21:3:131 21:4:177 22:1:13 22:2:55

loyalists hist, bk rev CTN 10:2:351

Rev War patriots geneal biogs, bk rev CTN 10:2:342

state lib resources CTN 7:2:163

Stonington, First Cong Ch hist 1874, bk rev CTN 8:1:37

hist 1900, bk rev CTN 10:3:523

surnames of early settlers CTN 10:1:33

Wallingford, fams geneal 1870, bk rev NYR 10:4:245 GH 33:3:98 MQ 45:2:91 CTN 12:1:173

early fams geneal supp CTN 12:1:30 NGS 67:2:156

Wellington, hist, bk rev CTN 10:4:706

West Hartford, hist CTN 9:4:483

Westbrook, First Cong Ch recs 1725-1899 & cem inscr, bk rev CTN 12:4:699

western CT geneal res guide CTN 8:1:15

Weston, hist, bk rev CTN 12:3:534

Willington, hist, bk rev CTN 10:3:521

Windham Co, hist v1-2, bk rev CTN 8:4:541

Windsor, hist v1 (1892), bk rev CTN 9:1:130

hist v2 (1892), bk rev CTN 9:4:606

witchcraft trials, bk rev NYR 110:4:277 CTN 11:4:697

Woodbury, hist 1854, bk rev CTN 10:4:704

CONNELL, John m1802 w Eleanor Sweasingen, WV, fam rec NSN 4:4:30

CONNER, Nathan b1821 w Elizabeth Buell, VA, OR, biog notes ORB 17:8:72 17:9:82

CONNERS, George Wellington b1868 w Nellie Victoria Amey, Can, biog FAM 18:1:11

CONNOR, James b1732 w Abigail,

ME, geneal DE 3:4:12

CONRAD, Henry b1832 w Phebe Ann, Bible rec MI 24:2:44

CONVICTS, Eng convicts in Am as refugees from injustice GJ 8:3:125

COOK, Benjamin bc1675 w Bridget, NJ, geneal GNJ 54:1:1 54:2:127

Claude John b1912 w Gertrude Effie McKie, KS, IA, anc ch OG 4:2:39

Corydon b1842 w Elizabeth Kelly, Scot, PA, IN, Bible rec HG 19:2:30

fam geneal, bk rev GE 49:9

James S m1825 w Eunice Hunt, IN, Bible rec HG 19:2:29

Jonathan b1793 w Frances Harris, Bible rec FF 8:3:62

Walter b1625, MA, geneal IG 15:3:75

William Sr b1613, Eng, VA, geneal, bk rev GH 33:3:104

COOKE, fam of OH, geneal, bk rev REP 19:4:166

Thomas f1621, Eng, VA, notes on NGS 67:3:211

COOLEY, Miller Wisdom b1822 w Elizabeth Hill, KY, MO, OR, geneal RED 12:1:9

COON, fam of PA, geneal, bk rev GH 33:5:83

COOPER, Chandler b1823 w Alvira, OH, OR, biog notes GFP 29:2:33

Elizabeth Ann d1882 h Ebenezer V Cooper, cem inscr OC 16:4:130

fam of GA, fam recs GP 16:4:186

The Cooper Collection, 19 Crinkleroot CT, The Woodlands TX 77380

Thomas w Ann Locke, IL,fam recs FF 8:2:69

Thomas H b1851 w Mary Louise Scott, MO, OR, biog notes ORB 18:2:30

COPELAND, Amos b1803 w Mary Short, Sarah (Strow) Burd, KY, Bible rec KA 14:4:224

Fred Lavonne b1940 w Janet Coline Officer, TX, anc ch

NGI 3:2:114

Samuel b1757 w Lucy Proctor, MA, NH, ME, biog notes DE 3:1:24

COPPESS, Adam b1771 w Mary Mock, NC, geneal, bk rev GH 33:5:83 GE 47:13

CORBIN, Clement b1626 w Dorcas Buckminster, MA, CT, geneal v2, bk rev GH 33:3:105

CORCORAN, Daniel f1834 w Lucy Simmonds, Ir, Eng, OH, NY, Can, biog notes FAM 18:1:10

Dennis Duncan d1872 w_____, Elizabeth Granger, Ir, OH, Can, biog notes FAM 18:1:9

CORKER, William f1663 w Susan Blackmore, VA, notes on NGS 67:3:215

CORLISS, Augustus W, NE, notes on NW 2:4:137

CORN, Robert Jackson b1895 w Norma Eve Stephens, TX, anc ch GR 21:1:9

CORNELIUS, Clarence D b1892 w Eva LaPage, IL, anc ch KG 16:4:101

CORNELL, George Washington, AL, will 1825 OK 24:1:39

James b1832 w Roxanna Bacheller, MI, CO, biog notes BGS 4:3:23

CORNS, Horace Greeley b1849 w Mary E Bowser, OH, IN, anc ch REP 19:2:85

CORNUTT, Alfred b1812 w Mary Delph, VA, OR, biog notes ORB 17:8:71

CORNWELL, George Washington b1808 w Eliza D Lane, Bible rec THT 5:4:28

CORSON, William John b1800 w Elizabeth Williams, Can, biog notes FAM 18:1:10

CORWIN, Oliver b1810 w Jane Daugherty, OH, Bible rec REP 19:4:145

Phineas b1780 w Mary Magdalena Dovenbarger, IN, OH, anc ch REP 19:3:119

COTE, Remi m1846 w Marie Daigle, Can, anc ch AGE 8:1:29

COTHERN, Thomas James b1877 w

Maude Younger, KY, anc ch FF 8:2:25

COTHREN, Leander Howard Sr b1878 w Hazel Ruth Henry, IL, CO, anc ch FF 8:3:62

COTTEN, Jacob Benjamin b1849 w Mattie C Smith, MO, KY, TX, Bible rec GR 21:3:115

COUCH, James Riley b1884, biog notes OK 24:4:179

COUNTS, Thomas b1870 w Ida M Seeds, OH, anc ch REP 19:4:161

COURT, fam of MD, geneal MD 20:2:114

COURTNEY, John A b1847 w Mary Elizabeth Queen, WV, Bible rec THT 6:3:97

Wirt B b1870 w Frances J Romine, WV, Bible rec, biog notes & letters THT 6:3:97

COWAN, John w Miss McKinney, geneal, bk rev TOP 9:2:53

COWLEY, Henry Thomas b1837 w Lucy Abigail Peet, Mary A Davis, NY, WA, biog EWA 16:2:51

COWLISHAW, George b1856 w Ann Butler, Eng, CO, geneal, bk rev GH 33:3:106

COX, Edward K b1891 w Clara Bernice Agler, KS, IA, anc ch TOP 9:3:77

Thomas b1791 w Martha Cox, VA, OH, OR, biog notes ORB 18:3:61

COZAD, John J f1882, NE, biog notes AH 6:1:14

MARY FRANCES B1850, BIBLE REC AH 6:4:134

CRABTREE, William B m1880 w Docie H Caley, IL, notes on MGR 14:1:21

CRAFT, James Louis b1884 w Minnie Beatrice Childs, AL, anc ch NAS 18:2:37

CRAGG, fam of Eng & Can, geneal, bk rev FAM 18:4:228

CRAIG, Cleitus Francis b1910 w Marie Baumgartner, ND, MO, anc ch RRS 12:1:77

Craig Limbs, Box 645, Twain Harte CA 95383

George W b1845, KY, biog VQ 16:3:49

Thomas w Esther Meyer, PA, geneal, bk rev AG 55:2:125

CRAIN, Isaac Denton b1867 w Elizabeth Johnson, TN, anc ch THT 6:3:79

Jerry C b1828, TX, cem inscr AGS 20:4:148

Stephen f1775 w Mary Brinkley, VA, SC, Rev War pension appl GGM 74:303

CRANE, Joseph, IL letter 1852 DWC 5:2:36

Orrin J b1829, OH, biog notes AH 3:3:88

CRAVEN, fam of Eng & Am, geneal, bk rev YP 9:2:103

CRAWFORD, Clyde Leonard b1870 w Minnie Margaret Scott, MO, WA, anc ch OG 5:3:71

fam & related fams, geneal, bk rev OG 25:1:58

John F b1810 w Almira Zachry, MO, TN, AK, TX, Bible rec THT 2:2:17

William b1785 w Mary, NJ, PA, OH, geneal FF 8:2:56

CREATH, Robert b1777 w Ann Crawford, KY, IN, fam recs IG 15:2:59

CREEL, John Jr bc1770, VA, TN, IL, geneal FF 8:2:99

CRISS, Volliy b1893, Bible rec RES 11:3:84

CRISSINGER, William b1828 w Mary Baker, PA, TN, anc ch REP 19:3:127

CROCKETT, David, TX, letter 1834 THT 5:2:7

William b1811 w Sally Ann (Caldwell) Cole, OH, fam rec AH 3:2:42

CROEL, Joel Sr b1757 w Elizabeth Beamer, NJ, Bible rec GNJ 54:2:126

CRONE, Matilda, OH letter 1872 KN 2:1:21

CROOK, Jeremiah b1793 w Polly Arnold, SC, anc ch YP 9:2:65

CROSBY, George Sr d1731, VA will VAG 23:4:243

Mary bc1685 h Edward Mountjoy,

John Mauzy, Joseph Waugh, VA, biog notes VAG 23:4:247

CROSS, Daniel Gosnell b1809 w Phoebe Young Howell, PA, OH, anc ch REP 19:4:166

Judson N f1862, OH, biog notes AH 3:1:13

CROSSETTI, Franklin M m1870 w Mary A Driggs, Bible rec CTN 11:4:596

CROSSLEY, John Bennett b1892 w Rena Mildred Jones, KS, IL, CO, anc ch BGS 11:2:86

CROSWELL, Thomas b1633 w Priscilla Upson, MA, geneal, bk rev CTN 10:1:156

CROUCH, John f1756 w Sarah Barbary, Elizabeth Cloud Lane, VA, NC, TN, geneal FF 8:3:83

CROWDER, fam of IL, fam recs CI 15:2:20

CROWE, Edward Berry b1871 w Mary Frances Walton, Bible rec KA 14:3:166

CROZIER, James f1808 w Sarah Ann Jardine, geneal, bk rev SCS 14:2:52

CRUME, Uriah b1852 w Alice Josephine Daniels, IL, MO, NM, fam rec NMG 18:3:83

CRUMMETT, Charles Jones Sr b1870 w Mary Etta Brann, ME, anc ch RED 12:2:9

CULBERTSON, fam of IL, misc recs FF 8:1:38

William Homer b1875 w Anna Irene Boaz, MO, anc ch FF 8:2:25

CUMBLE, Rufus Charles b1854 w Rachel EuDora Blaylock, GA, AR, anc ch THT 7:1:20

CUMMINS, fam of KY, geneal, bk rev NGS 67:3:220

CUNNINGHAM, Bertram G b1851, ME, Bible rec DE 3:1:20

George William b1865 w Elsie Luella Logan, Bible rec CI 14:2:65

James M b1814 w Sarah D Standefer, Elvira C Coffey, Bible rec NAS 18:1:9

Nancy Jane (Kinsey) b1820 h

Robert Cunningham, IL, biog notes IL 11:3:134

Phoebe bc1760 h Thomas Cunningham, WV, biog DAR 113:5:542

Washington T d1897 w Lucy A Lamon, VA, IL, Bible rec NSN 4:1:2

William b1738 w Dorothy Colby, Mrs Betsey Hough, ME, biog & fam notes DE 3:2:24

William b1825 w Annah M, ME, Bible rec DE 3:1:20

CURRIER, Albertus E d1929 w Lettie O Morse, ME, Bible rec DE 3:1:12

CURREY, Edward b1778 w Elizabeth Smith, Bible rec KA 14:4:227

CURRY, Jesse J f1928 w Neva M Britton, OR, KS, anc ch TB 6:3:18

William b1748 w Charity Lockwood, NY, PA, geneal, bk rev CTN 10:4:700 11:1:47 12:1:181 NYR 110:3:183

CURTIS, Edward Sheriff bc1868 w Clara Phillips, WI, WA, biog notes TST 12:15:1

CUSHEN, Edward d1893 w Bridget Ryan, Ir, IA, Bible rec HH 14:3:151

CUSSEN, John b1864, IA fam rec HH 14:3:151

CUSTER, fam of PA, geneal (1944), bk rev GH 33:6:86 KCG 20:3:151

CUSTIN, Benjamin b1780 w Rosannah, Phebe, Bible rec CTN 11:4:594

Robert b1809 w Ruby Kelso, OH, Bible rec CTN 12:2:237

CUSTIS, fam of VA, geneal CLG 10:1:25

CZECHOSLOVAKIA, gazetteers guide GH 33:1:9

geneal res guide GH 33:6:9 NGI 3:1:40

geneal res guide, bk rev GH 33:3:97 TST 12:5:37 GE 49:8 VAG 23:2:151 NYR 110:2:120 WCK 12:1:18 DM 42:4:183 CDS 16:3:3

DAGGETT, William, ME, geneal, bk rev CTN 9:1:125

DALBEY, Aaron b1796 w Christiana Prong, PA, Bible rec IG 15:3:95

DALE, S W b1875 w Sallie, WI, TN, TX, Bible rec WI 26:2:72

DALEY, Edward Barber b1825 w Nancy Ann Hunt, NY, CA, biog VQ 16:2:23

DALL´AVA, Nocola f1842 w Julia, Italy, MA, geneal, bk rev NGS 67:2:148

DANDRIDGE, Martha b1732 h Daniel Parke Custis, George Washington-US Pres, VA, biog DAR 113:2:136 113:5:528

DANFORD, Ambrose b1784, MD, OH, biog REP 19:3:95

John b1838 w Nancy Jane Battin, OH, Bible rec REP 19:3:99

Michael b1803 w Mercy Dandord, OH, Bible rec REP 19:3:99

DANHAUER, fam of KS, geneal, bk rev GH 33:4:117

DANIEL, Simon d1722 w Sarah,, MA, will abstr with VA connections RRS 12:2:226

DANIELS, Alsace Lorraine d1977, geneal, bk rev GH 33:4:117

DARBY, George b1872 w Maude Ashford, OR, anc ch TB 6:1:22

DARLING, Benjamin f1829 w Sarah Proverbs, ME, fam rec DE 2:5:8

DARNALL, David d1702 w Margritt, MD, VA, geneal v2, bk rev GH 33:5:83

DARROW, Archie b9101 w Lillian Jeanette Parker, WA, anc ch WB 9:3:116

DAUGHERTY, fam of AL, biog notes VL 13:3:121

DAVENPORT, fam of CT, geneal notes CTN 12:3:406

Jack Smith b1784 w Lucy Keen, Bible rec KA 14:4:226

DAVIDSON, Daniel P b1842 w Mary F McMullin, Bible rec CI 14:1:8

Grace (Menzies) b1836 h William Davidson, Scot, UT, fam rec SCC 16:1:2

Martha Susan f1864 h Samuel Teague, NC, IN, letter DC 16:1:16

DAVIS, Amasa Calvin b1912 w Nina Louise Miller, CA, anc ch RED 11:4:2

Arthur d1836 w Mary (Townsley) Penner, NJ, fam rec MGR 14:1:43

Charles Herring f1857 w Elvira Van Dressen Belding, NY, geneal NYR 110:4:209

Daniel C b1838 w Isabell R Laughlin, WA, biog notes ORB 17:9:83

David b1793 w Mary McDowell Martin, NC, TN, IL, Bible rec & biog CI 12:2:45

fam of PA, MD, VA, OR, geneal, bk rev NGS 67:2:149 GFP 29:1:5 DM 42:3:136

Harry Clayton b1875 w Harriet B O´Connell, MA, CA, anc ch OC 16:3:96

James C b1796 w Sally Johnston, Bible rec CI 15:1:5

John Felix b1857 w Lelia Eugenia Walkup, TX, NC, anc ch GR 21:3:97

John Henry Newton b1876 w Ouida (Jensen) Ryder, IL, CO, anc ch BGS 9:3:44

Nancy Ann (Cody) f1868, IL, Bible rec TA 14:3:67

Oliver, ME, 1846 church trial DE 3:1:14

Robert, OH, letter 1864 BGS 9:4:33

Samuel m1850 w Elizabeth M Witter, NY marr cert THT 3:1:29

Samuel M d1910 w Sarah Pierce, IL, obit MCH 7:2:45

Thomas C b1821 w Nancy Ann Hines, MO, OR, biog notes GFP 29:3:53

Thomas Rollin b1878 w Effie Abbie White, TX, anc ch GR 21:4:141

William b1770 w Nancy Norton, MD, VA, Bible recs BGS 10:2:21

William d1836 w Jane Allen, ME,

fam rec DE 3:1:26

DAVOLT, Adam b1785 w Frances Whisenand, geneal, bk rev TB 6:3:22

DAWSON, Arlto Franklin b1864 w Sophia F Montz, IA, MN, NE, anc ch MIS 11:4:58

John b1839 w Sarah Blackburn, Eng, RI, CO, biog notes & geneal BGS 5:3:12 9:4:27

Joseph Benjamin b1899 w Christabelle Elizabeth Craig, KS, CO, anc ch PGB 11:6:61

DAY, David Bounel b1828 w Ann Maria McFarland, geneal, bk rev YP 9:3:166

Ephram Abraham b1826 w Susana Smith, Mrs Elizabeth Armstrong, PA, IL, Bible rec CI 14:4:127

fam geneal, bk rev CTN 11:3:517

fam of ID, geneal, bk rfev CDS 16:5:46

Giles m1808 w Hannah Cutler, Bible rec CTN 11:4:592

DEAL, Peter Sr b1754 w Margaret Stein, VA, PA, geneal LM 20:37

DEAN, Aylett b1794 w Ann F Jones, VA, anc ch YP 9:2:65

Aylett b1794 w Ann F Jones, Bible rec GR 21:4:159

Cecil Elmer b1891 w Olive Rosa Swiger, OH, anc ch RRS 12:1:92

John b1817 w Eliza A Hunnewill, ME, fam rec TRI 19:3:49

DE BACKER, John b1827 w Marie Fouse, Belgium, Ger, CO, biog notes BGS 4:4:33

DE BREBEUF, Jean b1593, biog JMS 2:2:30

DECATUR, Stephen b1779, PA, biog notes DAR 113:5:532

Susan (Wheeler), geneal, bk rev PGB 11:9:101

DEERMAN, Richard bc1720 w Elizabeth, NC, geneal NAS 17:3:75

DEETER, Edward David b1863 w Emma V Franz, OH, IN, CA, anc ch BGS 11:2:82

DE FORE, John Wilbur b1911 w Evelyn Lucille White, CO, IL,

KS, anc ch THT 6:3:64

DE GAYNER, Ralph b1909 w Marie M Seeger, MI, WI, anc ch PF 8:3:58

DELAWARE, Lynch-West fam cem inscr NGS 67:2:142

misc pioneer fams, bk rev BR 6:3:96

New Castle Co, black birth recs 1810-1853 NGS 67:4:264

wills 1682-1800, bk rev REP 19:4:168

DELL'API, Agastino b 1885 Italy, NJ, biog notes FH 2:2:37

DE MARCELLIN, Edward Preble b1805 w Caroline Slocum, NY, Bible rec & photo album GFP 28:10:187

DENCKER, Carl, Denmark, geneal, bk rev IG 15:1:8

DENISON, geneal supp, bk rev CTN 12:1:174

George W b1751 w Theoda Brown, CT, Bible rec CTN 7:2:319

Lewis, PA wil 1843 LL 15:1:36

DENMARK, geneal guidebook & atlas 1969, bk rev OG 1:3:88

probate recs guide GJ 8:1:12

surnames, notes on TST 12:10:37

DENNISON, George b1699 w Abigail Haraden, MA, geneal, film rev GH 33:6:91

DENNY, Walter d1842, IN, biog notes MIS 11:4:52

DENSON, fam of VA, geneal, bk rev REP 19:3:134

Jordan d1806, VA, geneal, bk rev VAG 23:1:141

DENYS, Nicholas b1588 w Marguente DeLa Faye, anc ch AGE 8:3:97

DE RICHEBOURG, Claude Phillipe w Ann Chastain, France, VA, SC, biog DAR 113:9:1012

DERRICK, Ernest b1890 w George Ethel Moran, TX, anc ch STK 7:3:138

DEVAUX, Alfred b1851 w Ellen Guillaume, Bible rec ACL 4:1:9

Jesse b1888 w Cecelia Springer, IN, Bible rec ACL 4:1:9

DE VAUX, Nicholas m1667 w Mrs

Marie Sy Petilion, Ger, fam rec NYR 110:2:100

DEWEY, George b1837, Admiral, VT, biog & geneal, bk rev GH 33:2:83

Levi M b1818 w Mary A Ramsdell, NY, MI, Bible rec DM 43:1:40

Pelatiah f1746 w Sarah Norton, CT, Bible rec WB 10:2:61

DEWOLFE, Helen Alida (Marsh) b1847 h Augustus H DeWolfe, OH, obit AH 4:3:95

DEXTER, Teasdale b1853 w Clara Ruth Whipps, Can, KS, anc ch KK 17:1:4

DHONAU, Jacob b1808 w Frederika Philippa Schmitz, Anna Elizabeth Kampf, Ger, IN, geneal, bk rev GH 33:5:84

Peter b1812 w Mary Elizabeth Endres, Ger, KY, geneal, bk rev GH 33:5:84

DIAL, Isaac M b1808 w Jane Patton, SC, TN, Bible rec BGS 9:3:26

Morris f1882 w Samantha Josephine Riley, IL, fam rec FF 8:2:39

DIBBLE, Charlotte b1875 h Fred Tareton, OH, auto AH 1:3:10 2:2:55 2:3:74 2:4:110 3:1:8 3:2:63

DICE, Jonas M b1843 w Fanny Brechbill, PA, geneal, bk rev GH 33:6:86 FP 22:4:211 KCG 20:4:206

DICK, Charles William b1825 w Anna Roseta Herman, Ger, OH, IL, biog notes MCH 7:4:97

DICKERSON, Philemon, NY, geneal, bk rev NYR 110:2:119

DICKEY, James Noel b1823 w Colley Bolejack, TN, OR, biog notes ORB 17:5:48

DICKINSON, Emily b1830, MA, biog notes TST 12:19:41

Francis Coleman b1833 w Ermina G Chapman, IL, biog MKT 2:4:70

John b1602 w Elizabeth (Howland) Hicks, Eng, MA, NY, geneal, bk rev REP 19:3:137 notes on MQ 45:3:150

Nathaniel b1600 w Mrs Anna Gull, Eng, CT, MA, geneal supp, bk rev CTN 12:2:366 REP 19:4:173

DICKMAN, Henry William C b1810 w Becke A Koenenkamp, Ger, NY, OH, anc ch REP 19:4:159

DICKS, Peter bc1660 w Esther Maddock, Eng, PA, geneal, bk rev GH 33:2:83 IG 14:1:5 KCG 20:2:87

DICTIONARY, geneal dict & index to US counties, bk rev GH 33:5:69 TST 12:19:39 IL 11:3:180 GGM 73:165 TSP 3:1:37 VAG 23:3:234 KCG 20:4:208

DILLARD, James T b1825 w Martha Broughton, AL, Bible rec & marr cert VL 14:1:8

DILLINGER, George f1744 w Catherine, Switz, VA, geneal, bk rev REP 19:4:169

DILLINGHAM, John bc1630 w Elizabeth Feake, MA, anc ch YP 9:4:205

DILLON, Jacob b1818 w Cynthia A Hodson, OH, IL, notes on LL 15:1:37

DILTS, Charles b1867 w Susan Harper, OH, anc ch REP 19:1:32

DIMOCK, Joseph, Can, diary 1796-1844, bk rev GN 2:7:210

DINGMAN, James W b1885 w Ethel Vandeventer, IL, IA, anc ch ACL 4:4:84

DIRECTORY, archives & mss repositories in US, bk rev GJ 8:4:212 REP 19:4:176 AW 5:1:27

geneal periods 1979, bk rev GH 33:2:71 TST 12:7:46

geneal soc in US & Can 1976, bk rev OG 3:2:58

geneal soc in US & Can 1978, bk rev BCG 8:4:80

geneal soc, lib, period & professionals 1979 GH 33:4:15

hist soc in US & Can, bk rev GJ 8:1:52

news geneal columns 1979, bk rev MQ 45:4:231 GJ 8:4:216 BB

11:4:69

professuonal genealogists, bk rev TST 12:34:38

ship pass lists 1890-1930 NY & 1904-1926 elsewhere, bk rev OG 5:3:88

state & local hist periods, bk rev OG 5:1:28

DIRKS, fam geneal, bk rev TB 6:2:22

DISHMAN, Cahristopher Columbus b1844 w Mary E, Bible rec GR 21:4:157

Robert Eugene b1844 w Amanda Clark, MO, TX, Bible rec GR 21:4:156

DISHNER, William J b1847 w Mary C Helbert, TN, Bible rec THT 3:1:9

DISPIONIT, Johann Jacob bc1715, Ger, PA, geneal, bk rev REP 19:1:41

DISTRICT OF COLUMBIA, early recs in US Archives, notes on PGB 11:7:77

DITMORE, Henry b1798 w Abigail Holmes, fam reg NAS 18:1:11

DIVELEY, George Washington d1899 w Charlotte Radliff, IL, fam rec FF 8:2:49

Henry f1871 w Jennie May Radliff, IL, geneal FF 8:2:48

DIXON, Joseph m1876 w Mary Yuill, Can, marr cert & fam letters YV 11:4:177

DOANE, Charles West b1863 w Josephine Browning, IA, IN, CA, anc ch RRS 12:2:213

fam of MA, reunion minutes 1976, 1978, bk rev GH 33:6:86

Reuben f1769 w Ruth Chapman, MA, geneal MQ 45:4:196

DOBSON, John F b1859 w Sarah J Kenyon, IL, IA, Bible rec HH 14:2:83

DODD, Andrew Jackson b1846 w Frances Arabille Brightwell, MO, KS, fam rec MGR 14:2:94

Bernett b1836 w Charlotte Ereckson Peterson, IN, CO, geneal & biog notes BGS 5:2:9 9:4:19

Josiah b1740 w Mary Luttrell,

VA, TN, fam rec & will 1809 MGR 14:2:96 14:4:175

DODGE, John b1816, Eng, geneal, bk rev GH 33:4:117

NH, WI, geneal, bk rev CTN 11:1:44

geneal v2, bk rev CDS 16:4:11 NGI 3:2:107

Oliver f1774 w Abigail Harris, Bible rec REP 19:3:113

DODSON, William Abraham m1877 w A E Mulligan, MO, Bible rec GR 21:4:155

DOEGE, Otto Ludwig b1876 w Sophie Hulda Quade, Ger, TX, anc ch GR 21:4:143

DOGGETT, Thomas, NH, WI, MA, geneal supp, bk rev CTN 9:1:125

DOHNER, fams of Switz & PA, notes on EWA 16:4:149

DOISE, Augustin b1848 w Pauline La Fargue, LA, anc ch YP 9:2:66

DONALDSON, John F f1880 w Susan Hicks, KY, anc ch FF 8:4:42

Moses M d1896 w Elizabeth, IL, fam rec FF 8:2:31

DONNELL, Alonzo McWilliams b1885 w Lottie Palmer, MS, anc ch AGS 20:2:72

R P f1855, TN, letter IL 11:3:167

DOOLEY, Thomas bc1735 w Rebecca Sharpe, VA, KY, geneal KA 15:1:21

DOONEY, fam of Ir & New Zealand, geneal, bk rev IR 11:1:70

DORAN, William John b1886 w Elizabeth Bryan Smart, MO, anc ch BGS 10:4:45

DOREMUS, Cornelius b1714 w Antije Young, NJ, fam rec BGS 10:4:29

fam of NJ & NT, geneal, bk rev NYR 110:4:250

DORN, Max George Henry b1896 w Hattie Hannah Grossklaus, WI, anc ch NGI 3:1:38

DORRIS, John W b1806 w Elizabeth L Clements, SC, GA, fam rec DCG 2:10:9

DORSEY, Hugh B b1880 w Sarah

Brown, TX, notes & cem inscr THT 5:2:1

DOTY, Daniel b1765, NJ, OH, biog notes TST 11:50:44

Ralph J b1883 w Bertha E Eherenman, IN, anc ch ACL 4:1:14

DOUCET, Louis Joseph w Georgianna Cormer, geneal, bk rev AGE 8:3:91

DOUGAN, Robert b1811 w Cemantha Hannum, KS, anc ch TAK 9:2:31

DOUGLAS, William Orville b1898, WA, Justice US Supreme Court, biog & geneal notes YV 11:1:5

DOUGLASS, Thomas W b1798 w Delila Payne, Bible rec IG 15:1:5

DOUTEE, geneal CTN 7:2:305

DOWDA, Neil Eugene b1925 w Doris Jolene Allen, CO, anc ch BGS 11:4:177

DOW, Milton b1855 w Isabel McAfee, KS, NM fam rec NMG 18:2:52

Peggy f1853 h Lorenzo Dow, photo & biog notes GP 16:1:1

DOWDALL, James b1826 w Mary Stevens, fam rec CI 14:3:99

DOWEY, Thomas b1776 w Margaret Tracey, geneal, bk rev REP 19:1:41

DOYLE, Thomas White Jr b1791 w Betsey Welhim Bagley, geneal DE 2:5:16

DRAPER, Robert m1879 w Sarah Brown, marr cert BCG 7:3:46

DRESBECK, William Francis b1894 w Florence Ann Schweitzer, NY, CA, anc ch WB 9:4:162

DREES, John Bernard b1852 w Emma Jane Lucy Force, Prussia, NY, IL, geneal FF 8:2:44

DRIGGS, gam of Am, index part 2, bk rev CTN 9:2:313

Joseph b1718 w Rachel Johnson, Bible rec CTN 11:4:595

DRISKILL, Thomas T w Pollyann, MO, letter 1836 AB 7:3:58

DROMEY, James bc1800 w Catharine Mahoney, Ir, geneal, bkrev GH 33:1:91

DUBOURG, Maguire L b1849 w Maggie Howe, NY, KY, Bible rec MD 20:4:342

DUBS, Heinrich f1729 w Ann Marie, Switz, PA, geneal DM 43:1:7 43:2:55

DUCK, Daniel b1783 w Jane Garbutt, Eng, IL, Bible rec NSN 4:3:24

DUDLEY, Stephen Amos b1807/8 w Salome Collins, Bible rec CTN 12:2:231

DUGGAN, Thomas Hinds b1815 w Elizabeth Berry, MS, TX, fam rec THT 1:2:13

DULANY, fam geneal, bk rev LL 15:3:142

H B m1886 w Georgie E Slover, TX marr rec THT 1:2:3

DUNAGAN, Stephen Reed Jr b1861 w Delilah Ann Conner, AL, NM, fam rec NMG 18:2:51

DUNAHAY, Samuel b1848 w Angel Carothers, Ir, PA, OH, geneal, bk rev REP 19:3:134

DUNCAN, Alexander Sr bc1791, Bible rec TB 6:3:13

Jacob f1850, Bible rec TB 6:3:13

William Watts b1800 w Mary Barnwell, GA, fam rec DCG 2:10:7

DUNIVAN, John b1793 w Frances Hughes, IN, geneal, bk rev IG 14:1:5

DUNLAP, James Carmachan I b1740 w Jane Wills, Ir, KY, fam rec KA 15:1:36

James Carmachan III b1810 w Patsy Hainline, Mary Horn, Mahalah G Morrison, Bible rec KA 15:1:38

James W b1822 w Maranda Warren, Bible rec DM 42:4:174

DUNN, fam of TN, notes on THT 5:1:31

DUNNING, Ezra d1796 w Ruby Murray, Bible rec CTN 12:3:418

Rufus B b1786 w Roxa Fellows, Bible rec CTN 12:3:415

DUNTON, Robert f1644 w Anna Felch, MA, fam rec DE 3:2:14

DUPULE, Frederick Augustus b1875
w Helen Bernadette Kobel,
Can, MI, anc ch AGE 8:4:124

DURFEE, Josepah d1801, Can,
loyalist, biog, bk rev GN
2:6:172

DURHAM, William Lawrence b1891 w
Laura Leona Wyatt, TX, anc ch
NAS 17:4:95

DURRANCE, Samuel bc1680, geneal.
bk rev GGM 71:7

DURRELL. Philip f1689. NH. ME.
geneal NER 133:1:40 133:2:118
133:3:216 133:4:280

DUSENBURY, Hendrick b1658 w Mary
Thorn. NY. anc ch CLG 10:1:53

DWINNELL. Thomas b1672 w Diahah
Brimsdell. MA. fam rec DE
3:1:10

DYAR. Lydia d1776. MA. cem inscr
DM 43:1:18

DYER. Eliphalet b1721. CT. biog,
bk rev CTN 11:3:524

John f1763, PA. diary excerpts
BGS 11:3:119 11:4:168

Nina Canema (Cummins) b1866 h
Thomas Jefferson Dyer, IA,
KS, obit MGR 14:4:181

DYKE, Wiliam A b1833 w Mary
Jane, PA, Bible rec CI
14:4:127

EAHEART, Abram, VA, letters 1836
DG 25:2:98

EARLE, John bc1612. VA, geneal,
bk rev CTN 7:3:363

EARLY, fam recs IL, bk rev IG
14:1:5

EARNEST, Amos b1812 w Marya
Baker Willson, TN. Bible rec
BWG 8:1:40

EARP, Alex b1832 w Mary Ethel
Decker Nation. AL, TX cem
inscr THT 4:1:28

EASH, Jacob b1774 w Susannah
Miller. PA. geneal. bk rev LM
20:1:5

EASLEY. John Mayberry w Mary
Watkins. MS. geneal. bk rev
WCK 12:2:34

Robert w Ann Parker. geneal. bk
rev GH 33:1:92

EASTEP. fam of AL, bk rev CI
13:3:115

EASTERWOOD. Washington b1824
w Susan Lee, TN. OR. biog
notes ORB 17:6:61

EASTHAM, William L b1878 w Ora
Bell Crawford, TN, TX. OK.
anc ch RRS 12:2:214

EATON. fam of VT. OH. MN MN
10:1:28

Francis f1620. "Mayflower"
geneal. bk rev CTN 8:4:538 TB
6:4:31

EBBERT. Clarence b1871 w June
Flood Douglass. OH. WV. anc
ch OC 16:1:30

Jeremiah b1843 w Susanna Mc-
Williams, Bible rec DC
16:1:19

John William b1832 w Lunica,
fam rec GFP 28:6:110

EBERT, Alvin Clay, letter 1862
VQ 16:4:63

EBY, fam of Switz, Ger, & PA,
geneal, bk rev CTN 9:2:311
9:4:608

James Brian b1896 w Anne Davis,
PA, MD, TX, auto, bk rev CI
12:3:113 MCH 7:4:118 BGS
8:4:33

ECCLESTON, Henry Harrison b1811
w Belinda Richardson, NY, IN,
OR, biog notes ORB 17:8:71

EDGERTON, Thomas b1735 w Elizabeth Saint, NJ. geneal, bk
rev REP 19:3:135

EDWARDS, fam of Wales & VA,
geneal, bk rev HTR 22:1:5 REP
19:1:41

James Simon b1857 w Alice
Porter, IL, fam recs VQ
16:4:54

Miles b1825 w Margaret Ann Mc-
Larty, GA, fam rec DCG 2:10:5

William b1789 w   , Sarah
Lockhart, NC, VA, MS, fam rec
AGS 20:2:77

EGAN, Valentine f1779, Ir, MD,
geneal, bk rev GH 33:3:106
TST 12:23:48 KWC 20:2:88 CDS
16:4:13

EGGLESTON, Oscar Perry b1861,
MI, geneal, bk rev AH 6:1:27

EHRENBERG, Gus f1914, biog MKT
2:1:10 2:2:27

EICHHOLTZ, Johan Jacob b1712 w
Anna Catherine Reichert, Ger,
PA, geneal, bk rev REP
19:1:45 IL 11:2:80

EICHELBERG, Robert Elmer b1911 w
Lois Phyllis Morehouse, MN,
MT, anc ch BGS 11:4:179

EICKMEYER, Andrew b1833 w Louisa
Ladwig, Ger, MN, NE, WA,
Bible rec AB 8:2:29

ELDRIDGE, William Case b1809 w
Lucinda, Mrs Abigail Robina
Robinson Nash, IL, MI, notes
on FG 21:1:13 21:2:43

ELIASON, fam of Nor & Am,
geneal, bk rev GH 33:1:92

ELLICOTT, Andrew f1730 w Ann
Bye, PA, geneal (1882), bk
rev GE 46:8

ELLIOTT, Clarence b1894 w Clora
Sallee, KY, IL, biog notes
MCH 7:4:98

John Anderson b1850 w Mary
Elizabeth Hills, IA, Bible
rec ORB 17:6:54

ELKINS, George Maz b1876 w
Frances Osborne Martin, TX,
NM, fam rec NMG 18:3:82

ELLIS, Isaac Chase b1833 w
Martha A Conner, Eva E Toell-
ner, WA, Bible rec OG 4:4:104

Leonard Herbert b1913 w Mamie
Geneva Trull, WA, anc ch WB
9:4:147

William H f1857 w Eliza Jane
Pickerill, KS, biog MGR
14:1:17

ELLISON, Arthur b1767 w Sarah
Smith, Ir, KY, OH, geneal, bk
rev REP 19:4:176

ELLSWORTH, Josias, CT, geneal,
bk rev CTN 9:3:469

Oliver b1745, CT, biog, bk rev
CTN 12:3:538

ELWELL, Robert d1683 w Joane,
Mrs Alice Leach, MA, geneal
CTN 11:4:706 12:2:221

ELWOOD, Ira Elmer b1893 w Myrtle
Estella Comstock, NE, anc ch
NW 2:3:94

EMERY, Olen Arthur b1917 w Ardis

Elizabeth Loury, IL, WA, anc
ch TRI 19:1:5

Sarah Ann (Smith) f1811 h David
Emery Jr, MA, auto & geneal
notes (1879), bk rev NGS
67:1:74

EMMONS, Isaac Bird b1822 w
Harriet Rebecca Walling, CT,
IL, letters OC 16:2:52

ENGELS, Peter b1782 w Hester
Auter, PA, KY, AR, geneal, bk
rev TST 11:42:30

ENGLAND, Bristol, emig to Am
1654-1685, bk rev REP
19:4:168

indentured servants emig to
Am 1654-1686 GJ 8:1:24

Brythonic & Cymric Celts res
project EG 12:290

Clyde Mitchell b1894 w Ida
Lillie Mae Ramseur, NC, anc
ch PGB 11:10:108

discovering your fam tree, bk
rev TB 6:2:19

geneal gazetteer, bk rev CTN
11:4:697

geneal notes on Col Am fams NGS
67:1:58 67:3:210 67:4:287

geneal res v2,3, bk rev OG
2:3:88 2:4:118

geneal res guide OC 16:3:77 WB
9:4:149 BGS 9:3:1 GR 21:3:113
CTN 9:3:479 TS 21:4:127 AH
2:3:87 KN 2:1:3 2:3:19 KCG
20:2:78,80 PGB 11:10:109

geneal res guide with regional
societies BCG 5:2:22

handbook of fam hist, bk rev
FAM 18:4:227

HRH Prince Charles, geneal v1-
2, bk rev NGS 67:1:64

imms to Am in Eng recs, bk rev
OG 3:3:88

in search of British ancestry,
bk rev CTN 7:4:520

intro to geneal res, bk rev TST
12:1:52 NYR 110:2:121 DM
42:4:185 CTN 11:4:696 NGS
67:3:226 GH 33:1:81 AG
55:2:127

John B b1823 w Mary B Cayce,
VA, KY, biog VQ 16:3:49

Joseph, MD, geneal v2, bk rev

NGS 67:2:149

Liverpool, direct 1774 BCG 8:4:84

emig to Am 1697-1707, bk rev REP 19:4:167

lives & times of our ancestors, bk rev FTR 20:4

London, geneal sources SCC 16:2:21

inner London area parish reg 1538-1837, bk rev NYR 110:1:56

outer London area parish reg 1538-1837, bk rev NYR 110:1:56

Louis Orville b1897 w Mary Ellen Edgmond, IL, MO, MT, anc ch THT 6:3:84

news in microform BCG 5:4:32

Public Rec Office, geneal res guide TST 12:11:38

Richmond, hist, bk rev FAM 18:1:39

surnames guide GJ 8:3:163

titles of honour, notes on AG 55:2:111

tracing your ancestors, bk rev GN 2:6:173

wills, res guide, bk rev CTN 7:3:360

wills index prerogative court of Canterbury 1700-1850 vl A-Bh, bk rev NGS 67:3:221

ENGLISH, Maggie b1855, OH, Bible rec ACL 4:4:77

ENLDE, Denver James b1902 w Dona Belle Hall, MO, anc ch RRS 12:1:83

ENSIGN, James f1632 w Sarah Elson, Eng, MA, CT, geneal, bk rev GH 33:2:84

ENSWORTH, Joseph d1770 w Mary, fam rec BGS 10:4:28

EPLEY, David b1822 w Delila Helton, Bible rec THT 5:1:29

John dc1795 w Rosina, PA, geneal DM 42:3:99

ERB, Lucy (Haines) b1825 h John Erb, PA, TX, obit THT 2:1:31

ERICKSON, Peter E f1891 w Anna, Bible rec PR 3:3:50

ERSKINE, William Richard b1876 w Lillian Velma Cogdell, TX,

anc ch THT 6:3:66

ERVIN, Stephen Hoyt b1903 w Ruth Estelle Thompson, KS, TN, CA, anc ch SN 5:4:2 5:5:3 5:6:3

ERWIN, Patrick d1835 w Malinda Taylor, Ir, TN, biog & Bible rec BWG 8:1:27

ESTEB, Virgil Lawrence b1911 w Ruth Mary Shimondle, OR, anc ch ORB 19:1:12

ESTES, Aaron f1845 w Elizabeth Wilson, TN, MO, TX, fam rec THT 1:2:14

Edwin Joel b1870 w Anna Elizabeth Calkins, IL, AR, anc ch BGS 9:3:45

Peter Harris bc1775 w Esther Hiatt, VA, KY, geneal, anc ch BGS 3:3:7 9:3:18,45

ETHEREDGE, Thomas b1802 w Jane Camel, VA, fam rec HH 14:3:149

ETHRIDGE, Ben Quitman m1887 w Martha Ann Saunders, MS, TX, biog notes THT 2:2:9

EUCKER, John b1856 w Carrie Caroline McLaughlin, OH, anc ch REP 19:4:156

EUROPE, geneal res guide TST 12:19:38 12:20:46

EVANS, fam, misc names, bk rev TB 6:4:29

Mary Elizabeth (Erwin) b1854 h John William Evans, KY, Bible rec ANC 14:2:56

EVARD, Ami C m1880 w Mary L Evard, MI, Bible rec ACL 4:1:8

Orville C b1912 w Mary C Woods, IN, anc ch ACL 4:4:85

EYESTONE, fam of IL, misc fam recs FF 5:1:63 8:3:64

FACKLER, Matthias C b1837 w Elizabeth A, Bible rec OHR 20:3:140

FAIRBROTHER, fam of ME DE 3:3:24

FAIRCHILD, Edward Eugene b1840 w Josephine Clary, MA, geneal, bk rev GH 33:4:117

Robert Jackson b1846 w Mary Ann, MS, Bible rec GR

21:4:154

Zerah, reinterment 1929 IN TSP 3:1:35

FIARHURST, Guy b1832 w Louisa M Simpson, Eng, NJ, CO, geneal BGS 10:2:13

FANCHER, Henry b1856 w Ida May Vrooman, NY, MI, WA, Bible rec RES 11:3:84

FARBER, Philip f1806 w Margaret Wallace, OH, geneal, bk rev REP 19:1:39

FARCY, Grislain Emanuel m1926 w Helen Kellogg, WA marr cert RES 11:4:160

FARLOW, Nathan f1829 w Ruth Carter, PA, NC, biog notes QY 6:4:1

FARMER, David w Rachel, IN will 1829 LL 15:2:55

FARNSWORTH, Ezekiel Harker, geneal, bk rev BGS 11:2:75

Francis Porter w Eleanor Adelaide Wells, CT, geneal, bk rev CTN 12:1:174

FARRAR, Ephraim b1755 w Lovina, Bible rec CTN 10:2:367

FARRINGTON, fams of MA & NY, geneal, bk rev IL 11:1:58

FARRIS, Frederick b1822 w Mary J, TN, fam rec AGS 20:2:76

Mary Jane b1837 h John A Gills, Bible rec THT 6:2:29

W L m1891 w Q V Sorrels, TX, Bible rec THT 2:2:19

FAULKNER, George Wilford b1875 w Fannie Elizabeth Parker, TX, anc ch THT 6:3:69

Ira Leeman b1900 w Martha Mae Hershey, TX, NM, fam rec NMG 18:4:123

Luvisa Jeanette Simpson b1843 h George Faulkner, TN, MO, TX, diary 1900 THT 5:2:9

FAUST, Henry Howard b1894 w Maude Hoovel Baker, WA, anc ch TB 6:3:17

FAY, William m1818 w Caroline, KS, Bible rec KK 17:2:28

FEATHERHUFF, Michael b1833 w Elizabeth Hengst, Ger, IN, IL, geneal CI 15:1:9

FEATHERSTONE, marrs in VA 1764-

1815 NER 23:1:3

FEILER, fam of Poland & Am, geneal, bk rev NGS 67:2:153

FENTON, Ebenezer m1740 w Mehitable, CT, biog notes CTN 7:2:312

James A b1831 w Phebe E, Bible rec CI 15:3:87

Jeremiah b1764, VA, PA, geneal, bk rev TST 12:28:40

FERGUSON, Charles H b1793, GA, geneal FH 2:2:72

FERRELL, Alva John b1918 w Doris Fern Hankins, NE, anc ch NW 2:2:55

FERRIS, John b1723 w Hannah Mead, CT, NY, geneal NYR 110:4:207

FERRY, Charles, geneal, bk rev CDS 16:4:11

FEW, Richard bc1625, PA, geneal, bk rev WPA 5:2:77 NGS 67:2:149

FIFIELD, Abigail (Weare) b1676 h John Fifield, NH, biog notes AG 55:1:18

FILLMORE, Asa w Priscilla Burk, Can, geneal, bk rev GN 2:7:210

Millard b1800 w Abigail Powers, NY, anc ch SCS 16:2:49 16:4:110

FINCH, geneal, bk rev CDS 16:1:3

FINNEY, Elizabeth (Davidson) f1870, Eng, CO, Keepsake bk BGS 10:3:28

FISH, Amrose b1615 w Hannah (Miller) Fish Tobey, CT, geneal CTN 7:3:477

Chalres f1850 w Catherine Johnson, Can, fam photo FAM 18:2:84

David b1780 w Anna Hardy, MA, fam rec CTN 11:3:406

Henry Carlos b1824 w Hannah W Coes, Delia A Hardy, Amanda Malvina Stone, VT, MA, Bible rec CTN 7:2:315

Nathan b1779 w Naomi Phillipes, GA, Bible rec GGM 74:295

FISHER, Anna Marie b1896, IN, auto, bk rev CDS 16:1:4

Buford Dwain b1918 w Florence

Anita Sandoz, NE, anc ch NW 2:2:56

James w Jane Atkinson, PA, OH, geneal, bk rev TST 12:31:40

John f1841 w Elizabeth Webuer, OH, anc ch REP 19:1:35

FISHLINE, John Christian f1920 w Anna Christine Matzen, Denmark, NE, Bible rec NA 2:2:41

FITCH, James b1649 w Elizabeth Mason, CT, biog NER 133:2:102

Thomas m1680 w Abigail Goodrich, CT, fam recs CTA 21:4:193

FITZNIGEL, William dc1134, Eng, geneal EG 12:264

FITZPATRICK, James b1820 w Margaret Veek, Bible rec GFP 28:5:89

FLEENER, Jacob William f1740 w Mary Susannah Hope, Ger, PA, geneal, bk rev NGS 67:2:150

FLEENOR, Jacob William m1873 w Mary Susannah Hope, KS, geneal, bk rev YP 9:3:166

FLEER, fam of Prussia & Am, geneal vl, bk rev CDS 16:2:6

Friedrich Wilhelm b1898, geneal v4, bk rev CDS 16:2:6

FLEMING, fam of KY, geneal, bk rev BR 6:3:96

Thomas M dc1800, KY, death cert VA 17:1:22

FLETCHER, Adam b1862 w Clara Alma Wells, IA, IL, KS, anc ch BGS 10:2:35

FLORIDA, Clearwater, McMullen cem inscr LL 14:3:138

West Palm Beach, census 1900 ANC 14:2:64 14:3:81 14:4:113

FLOWERS, James b1743 w Theodoaia Bagby, VA, fam & Bible rec KFR 7:97

FLOYD, John Granville b1929 w Laura Frances Perry, VA, AZ, ID, anc ch TRI 17:2:38

FOGLER, Henry m1812 w Barbara Cline, OH, marr rec FF 8:1:50

FOLEY, Thomas b1804, VA, KY, geneal, bk rev GFP 28:7:127

FOLLETT, Seaborn, CT, geneal CTN 7:2:303,314

Walter b1768 w Martha Johnson, NH, geneal CTN 8:1:158

FOLLIETT, George b1804 w Gloryinda Kirk, Bible rec CTN 11:2:218

FOOT, Jonathan Sr b1737 w Lydia Baldwin, Bible rec CTN 12:2:414

FOOTE, Elizabeth dc1683 h Nathaniel Foote, Thomas Welles, MA, notes on AG 55:1:28

FOOTMAN, William Sr f1888 w Jane Mann, Eng, NY, CA, biog notes LL 14:4:187

FORBES, Orrin b1809 w Julia, Bible rec CTN 7:2:318

FORD, Lemuel b1788 w Hannah McDowell, VA, diary 1835, notes on TST 12:8:45

Leslie Lyle b1922 w Doris Marie Anderson, KS, anc ch KK 17:3:44

Nathaniel b1795 w Lucinda Duncan Embree, VA, MO, OR, biog notes ORB 18:3:61

William Alfred b1869 w Margaret Catherine Lacey, MO, TX, OK, anc ch NAS 17:3:66

FOREMAN, name & fam res, bk rev TB 6:3:23

FORNEY, John b1824 w Louisa Krob, IL, biog MH 6:1:1

FOSTER, David L b1780 w Annny Beard, IL, fam rec IL 11:3:168

David Montague b1823 w Annie Laurie, Eunice Ann Raymond, NY, Can, MI, geneal FG 21:3:48

fam rec OC 16:1:21

Herschel b1801 w Clara McGeoch, Bible rec HH 14:2:87

FOWLER, James Ray b1916 w Carol Marie Clark, TX, CO, anc ch BGS 11:1:39

FOX, Olen b1907 w Barbara Elizabeth Baxley, OH, CA, anc ch BGS 10:1:37

FOX TAYLOR, Nancy Jane h Jack Martin, John White, GA, TN, biog GP 16:1:41

FRAME, Josepah Sr b1757 w Hannah Underwood, PA, anc ch REP 19:3:120

FRANCE, geneal recs guide, bk
rev GH 33:1:72
geneal res guide GE 46:1 SCS
14:1:19
geneal terms STC 2:1:24
recs of geneal value, guide, bk
rev TST 11:52:45
Waldensians, hist ITG 2:36
FRANCIS, Caleb b1808 w Mrs Ma-
linda (Thompson) Jones, KY,
OH, anc ch REP 19:1:35
Frank m1882 w Bettie P Johnson,
NE, Bible rec KK 17:1:8
John M f1776, Eng, NY, biog
notes BGS 11:2:66
FRANK, Graham f1756, Eng, VA,
fam notes NGS 67:4:290
FRANKLIN, William b1784 w Hannah
Hackney, NJ, OR, biog notes
ORB 17:7:63
FRANTZ, Michael II b1764 w
Marian Elizabeth, Bible rec
TB 6:2:8
FRANZEN, Dean Sanford b1930 w
Esther Pauline McDaniel, KS,
anc ch TOP 9:2:40
FRAZER, Mary (Taylor) b1745 h
Persifor Frazer, PA, biog DAR
113:7:766
FREAME, Thomas bc1650 w Mary
Rowell, Eng, MA, biog notes
AG 55:1:44
FREDENBURG, Isaac Jr b1794 w
Dorcas Bassett, NY, OR, anc
ch HJA 6:3:49
FREEMAN, James b1842 w Nannie A
Miller, KY, biog VQ 16:4:60
John b1627 w Mercy Prence, MA,
anc ch YP 9:4:205
Lyman Henry b1885 w LaVerne
Galloway, IL, anc ch TAK
9:2:32
Robert Lon b1891 w Flossie
Woolridge, MO, anc ch THT
7:1:11
FREER, Romeo Hoyt b1815 w Lillie
Fuller, Mary Iams, OH, biog
notes AH 4:2:61
FRENCH, Charles Creighton b1784
w Mercy Gray Gilpin, Bible
rec PR 3:4:70
Eugene H b1910 w Catherine A
Tatem, CT, anc ch ACL 4:2:28

Frank G b1867 w Christena
Lynds, ME, Can, anc ch RED
12:1:11
Jerome b1834 w Esther Thomas,
OH, anc ch REP 19:4:160
Thomas, geneal, correction to
GNJ 54:2:49
FREY, Charles b1826 w Mary
Maier, Ger, IA, IL, CO, ge-
neal BGS 11:3:104
FRETZ, Abraham b1813 w Elizabeth
Rawn, Bible rec WB 9:4:159
FREY, Frederick William b1868 w
Rosina Robersch, SC, NC, anc
ch NW 2:2:61
FRIDAY, George Thomas b1854 w
Emma Jane Daniels, AL, LA,
biog notes THT 6:1:12
FRISBIE, Annie d1883, NE, cem
inscr NA 2:2:45
Levi Cornell b1821 w Adelayda
Vallejo, NY, CA, anc ch & fam
rec SPG 31:564
FROELICH, Leonard b1720 w Cath-
erine, Switz, geneal, bk rev
REP 19:4:174
FROST, Pleasant Miller b1844 w
Sarah M Christina Gowan, MO,
TX, Bible rec CSB 14:4:160
FRY, Monroe Bert b1899 w Eva
Dula Gailey, TX, anc ch THT
6:3:80
FUDGE, Conrad bc1770, VA,
geneal, bk rev GH 33:5:84
FULK, Jacob b1815 w Catherine
Foss, OH, anc ch REP 19:1:31
FULLER, Harold Leonard b1896 w
Marian Elizabeth Howard, MI,
anc ch BGS 10:2:37
Samuel f1620, "Mayflower"
geneal, bk rev CTN 8:4:538 TB
6:4:31
FULLERTON, fam of Am geneal, bk
rev OC 16:2:69
FULTON, Deborah (Thompson) f1810
h Robert Fulton, PA, letters
BGS 11:3:118
James, OR letter 1850 AB 8:1:13
John b1768 w Jean Reid, VA,
Bible rec VAG 23:1:15
FUNK, Jacob w Frances, VA, will
1746 THT 1:2:8
John Fretz b1835, biog notes MH

6:2:17

FUQUA, Charles Marion b1869 w Pink (Martha) McKee, IN, FL, anc ch HJA 6:4:38

FURLONG, geneal, bk rev LL 15:3:142

FUSON, William b1762 w Hannah Bates, VA, OH, geneal, bk rev REP 19:4:172

FUZUA, fam of VA, geneal, bk rev NGS 67:2:150

FYLER, fam of CT, geneal, bk rev CTN 7:2:294

GABLER, Johan Michael b1831 w Margaretha Nau, Bavaria, NY, geneal, bk rev GH 33:1:92

GAGAN, J F b1854, MO, auto BGS 10:3:27

GALL, George Friedrich b1848 w Louise Steinaker, VA, NY, CO, Bible rec BGS 5:3:17

GALLATIN, J H b1834 w Miriam J Grant, OH, Bible rec TS 21:3:84

GALLAWAY, George Taylor b1877 w Cloa May Erb, MI, IA, TX, anc ch THT 6:3:68

William Ragan b1825 w Sarah Jane (Gallaway), GA, Bible rec THT 7:2:96

GALLUP, John f1630, Eng, MA, biog notes BGS 6:2:16

GAMBLE, James L b1824, NY, letter WI 25:3:136 25:4:191

GANLEY, John w Bridget Mulloy, Ir, Bible rec IR 11:2:84

GANNETT, Matthew w Hannah, MA, geneal 1976, bk rev CTN 10:4:699

GARDENHIRE, Walter M b1803 w Mary Powers, geneal FF 8:1:29

GARD, Thomas B m1857 w Laura Buskirk, OH marr cert SCS 16:2:51

GARDNER, William, GA, AL, MS, geneal, bk rev GGM 71:6

GARLINGTON, Christopher f1638, VA, geneal, bk rev BGS 8:3:32

GARMAN, John b1814 w Elizabeth Holzner, Switz, NY, OH, geneal, bk rev GH 33:6:87

GARREN, fam of IL & IA, misc cem inscr CI 14:4:129

Phillip bc1812 w Celia Motsinger, IN, IL, IA, biog CI 13:4:151

GARRETT, Andrew b1823, cem inscr OC 16:4:130

Hugh b1850 w Matilda Austin, Ir, IL, KS, fam rec FF 8:2:36

James Garfield b1880 w Florence Lucille Blood, MA, NH, anc ch FF 8:2:26

Samuel Nelson b1887 w Annie Kristine Akerholm, anc ch GR 21:4:143

GARTON, Thomas f1684 w Mrs Ann (Tye) Brodhead Nottingham, NY, geneal NYR 110:2:134

GARY, George E f1890 w Maggie Webster Laird, OH, notes on peers AH 4:2:50

GASS, Patrick bc1771, WV, biog notes WPA 5:1:34

GASTINEAU, Job bc1760, VA, geneal, bk rev KY 21:3:115

GASTON, fam of AL, geneal, bk rev CDS 16:2:5

GATES, Catherine (Harden) b1766 h William Gates, NC,TX, fam rec THT 1:2:15,16

Charles b1794 w Manerva Fletcher Hanks, OH, TX, fam rec THT 1:2:15

Jared b1786, NYa, geneal, bk rev CTN 8:1:36

GAULT, John b1800 w Nancy McKinney, PA, OH, Bible rec OHR 20:3:102

GAY, David b1738/9, MA, ME, geneal NGS 67:2:85

GEBHART, Simon b1816 w Margaret Knable, biog notes LM 20:4:7

GECK, Jacob C b1869 w Anna M Angermeier, Ger, MI, anc ch BGS 9:4:38

GEE, Peter b1615 w Grace, Eng, MA, geneal AG 55:2:100

Ralph Marion b1896 w Gladys Victoria Lawson, NE, anc ch WB 9:3:115

GEMMELL, John b1693 w Agnes Wylie, Scot, geneal, bk rev GH 33:4:117 KCG 20:2:93

GENTRY, Gentry Fam Gazette &
    Geneal, 6151 Tompkins Dr,
    McLean VA 22101
GEORGE, John f1635, VA, geneal,
    bk rev NGS 67:2:151
    Otto, AK, auto, bk rev CDS
    16:4:10
    Stephen b1802 w Eliza
    Brown, Bible rec CTN 12:2:234
GEORGIA, Americus, hist 1832-
    1975, bk rev CDS 16:2:6
    Andersonville, death reg NGI
    3:1:47 3:2:125 3:3:189
    Atlanta, geneal lib for blind,
    descr TST 11:50:44
    Archives, fam exchange cards
    KCG 20:4:197
    Baldwin Co, hist 1925, bk rev
    GH 33:2:75
    tax list 1810 GGM 71:11
    Bibb Co, marr bk A 1827-1839
    GGM 71:21
    will bk A 1823-1855 GGM 74:245
    Brooks Co, hist 1858-1948, bk
    rev GH 33:1:75
    Bulloch Co, common school fund
    GGM 74:253
    Inferior Court minutes bk X
    GGM 71:31
    Butts Co, deed bk B GGM 73:167
    estate recs 1826-1841 GGM
    71:41
    hist, bk rev GGM 73:164
    recs 1836-1845 GGM 73:173
    Camden Co, tax list 1809 GGM
    74:261
    Campbell Co, Pumpkintown Dist
    1870 DCG 2:10:16
    will abstr bk A GGM 71:51
    Carroll Co, early marr recs GP
    16:1:43 16:2:87 16:3:139
    Charlton Co, hist 1932, bk rev
    GH 33:2:76
    Chatham Co, early recs GP
    16:1:9 16:2:81 16:3:117
    16:4:153
    Cherokee Co, early marr recs GP
    16:1:37 16:2:91 16:3:129
    16:4:183
    Clayton Co, census 1860, bk rev
    GGM 73:163
    Cobb Co, bond bk 1833-1855 GGM
    71:63

Coffee Co, hist 1930, bk rev GH
    33:2:76
Col conveyance bk abstr 1750-
    1761, bk rev GH 33:3:98
Col roll list, bk rev CDS 16:6:41
Col recs bk J 1755-1762, bk rev
    GH 33:3:98 GE 43:12 NYR
    110:1:57 GGM 71:6 CDS 16:2:4
Columbia Co, deeds & will
    abstr, bk rev GH 33:4:110
    deeds & will abstr to 1790, bk
    rev YP 9:4:229
Covington, architectural hist,
    bk rev CDS 16:2:3
Dodge Co, hist 1932, bk rev GH
    33:5:72
Dougherty Co, hist 1924, bk rev
    GH 33:2:76
Early Co, early recs GP
    16:4:147
    marr bk 2 GGM 73:177
Effingham Co, early recs GP
    16:1:27 16:2:69 16:3:107
    16:4:159
Emanuel Co, appraisement of es-
    tates 1812-1841 GGM 71:73
    estray bk 1841-1889 GGM 71:76
    hist 1812-1900, bk rev GH
    33:2:76
    registration of marks & brands
    1841-1899 GGM 71:74
Floyd Co, early marr recs &
    biog notes GP 16:2:51
    16:3:113 16:4:188
Fort Stewart, misc cem inscr
    NGI 3:1:29
Franklin Co, deeds index 1784-
    1860, bk rev GH 33:4:110 GGM
    73:164 KCG 20:3:147
Fulton Co, hist 1934, bk rev GH
    33:2:76
geneal magazine v1-8 1961-1969,
    bk rev NGS 67:4:305
Gilmer Co, census 1850, bk rev
    GH 33:3:99 NGI 3:1:32 OC
    16:2:69 GE 49:10 NYR
    110:3:181 GGM 73:163 CDS
    16:1:33
Gordon Co, marr recs 1881-1884
    GGM 71:77
Gwinnett Co, Elisha Winn house
    hist, bk rev GH 33:4:111
    misc hist tours 1968-1974, bk

rev GH 33:5:73

Habersham Co, wills abstr 1820–1850 bk 4A,5 GGM 73:187

Hartwell, news abstr GGM 74:279

imm hist, bk rev BGS 10:4:33

indexes to state census reports 1838–1845, bk rev GH 33:3:98

indexes to seven state census reports for counties 1838–1845, bk rev CDS 16:1:22

Irwin Co, hist 1932, bk rev GH 33:2:77 CDS 16:5:46

Jackson Co, geneal column abstr, bk rev KCG 20:4:211

misc recs, bk rev GH 33:4:111

geneal news column abstr, bk rev GH 33:6:76

Jefferson Co, early will abstr GP 16:1:47

hist 1927, bk rev GH 33:2:77

Lincoln Co, census 1800, bk rev GH 33:3:99 CDS 16:1:3

census 1850 REF 2:1:10

grantor deed index 1796–1860 GGM 73:193

Lowndes Co, hist 1825–1941, bk rev GH 33:2:77

Lumpkin Co, hist 1832–1932, bk rev GH 33:2:77 CDS 16:5:47

Macon Co, hist 1933, bk rev GH 33:5:73

misc abstr court recs 1898 MCR 10:4:93

misc county records, Cuyler collect GGM 73:213

misc fams, notes on FH 2:2:70

misc res guides GE 42:4

Monroe Co, marr bk A GGM 74:265

Montgomery Co, census 1880, bk rev GGM 73:163

natives in TN 1850 GGM 74:287

Pickens Co, hist 1935, bk rev GH 33:2:77

Rev War, continental establishment GP 16:1:33

hist, bk rev CDS 16:1:33

index to Saffell's recs (1858) GGM 73:212

soldiers & their desc GP 16:1:15 16:2:63 16:3:99 16:4:165

Wilkes Com Kettle Creek battle, bk rev GGM 71:10

Richmond Co, early recs GP 16:1:3 16:2:57 16:3:133 16:4:177

marr licenses 1785–1849 GGM 71:81

selected news columns (Wilcox), bk rev CDS 16:2:6

Talbot Co, will vA GGM 73:197

Telfair Co, hist 1812–1949, bk rev GH 33:2:78

Turner Co, hist 1933, bk rev GH 33:5:73

Whitfield Co, marr recs bk A GGM 71:93 74:273

Wilkes Co, early recs GP 16:1:21 16:2:75 16:3:123 16:4:171

Wilkinson, hist (1930), bk rev GH 33:2:78 YP 9:4:230

GERARDI, Anthony b1901 w Emma Cavagnaro, anc ch ITG 2:43

GERKING, Ida, NE letter 1883 BGS 3:3:19

GERLACH, Henry b1814 w Margaret Hager, Ger, OH, REP 19:1:30

GERMAN GENEALOGY, Am geneal resources in Ger archives, bk rev OG 5:2:58

beginner;s res guide TST 12:28:39 12:29:46 12:30:38 12:31:39 12:32:37 FAM 18:1:23

emigs to CO from Russia BGS 4:1:27

geneal handbk of Ger res, bk rev NGS 67:3:220

geneal res guide, bk rev OG 2:4:118

Ger ancestors in VA, notes on GCB 79:1:1

Germans from Russia JG 4:4:25

handbk of Ger research, bk rev OG 5:3:88

mercenaries from Hessen Hanau who remained in Can & US after Am Rev, bk rev SCS 15:3:89

notes on MCR 10:4:95

Palatine emig (1937), bk rev CTN 9:3:473

Palatine guide, bk rev CTN 8:4:543

res guide to Ger collect of Geneal Soc of Utah, bk rev GER 18:40

surname listings GER 18A:24 18B:54

GERMANY, Archives, geneal res guide, bk rev OR 24:2:74

Bischwiller, hist, bk rev REP 19:3:135

East Ger, geneal res tips BGS 8:2:1

geneal res guide, bk rev GE 43:11 GJ 8:4:212 ACL 4:1:6

Ger alphabet GR 21:3:116

index to towns & cities v4, bk rev CTN 9:3:467

Palatine Menn hist 1693-1698 PM 2:2:17

Prussia, hist GER 16:446

Schleswig-Holstein, emig to Am, notes on TST 12:25:48

surname changes AG 55:2:93

GERNERT, James b1837 w Sarah Jacoby, PA, anc ch REP 19:1:29

GERRISH, James bc1899 w Mary Ann, Eng, OR, biog notes GFP 29:3:51

GERSTENBERGER, fam geneal, bk rev CI 15:4:155

GHARNA, Robert F b1902 w Jean Frances Henderson, IL, anc ch FF 8:2:27

GIBBONY, Jones b1810 w Rachel Wells McCall, MD, OH, geneal 1945, bk rev REP 19:4:168

GIBBS, Julius d1834 w Aggy, VA, KY, pension appl BR 6:4:160

GIBSON, Charles d1882 w Clarissa McDaniel/McDowell, Mrs Phoebia McCulloch, AL, biog notes VL 13:3:122

Charles Reese b1842 w Sallie N Ellis, Emma Driskill, AL, biog notes VL 13:4:170

Hugh Fisher b1868 w Dorothy Isabel Paddock, WI, anc ch ANC 14:4:134

James b1752 w Elizabeth Jepson, Esther, ME, biog notes DE 3:4:8

Samuel b1846 w Laura Jane Kirkland, Bible rec THT 3:2:18

GIDDENS, fam of Am, geneal, bk rev GH 33:5:84

GIFFORD, Daniel Db1792 w Martha

Buckbee, NY, Bible rec CTN 11:3:405

William d1687, MA, geneal NER 133:1:49 133:2:134 133:3:211 133:4:294

GIGNILLIAT, fam of Switz & SC, geneal, bk rev NGS 67:3:219

GILBERT, Ephraim d1779 w Maria Bullis, Selina (More) Woodford, CT, NY, geneal CTN 10:2:360

George Treadway b1811 w Sarah Louise Wilson, MD, anc ch REP 19:3:128

Stephen W b1839, MI, Bible rec MI 24:3:78

Theodore b1729, Bible rec WI 25:3:128

GILBREATH, Joseph Marion b1844 w Mary Annie Bailey, AL, Bible rec PT 21:2:49

GILDEMEESTER, Vincent b1812, Can, biog notes FAM 18:2:67

GILLESPIE, David Rayner b1882 w Dora Chaplin, OH, KS, CO, anc ch BGS 10:2:38

John L b1837 w Malinda C Choat, Bible rec FP 22:1:8

GILLHAM, Charles b1786 w Corinda (Clarinda), Bible rec CO 40:3:97

GILLILAND, fam of KS, geneal, bk rev GH 33:4:117

John Berry b1790 w Jane McFerrin, VA, TN, geneal, bk rev GH 33:5:85

Samuel f1775 w Elizabeth, geneal, bk rev REP 19:1:42

GILLISS, James Melville f1858, biog, bk rev REP 19:4:168

GILLS, John Anderson b1863 w Katie, Bible rec THT 6:2:29

GILMORE, Baptiste b1776 w Sally Mooers, NH, WV, anc ch DE 3:2:23

Morris m1829 w Elizabeth Blazer, Bible rec KN 2:2:33

Robert Foster b1903 w Frances Elizabeth WQitter, OH, anc ch CPY 8:2:48

GILPIN, fam of KY, geneal 1929, bk rev TB 6:2:20

GILSTRAP, Nancy (Wright) b1779 h

Richard Gilstrap, NC, KY, IN, obit CI 13:4:152

GIRARD, Melissa m1872 h John Case, John F Fine, Bible rec AH 3:4:113

GLACKEN, Amm d1888, KS, biog notes IL 11:4:194

GLACKIN, James Hickerson b1831 w Matilda Lancaster, KY, IL, biog & fam notes IL 11:2:99

 Richard A f1921 w Sarah, IL, Can, Il biog notes IL 11:1:32

GLANTZ, Raymond b1908 w Alma Freda Amend, NE, MT, anc ch THT 6:3:83

GLASCOCK, William D bc1815 w Salina A, VA, AL, TX, fam rec & biog notes AGS 20:3:84

GLASS, Julius Franklin b1889 w Adele Davidson Ellis, AL, anc ch GR 21:1:8

GLAZENBROOK, John dc1825 w Judith R, VA will VAG 23:3:223

GLAZIER, John bc1637 w Elizabeth Gorge, Eng, MA, geneal DM 43:1:3 43:2:51

 GLEASON, EWlijah f1802 w Symthia, Bible rec CTN 11:4:595

GLEDHILL, James b1793 w Eliza Nash, Eng, NY, geneal, bk rev GH 33:1:92 NYR 110:3:183

GLENN, fam of TX, notes on YP 9:2:73

GLOVER, Chesley b1761 w Mary Guerrant, VA, Bible rec BGS 10:4:21

GODFREY, John b1762 w Eleanor Cromie, Ir, biog nootes IR 11:1:30

 John Fermor b1828, Ir, hunting diaries IR 11:2:107

GODIN, Majorique b1873 w Emilie Allard, Can, anc ch AGE 8:1:32

GODING, Amasa d1916 w Mary Smith, Dorcas (Goss) Rowe, ME, fam rec DE 2:5:12

 Rufus Henry b1853 w Jessie Fremont Hurd, ME, anc ch NW 2:3:95

GODWIN, Roberson J d1920 w Ida Green, Ada, Bible rec THT

2:2:15

GOERTZEN, Gerhard f1875 w Helena Reddecopp, Russ, Can, geneal, bk rev BCG 6:1:8

GOETHALS, fam of Neth, notes on LL 15:1:6 15:2:72

GOHN, John d1769 w Anna Rosina Crantzdorf, Ger, PA, geneal, bk rev GH 33:5:83

GOLAY, David Ph b1789 w Rachel McIntosh, IN, Bible rec HJA 6:1:46

GOLD, fam Bible rec MGR 14:4:156

GOLDEN, fam of AL, bk rev CI 13:3:115

GOLDHAWK, Thomas Howard b1898 w Bertha Aurora Goyer, Can, MI, anc ch BGS 11:1:40

GOLDSBY, Peter R f1864, LA, misc notes THT 2:1:20

GOOD, Jacob f1779 w Mary Bosley, MD, PA, geneal, bk rev GH 33:3:106

GOODALE, Benjamin Ellsworth m1906 w Hildur Lidstrom, Sweden, NY, Bible rec CO 40:2:44

GOODMAN, Henry Mandeville b1828 w Sally Elliott, Bible rec KA 15:2:103

GOODPASTURE, Hamilton b1811, IL, KS, biog notes & anc ch SCC 16:3:68,70

GOODRUN, William B w Dixie, FL, TX, biog notes STK 7:1:31

GOODWIN, Alfred d1847, NY obit MIS 11:4:60

 James B b1817 w Maria H, Isabel Nichols, fam rec & obits MIS 11:4:60

GORDON, John b1739 w Mary Duke, PA, geneal, bk rev REP 19:4:169

GORGES, Thomas f1640, ME, letters of governor, bk rev DE 3:1:33

GORTON, Samuel b1592 w Mary Mayplett, Eng, MA, RI, biog notes BGS 7:1:21

GOTTFRIED, Philipp bc1800 w Barbara Herthel, Ger, OH, anc ch REP 19:1:30

GOULD, Noah Miller b1810 w Rachel Donnell, ME, geneal IL

11:2:91

GOZA, Harry Edward b1897 w Jeannette Marion Fuqua, FL, OH, CA, anc ch RRS 12:2:217

Julius Echols b1875 w Cora Maude Oxley, IL, FL, GA, anc ch HJA 6:4:37

GRAFTON, Josepah w Mary Moore, geneal 1928, bk rev TB 6:4:21

GRAHAM, George b1766 w Elizabeth Lazembee, Eng, NY, OH, geneal, bk rev REP 19:1:45

Jasper b1829 w Julie Ann Strickland, OH, anc ch REP 19:4:157

Ralph b1806 w Hannah Burdick, NY, OH, anc ch REP 19:1:27

GRAMELSPACHER, Joseph b1848 w Mary Otillia Bettag, IN, anc ch THT 7:2:73

GRAMLICH, Alvin f1855, NE, biog notes NA 2:1:20

GRANT, Aaron R b1820 w Mahala Ann Libby, ME, Bible rec DE 2:5:19

Julia Dent f1898 h Ulysses S Grant, US Pres, geneal, bk rev REP 19:4:167

GRAVES, Frank Orien b1890 w Hazel Elizabeth Bell, IA, MT, WA, anc ch OG 4:3:69

Henry Marshall b1840 w Carrie A Hull, IA, Bible rec HH 14:2:86

Thomas M b1824 w Martha Fleming, Susanna M Wilson, Naunie E Harding, KY, biog VQ 16:3:48

GRAY, Asa Harland b1890 w Bernice Melissa Lawrence, ME, anc ch AG 55:2:113

C H, TX, letter 1861 YP 9:2:69

Clarence Truman b1877 w Bessie Lee Stretcher, KS, IN, TX, anc ch THT 7:1:13

fam of NC & VA, geneal, bk rev KY 21:1:32 GGM 71:8 SCS 16:2:59 RRS 12:X:2 CDS 16:3:6

James Addison b1838 w Georgia Mary Bradley, AK, anc ch & Bible rec YP 9:2:68,71

John d1751 w Agnes, VA, NC, geneal, bk rev IL 11:3:181

TSP 2:4:2

Jonathan b1785 w Phebe Grimes, KY, Bible rec VL 13:3:123

Richard Gerald b1919 w Eloise Addington, IL, GA, anc ch PGB 11:5:48

W J b1842 w Mary T Brandon, Bible rec YP 9:3:148

William Iliff b1891 w Maudie Ellie Swopes, AR, MO, anc ch TB 6:2:30

GRAYBILL, John f1755 w Barbara Darradinger, PA, biog & fam notes PM 2:2:4

GREEN, George f1800, OH, geneal, bk rev TST 12:21:56 GH 33:5:85

Henry f1841 w Blandina DeWitt, NY, geneal ANC 14:4:118

James bc1760 w Sarah Hix, IL, fam rec FF 8:2:32

GREENE, fam of ME, geneal, bk rev CTN 8:4:540

GREENLEE, fam cem inscr OH AH 3:4:110

GREENWOOD, Otto August b1887 w Frieda Minna Appel, Ger, ID, anc ch OG 5:1:40

GREGG, Cristy b1808 w Mary Merrill, NH, Bible rec CO 40:3:98

GREGORY, Godfrey b1777 w Roseanna, Bible rec KA 14:3:164

Mercy (Lawrence) b1739 h Isaa Gregory, MA, fam rec MI 24:2:39

GRIDER, James Elmer b1835 w Martha Jane Thurman, OH, MO, IL, Bible rec IG15:3:96

Martin b1779 w Sally Moore, Bible rec MCH 7:3:73

Tobias b1800 w Sarah Johnson, KY, IN, obit MCH 7:3:76

GRIFFITH, Daniel b1726 w Mary Aldridge, MA, NY, anc ch THT 7:2:76

Thomas b1797 w Hannah Burget, Bible rec RRS 12:2:225

GRIFFITHS, Herman Thomas b1917 w Bertha Emma Purchase, IA, MO, NE, anc ch ORB 18:4:97

GRIGSBY, William Rice b1903 w Evalee Potts Reed, GA, anc ch

NAS 18:2:35

GRILL, Richard f1707 w Sarah Ligon, VA, marr data VA 17:2:65

GRIMES, fam of NC, letters 1862 DG 25:3:177

GRIMM, John Jacob b1793 w Catherine Burkhardt, OH, anc ch REP 19:4:159

GRISSETT, fam of NC, geneal NGS 67:2:111

GRISWOLD, The Griswold Linkage, 5721 Antietam Dr, Sarasota FL 33581

GROEZINGER, Christian b1854 w Rosina Rendecker, IL, obit IL 11:2:98

GROSS, Walter J b1907 w Lillian I Franklin, WA, IN, anc ch ACL 4:1:15

GROKENBARGER, Adam m1844 w Comfort J Williams, OH, marr return AH 2:2:38

GROND, George Fredeick w Ann Marwin, Fr, Can, Bible rec GN 2:8:245

GROSS, Andrew f1782 w Christine, Russ, Geneal, bk rev TB 6:1:33 6:2:23

Norman J b1889 w Eva Mary Cleveland, KS, anc ch TOP 9:1:11

Paul F b1864, Russ, Am, biog, bk rev TB 6:2:23

GROSSE, Otto Herman Oswald b1852 w Emilie Emma Dohmeyer, bible rec RED 11:3:15

GUEDRY, Ursin d1924 w Julia Hughes, TX, Bible rec YP 9:2:72

GUENTHER, Johann Michael Julius b1823 w Dorothea Kiefer, Ger, OH, anc ch REP 19:1:31

GUNDERMAN, Lawrence b1829 w Anna Maria Strasser, Ger, OH, AR, geneal, bk rev GH 33:3:106 KCG 20:2:88

GUPTILL, Ronald b1934 w Katherine Howard, CA, anc ch RED 12:2:2

GUSTOFSON, Otto m1871 w Eva Charlotta, Sweden, NE, Bible rec LL 14:1:27

GUTHRIE, Robert b1844 w Isabella Stewart, Scot, Can, IL, biog notes VQ 16:2:24

GUZAK, Joseph P b1930 w Betty J Arnold, IL, IN, MI, anc ch NGI 3:3:177

GWYNNE, Hugh bc1619 w Elizabeth Fielding, VA, anc ch YP 9:3:126

HACKLEY, fam of VA & KY, geneal, bk rev WCK 12:4:66

HADA, David Leroy b1927 w Thelma Joyce Rader, OK, anc ch TA 14:3:77

HADLEY, Calvin Spencer b1893 w Jessie Josephine (Johnson) Perryman, KS, MO, WA, anc ch OG 4:4:99

HAGADORN, fam of NY, geneal, bk rev CTN 8:1:39

HAGEMAN, Cornelius w Henriette Heenskerk, Alida Maria Swedenryk, Holland, geneal SGS 29:4:317

HAGEN, Karl f1779, Bavaria, biog notes TST 12:3:40

HAHN, Byron George Sr b1886 w Alice Amelia Healey, MA, ME, anc ch CPY 8:1:24

HAIN, George w Veronica, PA, geneal, bk rev TS 21:1:27

HAKE, William C b1832 w Emeline Davis, OH, WI, CO, geneal BGS 11:2:55

HALBERT, fam of AL, bk rev CI 13:3:115

HALE, Milton b1821 w Susannah Brown, IN, OR, biog notes ORB 17:8:72

Richard b1717 w Elizabeth Strong, CT, fam rec BGS 10:4:29

Samuel bc1615, Eng, CT, geneal 1952, bk rev TST 12:1:52 NGS 67:1:72 MQ 45:4:226 CTN 11:3:529 CLG 10:3:182 AG 55:1:57

HALEY, S S b1842 w Mary A Mills-Crawford, AR, Bible rec THT 5:1:28

HALL, Alfred Roe b1869 w Florence Geva Hinman, MI, anc ch ANC 14:4:135

fam of TN, marr rec CI 14:3:89

Hall of Fame, 19 Crinkleroot Ct, The Woodlands TX 77380

Harriet (Pool) mc1819 h Briton Hall, LA, TX, BLWT appl lists ch YP 9:1:7

Ira Baker b1812 w Amanda Olmstead, CT, OH, anc ch REP 19:3:116

James W w Hannah T, AL, will 1834 DG 25:1:35

John bc1847 w Sarah Brooks, GA, biog notes FTR 20:5

John Milton b1896 w Neva Marguerite Cady, MO, IL, anc ch THT 6:3:73

Owen Lovejoy, geneal, bk rev BGS 11:2:75

Philo S b1805 w Sarah Jewell Hawley, VT, OH, IL, fam rec FF 8:2:45

William f1780 w Sarah, NJ, IN, Bible rec HJA 6:1:46

HALLIDAY, Walter m1673 w Katherine Hunter, MA, geneal, bk rev CTN 7:3:361 7:4:516

HALSEY, Jerome f1832 w Hannah, NY, Bible rec MGR 14:2:61

HAMELTON, David L b1786, MO cem inscr CI 12:2:75

HAMILTON, fam of KY, geneal, bk rev BR 6:3:96

James f1765, VA, Eng, notes on NGS 67:1:62

John b1808, ME, Bible rec DE 3:2:21

HAMMER, Guy Warden b1896 w Grethel Enola Taylor, MO, TX, anc ch THT 7:1:8

HAMMON, Heman Bangs b1833 w Lucy Wood, OH, biog notes REP 19:1:18

HAMMONDS, James William b1870 w Nancy Rebecca Farnsworth, TN, TX, anc ch THT 7:1:18

HAMPEL, Michael b1832 w Katherine Kessler, Ger, MO, AR, geneal, bk rev GH 33:3:106

HAMPSHER, Howard Monroe b1896 w Florence Isabella Golden, OH, anc ch KN 2:4:25

HAMPTON, John m1802 w Elizabeth Snider, GA, geneal, bk rev FP 22:4:209

HAMSCHER, John f1772, Ger, PA, geneal YP 9:1:17 9:2:113 9:3:170 9:4:231

HAMSHER, Daniel b1760 w Catherine Elizabeth Waldman, PA, NY, anc ch CLG 10:1:55

John d1785 w Lydia Hakart, PA, fam rec YP 9:1:18

HANBURY, fam of VA, notes on NGS 67:1:60

HANCOCK, Jacob Secor b1810 w Jane Van Vlack, Bible rec KK 17:4:78

HAND, Nathaniel b1739 w Esther Mulford, Bible rec CTN 12:2:230

HANEY, Martin H b1867 w Carrie Rigney, IL, obit MCH 7:4:111

HANFORD, Jeffrey bc1583 w Eglin (Hatherly) Downe, Eng, geneal CTA 21:3:107

Thomas f1637, geneal supp CTA 21:3:107 21:4:155 22:1:1 22:2:53

HANKINS, Thomas B b1846 w Lizie Hill, Bible rec CI 14:4:146

HANKINSON, William b1785 w Mary Ellinor, NJ, anc ch REP 19:3:131

HANKS, Hilaire Jefferson b1858 w Marguerite Azema Louviere, LA, anc ch AGE 8:2:62

Isabella bc1774 h Peter Hanks IV, Calvin Merry, TX, IN, fam rec THT 1:2:17

Joseph bc1730 w Nannie Ann Lee, VA, KY, geneal CI 15:3:92

Joseph b1791 w Almira, NY, Bible rec NYR 110:1:15

HANLIN, Patrick f1776 w Margaret, Ir, PA, VA, OH, geneal, bk rev REP 19:4:169

HANLON, fam of VA & OH, geneal, bk rev REP 19:4:167

HANNA, John W b1819 w Catherine Shade, NY, OH, IL, anc ch REP 19:3:127

HANSON, fam of NH & ME, geneal, bk rev DE 3:2:30

fam of NY, geneal NYR 110:1:16

Hans f1670 w Hannah, DE, geneal, bk rev GH 33:1:92 GJ 8:2:116 NYR 110:2:122 AG 55:2:128

HARDEMAN, fam geneal 1750-1900, bk rev CDS 16:2:5

HARDER, fam of NY, fam rec DM 42:3:102

HARDEY, George Henley b1818 w Jane Robinson, MD, MO, geneal MD 20:1:24

HARDIN, Augustine B dc1871 w Mariah Devers, TX, heirs YP 9:1:10

E H b1845 w A E King, Bible rec & fam reg NAS 18:1:10

fam recs KY KA 15:2:98

fam recs VA KA 15:2:99

John f1782, VA letters KA 14:4:35

Susan (Waggoner) h Robert Hardin, NC, GA, biog notes & letter 1874 MCH 7:2:46

HARDY, Levi b1735 w Sally Borden, MA, PA, Bible rec CTN 11:2:217

HARGRAVE, Peter w Mary Thomas, geneal supp, bk rev LL 15:1:23

geneal, bk rev LL 15:1:23

HARLEY, Olin b1850 w Anna Rachel Ulrey, IN, anc ch ACL 4:3:56

HARLOW, Mahlon Hall b1811 w Frances Burrus Tandy, KY, MO, OR, biog notes ORB 17:9:82

HARMON, Thomas b1774 w Jane McCallister, VA, anc ch REP 19:4:156

HARPEL, Philip b1759 w Mary, Ger, PA, fam rec BGS 8:1:21

HARPER, Elias m1854 w Amanda Kemp, Bible rec GFP 28:10:190

Finis Burke b1905 w Roberta Gertrude Cox, TX, anc ch AGS 20:2:61

John b1787 w Sarah Hurst, SC, geneal SGS 29:4:309

HARPINE, Elliot Homer b1885 w Phoebe Ardner, VA, OH, MT, anc ch NW 2:4:126

HARRINGTON, Dever S m1907 w Lydia F Miles, NY, marr cert THT 4:2:16

Frederick w Anna Truesdelle, OH fam cem inscr AH 3:3:77

HARRIS, A J (Jack) b1844 w Harriet Perkins Owen, AL, biog notes VL 14:1:23

David Saunders Jr b1879 w Pauline Isadora Brown, KY, anc ch THT 6:3:57

Hiram b1803 w Lucinda D Kingsley, Bible rec ORB 17:5:44

James Winter b1839, Eng, geneal, bk rev NW 2:4:134

Nancy D (Stovall) b1814 h David Huston Harris, TN, OR, biog notes ORB 17:5:47

Roy Lee b1947 w Rebecca Mae Fry, OK, CA, anc ch WB 10:2:67

HARRISON, Benjamin, geneal, bk rev TB 6:2:19

Richard w Anne, NC, letter 1781 NCJ 5:2:95

HARRYMAN, Elijah, geneal, bk rev OG 5:1:28

HART, Jesse m1886 w Mrs Mary L Smith, TX, Bible rec THT 5:1:30

William f1800 w Polly, VA, fam rec VAG 23:3:199

HARTLEY, John Thomas b1856 w Cornelia Texona Coplin, TX, Bible rec THT 2:2:17

HARTOUGH, fam recs, bk rev HH 14:3:162

HARVEY, fam geneal, bk rev CI 15:4:125

Jeremiah m1803 w Charity Masters, KY, biog CI 15:4:153

William b1741 w Margaret Duncan, Scot, VT, geneal, bk rev RES 11:4:148

HASKELL, John W b1810 w Mary A Williams, NY, OH, PA, Bible rec AH 5:3:98

HASKIN, Ernest Harley b1880 w Lydia Amelia Weirich, IL, WI, OR, anc ch NGI 3:2:115

HATCH, fam of MD, geneal, bk rev AGS 20:4:145

HATCHER, John Andrew b1853 w Mattie J Bullock, TN, obit BWG 8:1:42

HATHAWAY, Jeremiah S b1824, NY,

MI, WA, obit TB 6:2:9

HATHEWAY, Erastus b1789 w Mercy Norton, MA, Bible rec THT 2:1:9

George Whitfield b1831 w Jane Moore, OH, KS, biog THT 5:3:22

HATZENBUEHLER, George W b1875 w Nannie Lou Hawpe, IL, TX, anc ch YP 9:3:128

HAUBOLD, Charley b1872 w Anna Pery Lee, IL, OH, NE, CO, anc ch BGS 9:3:46

HAVENS, fam of NY, geneal, bk rev CTN 8:1:35

HAVNER, William Marvin b1900 w Edna Elizabeth Campbell, NB, WA, anc ch TRI 17:1:7

HAWAII, Kahuna sorcerers, hist, bk rev CDS 16:4:11

vr guide 1826-1896 GJ 8:3:159

HAWKES, William b1865 w Susan R Jones, Eng, anc ch KN 2:1:36

HAWKINS, Amos bc1770 w Rachel Jones, Eng, KY, Bible rec GL 13:1:20

Joel b1785 w Betsey Raynor, Bible rec DM 43:1:12

William b1800 w Anna Eddy, DE, NY, IN, geneal THT 5:2:14

HAWORTH, Edward Carlyle b1894 w Mabel Ella Andrews, NC, IA, CO, anc ch THT 6:3:70

HAWVER, John Wesly b1851 w Jennie Finnity, IL, Bible rec CI 15:3:84

HAXTONE, James f1689 w Mary, MA, RI, geneal, bk rev GH 33:4:117

HAY, John b1809 w Susan Flick, PA, geneal LM 20:3:3

HAYBRON, Richard b1819 w Rachel Gregory, OH, anc ch REP 19:1:26

HAYEK, James b1900 w Elizabeth Ann Sedlak, Czech, NE, anc ch BGS 11:2:84

HAYES, Rutherford B d1893 US Pres w Lucy Webb, OH, geneal CTN 12:2:202

William m1802 w Lucy Gatewood, Eng, VA, KY, geneal, bk rev TST 12:32:38

HAYFORD, Samuel Jr b1807 w Lucinda Clark, Can, OH, anc ch REP 19:1:38

HAYNAM, Thomas b1788 w Barbara Rule, MD, PA, anc ch REP 19:2:86

HAYNES, James H b1843 w Mary Lou Spires, Hester, KY, Bible rec KA 14:3:167

Milliner b1799 w Susan W Skillman, VA, KY, Bible rec KCG 20:2:69

HAYS, Asa Walker Jr b1924 w Mildred Louise Stout, WA, KS, anc ch WB 10:2:66

Robert f1806 w Betsy Adams, SC, OH, geneal, bk rev TST 12:9:45

HAZELTON, Stephen b1707, NH, geneal, bk rev DM 43:1:44

HEADLEY, John b1818 w Lydia Murry, OH, Bible rec AH 1:3:7

HEALEA, William m1889 w Mary C Livingston, Marr cert GL 13:3:71

HEALY, William Milton b1835 w Clarissa Caroline Collar, VT, MI, geneal, bk rev BGS 9:2:34

HEARD, Daniel m1765 w Lydia Littlefield, ME, child DE 3:4:21

fam geneal, bk rev GE 49:9

Osborne Overton b1890 w Mary Kerr Dunlop, MD, ID, biog EWA 16:3:77

HEATH, Wilson m1758 w Rachel, MD, Bible rec MMG 2:2:84

HEBERT, Clarence Jay b1911 w Florence Marie LeBlanc, LA, anc ch AGE 8:2:67

Jean Sarazin b1818 w Veronique Guidry, anc ch AGE 8:3:99

HEDGES, William b1828 w Phebe Gifford, NY, Bible rec CTN 11:3:406

HEER, Samuel b1832 w Catharine Wilhelm, Ger, OH, anc ch REP 19:1:38

HELD, Philip A bc1813 w Philippine Schaffer, Ger, OH, anc ch REP 19:1:38

HELDRETH, fams of VA, geneal, bk rev GH 33:2:84

HELLYER, Cordelia b1869 h Mr Williams, IA, biog notes BGS 6:3:5

HELM, James Wilbur b1849 w Carrie Judson Vest, OR, WA, biog YV 11:1:34

HELMLINGER, Jacob bc1816 w Elizabeth Lewis, Ger, OH, anc ch REP 19:3:129

HEMANN, Henry b1842 w Wilhelmina Schuster, Ger, IL, geneal FF 8:1:31

HEMPEL, Michael b1832, Ger, MO, geneal, bk rev KCG 20:2:88

HEMPHILL, Catherine A b1844 h John Carman, Adam Barnhart, John Crawford, OH, PA, notes on CPY 8:2:34

HEMRY, John Sr w Catherine, OH, geneal, bk rev KCG 20:4:204

HENDERSON, Alfred m1897 w Sarah Carrie Graham, PA marr cert KN 2:1:16

Dallas Glenn b1923 w Betty Clay Mobley, AR, anc ch RRS 12:1:91

John Sr b1780 w Sarah, NJ, fam rec KN 2:1:29

Tyra Green b1823 w Mary Lucinda Conner, MS, TX, fam rec THT 1:2:18

HENDRICK, Edward H b1817 w Jemima E Hancock, KY, Bible rec LL 14:2:70

HENDRICKS, John William b1899 w Agnes Marie Mickelson, CO, WA, anc ch TB 6:3:14

HENDRICKSON, James Ridgeway, geneal, bk rev GH 33:2:84

HENGST, John Lewis f1859 w Elizabeth Messerschmidt, Ger, IL, geneal CI 15:1:9

HENRICI, John Philip f1750 w Anna Catharina Mingler, Ger, Can, Bible rec GN 2:8:244

HERALDRY, Am Armory (1927), bk rev BGS 9:3:37

Anglo-Norman armory hist, bk rev GH 33:2:72

British fams (Burke) 1884, bk rev CTN 10:1:156

Cath Ch hist heraldry, bk rev ITG 2:55

heralds & hist, bk rev AG 55:2:127

notes on SCS 14:1:2 15:3:74

papal heraldry, bk rev ITG 2:55

Scottish, bk rev BGS 9:3:37

world heraldry, bk rev CTN 7:3:360

HERBERT, John m1656 w Mary Bennett, Eng, VA, geneal, bk rev VAG 23:2:142 GH 33:5:85 KCG 20:4:206

Thomas d1844 w Zilpha Murphy, NJ, IN, obit NSN 4:1:6

HERITAGE, William Howard Sr b1903 w Caroline Helene Roth, NJ, anc ch AW 5:2:52

HERNDON, Hollis Rodney b1909 w Flora Elizabeth Self, TX, anc ch THT 7:2:67

HERRIDGE, Collingsworth Hightower b1878 w Mary Annie Byrnes, TX, anc ch THT 6:3:87

HERRMAN, Katharina b1839 h J B Geyer, notes on CPY 8:3:71

HERRON, James b1807 w Elizabeth Brisbin, Bible rec & diary CI 14:4:133

HERYFORD, Dallas Marshall b1896 w Rose Luvada Mason, MO, KS, anc ch ROP 9:2:45

HERZER, Philip f1820 w Miss Bonnet, Ger, SD, KS, biog notes BGS 10:3:31

HESLETINE, Charles f1764, MD, notes on NGS 67:3:210

HESSON, Samuel b1809 w Eliza J Lamp, OH, anc ch REP 19:1:32

HESTER, Jesse Handley b1905 w Mamie L Dix, AL, GA, anc ch NAS 17:3:70

John f1740, KY, geneal supp, bk rev CTN 9:2:314

HEUSTON, fam of NE & OK, geneal, bk rev BGS 8:1:27

HEWITT, Joseph b1838 w Hellen C Thayer, NY, Bible rec NYR 110:3:163

HICKS, fams of MA, geneal, bk rev CTN 10:1:158

James Thomas b1801 w Catherine Harris, Cynthia Landers, NC, IL, geneal FF 8:1:35

John Robert b1867 w Rose Jane

Cocherell, IN, anc ch REP
19:3:121

Thomas b1744, fam rec HH
14:3:150

HIDY, William b1796 w Barbara
Henkle, Catharine (Parrot)
Wilson, VA, IN, anc ch REP
19:3:126

HIGDON, Joseph B b1837 w Ann
Eliza Miller, TN, WA, obit TB
6:2:9

HIGGINS, Alfred Norris f1881 w
Lucy Belle Watson, IL, fam
rec FF 8:2:43

HIGH, Ivan Harold b1896 w Ida
Gladys Morrison, IL, anc ch
FF 8:3:58

HILDERBRAND, Adam bc1864 w
Elizabeth Jones, Ger, IA, LA,
anc ch YP 9:1:3

HILDERBRANDT, George b1874, cem
inscr SGS 29:4:344

HILDYARD, Yoonne b1916, CA, auto
MKT 2:3:46

HILE, John Henry b1816 w Lovina
Kirkendall, OH, anc ch REP
19:4:157

HILER, William Napoleon b1853 w
Elizabeth Tina Slaughter, LA,
NM, fam rec NMG 18:4:121

HILL, George m1812 w Mary Ann
Baldwin, KY, BLWT & pension
claim KA 14:4:222

Harriet b1802 h William Henry
Johnson, CT, OH, geneal AG
55:1:55

Hill Heritage, Box 1791, Portland OR 97207

Jemima d1820 h Benjamin Bowker,
MA, geneal MQ 45:4:204

Robert f1705, Eng, MD,notes on
NGS 67:3:211

Samuel Branson bc1865 w Mary
Frances Hill, MN, WA, biog
notes QY 6:1:1

William bc1640 w Mary Spivey,
Eng, VA, NC, geneal QY 6:2:1
6:3:7 6:4:9

HILLIS, Thomas bc1804 w Anna
Quinn, Ir, MI, geneal, bk rev
GH 33:1:92

HILLYER, Robert, IA letter 1863
BGS 6:2:15

HILTON, Edward, NH, geneal, bk
rev TB 6:4:30

James, ME, 1795 will DE 2:5:9

William b1585 w Mary, Frances
White, Eng, MA, anc ch DE
3:2:22

HINCKLEY, Samuel f1635, MA,
geneal, bk rev MQ 45:3:163

HINKLEY, Joel f1850 w Margaret
Coombs, ME, geneal, bk rev MQ
45:4:226

HITCHCOCK, fam of CT, geneal, bk
rev NYR 110:1:57

HITE, Jost b1685, Ger, NY, PA,
VA, biog, bk rev GJ 8:4:220

HOAR, Benjamin f1815, NY, pet
for name change to Whitney TS
21:3:89

HAOBART, Jonas b1744 w Betty
Kemp, MA, anc ch OC 16:2:64

HOCHWARTER, Adam b1742 w Catherine Krohn, Ger, PA, anc ch
CLG 10:1:56

HOCKADAY, Edmund, VA 1790 will
VAG 23:1:54

HODGE, Alexander b1762 w Ruth
Hodge, PA, TX, fam rec THT
1:2:19

Samuel b1779, w Nancy Trigg,
Margaret Jane Allison, Sally
D Brown, TN diary & fam recs
THT 5:4:29

TN, TX, fam rec GR 21:3:91

HODGES, Daniel M b1809 w Eliza,
Nancy Ann Preuit, Martha
Preuit, SC, AL, biog notes VL
14:1:23

fam of Co Limerick Ir, geneal
IR 11:2:77

HODSON, Cynthia A b1821 h Jacob
Dillon, OH, IL, obit LL
15:1:38

HOECKER, August Charles Sr b1906
w Florence Schweizer, NY, anc
ch BGS 10:3:40

HOELSCHER, Anton b1791 w Anna
Maria Katherine Daldrop, Ger,
TX, geneal, bk rev GH 33:4:118

HOFFMEYER, Heinreich Adolph
b1801 w Dorothea Elisabeth
Frick, Ger, NY, MI, fam recs
CPY 8:2:42

HOFFMIRE, Henry f1843 w Catherine, Ger, IL, geneal FF 8:2:65

HOGG, Joseph Lewis b1806 w Lucanda McMath, TX cem inscr THT 4:1:28

HOLL, Raymond S b1893 w Birchel L Smith, IN, TX, OK, anc ch ACL 4:2:35

HOLLAND, geneal res notes SGS 29:1:51

William b1819 w Martha J Miller, Martha Martin, TN, KY, biog VQ 16:3:47

HOLLBROOKS, Charlotte d1840 h G C Hollbrooks, OH, cem inscr AH 3:3:77

HOLLIBAUGH, Dean Walter b1927 w Mildred Erma Rogers, NE, anc ch NW 2:4:130

HOLLIDAY, Anna Maria d1855, MO, will TS 21:3:82

Anna Nancy d1853 h Richard Holliday, VA, MO, will & biog notes TS 21:3:82

HOLLINGSHEAD, Robert b1797 w Elizabeth, fam rec GNJ 54:2:82

HOLLINGSWORTH, Leon S b1896, geneal card file, bk rev NGI 3:4:208

HOLLISTER, Storrs W b1853 w Eva E Buss, WI, Bible rec PR 3:2:24

HOLLOWAK, Stanley Adam b1915 w Martha Lee Murphy, MD, anc ch MD 20:3:235

HOLLOWAY, Henry Miller b1807 w Nancy Monday, KY, IA, anc ch REP 19:3:126

Simpson b1798 w Charlotte, MO, KS, TX, fam rec THT 1:2:20

William b1770 w Nancy Boswell, Bible rec BWG 8:1:30

HOLMAN, Abraham b1818 w Leah Dresbach, OH, geneal supp, bk rev REP 19:4:177

HOLMES, Elmer A b1878 w Edna A Abbey, IA, MN, Bible rec TB 6:1:20

James f1850, GA, PA, CT, bk rev CDS 16:1:5

HOLTON, William Calvin b1835 w Amanda J Thurman, TN, KY, IL,

biog notes MCH 7:4:104

HOMAN, John d1797 w Elizabeth Oxley, VA, anc ch TAK 9:2:33

HOOK, J A m1884 w Maggie Dick, IL, biog notes MCH 7:4:113

Jacob m1784 w Elizabeth Campbell, Bible rec MD 20:4:344

Jacob b1804 w Susannah Fredrick, Bible rec MCH 7:4:112

HOOKER, Benjamin w Ann Frizelle, NC, TN, geneal & supps, bk rev GH 33:5:85

Sarah (Whitman) d1837 h Thomas Hart Hooker, Seth Collins, biog notes CTN 7:2:162

Thomas b1586, CT, biog, bk rev NER 133:1:57

HOOPER, fam of TN, notes on THT 5:1:31

HOOSIER, fam recs v2, bk rev GH 33:3:99

HOOVER, Solomon H, PA, lewtter 1863 ANC 14:4:129

HOPKINS, Susan (Dodd) b1818 h Robert Duncan, Eli Hopkins, KS, fam rec MGR 14:4:179

HOPPER, George R b1845 w Martha J Hurt, Elvira J Merritt, IN, CO, IL, auto & fam data BGS 10:1:22 10:2:19

Otis Frances b1912 w Margaret Ellen Jacobson, MT, anc ch BGS 11:4:180

HOPPING, John bc1647 w Rebecca (Hand) Smith, Eng, NY, geneal, bk rev CTN 7:3:361 12:4:699

HORNBECK, Conrade w Frederike E, fam rec LL 14:1:28

HAORNE, John S d1891, NH cem inscr FG 21:1:9

HORST, fam of PA & OH, geneal & anc ch OHR 20:3:115

HORTENSTINE, Henry, VA, IL, 1857 pers property sale MCH 7:3:85

HORTON, Solomon b1736 w Anna, Can, Bible rec GN 2:5:140

Stephen w Jane Horton, NY, geneal, bk rev NYR 110:4:249

Thomas b1602 w Mary, Eng, MA, geneal, bk rev CTN 9:2:315

William w Mary, NY will 1729 LL 15:3:138

HOTCHKISS, fam of CT, geneal CTN 12:2:218

HOUSE, Samuel b1610, Eng, MA, geneal 1952, bk rev TST 12:1:52 MQ 45:4:226 CTN 11:3:529 NGS 67:1:72 CLG 10:3:182 AG 55:1:57

HOUSER, Mary Ann m1864 h William Eggers, IL, IA, geneal, bk rev KCG 20:4:205 GH 33:3:108

HOWARD, Clarence Edward b1881 w Lucia Pierce Barber, NY, CT, anc ch BGS 11:2:85

  fam of AL, geneal, bk rev CDS 16:2:5

  Leicester b1809 w Mary Ann Hersey, Olive R Leach, ME, Bible rec DE 3:4:22

  Matthew A B b1824 w Sarah Crawford, Rachel Clark, GA, FL, geneal, bk rev GH 33:4:118

HOWE, John b1754, Can, loyalist, biog, bk rev GN 2:6:172

HOWELL, Edward b1584, Eng, MA, geneal, bk rev CI 14:3:110

  Joseph Ledem b1843 w   , Mary Carson, Martha Ellen Watson, IL, fam rec FF 8:2:43

HOWLAND, John f1620 w Elizabeth Tilley, Eng, MA, notes on MQ 45:1:23

  Joseph b1717 w Elizabeth Mitchell, MA, geneal MQ 45:1:70

HOXTON, fam of MD, VA, geneal MD 20:2:129

HUBBARD, Charles b1823 w Mary Cook, IL, OR, biog notes GFP 29:4:71

  Charles A b1832 w Alice, MO, OR, biog notes GFP29:4:71

  Goldman f1850, MO, OR, biog notes GFP 29:4:72

  Gideon bc1826, MO, biog notes GFP 29:4:72

  Mary b1754 h Oliver Burr, NY, fam rec CTA 22:1:49

HUBBELL, William White b1849 w Mariah H Light,MI, anc ch NGI 3:2:113

HUBBS, Albert F b1858 w Viola Bigler, MI, Bible rec MI 24:2:44

HUCK, Abraham b1824 w Nancy

Gentry, PA, Can, biog & geneal BCG 8:3:58

HUDSON, Frank M b1852, AL, TX, notes on FH 2:1:22

  Hudson Fam Assoc (South) Bulletin, Rt 7 Del Monte Pl, Longview TX 75601

  John Paria f1769 w Martha Henderson, Ir, MD, VA, geneal GR 21:2:78

  John T d1862, WI, biog notes BGS 10:4:26

HUESTIS, Edward Franklin b1906 w Vida Marlow, fam rec RED 12:1:8

HUGGINS, Martha Jane Shinall f1885 h Mr Shinall, Ezra Huggins, IL, biog notes IL 11:1:30

HUGHES, fam of AL, fam recs VL 13:4:158

  fam of TX, notes on YP 9:2:74

  William A f1866 w Margaret Jones, IL, biog notes GL 13:1:3

  Willis Andrew b1896 w Eula Jennie Swenson, KS, AZ, anc ch BGS 10:3:41

HUGHSTON, Archibald Patrick b1873 w Mary Emma Lively, AL, TX, anc ch THT 6:3:58

HUGUENOT, settlements in Col Am NGI 3:2:103 3:3:163

HULIN, Lester, diary 1847 IA to OR ORB 18:1:8 18:2:28 18:3:62 18:4:87

HULL, John Williams b1868 w Mary Brainard Howell, NY, anc ch ANC 14:2:51

  Richard f1634, MA, CT, geneal (1912), bk rev CTN 12:2:365 CDS 16:6:42

  Samuel Smith b1835 w Rebecca J Thompson, Lucy Kirkwood, Rebecaha (Hull) West, MO, AK, Bible rec THT 1:2:32

  William Emerson b1900 w Violet June Dubeau, TN, MN, AZ, anc ch THT 6:3:89

HULSE, Henry Adelbert b1836 w Caroline Mallion, OH, OR, geneal SGS 29:3:223

  James Reeves Jr b1828 w Eleanor Stipp, OH, anc ch REP 19:4:160

HUMPHREY, Michael bc1620 w Priscilla Grant, Eng, CT, geneal v3, bk rev GH 33:2:84

HUMPHRIES, Jake b1895 w Myrtle Irene Gills, AR, TN, anc ch THT 6:3:90

HUNGARY, gazetteers guide GH 33:1:5

geneal res guide GH 33:6:9

HUNGERFORD, William W b1860 w Addie I Halsey, NY, Bible rec MGR 14:2:61

HUNT, Daniel b1723 w Mary Trussell, VT, geneal, bk rev CTN 9:4:609

fams of Canada, geneal, bk rev CTN 11:2:341

fams of KY, bk rev WCK 12:4:66

fams of VT, geneal, bk rev CTN 10:2:345

Jonathan b1637 w Clemence Hosmer, MA, CT, VT, geneal, bk rev CTN 10:4:700

Samuel Perry b1825, NH, VT, geneal, bk rev CTN 11:3:525

Thomas b1717, geneal, bk rev CTN 12:3:534

Uriah b1774 w Sarah, TN, fam rec BWG 8:1:31

William b1781 w Elizabeth, NC, Bible rec HG 19:2:29

HUNTER, Daniel K, AL, minister's credentials 1826 VL 13:3:136

Duncan f1784, NY, notes on NGS 67:3:214

George b1755 w Phoebe Bryant, Scot, PA, biog DAR 113:5:500

Thomas J m1881 w Hattie E Anthony, Bible rec PR 3:1:4

HUNTLEY, John b1647, MA, CT, geneal, bk rev CDS 16:5:45

HUNTINGTON, Samuel b1731, CT, biog, bk rev CTN 11:3:524

HUNTLEY, John f1647 w Sarah, Jane, Mary, MA, CT, geneal, bk rev GH 33:2:84 CTN 12:1:183

HURLBUT, Orrin bc1797 w Lois Smith, CT, Bible rec AH 1:2:16

HURTT, fam of MD, fam recs PGB 11:6:63

HURTY, George Edwin b1895 w Mildred Jean Rockey, IN, KS, anc ch KK 17:2:24

HUSCROFT, William Roger b1830 w Jane Fisher, Eng, UT, Can, biog BCG 5:1:29

HUSS, Abraham b1818 w Jane Bodle, PA, IN,a anc ch REP 19:2:84

HUTCHINS, Jacob f1776, MA, biog, bk rev CTN 9:3:468

John d1685 w Elizabeth, MA, geneal, bk rev CTN 9:3:317

Strangeman b1707 w Elizabeth Cox, VA, NC, geneal, bk rev GH 33:6:87 GE 47:11 TS 21:2:75

William Jr b1767 w Lucinda Aseneth Allen, Mary Cowdrey, MA, NY, OH, biuog notes AG 55:1:27

William Jennings Bryan b1894 w Bennie Ward Williams, MS, TX, anc ch KG 16:1:18

HUTCHINSON, Elizabeth b1700 h Caleb Chappell, MA, fam rec CTA 22:1:48

Thomas H w Elizabeth, TN, will 1862 DG 25:3:180

HYATT, Alvin d1835 w Abigail Gruman, Mrs Sarah Edwards, Bible rec CTN 10:2:368

HYNES, James F b1882 w Elizabeth E Gover, KY, anc ch RRS 12:1:213

IDAHO, early hist, bk rev CDS 16:3:6

Indians, hist, bk rev CDS 16:1:6

Market Lake, hist v2, bk rev GH 33:4:111

pioneer hist, bk rev CDS 16:3:5

IGO, Jacob bc1774 w Elizabeth Anson, MD, MO, KY, anc ch AGS 20:2:67

ILLINOIS, Adams Co, index to 1872 atlas, bk rev OC 16:3:110

Alton, misc names in news 1838 IL 11:2:84

archives, inv GE 49:12

inv, bk rev KA 14:4:255
res guide TST 11:41:29 12:36:22 IL 11:3:147 SCS 16:1:15
Arthur, news abstr 1910 MCH 7:4:91
Rosedale Meth Epis Ch hist MCH 7:4:105
Barrington, news obits 1890-1895 NSN 4:1:4
news obits 1896 NSN 4:5:45 4:6:54
Belleville, First Bapt Ch hist STC 2:1:19
Bethany, Church of Christ reg 1881-1905, bk rev CI 13:4:153
Black Hawk War 1831-1832 v2, bk rev IL 11:1:57
Bloomington, city cem hist GL 13:2:50
misc news abstr GL 13:1:4,7,13 13:2:35 13:3:77 13:4:99
revised ordinances 1861 GL 13:1:29
Blount Twp, Bethel cem inscr IG 14:2:47
Grimes cem inscr IG 15:2:62
Fairchild cem inscr IG 15:1:9 15:2:64 15:3:70
Johnsonville, Finley's Woods, Humphrey-Stewart cem inscr IG 15:2:63
Pentecost cem inscr IG 14:3:83
Blue Mound, hist, bk rev CI 14:4:150
Bond Co, census 1840 CI 13:4:133 14:1:11
Greenville cem inscr CI 15:3:107
hist notes CI 14:1:26
Hurrican Fork, Bapt Ch in Christ, minutes 1818 BGS 6:1:4
Maxey cem inscr CI 11:2:54
Bureau Co, census 1850, bk rev TRI 19:2:31
hist (1885), bk rev CI 15:2:30
Calhoun Co, cem inscr, bk rev GH 33:2:78 TST 12:3:36
Carlock, area cem inscr, bk rev GH 33:6:77
Carroll Co, Savanna, hist, bk rev IL 11:3:180

Carrollton, hist, bk rev VAG 23:4:312
Cass Co, cem inscr, bk rev GH 33:1:83
cem inscr, 1966, bk rev TST 12:10:38 CDS 16:6:43
hist, bk rev GH 33:6:77 TST 12:32:38 KCG 20:4:211
Catlin Twp, Hickman cem inscr IG 14:3:82
census 1850, bk rev TB 6:2:18
census 1900, microfilms list IL 11:4:224
Champaign Co, early settlers biog notes IG 15:2:47
Chenoa, high school class notes GL 13:2:39
Chicago, area incorporated municipalities CHG 11:1:5
cems list NSN 4:2:13
Ger Luth churches 1865-1900, geneal res guide CHG 11:1:10
high school students 1868 NSN 4:3:26
high school students 1872 NSN 4:4:35
misc geneal sources TST 12:2:44
news abstr vr 1847, bk rev NGS 67:3:222
public school teachers 1867 NSN 4:2:15
soldiers & patriots biog notes (1892) CI 15:1:26
surname index to census 1850, bk rev KA 15:1:63
Christian Co, Bear Creek Twp, Cath cem inscr CI 15:1:30
Liberty Christian Ch, hist (1881) CI 15:2:27
Morganville, annual picnic CI 11:3:94 11:4:129
Mosquito Twp, Sycamore School CI 11:4:125
Mt Pleasant cem (Church of God) cem inscr CI 15:2:27
Pleasant Grove school recs 1892-1893 CI 13:3:113
Clark Co, Westfield, York cem inscr CI 15:2:25
Clay Co, early marrs CI 14:3:85
mort sched 1860 & 1870, bk rev GH 33:1:83

Clinton Co, East Fork Twp, hist, bk rev IL 11:2:116

Coles Co, census 1860, bk rev IL 11:4:237

Cook Co, Jefferson Vols 1861 IL 11:2:72

natural recs guide CHG 11:1:18

Jefferson Twp, Mt Olive cem inscr CHG 11:1:15

county courthouse res guide, bk rev GH 33:5:70

counties, list STC 2:1:40

origin & hist with maps, bk rev TB 6:2:18

Crawford Co, cem inscr, bk rev CI 12:4:155

census 1850 index CI 12:3:91

marr recs 1843-1844 IG 14:3:70

mort sched 1860 & 1870, bk rev GH 33:1:83

Palestine, Kitchell cem inscr CI 15:2:28

Cumberland Co, notes on res SGS 29:1:27

Wright Community cem inscr CI 14:1:9

Danville, Cline/Milner cem inscr IG 15:3:72

Hooten cem inscr IG 15:3:73

Lamb cem inscr IG 15:2:61

Darnstadt, Dial cem inscr STC 2:1:38

De Kalb Co, census 1850, bk rev TRI 17:3:46

index to plat bk 1892, bk rev IL 11:1:57

Sandwich, Somonauk United Pres Ch hist, bk rev MKT 2:2:35

De Witt Co, Barnett Twp, Elm Grove elementary school recs 1899-1911 DWC 5:4:115

cem inscr CI 15:2:11

Clinton, Meth Epis Ch scholars 1859 DWC 5:2:33

Clinton, news abstr 1863 DWC 5:1:21

Clinton, news abstr 1864-1866 DWC 5:2:52 5:3:77 5:4:105

Clintonia Twp, tax list 1861 DWC 5:2:39

natural recs DWC 5:1:1 5:2:34

misc news vr abstr DWC 5:2:35,38 5:3:63 5:4:94

Santa Anna Twp, tax list 1861 DWC 5:4:97

Wapella Twp, tax list 1861 DWC 5:3:70

Douglas Co, biog notes c1900 IG 14:2:40

Garrett Twp, Taylor cem inscr CI 15:4:143

Du Page Co, geneal sources, bk rev NGS 67:4:306

lib geneal guide, bk rev GH 33:4:111 IL 11:2:115

early recs 1737-1769 STC 2:2:52

Edwards Co, mort sched 1860 & 1870, bk rev GH 33:1:83

Effingham Co, King cem inscr CI 13:4:125

King cem inscr supp CI 14:1:27

Eggingham Co, mort sched 1860 & 1870, bk rev GH 33:1:83

Elgin, Elgin high school archives, descr IL 11:1:5

Elwin, Elwin Meth Epis Ch report 1904 CI 15:3:90

Elwood Twp, Cumberland Pres (Liberty Church) cem inscr IG 14:4:101

Evanston, unclaimed letters 1897 LL 15:4:182

Fayette Co, Avena Twp, Crum's Chapel & cem inscr CI 13:3:102

Avena Twp, St Bonaventure Ch bapt 1859-1862 & hist CI 14:4:123

Bear Grove Twp, cems inscr FF 8:1:1H

Bear Grove Twp, Elm Grove scholars 1899 THT 3:1:32

Bear Grove Twp, first land entries FF 8:2:79

Bear Grove Twp, geneal notes & hist FF 8:2:73

Bear Grove Twp, hist FF 8:2:73

estate recs FF 8:1:13 8:2:13 8:3:13 8:4:13

Kaskasia Twp, Britton cem inscr CI 15:1:29

Logue cem inscr CI 13:4:124

marr recs FF 8:1:5 8:2:5 8:3:3 8:4:3

Pope Twp, Bear Creek cem inscr CI 12:3:84

Sefton Twp, Buchanan School
recs 1899 CI 11:1:10

Wilberton Twp, Pryor cem inscr
CI 15:1:29

Ford Co, almshouse reg 1897-
1936 IL 11:3:135

Fulton Co, cem inscr v3, bk rev
CI 12:3:113

census 1850, bk rev IL
11:4:234

early marr recs CI 11:2:59

Fairview Twp, cem inscr v4, bk
rev IL 11:4:234 GH 33:6:78

Joshua Twp, cem inscr v4, bk
rev IL 11:4:234 GH 33:6:78

Norris, Norris cem inscr CI
12:1:10

geneal abstr from state laws
1836-1839 IL 11:1:19 11:3:155

geneal soc list IG 14:2:61 STC
2:1:42

geneal res guide, bk rev GH
33:5:70

Geneva, hist, bk rev GJ 8:3:171

Greene Co, Carrollton, hist, bk
rev KN 2:2:32

farm direct 1918, bk rev IL
11:2:116

hist, bk rev VAG 23:4:312 KN
2:2:31

settlers hist 1830, bk rev VAG
23:4:312 KN 2:2:31

White Hall, hist 1879, bk rev
KN 2:2:32 VAG 23:4:312

Grundy Co, census 1850, bk rev
REP 19:1:43

Hamilton Co, public school
teachers 1900, notes on IL
11:1:1

hist notes IL 11:2:81

Hardin Co, census 1850, bk rev
TRI 17:3:46

deaths 1887 TSP 2:3:27

obits abstr TSP 2:3:15

Henderson Co, vr 1879 IL
11:4:195

Higginsville cem inscr IG
14:3:80

hist landmarks in southern IL
DAR 113:4:332

hist notes BGS 6:4:1

how to research a fam with IL
roots, bk rev SCS 14:2:51

IL Vol Infantry 124th Reg,
direct of survivors 1886 BGS
8:4:29 9:1:27

imm from OH 1830-1860, bk rev
REP 19:3:133

Iroquois Co, census 1850, bk
rev IL 11:4:238

Jackson Co, Carbondale Twp, cem
inscr v2, bk rev IL 11:4:236

MaKanda Twp, cem inscr v1, bk
rev IL 11:3:180

Jasper Co, mort sched 1860 &
1870, bk rev GH 33:1:83

Jefferson Co, Rome Twp, Ebenezer cem inscr CI 11:3:83

Jersey Co, farm direct 1918, bk
rev IL 11:2:116

Jo Daviess Co, cem inscr v1,2,
bk rev IL 11:4:233 GH
33:4:111

Johnson Co, Peterman cem inscr
CI 14:1:28

Kane Co, biblio of hist &
geneal materials IL 11:4:213

Burlington Twp, cem inscr, bk
rev IL 11:3:182

census 1840 index IL 11:2:65

census 1850, bk rev GH 33:5:73
TST 12:25:48 IL 11:4:238 NGI
3:3:169

Elgin, biblio of hist & geneal
materials IL 11:4:215

Elgin, Civil War nets birth &
death dates IL 11:4:200

Kankakee Co, census 1860 TAK
9:2:11

Kankaskia, Fr hist, bk rev DM
43:1:46

Knox Co, agricultural patents
1860 KIL 7:3:83

archives inv descr KIL 7:1:7

Copley Twp, cem inscr, bk rev
IL 11:1:56

death recs index KIL 7:1:1
7:2:35 7:3:57 7:4:89

Haw Creek Twp, cem inscr, bk
rev IL 11:1:56

hist 1886, bk rev TB 6:2:18

Indian Point Twp, cem inscr,
bk rev IL 11:1:56

"Knoxville Journal" extracts
1849-1852 KIL 7:2:29 7:3:77
7:4:107

marrs females bk 1 KIL 7:1:9
7:2:41 7:3:65 7:4:95
marrs males bk 1 KIL 7:1:15
7:2:47 7:3:71 7:4:101
Ontario Twp, cem inscr, bk rev
IL 11:1:56
Orange Twp, cem inscr, bk rev
IL 11:1:56
Persifer Twp, cem inscr, bk
rev IL 11:1:56
Rio Twp, cem inscr, bk rev IL
11:1:56
stock recs KIL 7:1:21
Lahe Co, census 1850, bk rev IG
14:1:5
hist #1-3, bk rev IL 11:1:55
land atlas index 1876, bk rev
TS 21:4:173
Lawrence Co, mort sched 1860 &
1870, bk rev GH 33:1:83
Leroy, Horr school hist notes
GL 13:2:33 13:3:75
lib list CI 13:3:87
limestone houses hist, bk rev
VAG 23:4:312
Logan Co, Pleasant Valley cem
inscr CI 11:4:131
Lovington, Black Horse Tavern
hist MCH 7:1:1 7:3:61
Lovington Twp, Turner cem, surname index MCH 7:1:9
lower IL Valley, hist & geneal
sketches, bk rev KN 2:2:31
Macon Co, biblio CI 15:2:15
Decatur, bus firms 1923 CI
12:1:17
Decatur, Fairlawn cem, bk rev
CI 12:2:53
Decatur, geneal soc anc ch index CI 15:3:114
Decatur, high school classes
1867-1900, 1920 CI 12:4:125
13:1:14 13:3:112
Decatur, hist notes CI 15:1:22
Decatur, news extracts CI
14:2:67 13:4:130,146 14:1:32
14:2:67 14:3:101,106 14:4:132
15:2:23,54
Decatur, news extracts 1925-
1927 CI 15:1:25
Decatur, public school teachers 1865-1900 CI 13:1:8
estate recs 1851-1853 CI

15:1:32
estate sale 1853 CI 15:1:31
Frank Hays farm journal 1901-
1902 CI 15:1:19
George Pasfield farm goods
sale 1906 CI 12:3:106
Greenwood cem inscr, bk rev CI
12:3:90
Hickory Point Twp, Frank Hays'
farm journal 1900-1901 CI
14:4:143
misc recs 1837-1949 CI 15:2:3
15:3:100 15:4:131
pioneers CI 13:3:94,99
recs available CI 13:3:101
South Wheatland Twp, Elwin,
Meth Epis Ch membership roll
CI 11:3:100
tax list 1865-1866, bk rev GH
33:1:84 IL 11:1:58
vets graves reg, bk rev CI
13:4:153
Warrensburg, hist CI 13:3:111
Whitmore Twp, officers 1860-
1864 CI 15:2:21
Whitmore Twp, pet 1867 CI
14:4:125
Whitmore Twp, pet for railroad
cert 1868 CI 15:2:22
Whitmore Twp, town mtgs 1860's
CI 14:1:4
Whitmore Twp, voters 1869 CI
14:2:47
Madison Co, delinquent tax list
1838 IL 11:1:48
map of early trails CI 12:2:68
Maquon, hist notes KIL 7:3:63
"Maquon Breeze" residents 1898
KIL 7:2:53
Marshall Co, census 1850, bk
rev TRI 17:3:46
"Henry Times" draft roster
1917 IL 11:1:47
"Henry Times" mortuary rec
1899 IL 11:1:45
misc cem inscr IL 11:1:46
Mason Co, census 1850, bk rev
GE 49:9
McDonough Co, election list
1888 IL 11:4:210
Emmet Twp, Atkinson cem inscr
CI 15:2:26
McHenry Co, census 1850, bk rev

TB 6:4:31

McLean Co, Bellflower Twp, cem inscr v7, bk rev IL 11:1:56

Chenoa, class of 1913-1925, notes on GL 13:1:14

deaths with burials elsewhere GL 13:2:54 13:3:89 13:4:98

farm direct 1941 GL 13:1:5 13:2:47 13:3:73 13:4:107

Spanish War vets burials GL 13:1:11

Menard Co, census 1860, bk rev CI 14:1:29

Middlefork, Kickapoo Park, Cox cem inscr IG 15:2:55

Middlefork Twp, Ingersoll cem inscr IG 15:1:14

old Parllow cem inscr IG 15:1:13

militiamen 1790 CI 15:1:6

Millstadt, Trinity Luth Ch, marr recs 1848-1911 STC 2:1:27

misc fam corres IL 11:4:207

misc hist & geneal soc notes IL 11:1:52 11:2:107 11:3:165,177

misc jurors 1879 IL 11:3:175

Monroe Co, census 1850, bk rev IL 11:4:235

Montgomery Co, geneal soc surname index 1979, bk rev GH 33:5:74 IL 11:3:182

pioneer death notices CI 14:2:48

Traylor cem inscr CI 15:3:109

Morgan Co, cem inscr v1,2,3, bk rev IL 11:4:237

mort sched 1850, bk rev OK 24:2:74

mort sched 1860 v1, bk rev CSB 14:1:24

Moultrie Co, Ash Grove Twp, hist notes MCH 7:3:66,70

cem sites & map MCH 7:2:32

census 1860, bk rev TRI 19:2:32 CI 12:3:113

direct of tractor owners 1917 MCH 7:1:21

East Nelson, reg of electors & voters 1874 MCH 7:2:54

Gays, hist notes MCH 7:2:52

Gays, old settlers picnic 1912 MCH 7:2:47

Kellar cem inscr, bk rev TRI 19:2:31 CI 13:3:115

Lowe Twp, land & pers road tax 1876 MCH 7:4:101

Lowe Twp, voters 1869 MCH 7:4:115

Memorial Park cem inscr CI 15:1:28

post offices & postmasters MCH 7:2:48

Sullivan misc funeral notices MCH 7:1:12

Sullivan, misc news abstr MCH 7:1:20,22 7:3:86 7:4:107

physicians & dentists MCH 7:1:15

Sullivan, unclaimed letters 1907 MCH 7:2:56

Whitley Twp, hist notes MCH 7:2:31,34,41 7:3:65,68

Williamsburg, hist notes MCH 7:4:98

Moweaqua, hist, bk rev CI 12:4:155

Union Predestenarian Bapt Ch hist & recs CI 14:3:84 14:4:135

natives in CA 1893 CI 13:1:12

natives in MO 1860 IL 11:3:169

natives marr 1829-1854 in MO IL 11:2:79

Newell Twp, Huffman cem inscr IG 15:4:119

news in IL state hist lib 1979, bk rev TB 6:3:23

Oakwood, Shock cem inscr IG 15:2:64

Oreana, misc recs CI 14:3:102

Oquawka, old settlers assn list OC 16:4:117

pension appl 1888 IL 11:3:125

Perry Co, Swanick, Old Cem inscr CI 15:2:25

Piatt Co, direct of tractor owners 1917 MCH 7:1:21

East Frantz cem inscr CI 12:3:95

election of 1904 CI 15:3:88

Lintner School recs 1892-1910 CI 14:2:61

patrons direct 1875 CI 13:1:22

Willow Branch cem inscr CI 12:4:141

Pike Co, census 1850, bk rev IL 11:4:236 MCH 7:4:118

Pilot Twp, Trimmell cem inscr IG 15:4:116

pioneers from OH, biog notes OHR 20:4:173

pioneers hist & geneal, bk rev CI 15:4:155

Quincy, Woodland cem inscr to 1882, bk rev TB 6:4:29

RR hist, bk rev VAG 23:4:312 KN 2:2:32

regional archives depository system, descr TST 11:42:28 IL 11:1:17 GE 42:18

residents married in WV 1798 CI 14:3:84

Rev War, hist notes IL 11:2:93 IL Reg of Vols & landbounty granted HG 19:2:40

Richland Co, mort sched 1860 & 1870, bk rev GH 33:1:83

Ridgefarm, Bethel Ch cem inscr IG 14:1:6

Rock Island Co, Civil War soldiers recs IL 11:4:209 hist 1877, bk rev GFP 28:7:127

Rockford. public lib geneal sources & use IL 11:3:173

St Clair Co, Bethel Bapt Ch, hist & recs STC 2:2:73 claimants & land grants 1798 CI 11:2:70

Hecker, Evan St Marcus cem inscr CI 11:1:17

Shiloh Valley Twp, John Perschbacher cem inscr STC 2:2:68

Stookey Twp, Concordia United Ch of Christ, marr recs 1851-1900 STC 2:2:80

Stookey Twp, St George's cem inscr STC 2:2:98

Salem cem inscr IG 15:4:120

Sangamon Co, cems inscr v1-2, bk rev TB 6:2:20 census 1840 index v5, bk rev IL 11:2:116 hist of early settlers (1876), bk rev TB 6:3:25 probate recs 1827-1835, bk rev CI 12:1:9

Savanna, pioneer hist, bk rev

IL 11:2:115

Scott Co, marr lics 1839-1899, bk rev GH 33:1:84 TST 11:48:37 IL 11:1:53

Naples, Old Township cem inscr CI 12:2:58

Seminary Twp, first land entries FF 8:3:41 hist FF 8:3:31

Seminary cem inscr FF 8:3:1-L

Shawneetown, land dist recs 1814-1820, bk rev TB 6:2:15 CI 14:4:150

Shelby Co, cem inscr, bk rev CI 12:3:113 cem inscr v4, bk rev CI 11:1:27

Sanner Chapel hist, bk rev CI 12:2:53

Shelbyville news extracts CI 11:1:6   11:3:88   12:2:69 12:3:109 teachers, schools & addresses 1903-1904 CI 12:4:129

Wilborn Creek ch reg 1860-1874, 1889-1902, bk rev CI 13:4:153

Windsor hist 1880 MCH 7:3:77,82

Smithfield, autograph album 1880-1895 of Anna Caley MGR 14:1:21

soldiers biog notes 1892 CI 12:2:59 12:3:86 12:4:136 13:1:28 14:2:57 14:3:107

Springfield, news extracts CI 14:3:103 railroad telegraphers employed IL Central RR CI 12:2:65

Tazewell Co, cems, bk rev IL 11:1:56 census 1850 v2, bk rev IL 11:2:104

Delavan Twp, cem inscr, bk rev IL 11:2:114

Dillon Twp, cem inscr, bk rev IL 11:2:114

Elm Grove Twp, cem inscr, bk rev IL 11:2:114

Elm Grove Twp, Railroad Schoolhouse cem insc MH 6:2:19

Hopedale, Griesemer cem inscr

CI 15:1:28

territ papers abstr 1787-1803 IL 11:3:131

territ papers abstr 1809-1814 IL 11:4:187

transportation hist, bk rev CDS 16:1:6

Troy, First Troy Persb Ch recs 1842-1864 IL 11:3:149

Union Co, census 1820-1880 v1,2, bk rev GH 33:2:78 TST 12:3:36 IL 11:1:53

census 1850, bk rev TRI 17:3:46

Univ of IL, alumni recs IL 11:4:219

lib descr & use IL 11:2:73

misc alumni bef 1913, biog notes IL 11:1:41

Vance Twp, Bodkin cem inscr IG 14:4:114

Vermilion Co, census 1830 heads of households IG 15:2:40

Danville cem inscr (Amos Williams graveyard) IG 14:2:37

marrs 1869 IG 15:1:17

marrs 1870 IG 15:2:50

marrs 1871 IG 15:3:88

marrs 1872 IG 15:4:121

North Fork Sunday school recs 1848-1862 IG 14:3:76

personal property tax 1834 IG 15:3:77 15:4:106

Ross Twp, Bethel (United Brethren/Wiseman) cem inscr IG 14:2:51

vital recs legislation IL 11:2:102

Wabash Co, mort sched 1860 & 1870, bk rev GH 33:1:83

Wabash Railroad workers reunion 1923 CI 14:2:70

War of 1812, bounty lands recs, bk rev CSB 14:1:24 ACL 4:3:55 SCS 15:3:88

vets meeting 1869 with biog notes DWC 5:4:95

Warren Co, Roseville, misc cem inscr KIL 7:3:83

Wayne Co, Garden Hill Twp, Powers cem inscr CI 11:4:136

mort sched 1860 & 1870, bk rev

GH 33:1:83

wedding annivs over 50 years MCH 7:1:17 7:3:72

Wenona, Meth Epis Ch, bapt rec bk 2 GL 13:2:52 13:3:83 13:4:94

Meth Epis Ch, marrs rec bk 2 GL 13:1:22 13:2:51 13:3:83 13:4:94

Whiteside Co, census 1850, bk rev IL 11:4:237

Williamson Co, census 1860, bk rev IL 11:3:179

Winnebago Co, census 1840 index v5, bk rev IL 11:2:116

voters list 1836 CI 11:1:30

Woodford Co, census 1850, bk rev IL 11:4:239

Montgomery Twp, Stambaugh cem MH 6:2:20

INDEX, British index of geneal interests by surnames, bk rev NSN 4:5:43

Col Kinsmen from Plymouth Rocke to York Towne, bk rev NYR 110:3:186

geneal period v1-3 1932, 1948, 1953 (Jacobus), bk rev TB 6:4:30 GJ 8:3:173 SCR 3:2:1 OG 5:3:88 CTN 11:2:339

geneal period 1975 v14 (Towle), bk rev BB 11:2:18

geneal period 1976 v15 (Towle), bk rev TST 11:42:30 IL 11:1:54 VAG 23:1:67 NYR 110:2:121 YP 9:2:105 DM 42:4:183 TSP 2:3:37 NGS 67:1:74 AG 55:2:126

geneal period 1977 v16 (Mayhew), bk rev DE 3:4:27 TRI 19:4:69 SGS 29:3:246

geneal period literature 1960-1977, bk rev GJ 8:4:220

index to GER 1-16 GER 17A,B

NY recs collect to DAR lib, index 1972-1978, bk rev CDS 16:1:22

news indexes v2, bk rev TB 6:2:15

news indexes guide GJ 8:4:185

place names in 1850 census, bk rev WCK 12:3:48

survey of Am geneal period in-

dexes, bk rev GJ 8:1:51 NYR
110:2:120 WCK 12:1:17 DM
42:4:183 CTN 12:1:178 NGS
67:1:69 RRS 12:X:2 SCS
16:1:23 CDS 16:1:22 GH
33:1:81 VAG 23:1:67 AG
55:2:122

queries in TST 1978, bk rev TST
12:33:39

Rev War pension appl at
Archives, bk rev OG 3:2:58

topical index of geneal period
at St Louis MO geneal soc
1976, bk rev IL 11:1:55

INDIA, guide to British biog
sources, bk rev GH 33:6:76

INDIANA, Adams Co, hist 1918 bk
rev REP 19:1:40

Allen Co, early Irish settlers
ACL 4:4:70

Fort Wayne, geneal guide to
public lib CTN 7:4:522

Fort Wayne, geneal guide to
public lib, bk rev ACL 4:3:55

hist ACL 4:1:3

imms from KY 1850 ACL 4:3:47

Madison Twp, cem inscr, bk rev
ACL 4:4:75

maps ACL 4:1:19

Marion Twp, Herr cem inscr ACL
4:4:80

Monroe Twp, cem inscr, bk rev
ACL 4:4:75

Monroe Twp, map 1880 ACL
4:4:89

Monroe Twp, Monroeville, Masonic cem inscr ACL 4:3:60

Monroe Twp, Schlemmer cem inscr ACL 4:4:78

Pleasant Twp, Lindlag cem inscr ACL 4:4:79

St Joseph Twp, Pierr Settlement, map ACL 4:2:39

St Joseph Twp Pierr Settlement, St Michael's Ch cem/Ac-
adamie-Pierre cem inscr &
hist ACL 4:2:23,30

Washington Twp, Waters fam cem
inscr ACL 4:1:10

archives guide descr TST
11:41:29

Bartholomew Co, marr lic, orig
unclaimed HG 19:1:10

misc biogs HJA 6:4:22

probate rec 1 1823-1829 HJA
6:4:20

Boone Co, marr rec 1831-1844 HG
19:1:17

Brown Co, hist HJA 6:1:25 6:2:8

land recs HJA 6:1:13 6:2:7

wills bk A 1845-1875 HJA
6:1:25

census index 1840, bk rev TRI
17:3:46

Civil War, 6th Reg roster HJA
6:3:40

38th IN Vol Infantry 1861-1865
HJA 6:1:34 6:2:58

Clark Co, Clark grant hist HJA
6:1:3 6:2:3 6:3:4 6:4:3

estray recs 1811-1817 HJA
6:1:8

marrs 1824- HJA 6:1:9

St Clair fam cem inscr, annotated HG 19:2:31

Clay Co, Washington Twp, Nathan
Davis Walker fam cem inscr
NGS 67:2:97

Washington Twp, Richard Walker
fam cem inscr NGS 67:2:129

county courthouse res guide, bk
rev GH 33:5:70

county geneal sources HJA
6:2:43 6:3:45

county maps 1876, bk rev OG
5:4:116

Davis Co, hist 1886, bk rev TB
6:2:18

Dearborn Co, hist HJA 6:1:26

Manchester Twp, old cem inscr
HJA 6:2:38

Miller Twp cem inscr HJA
6:2:38

misc fam cem inscr HJA 6:2:38
6:3:44

natural recs HG 19:1:13

deaths from cholera 1849 HG
19:2:26

Decatur Co, marr bk D 1837-1840
HJA 6:2:33

mort sched 1850 HJA 6:2:32
6:3:13

probate rec A 1826-1848 HJA
6:4:45

will bk A 1822-1837 HJA 6:2:35
6:3:35 6:4:44

Delaware Co, archives, descr GE
43:15

Dubois Co, marr lic 1873-1895,
bk rev TSP 3:1:14

Elkhart Co, Benton Twp, Hire
cem inscr MIS 11:1:16

Clinton Twp, Pleasant Hill
School 1913 MIS 11:4:51

Jackson Twp, Whitehead School
1881 MIS 11:4:66

Locke Twp, Berlin School 1905
MIS 11:4:51

millers 1831-1837 MIS 11:4:53

Olive Twp, births 1874-1879
MIS 11:1:7

Olive Twp, Civil War enlistees
MIS 11:1:11

Olive Twp, deaths 1874-1879
MIS 11:1:8

Falls City, plan TST 12:20:47

Fayette Co, deaths HG 19:1:11

Floyd Co, hist HJA 6:3:38

marrs bk A 1819-1837 HJA
6:1:29 6:2:16 6:4:14

wills bk A 1819-1829 HJA
6:2:11 6:3:37

Fountain Co, Ferry book abstr
1830 IG 14:2:39

misc court recs 1826-1851, bk
rev GE 43:12

Van Buren Twp, Trinkle-Osborn
cem inscr IG 15:1:15

geneal res guide, bk rev GH
33:5:70

geneal sources from IN magazine
of hist, bk rev TS 21:4:173

Gibson Co, hist 1897, bk rev
TSP 3:1:39

Owensville, news abstr 1872-
1915 (1916), bk rev TST
11:42:30 GH 33:1:84 IL
11:1:54

Rev War soldiers burials, biog
notes TSP 2:3:8

Grant Co, hist notes GCB 79:1:2
79:2:13 79:3:22 79:4:31

marr recs bk C GCB 79:2:16
79:3:25 79:4:32

wills bk A GCB 79:2:17 79:3:26
79:4:33

Greene Co, deed bk A HJA 6:2:30
6:3:34 6:4:24

hist HJA 6:4:23

marr bk C 1833-1841 HJA 6:4:28

misc cem inscr HJA 6:4:39

will rec 1 HJA 6:4:25

probate bk A HJA 6:2:27 6:3:35

Walnut Grove, Walnut Grove Ch
hist HJA 6:3:33

Walnut Grove, Moode cem inscr
HJA 6:3:33

Highland Twp, McIntosh cem inscr HJA 6:3:34

guide to geneal recs, bk rev
ACL 4:2:25

Harmony, hist of Harmony Soc IN
1814-1820 v1, bk rev WPA
5:1:37

hist of Harmony Soc IN 1820-
1824 v2, bk rev BR 6:3:96 WPA
5:1:37

Harrison Co, wills bk A 1809-
1832 HJA 6:1:15 6:2:39

Henry Co, atlas & hist 1893, bk
rev GH 33:6:78

hist notes HJA 6:1:7 6:2:22

hist to 1816, bk rev ACL 4:2:25

Hist Soc Lib geneal sources
descr GE 47:1 48:1

Hopewell, misc cems inscr IG
14:4:106

Jasper Co, Gillam Twp, pioneer
chs & cems, bk rev GE 49:9

Jay Co, hist 1822, bk rev GH
33:6:79

Jefferson Co, Pisqah cem inscr
& index HJA 6:1:37 6:2:22

Shelby Twp, census 1860 HJA
6:1:31 6:2:19 6:3:7

Jeffersonville, land office
cert 1808-1812 KA 15:1:3
15:2:67

Jennings Co, misc early settlements BGS 8:3:6

Sandcreek Twp, truant officers
rec 1905 HG 19:1:4

Johnson Co, bus direct 1876 HJA
6:1:10

Deer fam cem inscr HJA 6:3:43

entry bk A 1823-1827 HJA
6:1:22

deed bk A 1824-1829 HJA 6:1:22

hist HJA 6:1:23

probate bk AA 1831-1945 HJA
6:1:20

Knox Co, atlas 1880-1903, bk

rev GH 33:1:84

early land recs & court indexes 1783-1815, bk rev CDS
16:3:5

Kosciusko Co, cem list MIS
11:4:59

Jefferson Twp, cem inscr v7,
bk rev GH 33:4:111

Plain Twp, cem inscr v7, bk
rev GH 33:4:111

Prairie Twp, cem inscr v7, bk
rev GH 33:4:111

Scott Twp, cem inscr v7, bk
rev GH 33:4:111

Laporte Co, Springfield Twp,
Shippeeburg cem inscr MI
24:4:137

Posey Chapel cem inscr PF
8:4:86

Lawrence Co, Bono Twp, atlas
entries 1876 HJA 6:3:28

Marion Twp, atlas intries 1876
HJA 6:3:28

natural recs HJA 6:3:29

Madison Co, vr descr GE 48:6

misc geneal recs, bk rev IL
11:4:239

misc news obits HG 19:4:79

Mishawaka, First United Meth
Ch, hist, bk rev GE 49:8

Monroe Co, census 1820, 1830,
1840 & 1850, bk rev GH
33:6:79

Ellettsville, fam cem inscr CI
12:4:140

Montgomery Co, natural appl
1850-1930, bk rev TSP 3:1:39

orig entry bk, bk rev TSP
3:1:39

natives in OH 1860 HJA 6:3:40
6:4:13

news extracts 1807 HG 19:1:1
19:2:36 19:3:56

New Carlisle, Maple Grove cem
inscr PF 8:3:66

Ohio Co, marr bk 1 1844-1881
HJA 6:3:15

probate bk 1 1844-1852 HJA
6:3:17

will rec 1 1843-1854 HJA
6:3:11

Ohio Valley, hist biblio, bk
rev CTN 10:2:346

Orange Co, marrs 1823-1825 HJA
6:1:35

Stamper Creek Twp, census 1860
HJA 6:4:7

will bk 1 1816-1852 HJA 6:3:39

Perry Co, hist 1916, bk rev WCK
12:3:47

Pike Co, natural recs HG
19:4:90

Posey Co, cem inscr 1814-1979,
bk rev GE 47:14

Pulaski Co, marrs 1839-1853 HG
19:4:95

Putnam Co, Warren, Bethel Meth
Ch cem inscr KN 2:1:16

Ripley Co, index to probate entries to 1850 HG 19:3:73

probate entries to 1850 HG
19:3:68

roster of geneal societies GE
43:13

Rush Co, mort sched 1850 HJA
6:1:39

mort sched 1850, index HJA
6:2:26

mort sched 1850, notes on HJA
6:1:39 6:2:24

Scott Co, maps 1889 HJA 6:1:42
6:2:10 6:3:18 6:4:10

land grants HJA 6:1:12

Shelby Co, Norristown, Norristown Union Ch building sub-
scribers HG 19:3:54

source bk v1, bk rev TRI
17:3:46

Spencer Co, Eureka, Baker Creek
cem inscr TSP 3:2:23

marrs 1855-1863 bk 4, bk rev
IL 11:4:237

state fair awards 1854-5 MCR
10:4:112

surname list TSP 2:4:5

Switzerland Co, land recs HJA
6:3:23

probate bk 1 1814-1824 HJA
6:3:21 6:4:32

marr recs 1818-1824 HJA 6:4:33

Lostutter cem inscr HJA 6:4:38

will bk 1 1823-1847 HJA 6:3:20

Tippecanoe Co, hist & atlas
1878, bk rev GH 33:2:78

Tipton Co, atlas 1874, 1928,
1975 & hist, bk rev GH

33:6:80

Union Co, atlas 1884, bk rev GH
33:6:80

Vanderburgh Co, ch recs vl, bk
rev GH 33:5:74 TST 12:20:48

Evansville, First Ger Meth Ch
(Fourth St M E ch) recs 1865-
1888 TSP 3:2:5

Knight Twp, Angel cem inscr
TSP 3:1:15

natural recs, court order bk F
TSP 2:4:11

natural recs, court order bk H
1850-1854 TSP 3:2:28

New Salem (campground) cem
inscr TSP 3:1:16

Oak Ridge cem inscr TSP 2:3:28

St Peters United Ch of Christ
cem inscr TSP 2:3:36

Saundersville, hist, bk rev
TST 12:15:31

Vermillion Co, Eugene Twp,
Brown fam cem inscr IG
14:1:15

Highland Twp, Harrison cem
inscr IG 15:1:16

Highland Twp, Hughes cem inscr
IG 14:3:84

Vigo Co, index to fam hists in
public lib IG 14:1:11

Wabash Co, epitaphs, bk rev GE
49:9

Warrick Co, Newburgh, Newburgh
Pres Cha recs 1840-1842 TSP
3:2:21

Ohio Twp, census 1850 TSP
3:2:26

St John the Evangelist Cath
cem inscr TSP 2:3:30

Washington Co, Gibson Twp,
Mount cem inscr HJA 6:1:19
6:2:24

Wayne Co, atlas 1893, bk rev GH
33:6:80

land recs HJA 6:3:25 6:4:41

misc recs TST 12:35:36

natural recs 1833-1840 HG
19:2:33

probate bk A 1818-1830 HJA
6:3:32 6:4:31

will bk 1 1812-1823 HJA 6:3:30
6:4:30

Wells Co, hist 1918, bk rev REP

19:1:40

West Lebanon, hist notes IG
14:2:43

Whitley Co, marrs 1830-1850 HG
19:3:60

INGALLS, fam of Eng, notes on AG
55:2:109

Robert A bc1555 w Elizabeth,
Eng, fam rec AG 55:2:110

INGHAM, F E f1888 w Dona Watson,
TN, TX, biog THT 4:1:28

John f1710, Eng, NJ, geneal, bk
rev CI 14:1:30

Joseph f1639 w Sarah Bushnell,
Eng, CT, geneal, bk rev BGS
8:1:26 OG 4:4:117

INGRAHAM, Hannah b1772, Can,
loyalist, biog, bk rev GN
2:6:172

INGRAM, George Washington b1901
w Gladys Lenore Hatchett, TX,
anc ch KG 16:1:17

Job, IL, scrapbook 1880-1882 GL
13:3:63 13:4:103

IOWA, Adair Co, Grove Twp, Grove
Center cem inscr HH 14:3:140

Washington Twp, Campbell cem
inscr HH 14:3:139

Bible recs in museums & libs
v2, bk rev CTN 11:1:45

Bible recs in museums & libs
v3, bk rev IG 15:3:71 GH
33:3:99 HH 14:3:162 CTN
12:2:363 TS 21:2:74

biog index to county hist vl,
bk rev GH 33:6:80

Collins, hist, bk rev HH
14:2:103

Decatur Co, Richland Twp, Young
cem inscr HH 14:3:142

Eden Twp, Mt Tabor cem inscr
HH 14:3:148

emigs to NE HH 14:3:134

Fremont Co, census 1870, bk rev
TB 6:2:17

geneal res guide TST 12:15:30

geneal res guide, bk rev GH
33:5:70

Hamilton Co, Stanhope, hist, bk
rev HH 14:3:162

Randall, hist, bk rev HH
14:3:162

hist atlas 1875, bk rev TB

6:4:27

hist soc publ, bk rev NGI 3:1:33

Linn Co, East Marion Twp, Martins Creek cem inscr HH 14:4:216

hist vl-2, bk rev IL 11:2:80

misc biog notes, bk rev CDS 16:4:10

Monroe Co, Mantua Twp, Smith cem HH 14:4:212

payroll 1861 Co F, 2nd IA Cavalry at CO BGS 4:4:32

pioneer biogs HH 14:1:45 14:2:92 14:3:153

Plymouth Co, Lincoln Twp cem inscr LL 14:4:190

Sioux, Little Sioux Twp, hist, bk rev GH 33:3:99 KCG 20:1:46

soldiers in NE 1884 NW 2:3:82 2:4:112

Story City, hist 1855-1976, bk rev HH 14:3:161

Wayne Co, abandoned towns HH 14:1:10

biblio of published sources HH 14:1:12

cemeteries list HH 14:1:11

death recs 1880-1897 HH 14:3:123 14:4:206

emigs westward HH 14:1:13

hist HH 14:1:5

Howard Twp, Thomas-Shane cem inscr HH 14:1:36

Jackson Twp, Ripper cem inscr HH 14:1:35

marrs 1851-1865 HH 14:1:19

old settlers assn list HH 14:1:40 14:2:61

South Fork Twp, Jones cem inscr HH 14:1:28

Union Twp, McDaniel cem inscr HH 14:1:34

Union Twp, Ryan cem inscr HH 14:1:35

Walnut Twp, Hickerson-Stacker cem inscr HH 14:1:33

Washington Twp, Woods cem inscr HH 14:1:37

Wright Twp, Adcock cem inscr HH 14:1:33

Wright Twp, Brown fam cem inscr HH 14:1:33

Wright Twp, Jones cem inscr HH 14:1:34

Winnebago Co, Forest City, Scandinavian Meth Epis Ch, bapt recs HH 14:4:185

hist HH 14:4:172

marrs 1865-1880 HH 14:4:178

persons liable to do mil duty 1876-1892 HH 14:4:189

Woodbury Co, Grange Twp, cem inscr HH 14:2:71

Grant Twp, Peiro Bethel cem inscr HH 14:2:74

Lakeport Twp, Walnut Grove cem inscr HH 14:2:79

Liberty Twp, cem inscr HH 14:2:71

Oto Twp, Wellington cem inscr HH 14:2:79

Rock Twp, Rock cem inscr HH 14:2:78

Wolf Creek Twp, cem inscr HH 14:2:80

IREDELL, James b1751 w Hannah Johnson, Eng, NC, biog DAR 113:9:994

IRELAND, abstr of misc Neale & O'Neill wills, admin & marr bonds IR 11:1:27

army deserters 1840-1860 at New Zealand IA 11:1:4

basic geneal res guide, bk rev GJ 8:1:53 GH 33:1:81

Co Cork, Kilmeen, Castleventry Parish, hist, bk rev IR 11:1:71

Co Down, cem inscr vl-16, bk rev NGS 67:1:65

cem inscr v17, bk rev GH 33:2:73

Newry, First Pres Ch rec 1779-1796 IR 11:1:45

Newry, First Pres Ch rec 1809-1822 IR 11:2:121

Co Meath, Dunboyne Ch of Ireland, mem tablets & cem inscr IR 11:1:54 11:2:137

Co Westmeath, house furnishings 1742 IR 11:2:86

cultural heritage guide for Am, bk rev GH 33:2:73 KCG 20:2:91

Dublin, medieval hist 840-1540, bk rev IR 11:2:153

Reg of Deeds biblio NSN 4:3:23

emig misc articles on Irish in Am 1906-1930, bk rev TST 12:18:38

geneal res, biblio ACL 4:4:75

guide EWA 16:2:65 16:3:101 16:4:133 IRA 13:236,241 SCS 15:1:7 BCG 6:1:3

heraldry IRA 13:256

index to Irish fams, bk rev GH 33:3:97

Irish heritage, series of maps & histories, bk rev IR 11:1:72 11:2:154

Irish settlers in Am vl-2, bk rev NGS 67:3:224

James Peter b1897 w Nancy May Isabell Swetland, IL, anc ch FF 8:3:61

Jonathan b1829 w Catherine Lee, IN, IA, Bible rec HH 14:2:85

list of current articles of geneal interest IR 11:1:75

manual for Irish geneal, bk rev CTN 12:4:701

misc maps, bk rev ACL 4:4:75

Munster Province, ch maps, bk rev IR 11:1:70

county maps, bk rev IRA 13:279

natives in MI census 1860 DM 42:4:175

news in microform BCG 5:4:32

Offaly, sources for hist, bk rev IR 11:2:153

parliamentary papers printed recs 1613-1800, bk rev IR 11:1:73

primer for Irish geneal res, bk rev OG 4:4:117

printed court reports guide NSN 4:6:52

surnames guide GJ 8:1:9

Ulster, fam res, bk rev AH 6:1:27

geneal & hist soc publ, bk rev VAG 23:1:72

linen drapers 1750-1764 IA 11:1:9

Scotch-Irish pioneers (1910), bk rev ACL 4:4:75

ISRAEL, geneal res guide JJG 3:4:11

ITALY, geneal res guide NGI

3:3:157 CTN 11:2:204 GH 33:6:9

emig to Am, geneal res guide, bk rev ITG 2:55

fam res guide, bk rev ITG 2:55

geneal study of Royal House of Savoy ITG 2:50

Genoa, geneal res guide ITG 2:34

guide to geneal recs, bk rev ITG 2:55

surnames ITG 2:31

IVEY, Robert Mecklenburg William b1799 w , Lecy Lynn William, NC, TN, Bible rec HTR 22:4:130

IVY, David Lawrence b1900 w Cecile Bernadette Pecot, LA, TX, anc ch GR 21:1:7

JACK, Mary P h Mathew Jack, IL letter 1863 BGS 3:4:11

JACKSON, Billy Bob b1902 w Petra Ila Hartsell, MS, TX, anc ch OC 16:2:64

Charles b1791 w Sarah Drake, VA, Bible rec RRS 12:2:224

Clarence Earl b1900 w Pearl M Neely, GA, anc ch NAS 18:2:35

John f1848 w Mary Amery, Eng, TX, biog (1908), bk rev CI 11:4:158

Mark b1827 w Melvina Jane Swagarty, Tracy Jane Durham, TN, AK, fam rec OK 24:2:70

Peter, TX headright cert 1838 VL 14:1:18

JACOBY, John b1822 w Serena Ray, fam rec MIS 11:4:65

JAMES, Godfrey Hunter b1897 w Margaret Elizabeth Moseley, KY, anc ch RRS 12:1:85

William Strauder b1889 w Sarah Nancy Elizabeth Rogers, AL, anc ch NAS 18:1:4

JAMESON, James P b1840 w Mary E Henlan, PA, CO, Bible rec 8:1:10

John f1800 w Ann, Ir, PA, geneal, bk rev REP 19:4:169

Samuel d1816 w Margaret Harper, Ir, VA, geneal, bk rev REP

19:4:167

JANSON, George m1688 w Mary Edwards, Eng, VA, notes on NGS 67:4:290

JAPAN, cultural hist, bk rev CDS 16:2:5

geneal res guide GJ 8:1:43

bk rev GH 33:5:69

JAQUA, Richard bc1787 w Elizabeth Wilsee, NY, Can, OH, anc ch REP 19:2:87

JARAMILLD, Alfego bc1820 w Maria Antonia Sanchez, NM, fam rec NMG 18:2:53

JARVAS, fam of VA, notes on AW 5:1:7

Henry Clay m1869 w Minnie F Halderman, IA, Bible rec BGS 4:3:10

JASINSKY, John Frederick b1790 w Mary Magdalena Rudy, OH, ledger & fam rec REP 19:4:146

JENCKES, Joseph b1603 w Mary Tervyn, Eng, MA, biog notes BGS 6:1:8

JENKINS, Joel bc1614, MA, geneal, bk rev CTN 11:1:46

Kennark Ellis b1882 w Mary Sharlott Hammack, AR, OK, anc ch NAS 18:2:34

Obadiah b1650 w Mrs Mary (Jones) Lewis, MA, geneal LL 14:1:30

JENSEN, Alfred Holger b1887 w Muriel Grace Williams, Denmark, MT, anc ch THT 7:1:27

JETTE, Philoctede b1859 w Zoe Felicie LesPerance, anc ch AGE 8:2:59

JEWISH GENEALOGY, fam historians handbook, bk rev SCS 15:4:117

first Am Jewish fams geneals 1654-1977, bk rev NER 133:4:313 NYR 110:2:121 NGS 67:2:155

guidebook, bk rev OG 4:4:117 NGI 3:2:109 SCS 15:3:87

how to trace your Jewish geneal, bk rev ACL 3:4:24

Leo Baech Institute Lib NY, guide TST 12:7:45

misc fams from Poland geneal, bk rev NGI 3:2:107

practical guide to geneal, bk rev JJG 3:1:4

res guide JTG 3:4:11

sources for res SCS 16:2:63

yizkor books/memorial books, biblio JJG 3:2:7 3:4:24

geneal source JJG 3:2:3

JIRASEK, John Adolph b1882 w Rosa Hosek, TX, anc ch GR 21:2:50

JOHNS, James McClellan b1834 w Elizabeth Ann Darby, Mrs Margaret Biggs, OH, OR, biog notes ORB 17:9:84

Mortimer b1850, IN, biog notes GE 48:5

JOHNSON, Bible rec PR 3:3:50,51 FP 22:1:10

Caleb b1798 w Sarah Keller Ensminger, NJ, OH, IL, diary 1824 STC 2:2:49

Ellison Carl b1831 w Nancy Jane Gilliam, TN, OR, biog notes ORB 18:2:27

fam of Isle of Wight Co VA, geneal vl, bk rev NCJ 5:4:258

fam of MO, geneal, bk rev GH 33:6:87

fam of VA, geneal, bk rev GFP 29:1:5

Harriet (Smith) b1807 h Abraham Johnson, NY, Can, photo & biog notes FAM 18:2:86

James Harris, letters 1871 BGS 3:1:3

John b1742, Can, loyalist, biog, nk rev GN 2:6:172

Joseph B bc1787 w Sarah Kent, PA, anc ch REP 19:4:158

Joseph Eggleston b1873 w Beulah Beatrice Cardinell, TX, NE, anc ch GR 21:1:8

Matthew b1825, TN, biog notes NCJ 5:2:96

Peter J b1833 w Mary S, Sweden, CO, biog notes BGS 5:2:10

Robert b1616, VA, geneal, bk rev GE 47:11 VAG 23:4:307 CTN 9:1:124

Samuel, ME, 1843 letter DE 2:5:4

Sarah Ann Olds, letters 1857-1887, bk rev BGS 5:2:20

Stephen d1786 w Elizabeth Diodate, Mrs Mary Gardiner Blaque, Abigail Leverett, NJ, CT, biog notes CTB 44:1:17

Stewart b1776, DE, RI, geneal, bk rev GE 42:10 GJ 8:2:116 CTN 11:1:41

William Martin b1840 w Mary Elizabeth Bowhay, MO, KS, geneal KK 17:1:26

Zachariah bc1751, MO, KY, geneal, bk rev KY 21:3:115

JOHNSTON, Albert Newcomb b1869 w Kate McGregor Martin, WI, MI, anc ch BGS 9:3:47

Archibald b1775 w Betsy Booth, Bible rec CI 15:1:4

fam of Scotland & VA, geneal, bk rev CTN 10:4:700

J Elmer, letter 1899 BGS 5:1:18

John W b1861 w Delpha Rebecca Hunt, IL, KS, anc ch BGS 10:4:41

JOINER, Asa, GA, geneal, bk rev GGM 71:10

JONAS, Guy Norman b1911 w Jessie C Snow, TX, anc ch NAS 17:4:97

JONES, Allen b1864 w Nellie Babcock, Jessie Hopkins, Emily Black, IL, obit CI 15:2:26

Amos d1827 w Ann, MD, fam recs MD 20:1:89

Andrew b1764 w Margaret Wolfe, OH, anc ch REP 19:3:119

Clarence J Sr b1892 w Palmyra Pontif, LA, fam recs AGE 8:1:22

fam geneal, bk rev OC 16:1:33

fam of GA, geneal, bk rev CTN 10:4:705

Harold Lewis b1879 w Edith C Todd, SD, WI, anc ch BGS 9:3:48,49

Hendley, VA, GA, geneal, bk rev GGM 71:6

James f1807 w Jane Slaughter, VA, biog VAG 23:4:287

Martin William b1785 w Rhoda, NC, TN, TX, geneal BGS 9:2:19

Merton Edward, geneal, bk rev CTN 9:4:604

Richard b1835 w Alce Ann Ellma-

ker, Nancy Elizabeth Gaskiee, TN, WA, OR, biog notes ORB 17:7:64

Richard f1853, lwtter OR to TN ORB 18:1:7

Robert Franklin b1855 w Leana Cordelia Sims, Bible rec TB 6:4:14

Russell Richard b1912 w Ruth Florence Booser, AR, PA, CA, anc ch BGS 11:3:131

Samuel Jacksoan b1892 w Verdie Crawford, TX, OR, anc ch ORB 17:6:57

Thomas R b1835 w _ , Martha Brame, Martha Simpson, TN, KY, biog VQ 16:3:46

W B, CA, letter 1880 BGS 3:4:4

William Buchanan b1797 w Margaret W Hess, VA, KY, TX, anc ch THT 7:2:74

VA, TN, AL, Bible rec THT 4:3:15

William Wesley b1830 w Catharine Kinney, OH, anc ch REP 19:1:36

JORDAN, Cyrus Victor b1880 w Helen May Head, NY, anc ch THT 7:1:15

JOSEPH, Pascal Irving, NY, name change 1914 JJG 3:1:17

JOSSELIN, Ralph, Eng diary 1616-1683, bk rev NGS 67:4:310

JUDD, Amos b1804 w Lucy Cartwright, NC, MO, KY, TX, anc ch GR 21:4:137

Lovina Gertrude b1850 h William Jay Barber, MO, biog notes BCG 7:3:78

William Wesley b1813 w Rebecca L Sargent, OH, OR, biog notes ORB 17:8:72

JUDY, John b1813 w Mary C Allen, OH, anc ch REP 19:2:86,87

JUENEMANN, Adam b1864 w Elizabeth Baune, WI, obit MGR 14:2:92

Frank b1867 w Bernadine Baune, IA, obit MGR 14:2:93

JUNEAU, fam of Fr & Can, geneal, bk rev TB 6:3:20

JUNKIN, Joseph m1743 w Elizabeth Wallace, PA, geneal, bk rev

CI 12:2:53

KALBFLEISCH, Ludwig b1799 w Anna Maria, Ger, biog notes FAM 18:1:23

KALBFUS, Charles b1804 w Mary Ann Bowman, MD, PA, OH, anc ch REP 19:2:87

KAMENS, Daniel William b1912 w Gertrude Louise Morgan, WI, anc ch NGI 3:2:112

KANE, Michael b1876 w Minnie Bell, NJ, OH, Bible rec CI 14:2:52

KANSAS, Allen Co, misc small cems inscr KCG 20:3:120

Anderson Co, small unnamed cems inscr TOP 9:1:3

Bourbon Co, misc marrs 1871-1872 TOP 9:4:118

Brown Co, Willis, Kimberlin cem inscr MGR 14"2"63

Butler Co, Whitewater, Emmaus Menn cem inscr MGR 14:1:32 14:2:83 14:3:108

cem sites in 1906 by county TOP 9:1:6

Chanute, high school class rolls 1909 MGR 14:2:65

Village Creek, Reeves cem recs TB 6:1:17

Clay Co, hist biogs, bk rev TB 6:2:20

map & direct 1884 KK 17:4:81

Clyde, Cedar Hill cem inscr MGR 14:4:153

New Hope cem inscr LL 15:3:146

Davis Co, census 1857 KK 17:2:34

Denison, news abstr 1895-1896 TOP 9:4:99

Doniphan Co, Bendina, St Benedict's Ch, misc recs TOP 9:4:116

Douglas Co, Baldwin, autograph bk 1884-1888 WB 10:1:31

Stull, Stull cem inscs TOP 9:3:78 9:4:103

Elk Co, Longton, Busby cem inscr OC 16:3:105

Finney Co, Garden City, First Bapt Ch hist & charter mem-

bers 1887 TS 21:3:90

Ford Co, Concord Twp, West Hopewell, hist, bk rev TS 21:2:74

Geary Co, hist biogs, bk rev TB 6:2:20

geneal res guide, bk rev GH 33:5:70

Gray Co, Cimarron, school graduates 1899-1910 TS 21:3:85

marrs bk A 1887-1915 TS 21:4:135

Hodgeman Co, Bellefont, St Mary's Ch, hist notes TS 21:3:119

Jetmore, United Pres Ch recs TS 21:4:159

St Michael's Luth Ch marr reg 1900-1919 TS 21:1:11

Hutchinson, Reno Co common schools graduating class 1916 MGR 14:3:130

imms from OH 1873 AH 3:2:44 3:3:74

Jackson Co, Adrian cem inscr KCG 20:1:34

Little Cross Creek cem inscr KCG 20:4:185

Jefferson Co, abandoned cem inscr TOP 9:1:5

delinquent tax list 1873 TOP 9:3:70

marrs 1861-1867 TOP 9:1:23 9:2:54 9:3:66

Old Grantville cem inscr TOP 9:1:4

Johnson Co, Aubrey, census 1865 index JCG 7:3:69

Aubrey Twp, census 1865 index JCG 7:3:69

Gardner City, census 1865 index JCG 7:3:71

Gardner Twp, census 1865 index JCG 7:3:71

marr recs 1869 JCG 7:1:26

marr recs 1870 JCG 7:2:49 7:4:106

marr recs 1871 JCG 7:4:111

McCamish Twp, census 1870 index JCG 7:2:44

Olathe, census 1865 index JCG 7:4:119

Olathe Twp, census 1865 index

JCG 7:4:121

Oxford Dist, census 1865 index JCG 7:3:65

Oxford Twp, census 1870 index JCG 7:1:10

Shawnee Twp, Lenexa cem inscr JCG 7:4:126

Shawnee Twp, St John's cem inscr JCG 7:3:74

Labette Co, Iuka cem Civil War burials TS 21:4:134

marr recs 1867-1881 news abstr, bk rev GH 33:2:79

LaCrosse, hist & biog, bk rev TS 21:1:27

Lyon Co, Hartford cem inscr & news death notices, bk rev GH 33:2:78

Manhattan, hist notes 1878 KK 17:4:82

hist notes 1903 KK 17:4:83

Marshall Co, census 1857 KK 17:2:37

hist biogs, bk rev TB 6:2:20

McPherson Co, Conway, Monitor Ch of the Brethren cem inscr MGR 14:1:45

McPherson, McPherson Co 8th grade graduating class 1936 MGR 14:3:136

Neosho Co, cem inscr, bk rev GH 33:2:79

Erie Twp, records MGR 14:2:80

Offerle, Zion Luth Ch 1878-1978 hist, bk rev TS 21:2:74

Osage Co, marrs bk IA 1867 TOP 9:4:93

Phillips Co, burials of Civil War vets TOP 9:4:100

Pottawatomie Co, hist biogs, bk rev TB 6:2:20

census 1857 KK 17:2:36

Pratt Co, death recs 1888-1899 TS 21:3:93

Reedsville Village, hist, bk rev KK 17:3:70

Riley Co, Bellegarde cem (incl Deal-Wilder fam cem) inscr KK 17:3:64

cems map corr KK 17:1:3

College Hill School 1904 commencement KK 17:1:10

direct 1911 KK 17:1:11

geneal pay fund ordinance 1890 KK 17:1:10

hist biogs, bk rev TB 6:2:20

map & direct 1884 KK 17:2:30

Peach Grove, cem inscr KK 17:2:32

Peach Grove, Evan United Brethren Ch hist KK 17:2:33

Pleasant Hill cem inscr KK 17:1:9

Rooks Co, misc small cems inscr TS 21:2:66 21:3:109,110

Palco, Palco cem inscr TS 21:3:112

Plainville cem inscr TS 21:3:113

Slate cem inscr TS 21:3:107

Spring Branch cem inscr TS 21:2;64

Survey cem inscr TS 21:2:59

Rush Co, Bison, Lone Star cem inscr TS 21:1:17

marr bk C 1894-1904 TS 21:1:13

Russell, city historians TS 21:2:75

Sedgwick Co, probate court bk B marr licenses 1880-1881 MGR 14:1:39 14:2:68

Shawnee Co, index to landowners, 1873, atlas, bk rev TRI 19:2:31

land recs grantor-grantee index bk 1 TOP 9:1:19 9:2:50

probate court index bks I & II, bk rev TRI 19:2:31

probate court index bks III, IV & V, bk rev TRI 19:2:31

Topeka, news abstr TOP 9:3:85,88

Ruleton cem inscr TS 21:4:156

St Marys, hist, bk rev GH 33:1:84

Summer Co, Gore Twp, real estate & personal tax rolls 1890 MGR 14:2:59

Green Castle cem inscr (east) TS 21:4:157

Tecumseh, Hopkins fam cem inscr MGR 14:4:179,180

Wabanusee Co, hist biogs, bk rev TX 6:2:20

Wallace Co, Fairview Cem inscr TS 2:4:174

Washington Co, Civil War burials MGR 14:3:138
hist biogs, bk rev TB 6:2:20
Wellington, tax roll 1883 MGR 14:3:105

KARR, John b1759, geneal bk 1, bk rev CI 14:1:29

KASLER, Kelion b1788 w Mandana Pember, NY, anc ch REP 19:4:162

KAUFFMAN, John Andrew m1828 w Elizabeth Johns, Prussia, PA, TX, geneal, bk sev GH 33:6:87

KAY, Louis d1898, IL, obit KIL 7:2:54

KEAN, James b1803 w Cassander, Bible rec MD 20:3:238

KEARBY, John f1749 w Miss Owen, VA, geneal VAG 23:3:163 23:4:259

KEARnS, fam of PA, geneal, bk rev NYR 110:4:250
John f1853 w Margaret Groughbough, OH, IA, geneal 1911, bk rev HH 14:3:162
William H m1815 w Sarah King, MD, OH, geneal, bk rev REP 19:3:133

KEEFER, George b1733 w Catharine Lampman, NJ, Bible rec BCG 6:2:7

KEELER, Isaac f1776, notes on CTA 22:2:68

KEELING, Thomas b1674/5, VA, geneal, bk rev GH 33:5:86

KEENEY, Jonathan b1813 w Mary Catherine Shoemaker, IN, MO, OR, biog notes ORB 18:3:64

KEESEE, George F d1825, TN, will LL 14:4:171
Richard dc1793 w Ann, VA will LL 14:4:189

KEITH, Howard Martin b1912 w Esther Louise Nelson, IA, anc ch KG 16:2:46
James Sr bc1720 w Miss Norid, Scot, VA, geneal, bk rev GH 33:5:86 TST 12:20:48 IL 11:4:235 VAG 23:4:230 YP 9:4:227 HHR 22:4:127 SCR 3:2:22 NCJ 5:4:258 AW 5:4:114 TRI 19:4:69 TSP 3:1:37 GR 21:3:89 21:4:124 NW 2:4:127

IG 15:4:103 MGR 14:3:18 NGI 3:4:207 CTN 12:4:703 LL 15:1:23 VL 14:2:95 DWC 5:3:88 RES 11:2:47 TB 6:2:15 STK 7:2:58 SGS 29:2:155
Levi Parks b1836 w Charlotte Keith, IN, IL, anc ch HJA 6:2:40

KELCHNER, David b1798 w Elizabeth, PA, Bible rec CI 14:4:146

KELLER, Samuel b1803 w Catherine Beavers, PA, OH, anc ch REP 19:4:164
William b1824, IN, biog notes TST 12:17:1

KELLEY, Carter Jerrel f1854, KY, geneal 1926, bk rev WCK 12:4:63
Hiram f1845 w Catherine Marks, OH, anc ch REP 19:1:35
John Gilbert b1913 w Helen Mae Mire, LA, anc ch AGE 8:3:96

KELLOGG, Ezra, OH letter AH 4:3:90
William Hollis b1874 w Ethel Carrie Lamphier, PA, CO, anc ch BGS 11:1:42

KELLY, Daniel b1820 w Elizabeth, Scot, PA, Bible rec HG 19:2:30
James f1848 w Mary, Ir & NY, geneal NYR 110:1:7
James P b1824 w Lucinda Craven, Bible rec KA 15:1:39
William S, TX, letters from Ir 1894 STK 7:4:177

KEMMERER, Joseph b1817 w Elizabeth Matilda Johnson, PA, IL, geneal, bk rev GH 33:2:85 TST 11:45:29 IL 11:2:114 NYR 110:3:181 REP 19:3:134 KCG 20:3:148
Joseph b1817 w Elizabeth M Johnson, PA, OH, IL, geneal, bk rev REP 19:3:134

KENNAMER, James Allen b1829 w Matilda Maples, TN, TX, geneal, bk rev VL 14:2:96

KENNEDY, Matthew B b1839 w Bell J Carnahan, PA, IL, biog VQ 16:2:24

KENTUCKY, antislavery movement,

bk rev REG 77:4:300

Bible recs v1, bk rev GH 33:2:79

Boone Co, Burlington, Kelly fam cem inscr KA 15:1:44

Bourbon Co, brides' index to marrs KA 14:3:139 14:4:209 15:1:9 115:2:87
hist 1785-1865, bk rev KA 15:1:63
hist 1882, bk rev VAG 23:3:232 KY 21:1:71
Paris, Mt Olivet Cath cem inscr KA 14:3:169

Breathitt Co, Frozen Creek, Taulbee cem inscr KA 15:1:42

Butler Co, cems inscr, bk rev OC 16:2:67
census 1870, bk rev OC 16:3:107

Calloway Co, census 1860 BR 6:3:101

Campbell Co, delinquents list 1807-1809 KA 14:3:145
hist, bk rev KA 14:4:254 REP 19:3:138
St John's Evang Luth Ch, bapt 1862-1866 KA 14:3:133 15:4:73

Casey Co, misc land grants 1781-1836, bk rev BR 6:2:55

census index 1830, bk rev CDS 16:2:5

Christian Co, misc early marrs KFR 7:91

Civil War memoirs 1904, bk rev WCK 12:4:63

Clark Co, marrs 1793-1799, bk rev ACL 4:3:55

Clinton Co, census recs 1840-1850, 1860, 1870, bk rev KA 14:4:255

county courthouse res guide, bk rev GH 33:5:70

county map ACL 4:3:65

Covington, hist 1751-1834, bk rev KY 21:1:34

Crittenden Co, census 1870, bk rev IG 14:1:5

Daviess Co, deed bk A KY 21:1:60
Owensboro, Elmwood cem inscr KA 14:4:235

emigs to TX 1866, notes on MKT

2:2:24

fam group sheets, bk rev WCK 12:3:49 BR 6:2:55

Fayette Co, Cane Run Bapt Ch hist, bk rev KA 14:3:189
pioneer recs BR 6:1:1

Fleming Co, court house recs descr BR 6:1:28
misc deed abstr BR 6:4:159

Floyd Co, census 1840, bk rev GH 33:4:111

Frankfort, Ch of the Ascension (Epis) reg 1834-1890, bk rev BR 6:3:96

Fulton Co, cem inscr v2, bk rev GH 33:3:99

Gallatian Co, deed abstr 1797-1808, bk rev GH 33:1:85
marrs, bonds, consents 1799-1835 KA 14:3:146 14:4:203 15:1:15 15:2:79

geneal & biog v6 1885 (Perrin), bk rev WCK 12:3:46

geneal publ, bk rev VAG 23:2:148 NCJ 5:2:141

geneal res guide STC 2:1:1 CI 14:2:60

Grant Co, Dry Ridge, hist BR 6:2:50

Hancock Co, hist soc guide TST 12:6:44

Hardin Co, census 1850, bk rev WCK 12:4:65
Elizabethtown, hist, bk rev VAG 23:4:311 KY 21:4:159 KA 15:2:127

Harrisoan Co, Antioch, Antioch Mills cem inscr KA 15:2:108
Beaver Bapt Ch Graveyard cem inscr KY 21:4:130
hist (1882), bk rev VAG 23:3:232 KY 21:1:71
Oddville Meth Epis Ch cem inscr KY 21:4:136

Henry Co, marr bonds 1798-1851 BR 6:3:65 6:4:109
hist REG 77:4:285
hist (1942), bk rev BGS 8:4:34
hist v1-8A,8B (1995-1888), bk rev VAG 23:3:231 KY 21:1:70
hist & geneal v1-5 1885, bk rev BGS 10:2:31
hist notes 1889 TST 12:23:47

Hopkins Co, misc recs from William C Thomasson's book 1840-1848 KA 14:4:198,220,225

"Hopkinsville Gazette" abstr 1835-1836 KY 21:4:123

index to Confederate vets & widows pension, bk rev WCK 12:4:64

Jefferson Co, tax list 1793 KY 21:3:92

Jessamine Co, hist 1898, bk rev WCK 12:2:33

Hunter cem inscr KA 15:1:44

Nicholasville, Evins Graveyard cem inscr KA 15:1:43

Nicholasville, Wallace Graveyard cem inscr KA 15:1:43

Portwood cem inscr KA 15:1:44

Johnson Co, census 1850, bk rev BR 6:3:96

census 1880, bk rev KA 14:4:254

KY hist soc lib geneal resources descr BR 6:3:95

Knott Co, Mousie, Fred Martin cem inscr KA 14:4:231

Knox Co, hist, bk rev OG 5:2:58

Letcher Co, census 1850 & 1880, bk rev OC 16:3:110

Lincoln Co, marrs 1780-1850 & cem inscr, bk rev IL 11:1:54 OC 16:3:109

misc land grants 1781-1836, bk rev BR 6:2:55

Logan Co, Pleasant Run Ch, hist notes KCG 20:2:65

Stovall-Mason cem inscr KFR 7:96

Madison Co, census 1830, bk rev GH 33:1:85 KA 14:4:254

Marshall Co, cem inscr vl, bk rev GH 33:5:74

Oaklevel, Shemwell cem inscr KA 14:4:230

McCreary Co, hist, bk rev KY 21:4:158

misc biogs of western KY vl-2, bk rev TB 6:2:19

misc fams, geneal, bk rev KY 21:3:115

Morgan Co, West Liberty, Davis cem inscr KA 14:4:234

Muhlenberg Co, cems v2, bk rev

GH 33:1:85

census 1860, bk rev WCK 12:1:18

David Gross/Grundy cem inscr KA 14:4:232

hist notes, bk rev WCK 12:4:66

hist of blacks, bk rev WCK 12:2:24

Scott cem inscr KA 14:4:233

natives in IN 1850 ACL 4:3:47

Nicholas Co, apprent bonds NGS 67:3:177

hist (1882), bk rev VAG 23:3:232 KY 21:1:71

marrs 1800-1812, bk rev ACL 4:3:55

Ohio Co, geneal news columns 1969-1972, bk rev WCK 12:4:65

Walton's Creek Bapt Ch recs from 1814, bk rev WCK 12:2:35

Ohio Valley, hist biblio, bk rev CTN 10:2:346

Oldham Co, Westport, small cem inscr KA 14:4:239

people in OH news 1872-1873 KA 15:2:104

Perry Co, Buckhorn, Johnson cem inscr KA 15:1:41

Daisy, Cornett cem inscr KA 15:2:105

Pike Co, misc residents 1829 KY 21:2:43

pioneer geneal publ, bk rev IL 11:3:180 VAG 23:2:148

res notes TSP 3:1:15

researchers for hire WCK 12:1:8

Rev War, pensioners 1818-1832, bk rev ACL 4:3:55

Rockcastle Co, census 1810 & 1820, 1815 tax list, bk rev GH 33:6:81

saltpeter mining hist REG 77:4:247

Scotch-Irish settlers, hist notes TST 12:5:37

Scott Co, hist (1882), bk rev VAG 23:5:232 KY 21:1:71

Shelby Co, hist 1929, bk rev WCK 12:3:46

marrs 1792-1800, bk rev ACL 4:3:55

tax list 1792 KY 21:1:26

Simpson Co, census 1820 KFR

7:81

notes on KFR 7:86

vr 1852-1861 KFR 7:87

state resources for birth & death recs GE 48:11 BR 6:2:56

Taylor Co, Rev War plague BR 6:4:158

Todd Co, Coleman fam cem inscr REF 21:1:14

Morton fam cem inscr KFR 7:100

Trenton, Watts Graveyard cem inscr KA 14:4:240

topical index KY 21:1:3

Union Co, Cowan-Holeman fam cem inscr KY 21:1:72

Univ of KY lib, fam & local hist resources descr BR 6:3:63

Warren Co, emigs to IL BGS 6:1:4

Riverside, Log Ch cem inscr KA 14:4:195

Wayne Co, Burnett fam cem inscr THT 4:2:5

census index 1810-1880, bk rev OC 16:3:109

Meadow Creek Meth Ch cem inscr THT 6:3:106

misc court papers 1823-1824 KY 21:4:147

Powell cem inscr THT 5:3:3

Rolley Creek, Dodson cem inscr THT 6:3:109

Sumter, Bartheson-Miller fam cem inscr KA 14:3:174

Webster Co, census 1870, bk rev WCK 12:4:65

West Point, hist, bk rev WPA 5:2:78 KA 14:3:189

western KY biog notes 1904, bk rev WCK 12:2:33

Whitley Co, Corbin, Chestnut Grove cem inscr KA 15:1:42

Woodford Co, McCowan's Ferry Pike, McConnell fam cem inscr KA 15:2:107

KERBY, fam of Ir, notes on SGS 29:1:31

KERR, fam of NY 1786, notes on NGS 67:1:62

George b1857 w Sarah Lavina Adams, Can, RI, WA, geneal, bk rev CTN 9:2:313

James Sr, TX, will 1859 DG 25:3:182

KETCHUM, Richard Norman b1903 w Leah Louise Braden, IN, anc ch BGS 10:1:35

KETTMANN, Bernard Henry b1823 w Mary Pater, Ger, OH, geneal, bk rev GH 33:5:86

KEYSER, Andrew b1804 w Mary Brubaker, Bible rec GR 21:1:38

KIEFER, Louis Wilfred b1914 w Mary Frances Brown, LA, TX, anc ch AGS 20:2:74

KILGORE, James William f1760 w Elizabeth Jack, PA, geneal BGS 10:1:29

Alexander Jr bc1838 w Elizabeth Jane McDowell, Scot, Can, biog & letters BCG 6:1:2,4

KILLION, Isaac b1858 w Alice Millir, IL, fam rec GL 13:2:42

KILLOUGH, Isaac Sr d1838, TX, fam rec THT 5:1:12

KIMBALL, Jesse b1774, ME, Bible rec DE 3:1:12

William F b1826 w Mary J Day, VA, IA, Bible rec SGS 29:2:112

KIMBRELL, fam of AL, fam rec NAS 18:1:14

KINDER, Valentine b1759, Bible recs TB 6:4:15

KINCH, Niles Henry b1863 w Ardella Ruth Clark, KS, NE, Bible rec NA 2:2:41

KING, Boston bc1760 Can, loyalist, biog,bk rev GN 2:6:172

Edward W b1819 w Nancy Jane Cochran, TN, Bible rec BWG 8:1:39

fam of WV, geneal, bk rev BGS 8:4:32

Paolis b1791 w Polly Matthews, RI, CT, Bible rec CTN 10:2:364

Stephen Jonah b1857 w Sarah Ann Murray, NC, AL, anc ch YP 9:2:67

Thomas b1752 w Lucy Hyde, MA, fam rec NSN 4:3:25

KINKEAD, John L b1789 w Sarah Speers, NJ, VA, OH, biog

notes REP 19:2:77

KINNEAR, Stephen A b1813 w Mary Harris ?Williams, OH, geneal, bk rev REP 19:2:92

KINNICUTT, fam of IL, notes on FF 8:1:56

KINSMAN, Joseph Alexander b1850, Can, geneal, bk rev CTN 7:4:518

KINTNER, Edward b1879 w Glada Olis Snyder, OH, IN, anc ch RRS 12:1:94

KINZER, Jesse Andrew b1876 w Rosa Beatrice McLarty, GA, AR, anc ch THT 7:2:74

KIRBY, James bc1799 w Bridget McMahon, Ir, anc ch SGS 29:1:32

KIRK, fam cem inscr IL FF 8:1:38

KIRKPATRICK, Edwin Clarence b1878 w Dorie Dorado Long, KY, CA, anc ch OC 16:4:119

KITZMILLER, Abdiel Unkefer m1855 w Mary Jane Taylor, Bible rec BWG 8:1:41

KLAPROTH, Herman b1853 w Anna Louise Rohlfing, Ger, TX, anc ch THT 7:2:72

KLINGENSMITH, fam of PA, misc recs, bk rev TS 21:4:174

KLINGER, fam recs of PA, bk rev GE 42:11

KLOHR, Phillip b1841 w Christina Ruebsamen, Ger, IL, fam rec CI 15:1:18

KLONTZ, William b1820 w Anna Blair, VA, OH, anc ch REP 19:4:159

KNAPPER, Frederick d1934 w Ellen, Norway, MN, Bible rec PR 3:3:49

KNERL. Calvin A b1893 w Clara Ruth Diffendaffer, NE, anc ch NW 2:3:92

KNIFFEN, Charles Henry b1846 w Mary Jane Sniffen, Bible rec CTN 10:3:415

KNIGHT, Bertram D b1889 w Gertrue Elizabeth Wilkinson, TX, NM, geneal NMG 18:1:28

Thomas, PA, NJ, geneal, bk rev TB 6:1:33

William Edward b1885 w Eugenia

Gladys Bonney, MS, LA, anc ch GR 21:4:140

KNOWLES, John m1660 w Jemima Asten, NH, geneal, bk rev GH 33:6:88 KCG 20:4:205

Robert m1866 w Catherine Jane Kemper, Bible rec CI 14:3:96

Samuel b1768 w Sally (Downing) Nute, NH, anc ch OC 16:3:98

KNOWLTON, Samuel b1822 w Julia Ann Hadley, ME, OH, IA, anc ch DE 3:4:23

KNOX, Hugh McAllister b1792 w Anna Wright, PA, Bible rec MI 24:1:45

William b1767 w Margaret MacCollum, Nancy Smith, Ir, PA, geneal REF 21:1:5

KOCH, Fred f1878 w Catherine Adler, Katie Kimble, Russia, NE, OR, notes on NA 2:1:18

KOHN, Gaylen Duane b1931 w Vera Evelyn Patterson, KS, anc ch TOP 9:2:41

KOLKER, Reynold Edward b1898 w Gertrude Mary Fedde, IA, TX, OK, anc ch THT 7:1:22

KONWINSKI, Jakub b1759, Poland, biog notes PN 1:1:7

KOONTZ, fam of IN, letters 1834-1848 DG 25:2:100

KORNEGAY, Ed Augustus b1864 w Missouri Edwards, GA, MO, TX, anc ch THT 7:2:77

fam of NC, geneal THT 7:2:107

KRAEER, John Calvin b1925 w Evelyn Jean Kimbrough, KS, TX, anc ch AGS 20:2:52

KREIGER, Herman August b1814 w Amelia, Bible rec CI 14:4:142

KROPFF, John William b1863 w Carrie Maria Kosier, IL, KS, anc ch TOP 9:3:76

KUHN, Mary Katherine, TN will 1828 BWG 8:1:90

KYN, Joran, PA, geneal, bk rev CI 15:2:30

LABONTE, fam geneal, bk rev GH 33:1:91

LABROQUERE, Raimond f1727 w Jeannot de Charlas, Fr, Haiti, geneal MD 20:4:260

LACHANCE, famof Quebec, Can, notes on QBC 2:1:8

LACKNER, Joseph Albert b1888 w Kathryn Ault, NE, CO, anc ch BGS 10:3:45

LADD, Abner d1820, death notice NSN 4:5:43

LAING, Frederick William d1948 w Colina C A, Can biog BCG 5:1:3 5:2:1

LAKE, Taz Whitaker b1889 w Mary Sexton, TX, anc ch THT 6:3:66

LAKIN, Mary (Bacon) f1661 h John Lakin, Eng, MA, notes on CTN 8:3:478

LA LANDA, Jean Baptiste f1804 w Maria Rita Abeyta, Maria Polonia, IL, NM, fam rec NMG 18:2:52

LAMAR, Daniel E b1854 w Lenora J Reid, Bible rec IG 15:2:57

Thomas f1663, MD, geneal, bk rev NGS 67:1:70

LAMB, David bc1731, NY, geneal NYR 110:4:227

James Madison b1845 w Mary Alice Alexander, KY, IA, biog THT 5:3:23

Thomas Sr f1836 w Miss Adamson, NC, IN, geneal QY 6:4:3

LAMBERTON, George d1646 w Margaret (Lewen) Lamberton Goodyear, Eng, CT, biog notes BGS 11:3:116

LAMBKIN, Emory Best b1899 w Frances Terry Hawkins, GA, TX, anc ch THT 6:3:76

LAMMERT, Harry F b1892, NM, biog notes NMG 18:4:124

LAMONT, John b1759 w Elizabeth Sullivan, Bible rec CTN 11:4:595

LAMPHERE, George b1631 w Jane Hulet, Eng, RI, geneal, bk rev CTN 12:4:701

LAMPHIER, Benjamin b1799 w Mary Ann Francis, CT, NY, geneal BGS 11:2:64

LANAM, Jess Gordon d1919 w Julia Edna Sultz, CO, anc ch FF 8:2:72

LANDESS, Diana (Decker) h Abraham Landess, John L Fryer, OR fam rec GFP 29:2:36

LANE, Clarence Otto b1894 w Clara Isabell Tucker, IL, anc ch GL 13:3:67

Clarence Roe b1894 w Helen Augusta Henkel, KS, anc ch KK 17:4:77

James Sidney b1884 w Elura Morgan Fall, Can, WA, anc ch TB 6:4:22

John f1802 w Rachel Herod, PA, OH, Bible rec & biog CI 12:2:48

Parthenia b1829 h Leonard Washington Furr, GA, Bible rec THT 5:1:28

LANG, Joseph E, geneal, bk rev GH 33:2:85

LANGELLIER, Joseph w Marie Louise Levesques, Can, IL, marr contract 1800 DM 42:3:127

LANGSTON, John bc1710, VA, NC, SC, geneal, bk rev GH 33:3:106 OK 24:2:73

LANKFORD, Walter Addison b1911 w Gloria Wynne, VA, TX, anc ch THT 7:1:25

LANNING, Mary Eleanor (Powell) f1886 h David Martin VanBuren Lanning, fam recs LM 20:4:2

LANPHERE, George b1631 w Jane Hulet, Eng, RI, geneal, bk rev GFP 29:4:67

LANT, fam geneal, bk rev TSP 2:3:37

LARKIN, John bc1755 w Patience Gardiner, RI, geneal CTN 8:3:476

LA ROSE, fam of MN, death recs Rice Co MN 10:1:73

LARKINS, William E b1794 w Rachel Reed, PA, OR, biog notes ORB 17:9:83

LARSEN, fam of Den & Am, geneal, bk rev IL 11:2:115 CSB 14:1:22 CTN 12:1:173

LARSON, Bernhard Marinius b1852 w Elise Saxhaug, Norway, MN, geneal, bk rev TB 6:4:30

Helfred L b1896 w Mable D Tyler, Sweden, MN, SD, anc ch

OG 4:2:36

LATHROP, Charles Slothower b1884
w Letha Oliva Wynkoop, NE,
MO, IA, anc ch NW 2:3:93
fam of CT, geneal v1-4, bk rev
NYR 110:4:249

LATIN AMERICA, geneal hist
guide, bk rev GE 49:8 GH
33:2:73 VAG 23:2:151 WCK
12:2:34 DM 42:4:183 SPG
31:587

LAUGHERY, James J b1828 w Hannah
Malintha Halstead, NY, OH,
biog notes AH 5:4:124

LAUGHLIN, Samuel b1791 w Naomi
Morrow, Nancy Doughty, SC,
MO, OR, biog notes ORB
18:1:11

LA VALLY, John J bc1794 w Elizabeth Smith, VA, IN, OH, anc
ch REP 19:3:129

LAW, Samuel dc1906, Eng, Can,
OH, obit CPY 8:1:25

LAWLER, Henry Howard Sr b1884 w
Odile Clara Dean, TN, LA, anc
ch GR 21:2:49

LAWRENCE, Almira A (Rathbun)
d1877 h Levi Howard Lawrence,
Stephen Francis, PA, biog
notes REP 19:4:139

David b1730 w Sarah, Bible rec
CTN 12:3:417

fam of CT, fam recs 1746-1867
CTN 12:3:416

James F, letter 1858 BGS 3:1:4

James W bc1822 w Angeline Sni-
der, Can, NY, WI| TX, biog
THT 3:1:34

Joseph b1838 w Eliza Catherine
Black, VA, Bible rec SCS
14:3:69

Samuel b1739 w Rhoda Benedict,
CT, NY, biog notes BGS 2:2:7

Tryphena (Lawrence) b1735 h
Jonas Lawrence, will BGS
1:1:8

LAYTON, fam of KY, fam recs KA
14:4:215

LEACH, fam geneal, bk rev CI
14:3:110

LEACHE, fam of MD, notes on MD
20:3:180

LEAVITT, William f1825 w Ruth

Merrill, ME, KS, fam recs KK
17:1:6

LE BLANC, Hubert m1829 w Marguerite Samosette, Can., anc
ch AGE 8:4:127

Joseph b1878 w Genevieve Prene-
vost, MN, anc ch AGE 8:2:68

Paul b1878 w Angeline Lambert,
LA, anc ch AGE 8:2:63

Pierre f1772 w Marie Madeliene
Babin, LA, biog notes AGE
8:1:25

Pierre f1755 w Marguerite Amir-
ault, LA, geneal AGE 8:1:25

LE CLAIRE, Charles Homer b1918 w
Elizabeth Lucille Dugal, MI,
anc ch BGS 9:4:39

LEDBETTER, fam of VA, geneal, bk
rev GGM 71:6

LEDGERWOOD, Josepah b1836, biog
MKT 2:3:44

LEDUKE, Mollie, TN 1904/5
letters THT 6:2:43

LEE, fam of NC & VA, geneal,
bk rev OC 16:1:34 VL 13:3:147

Francis Russell b1881 w Clara
Jane Rusk, GA, anc ch ORB
17:9:84

John b1793 w Mary W Pressley,
SC, fam rec GGM 74:295

John b1876 w Sallie Mamie Bar-
din, TX, anc ch GR 21:4:134

Robert W b1800 w Martha
Thomeson Brankam, Bible rec
HH 14:2:89

Thomas m1796 w Anne Harrel, NC,
marr rec NCJ 5:4:263

LEER, Jacob f1776, IN, biog
notes MIS 11:4:52

LEES, Lot bc1815 w Hannah Ashton, Eng, anc ch EG 12:310

LEESEMAN, Charles John George
m1874 w Elizabeth J Schultz,
TX, Bible rec GR 21:4:152

LEGG, fam of AL, bk rev CI
13:3:115

John f1731 w Temperance Thayer,
fam rec AH 5:2:49

LEHR, Johann Peter bc1850 w
Katherina Loefler, Russ, MI,
geneal PF 8:4:77 9:1:8

LEIFESTE, August Sr b1812 w
Elizabeth Viedt, Ger, TX,

biog THT 6:1:14

LEHMANN, Clement m1713 w Anna Gerdraut, NY, geneal NYR 110:2:105 110:3:146

LEIGHTON, Joseph b1779, ME, Bible rec DE 3:1:12

LEMIRE, fam of WI, geneal, bk rev MN 10:1:42

LEMLEY, Jacob b1766 w Sarah, NY, PA, anc ch REP 19:1:37

LEMMON, James b1769 w Sarah Carr, Amy Rawlins, MD, KY, IN, IL, geneal CI 11:2:74

LEDNARD, Asa b1771, MA, Bible rec AH 4:3:84

LE VAN, Daniel f1727, Fr, PA, geneal, bk rev CTN 11:1:41
  Solomon b1778, DE, geneal, bk rev GE 42:10 GJ 8:2:116

LEVERING, Daniel b1784 w Mary Kearnay, NJ, PA, OH, geneal, bk rev REP 19:4:173

LEWIN, Philip f1692, MD, geneal PGB 11:8:83

LEWIS, Benoni b1843 w ___, Mrs Mary Malbern King, RI, obit RIR 5:4:9
  David R b1814 w Mary Redden, KY, OR, biog notes ORB 17:7:64
  fam & related fams of VA, MD, PA, geneal, bk rev REP 19:3:133
  fam of IN, geneal, bk rev TSP 3:2:4 KA 14:3:189
  fam of VA, geneal, bk rev KY 21:1:68 DM 43:1:47
  John w Isabella Miller, VA, geneal 1935, bk rev VAG 23:2:144 GH 33:2:85 TST 12:7:46 NYR 110:3:185
  Marion Jackson b1882 w Mary Corrilla Morrison, AL, anc ch NAS 17:3:68
  Robert f1635, Wales, VA, geneal, bk rev NGS 67:2:151
  Thomas W b1781 w Judith Maloy, TN, anc ch RRS 12:1:116

LIBBY, Richard b1762 w Sarah Ross, ME, Bible rec DE 2:5:19

LICHTENWALTER, Daniel b1787 w Rachel Baer, PA, OH, anc ch REP 19:4:162

LIDDELL, Adam d1872 w Annie, Eng, will SGS 29:3:209

LIEBFRIED, Harry Lentz b1852 w Eva Amelia Button, Ger, PA, MD, KS, geneal MGR 14:1:25

LIGGETT, Samuel F b1806 w Jane Stackhouse, OH, anc ch REP 19:3:125

LIGHTFOOT, Isaac b1806 w Emma Schooley, PA, OH, anc ch REP 19:3:130

LIGON, Thomas b1586 w Mary Harris, Eng, anc ch AGS 20:2:56

LIKENS, Jeremiah Doran b1837 w Mary Matilda Walsworth, OH, IN, Civil War diary & letters, bk   rev GH 33:4:118 CDS 16:4:13

LILLY, Orris bc1841 w Susan Catherine Staley, Nancy Brown, Jane Heltion, IL, pension cert MCH 7:3:80

LINAM, Walter Thorp b1900 w Frances Ruth Briscoe, OK, TX, AZ, anc ch THT 7:2:69

LINCOLN, Abraham (US Pres) b1809 w Mary Todd, anc ch TST 11:45:29

LINDBERG, Harry Edward b1883 w Ingrid Theresa Johansson, Sweden, IL, NB, MO, anc ch BGS 11:4:132

LINDESAY, fam of Ir, geneal, bk rev REP 19:3:134

LINDESMITH, Lonnie Lee b1906 w Julia Esta Morris, IN, anc ch FF 8:4:44

LINDLEY, Jacob Marion f1831 w Alsey Ruth Gibson, NC, KY, MO, TX, geneal, bk rev TA 14:1:19
  Joseph B f1923, AR, AL, MS, biog notes BGS 7:4:20

LINDSAY, fam of VA, geneal VA 17:2:59

LINDSEY, fam of NC, geneal, bk rev NCJ 5:3:214
  Micajah b1774 w Elizabeth McClurken, SC, MS, geneal AGS 20:2:54

LINN, Henry b1775 w Rebecca Cain, WV, IN, Bible rec HJA

6:2:37

LINSCOTT, Henry L b1808 w Betsey M Trafton, ME, Bible rec BGS 10:3:26

LINSLEY, John William w Lydia Chamberlin, MI, Civil War biog & fam rec MI 24:4:133

LIPE, Columbus Joshua b1843, IL, biog notes OC 16:2:54

LIPPERO, Thomas b1809 w Elizabeth, Bible rec CO 40:4:185

LIPSCOMB, Richard Travis b1884 w Leonora Gale, TX, anc ch GR 21:4:138

LITHUANIA, Polish fams, notes on PN 1:1:4

LITTLE, Clinton b1839 w Nancy Holman, Mary Jane Cleveland Camp, IL, Bible rec CI 14:4:128

LITTLEFIELD, Catherine b1754 h Nathaniel Greene, RI, biog MKT 2:4:64

LIVINGSTON, Robert Dee b1881 w Emma Adaline Farnsworth, IA, MO, CO, anc ch BGS 10:2:40

LLOYD, David f1800 w   , Esther Pearson, Mary Quinn, Jane Cooke Quinn, Can, PA, biog notes FAM 18:2:i

fam of Can FAM 18:4:i

LOBAUGH, John William b1872 w Grace Edith Earnest, WV, IL, KS, anc ch BGS 10:2:36

LOCKE, fam of IL, fam recs FF 8:2:69

Lue Washington b1898 w Ludie Mary McKee, LA, anc ch YP 9:4:204

LOCKWOOD, Edmund bc1625, CT, geneal, bk rev NYR 110:1:55 CTA 21:4:175 MQ 45:1:26 DM 43:2:87 CTN 12:1:74 AG 55:2:126

Isaac f1798 w Phebe Walters, NY, IN, geneal, bk rev GE 47:10

Joseph w Mary Wood, CT, biog notes CDS 16:2:17

Lebrand m1842 w Ann Louisa Benedict, NY, fam rec CDS 16:2:18

Mason Graves b1903 w Mae

Letitcia Hobson, TX, anc ch AGS 20:2:60

Mary m1770 h Nathan Knapp, CT, notes on CTA 22:2:69

LODEWIJK, Carel b1784, Can, biog notes FAM 18:2:67

LOEFFLER, Johan Martina f1854 w Johanna Christiana Zizelmann, Ger, TX, geneal, bk rev STK 7:2:58

LOEWEN, Peter A f1895 w Helena, Russ, Can, auto BCG 6:4:17 7:1:30

LOFTHOS, Henry Siver b1875 w Lule Harriet Fuller, WI, MN, anc ch BGS 11:1:46

LOGAN, David b1706 w Jane McKinley, Ir, PA, geneal, bk rev GFP 29:1:5

William f1792, SC, notes on NGS 67:1:62

LOGODZINSKI, Anna b1903 h Mr Rastetter, PA, biog notes PN 1:2:30

LOGUE, geneal, bk rev CI 12:2:75

LOHR, Philipp f1749, Ger, PA, geneal, bk rev REP 19:1:43

LONG, Frederick, PA, NC, court pet 1797 NCJ 5:3:149

John b1755 w Delilah, VA, Bible rec NGS 67:1:80

Joshua W m1853 w Julian Emery, IL, Bible rec BGS 5:3:16

LONGETEIG, fam of Norway, geneal, bk rev RES 11:3:82

LONGSTAFF, Gilbert bc1792 w   , Elizabeth Pratt, Eng, MI, geneal DM 43:1:13

LORING, Thomas b1725 w Zilpah Bradford, MA, Bible rec BB 11:2:27

LOSEE, John Henry b1840 w Josephine Caroline Roll, NE, Bible rec NA 2:1:23

LOSSEE, fam of Can & OH, notes on AH 6:4:135

LOUGHEAD, James S b1837 w Margaret Kingston, Can, Bible rec AH 4:4:134

LOUISIANA, Calcasieu Parish, census 1850 YP 9:1:27 9:2:83 9:3:161 9:4:214

Cane River, creole hist FH

2:2:78

geneal res guide NSN 4:2:10

New Orleans, Bell Plantation, ledger 1873 KN 2:3:47

Cath diorese 1704-1813, bk rev AGE 8:3:91

cotton company c1864 notes KN 2:1:29

Tensas Parish, marr recs 1850-1866 computer-indexed, bk rev YP 9:4:229

LOVE, John m1779 w Ann Updegraff, PA marr rec BGS 6:3:12

Samuel b1763, Bible rec HTR 22:2:47

LOVEJOY, Reuben, NY, letter 1881 NA 2:2:36

LOVELACE, William Douglas b1921 w Elizabeth Kneif, CA, anc ch KG 16:4:95

LOVELAND, Thomas f1683, Eng, CT, geneal, bk rev GH 33:1:93

LOWEREY, Mary Glover (Thompson) b1856 h Charles Emmet Lowrey, MI, CO, biog notes BGS 5:4:10

Charles b1820 w Catherine Hudgens, TN, anc ch YP 9:1:3

LOWRY, fam of PA, WA, Bible rec TRI 17:1:8

LUCIUS, Catherine (Shultz) b1810 h Peter Lucius, Belgium, OH, geneal v5, bk rev GH 33:1:93

Michael b1830 w Catherine Moes, MN, geneal v4, bk rev GH 33:1:93

LUCKEY, William b1799 w Martha Canny, KY, OH, anc ch REP 19:3:117

LUCY, fam of Europe & Am, geneal, bk rev KCG 20:3:152

LUDEMAN, Heye Hindrichs Janshen d1856 w Agthe Alken Westermann, Ger, IL, NE, geneal, bk rev GH 33:2:85 KCG 20:3:149

Robert William b1913 w Dorothy Lee Bowden, TX, AR, MO, anc ch THT 7:1:24

LUEBBERT, Charles b1879 w Lena Fayette Shane, OH, KS, CO, anc ch BGS 10:4:39

LUGLAND, Ole Olesen b1824 w Julia Nielsdatter, Nor, IL, anc ch & geneal IL 11:1:6

LUTHER, John f1630 w Elizabeth, MA, geneal, bk rev REP 19:3:137

John b1741 w Sarah Greennan, RI, Bible rec RIR 5:4:3

LUTTRELL, Richard b1735 w Sarah Churchwell, VA, Bible rec MGR 14:4:176

LYMBRIE, George f1636, VA, notes on NGS 67:1:63

LYNDE, fam of WI 1895, notes on MCR 10:3:71

LYON, fam of Am, geneal bk 4, bk rev CTN 9:4:603

LYONS, Eliab m1757 w Meriah Smith, MA, ME, geneal DE 3:3:20

LYTLE, Montgomery Bell m1878 w Alice Wharton McKittrick, KY, Bible rec TA 14:3:66

MC ADAMS, fam of OH, fam recs AH 4:3:103

MC ALLISTER, Lester S m1871 w Ella Welch, Bible rec FG 21:1:11

MC ANALLY, Charles f1693 w Houston, Scot, PA, geneal, bk rev GH 33:3:107

MC ARTHUR, James Marshall b1887 w Ruth Marie Wilson, KS, LA, anc ch GR 21:4:140

MAC BEAN, fam of Am, geneal, bk rev DM 42:3:136

MC BRIDE, Lewis b1797 w Rebecca Bowen, NJ, anc ch YP 9:3:129

MC CALMONT, Henry Conard b1808 w Rebecca Prather, Bible rec AH 4:2:43

MC CARTER, Robert A B b1812 w Sarah Ann Chance, Mariah Louise Meador, SC, TX, geneal, bk rev FP 22:4:211 VL 14:2:95 NCJ 5:4:258

William M b1826 w Harriet L Fenton, PA, NY, MO, KS, fam rec MGR 21:1:26

MC CASLIN, Mathew L b1822 w Miranda Haggerty, PA, NE, CO, geneal BGS 8:2:15

MC CAULEY, fam of LA, early recs AGE 8:1:26

MC CHESNEY, Thomas Clark b1835 w Martha Endora Cowdery, IL, geneal SCC 16:1:9

MC CLANATHAN, John f1727 w Martha Shaw, Ir, MA, geneal, bk rev CTN 12:3:533

MC CLELLAND, Thomas b1780 w Ann Kinnear, Scot, Ir, PA, anc ch REP 19:1:37

MC CLENATHEN, Gordon Arthur b1901 w Una Claire Powell, CA, anc ch AW 5:3:73

MC CLENDON, Lucinda bc1800 h Thomas Fincher, Zachariah Darden, GA, AL, anc ch AGS 20:2:65

MC CLENNING, Daniel m1806 w Thirza Gilbert, MA, geneal, bk rev CTN 10:3:520

MC CLESKEY, fam of TX, geneal, bk rev FP 22:4:209

MC CLUGHAN, Eilsa Frances (Shaw) b1854 h Samuel McClughan, Can, auto & fam rec BCG 6:3:27

MC CLUNG, John b1808 w Nancy J Wilson, Bible rec BWG 8:1:32

MC CLURE, John dc1846 w Mary Jane Cartee, MO, anc ch YP 9:1:4

John M b1854, Bible rec HH 14:3:159

Nathaniel S b1782 w Elizabeth Wilt, VA, OH, anc ch REP 19:4:165

Vincent Scott b1815 w Sarah Bruce, Sarah Tandy Benson, IN, OR, biog notes ORB 17:7:63

MC COLLUM, James b1806 w Lydia, IL, Bible rec CI 15:3:91

MC COMB, George b1816 w Annis Robinson, Ir, PA, OH, IL, biog CI 15:4:123

MC CORD, James bc1761 w Martha Burch, Ir, OH, geneal, bk rev REP 19:4:176

William Young b1816 w Harriet Weedman, TN, IL, biog DWC 5:4:91

MC CORDY, Samuel d1855 w Marianne Corey, Bible rec PR 3:3:50

MC CORKLE, Joseph b1753 w Margaret Snoddy, KY, OH, biog notes REP 19:2:80

MC CORMACK, John dc1768 w Anne, VA, fam recs IG 14:2:42

MC CORMICK, J Harvey b1845 w Eliza Sophronia Bollen, IL, WV, NV, CA, Bible rec VQ 16:2:27

MC COY, Sam bc1860, KY, AR, MO, biog & geneal, bk rev TST 12:22:40 GH 33:5:87 BR 6:2:55

MC CRACKEN, Clive d1905, WI cem inscr WI 25:4:213

fams of NC & TX, geneal, bk rev DG 25:3:188

Walter William b1898 w Minnie Vera Masters, OK, anc ch RRS 12:1:97

MC CREARY, Lewis b1825 w Martha Ann Shackelford, Margaret Hannah Mahurin, Margaret Eleanore Yount, OH, Bible rec CI 15:4:151

MC CRUM, C O b1828 w Sarah K Dunn, OH, Bible rec TOP 9:3:65

MC CUBBIN, Abraham b1817 w Sarah, Bible rec GFP 28:5:90

James bc1812 w China, VA, biog notes ORB 17:6:55

MC CULLOUGH, John David b1888 w Willie Leigh Taylor, AL, anc ch AGS 20:2:71

MC CURDY, William b1799 w Hannah McDermut, Bible rec WB 10:1:30

MC CUTCHEON, George Lafayette b1876 w Ola Maude Tarpley, TX, anc ch RRS 12:2:216

Samuel b1783 alias Samuel Weston, biog KCG 20:4:179

MC DOWELL, John Raymond f1905 w Winifred Davis, WI, photo & biog notes SCS 14:3:6

MC DONALD, Nathaniel Green b1818 w Rebecca Munkers, NC, MO, OR, biog notes ORB 18:2:30

William Archie b1905 w Katherine Elizabeth Curry, GA, anc ch NAS 17:3:69

William Clifford b1874 w Valeria Cleveland Bundren,

TN, AL, anc ch PT 21:4:126

MC DONOUGH, Frank w Carolyn Warner (Harris), CO, & related fams, geneal, bk rev GFP 28:5:87

MC DOUGALL, Daniel m1845 w Mary Nigh Hanks, NY, Bible rec NYR 110:1:15

MC ELROY, Charles Lynn b1919 w Enid Elizabeth McKinley, IL, anc ch GL 13:3:69

MC FARLAND, Elsie Ann (Rearick) h Robert McFarland, travel diary 1903 MO-CO TS 21:1:5

MC GAFFEY, Neal f1720, Ir, NH, geneal, bk rev BGS 8:2:29

MC GILL, fam of Ir, notes on TST 12:14:38

MC GINTY, John f1738 w Mary, Ir, VA, geneal, bk rev GH 33:6:88

MC GLASSON, William II dc1776 w Judith Ford, VA, geneal CI 11:3:91

MC GOVERN, James Patrick b1884 w Mattie Josephine Dorser, CA, anc ch RED 12:2:7

Thomas Francis bc1849 w Alice Elizabeth Hunter, Ir, CA, misc rec RED 12:2:8

MC GRAW, fam of NY, Bible rec MI 24:1:8

MAC GREGOR, T A b1840 w Judelle Trabue, KY, LA, biog VQ 16:4:57

MC GREGOR, Albert Alexander b1835 w Celia King, Happy C Cooper, AL, biog notes VL 19:2:68

MC GRIFF, James b1755, SC, GA, geneal, bk rev VAG 23:4:309

MC GUIRE, Merry d1796 w Rebecca Smith, SC, pension appl fam rec CI 14:2:56

MC HARGUE, Alexander f1745, PA, geneal, bk rev GH 33:1:93

MC HENRY, Henry b1762 w Martha Morrison, Bible rec IG 15:1:6

MC HUGH, John Alexander b1832 w Nancy Ford Pennington, Bible rec NAS 18:1:8

MC INTIRE, Ora Ethel d1939 h James E Williams, WV, biog THT 7:2:106

MC INTURFF, fam of PA & VA, geneal, bk rev CI 12:2:53

MAC KAY, clan MacKay hist, bk rev GN 2:8:249

MC KEE, James b1781 w Mary Riley, OH, geneal, bk rev REP 19:2:91

Kirk William b1915 w Edna Nora Sanstrum, OR, anc ch OG 3:3:66

MC KELLAR, Thomas G b1786 w Ruth Thorndike,ME, fam rec DE 2:5:13

MC KENNEY, John b1740 w Margaret, Can, Bible rec GN 2:7:209

MC KENZIE, Edgar m1895 w Anna Mary Evans, IL, biog notes MCH 7:1:18

MC KINLEY, Alexander b1833 w Sorro McGuick, Louisa Bell Hughes, OH, IL, Bible rec & obit GL 13:2:45

MC KINNEY, fam rec & letters KN 2:1:17 2:2:26 2:3:35

Silas m1847 w Fannie Melissa Clark Nelson, Mary C Burt, NY, South Africa, Bible rec CSB 14:1:27

William M b1832 w Sarah Jane Petty, TX, Bible rec THT 3:1:8

MC KITRICK, fam of Ir & Scot, geneal, bk rev NYR 110:4:250 IRA 13:280 SCG 13:51

MC LEAN, Daniel b1787 w Susanna Fobes jr, Deborah Loring, Scot, NY, Bible rec BB 11:2:28

MC LOUGHLIN, John, OR, biog, bk rev TB 6:3:24

MC MAHON, fam of Ir, notes on SGS 29:1:31

MC MANIGAL, Park Eldred b1903 w Marcia Blanche Spencer, NE, IA, anc ch RRS 12:1:75

MC MICHAEL, John W, letter 1864 SGS 29:2:115

MC MILLAN, Dougald f1751 w Sarah, Scot, NC, geneal ed 1, bk rev NCJ 5:2:140

MC MINN, Albert Richard d1908, CO, Bible rec BGS 7:1:9

MC MURTRY, Abner Sr d1885 w

Sarah H Hardin, Mrs Louise Tucker, TX, fam rec YP 9:1:11

William, KY, AL, geneal, bk rev YP 9:1:39

MC NAIR, John f1724, Scot, Ir, PA, geneal, bk rev CTN 11:1:43 CDS 16:2:4

MC NEAL, Thomas b1771 w Clarissa Polk, TN, biog notes AGS 20:2:44

MC NULTA, John d1900, NY, IL, biog notes GL 13:4:95

MC PHERSON, William b1813 w Mary, SC, AL, TX, Bible rec YP 9:2:75

MC QUERRY, James Madison b1890 w Anna Lois Harrison, MO, anc ch OC 16:3:98

MC ROBERTS, Maxwell William b1899 w Ruth Ellen Semans, OH, CO, anc ch BGS 10:2:41

MACKEY, Charles b1755 w Harriet Thomas, Bible rec CTN 12:2:238

MACY, Charles b1831 w Mary Jane Meadows, KY, KS, MO, Bible rec TA 14:3:70

James Willis b1884 w Elsie Abigail Medcalf, OH, MN, anc ch WB 10:2:70

Thomas f1635, Eng, MA, geneal, bk rev CTN 7:3:361

William b1790 w Polly, VA, Bible rec TA 14:3:70

MAHIER, Richard d1722 w Mary Savage, VA, MA, will abstr RRS 12:2:226

MAHON, Jeduthan Carter f1884 w Betsy Pruitt, IL, fam recs FF 8:2:70

MAIER, Fred Adolph b1904 w Norma Mae Goldsmith, TX, anc ch NGI 3:2:110

MAIN, Eleazer b1791 w Margaret Cole, VA, OH, anc ch REP 19:1:27

MAINE, ancester rolls of SAR & NSDAR, bk rev CTN 8:4:640

Arrowsic Island, misc fam cem inscr DE 3:2:28

Auburn, marrs 1902-1977, bk rev GH 33:1:85

Belgrade, misc recs DE 2:5:30

3:2:29

Berwick, marrs DE 3:1:9

Bowdoinham, misc vr DE 3:3:18

cem sexton's journal 1843-1847 DE 3:1:4 3:2:4 3:3:5

Chesterville, census 1830 DE 2:5:31

China, Clark cem inscr DE 2:5:22

Cousins Island, hist, bk rev DE 3:4:30

East Monmouth, Town Farm Road cem inscr DE 3:1:17

Easton, residents 1855 DE 3:2:13

Easton, voters list 1892 DE 3:1:11

Eastport town report 1881-1882 DE 3:4:11

geneal dict 1928-1939, bk rev CTN 9:2:315

geneal dict to 1699 (1928), bk rev TB 6:3:24

geneal hist 1909 v1,2,3, bk rev REP 19:4:172

Georgetown, marrs 1759-1773 DE 2:5:10

McMahan Island, fam cems inscr DE 3:1:13

Georgetown Island, misc fam cem inscr DE 3:2:28

Hartford, Fuller cem inscr DE 3:3:17

Hiram, Freewill Bapt Ch rec 1825-1826 DE 3:1:22

hist 1920, bk rev DE 3:1:33

index to fam data in Noyes Collect, LDS DE 3:2:12

Leeds, early residents DE 3:2:9

Lewiston, St Joseph Cath Ch, marr recs 1858-1978, bk rev CDS 16:4:12

Kennebec, pet 1752 DE 3:2:15

Littlejohn Island, hist, bk rev DE 3:4:30

Machias, hist, bk rev DE 2:6:29

natives in early TX DE 3:1:20

natives in IL 1881 DE 3:4:26

natives in VA census 1850 DE 3:1:13

New Vineyard, geneal hist, bk rev CTN 10:2:350

Newry, Sunday River cem inscr

DE 3:2:18

Oakland, Old Lewis cem inscr DE 3:3:22

obits of 200 Fr-Am, bk rev CTN 10:1:59

Penobscot Co, Rev War soldiers, deaths DE 3:1:24

Piscataquis Co, Medford, voters list 1915 TRI 19:1:8

placenames dict, bk rev DE 3:4:31

residents in MA 1802 DE 2:5:32

Rev War pensioners in 1819 DE 3:3:11

Sangerville, birth recs DE 2:5:24

surname index at state lib DE 3:3:9

Washington Co, misc fam cem inscr DE 3:4:10

Winthrop, hist, bk rev DE 3:1:33

York, lightstation hist, bk rev DE 3:3:29

MAINWARING, Alfred A, cert of natural MI 1900 FG 21:3:59

MANES, Samuel Joseph m1920 w Ada Beryl Darrow, WA, biog notes RES 11:4:149

MANN, fam of IL, geneal, bk rev YP 9:4:226

fam recs in Suffolk Eng ch recs 1813-1861 BCG 7:1:16

George Adam b1734, PA, VA, KY, OH, geneal, bk rev YP 9:1:38 DM 42:3:135

MANNING, Amos b1772 w Joanne Ball, NJ, Bible rec WB 10:2:63

MANTZ, fam of MD, geneal MD 20:3:192

MARBLE, Frank S d1817 w Sarah Pender, WA, obit TB 6:4:18

Harry Elton b1903 w Madeline Hyland, WA, anc ch TB 6:1:26

Luvisa Ganer (Greene) b1830 h Ansil S Marble, OH, IA, OR, obits TB 6:4:17

MARCH, Hugh bc1615 w Judith Knight, Dorcas Bowman, Sarah Cutting, MA, fam rec DE 3:3:13

MARCHANT, Harriet Matilda (Cas-

per) b1849 h Albert Gerge Henry Marchant, MO, geneal, bk rev KCG 20:4:207 REP 19:4:174 GH 33:3:107

MARCHBANKS, Bromet Davis b1920 w Bula Mae Roberson, OK, anc ch THT 6:3:91

MARDEN, fam of NH, geneal, bk rev CTN 7:4:518

MARION, William Woodrow b1918 w Neva Ann Holman, IL, anc ch FF 8:2:27

MARK, Jonathan b1795 w Susannah Plougher Blocher, OH, anc ch REP 19:3:131

MARKER, Charlotte Walsh, anc ch, film rev GH 33:6:92

MARKHAM, Albert Dewey b1897 w Alice Hyland Miller, IL, anc ch FF 8:2:27

MARKS, Solon b1827 w Theodora Smith, VT, WI, biog notes BGS 10:4:23

MARKSTEIN, Moritz f1887 w Johanna Mosner, Hungary, photo & biog notes JJG 3:4:28

MARLAR, John Thomas dc1803, MD, notes on NGS 67:1:63

MARLETT, William Carlow b1886 w Rosa Lee Hope, TX, AL, anc ch FF 8:3:60

MARLEY, John f1793, NY, notes on NGS 67:1:61

MARQUART, Oliver P b1882 w Bessie R Knepper, IN, anc ch ACL 4:2:33

MARSHAL, William bc1146, Eng, biog EG 12:266

MARSHALL James b1867 w Florence Margaret Munson, ME, NB, CT, anc ch DE 3:3:23

James Frank b1872 w Rose Jacobi, OH, MO, anc ch REP 19:3:122

Thomas Marcellus b1851 w Olive Augusta Hays, WV, NM, fam rec NMG 18:3:81

MARTIN, Agrippa D b1810 w Mary C Greggor, Elvra C Webb, OH, Bible rec AH 4:3:85

David, MD, PA, Bible rec NA 2:2:40

James b1793 w Barbara A Sigafoos, PA, OH, anc ch REP 19:1:32

John b1616 w Ann, Eng, VA, geneal, bk rev GH 33:5:86

John b1814 w Mary Barnhart, OH, anc ch REP 19:2:86

John Presley bc1776 w Nancy, PA, VA, geneal, bk rev GFP 29:4:67

Joseph Constant m1857 w Lucy Julia Pagnard, IN, Bible rec NW 2:4:118

Lulie E (Dyer) b1879 h A V Martin, AR, OK, obit MGR 14:4:178

Mary, TN letters 1829, 1837 & 1843 CI 14:2:53

Roland Alfred b1916 w Bernadette Henriette Langevin, Can, anc ch BGS 9:4:40

William b1814 w Nancy Robinson, KY cem inscr TSP 3:1:42

William f1852, Scot, NY, WI, biog notes BGS 7:3:15

William Kinney b1853 w Adelaide Jane (Rankin) Martin Franklin, TN, Bible rec BWG 8:1:29

MARTZ, Ronald Vaughn b1906 w Edith Mae Lewis, WA, IN, anc ch RED 11:4:17

MARVEL. Prettyman d1842 w Rebecca Carr, SC, IL, biog & fam rec DWC 5:3:61

MARWOOD, Horace Arthur b1894, biog notes BCG 7:3:46

MARYLAND, Anne Arundel Co, southern county cem inscr, bk rev PGB 11:9:101

Baltimore, black Republicans on City Council 1890-1931 MHM 74:3:203

Canton dist, hist, bk rev MO 20:2:135

city archives res guide MMG 2:2:49

George L Schwab funeral home recs, notes on MD 20:4:330

First & St Stephen's United Ch of Christ (formerly First Reformed Ch of Baltimore), bapt & birth recs 1816-1820 MD 20:3:225 20:4:300

First & St Stephen's United Ch of Christ (formerly First Reformed Ch of Baltimore), marr recs 1806-1838 MD 20:4:305

Lake Roland hist MHM 74:3:253

manual training hist MHM 74:3:238

natural index 1797-1853 MD 20:4:287

news abstr marrs & deaths 1796-1816, bk rev TST 11:48:44 VAG 23:1:69 NYR 110:1:58 MD 20:3:243 WCK 12:1:16 CTN 12:1:178 NGS 67:1:68 AG 55:2:124

"Sun" news marrs 1851-1869 index, bk rev TST 11:52:45 VAG 23:1:70 NYR 110:1:58 MD 20:3:243 WCK 12:1:16 NGS 67:1:68 AG 55:2:124

practicing medicine at the Almshouse 1828-1850 MHM 74:3:223

residents 1785-1795 NGS 67:3:202 67:4:283

yellow fever epidemic 1800 MHM 74:3:282

Baltimore Co, Green Spring Valley, hist & geneal vl-2, bk rev NGS 67:1:71

hist, bk rev MHM 74:4:367

Oella cem inscr MD 20:1:56

St John's Parish Christ Ch reg 1819-1861 MD 20:4:269

wills index 1659-1850, bk rev MMG 2:2:85

biog dict of MD legislature 1635-1789 vl A-H, bk rev MD 20:4:361

Calvert Co, wills 1654-1700, bk rev NGS 67:4:305

Caroline Co, soldiers in War of 1812 MD 20:3:184

court depositions & affidavits as evidence of age 1637-1657 MMG 2:2:68

deaths & births in the MD Penitentiary MMG 2:2:55

Elkton, letters unclaimed 1825 MD 20:4:323

first fams descendants, bk rev KCG 20:2:91

Frederick, Ger Reformed Ch cem,

notes on MD 20:4:330

Frederick Co, burials of Rev War soldiers MD 20:3:201

cem sites MD 20:3:211

census 1850, bk rev NGS 67:3:227 MMG 2:2:85

misc news abstr MMG 2:2:76

Monocacy Valley settlers 1707-1743 REP 19:4:143

geneal res guide TST 12:37:23 PGB 11:X:4

bk rev OK 24:2:73

Harford Co, Amos Jones fam cem inscr MD 20:1:89

non-associators 1776 BGS 11:4:167

St John's Parish Christ Ch reg 1819-1861 MD 20:4:269

Herring Creek Parish, St James, hist 1663-1799, bk rev YP 9:2:101

hist biblio MHM 74:4:358

hist of industrial slavery 1715-1865, bk rev MHM 74:4:368

Kent Co, census 1800 MD 20:2:138

marr lic 1796-1850 & ministers, bk rev NGS 67:4:304

marrs 1634-1777, bk rev CTN 10:1:157

misc early fams, bk rev GH 33:3:103

misc marr & death notices 1797-1798 MD 20:3:198

Montgomery Co, abstr of wills 1776-1825, bk rev CTN 11:1:46

atlas 1879, bk rev CTN 11:1:46

news abstr vl 1855-1856, bk rev NGS 67:3:223

"Sentinel" news abstr 1855-1856, bk rev MD 20:4:361

Prince George's Co, Bowie, hist of Belle Air, bk rev PGB 11:10:118

indexes of ch reg 1686-1885, bk rev PGB 11:1:4 11:5:49

slave transported to KY PGB 11:5:52

slaves registered & manumitted 1696-1803 PGB 11:3:24

Suitland, hist, bk rev PGB 11:8:90

will bk 1 1698-1770 abstr PGB 11:2:14 11:4:38

Rev War, naval barges hist, bk rev MHM 74:4:372

St Mary's Co, hist, bk rev PGB 11"3"28

Somerset Co, misc wills abstr CDS 16:3:1

source recs index, bk rev OK 24:2:74

Ukrainians of MD hist, bk rev MHM 74:3:301

Westminster, hist, bk rev MHM 74:3:300

MASON, William Absalom b1894 w Mahala Elizabeth Rush, IL, anc ch FP 8:4:72

MASSACHUSETTS, Amesbury, hist, bk rev NGS 67:1:74 AG 55:1:58

misc marrs & deaths KN 2:3:37 2:4:23

Barnstable, fams geneal (1888), bk rev MQ 45:4:229 CTN 12:4:702 NGS 67:4:308

West Barnstable cem inscr MQ 45:2:93 45:3:155 45:4:221

Bedford, First Parish (Cong) Ch, hist 1710-1834, bk rev CTN 11:2:342

Billerica, hist (1883), bk rev BCG 6:1:8

Boston, Archives of Chancery Archdiocese descr CTA 22:2:95

marrs & deaths 1630-1699 & births 1700-1800 (1993/1894), bk rev DM 42:3:135 MQ 45:4:231 CTN 11:3:528 NGS 67:1:73 AG 55:1:57

marrs 1700-1809 (1903), bk rev CTN 10:4:704

misc city documents 1720-1721 CDS 16:1:31

New England Home for Little Wanderers, orphan placement in IN HG 19:4:78

news abstr marrs 1792 NER 133:4:306

notarial recs 1644-1651 (Aspinwall), bk rev TB 6:3:21

census index 1800, bk rev NYR 110:1:54 DM 42:3:135 CTN 11:4:700 NGS 67:1:73

Concord, fams of, geneal

(1887), bk rev BGS 9:2:35

Cummington, hist, bk rev ANC 14:4:122

vr 1792-1900, bk rev MQ 45:4:228

freemen 1630-1691 (1849), bk rev NYR 110:1:54 NGS 67:1:72

geneal notes of first settlers (1856), bk rev CTN 11:4:698

geographic dict 1894, bk rev NYR 110:3:184 CTN 11:4:700 NGS 67:1:73

Hadley, geneal hist (1905), bk rev CTN 12:4:703 MQ 45:4:229 NGS 67:4:307

Harvard College, hist notes MQ 45:2:57

hist data re counties & towns MCR 10:4:96

Lancaster, early recs on microfiche, bk rev CDS 16:3:5

marrs to 1800 (1898), bk rev CTN 9:2:317 MQ 45:4:230

"MA Magazine" marr & death notices 1789-1796, bk rev DM 43:2:88

Massachusetts Bay Colony planters 1623-1636 (1846), bk rev CTN 8:2:318

MA Soc of genealogists CTN 9:4:639

"Mayflower", descs opf Francis Eaton, Samuel Fuller & William White, bk rev IL 11:3:178 CDS 16:6:43

descs of James Chilton, Richard More & Thomas Rogers, bk rev GH 33:4:112 IL 11:3:178 DM 43:1:44 NGS 67:4:303 TB 6:4:31 CDS 16:6:43 CLG 10:1:58

pass & settlement hist BGS 2:3:4

misc "Mayflower" desc (1977), bk rev TB 6:3:23

Merrimac, hist, bk rev AG 55:1:58 NGS 67:1:74

Newburyport, hist memories 1879, bk rev TST 11:51:37 AG 55:1:58

notes on Puritans & Pilgrims DAR 113:5:488

Old Post Road, hist & cem

inscr, bk rev REP 19:3:136

Otis, hist (Haskell), bk rev CTN 9:4:608

Pilgrim chronicles 1602-1625 (1844), bk rev CTN 7:1:129

Plymaouth, Burial Hill cem inscr (1892), bk rev CTN 10:4:705

Col court recs 1665 CDS 16:2:1

First Ch in Plymouth, hist & recs 1620-1859, bk rev CTN 8:1:38

marrs to 1650, bk rev CTN 11:3:527 AG 55:1:58

poverty in 18th century NER 133:4:243

reg of civil & mil lists 1802, bk rev GH 33:2:79 DE 2:6:32 CTN 12:1:180 CDS 16:2:3 RRS 12:X:2

Salem, hist vl-3 1924-8, bk rev CTN 9:3:472

Salisbury, misc marrs & deaths KN 2:3:37 2:4:23

Scituate, vr to 1850, bk rev TB 6:2:20

Springfield, early school recs DM 43:2:69

hist 17th century NER 133:3:163

Taunton, hist, bk rev TB 6:1:34

Yarmaouth, vr to 1850 vl,2, bk rev IL 11:3:179

MASSEY, geneal supp, bk rev WCK 12:4:66 FP 22:4:211

William w Catherine Taylor, IL, letters c1847 BGS 2:1:5

MATHEWS, Joel Nelson b1845 w Rachel Luraney Renfroe, GA, anc ch YP 9:2:67

MATHIAS, fam of VA& WV, geneal, bk rev REP 19:4:174

MATTHEWS, Mark b1824 w Elizabeth Jane Shearn, Eng, OH, anc ch REP 19:1:26

William bc1788 w Priscilla Bankston, VA, GA, fam rec DCG 2:10:2

MATTIX, Chester Leroy b1918 w Opal Catherine, KS, anc ch TOP 9:1:14

MAUGANS, Conrad bc1735, MD, geneal, bk rev REP 19:1:43

MAULDIN, Elihu C b1809 w Eliza Biggs, SC, TX, obit THT 7:2:105

Walter Gabriel b1887 w Alma Anna Arrant, TX, anc ch THT 7:2:71

William Henry b1856 w Minnie A, Callie C Bemis, TX, AZ, NM, biog notes THT 2:1:25

MAUPIN, Henley b1855 w Ida Clarke, Minnie Adella Peters, OR, biog notes ORB 17:9:84

MAURER, Peter b1787 w Mary, IL, biog MH 6:3:29

MAXFIELD, Hiram f1840 w Jane, TN, IL, heirsin probate 1877 CI 15:1:33

MAXWELL, John C b1802 w Sara Jane Hickey, VA, OR, biog notes ORB 18:2:27

MAY, John f1640, Eng, MA, geneal 1878, bk rev GH 33:4:118 CTN 12:1:183

MAYER, Charles Milton b1885 w Susie Elter, IA, NE, anc ch NW 2:3:98

Jacob w Regina Schram, Ger, Russ, SD, geneal, bk rev TB 6:2:23

MAYFIELD, Luke b1777 w Delila Gore, SC, Bible rec GGM 74:298

MAYHEW, George Washington b1803 w Mary Pattin, OH, anc ch BGS 10:4:43

Nathaniel b1725 w Mary McFadden, MA, ME, fam letter DE 3:3:10

geneal, bk rev BGS 5:2:19

MAYNARD, Moses Putney b1819 w Angelina Armstrong, Elizabeth Watkins, NY, WI, Bible rec YV 11:3:142

MAYO, Henry Hunt b1810 w Louisa Winston, Bible rec BR 6:2:60

Mercy f1738 h John Cole, MA, geneal MQ 45:4:201

MAZE, William H d1855 w Frances Ann, IL, probate & fam recs IG 14:4:130

MEECH, Gordon b1771 w Lucy Swan, CT, Bible rec CTA 21:3:122

MEEK, Meek-Meehs Newsletter, Box 7151, Washington DC 20044

MEIGS, Lumas b1795, VT, Can, geneal, bk rev CTN 11:3:525

MELANCON, Aime m1865 w Marie Elvina Perillou, LA, anc ch AGE 8:3:98

MELVIN, Nathaniel P w Sarah Rowe, Bible rec BGS 8:4:13

MENDENHALL, Albert D b1857 w Lenora J (Reid) Lamar, Bible rec IG 15:2:57

geneal notes QY 6:1:9 6:2:9 6:3:10 6:4:11

Willie b1891 h A B "Cowboy" Mendenhall, TX, obit THT 5:2:1

MENNONITE, Amish, hist, bk rev PM 2:3:24

misc documents PM 2:3:12

pioneers in OH, bk rev CDS 16:5:47

pioneers in Switz & Europe, bk rev CDS 16:5:47

biblio 1631-1961 v1-2, bk rev PM 2:1:22

hist lib IN, descr TB 6:4:4

hist notes SCS 14:4:92

hist of Anabaptists from Russ to Am, bk rev TB 6:2:22

Hutterite Menn hist, bk rev TB 6:2:23

Lancaster Menn Conf hist soc JG 4:3:7

lib PA, guide TST 12:1:52

scrapbook of migration from Russ 1870-1885, bk rev TB 6:2:22

Swiss Menn fam names annotated JG 4:3:24 4:5:27

MERCER, fam of IN, fam rec KN 2:1:23

John C b1827 w Miss Castillo, KY, biog VQ 16:4:59

Robert b1759 w Eleanor Tittermary, NJ, geneal, bk rev NGS 67:2:152

MERCHANT, Robert b1797 w Lucretia Stewart, Scot, IN, OH, OR, cem & biog notes GFP 29:2:34 29:3:51

MERRICK, John b1826, CT, MN, auto notes, bk rev CTN 11:4:702

MERRIFIELD, John b1782 w Elizabeth, TX, biog notes DG 25:3:162

MERRILL, fam of OH, misc letters 1866 AH 6:1:31

John d1682, MA, biog notes DE 3:1:18

Moses d1840, NE, notes on NA 2:1:28

Nathaniel d1655 w Susannah Willerton, MA, fam rec DE 3:1:18

Trumbull S b1810, CT, OH, biog notes AH 1:3:30

MERRITT, Fred M, NE, notes on NW 2:2:58

MERSHON, Henry bc1672, NY, NJ, geneal, bk rev GJ 8:2:118

MERWIN, Miles f1630, CT, geneal, bk rev CTN 12:4:696

METHODOLOGY, abbreviations used in queries NW 2:2:51

Am pedigree building, bk rev OG 3:1:28

ancestor detecting, bk rev TST 11:40:28 IL 11:1:56 AG 55:2:124

anthology of geneal 1958, bk rev SCS 15:3:86 ACL 4:1:6

automated documentation communication format GJ 8:1:34

basic guide to geneal, bk rev GH 33:2:71 FH 2:3:96 MGR 14:1:10

begin climbing your ancestree, bk rev GH 33:4:109

beginner's guide to geneal, bk rev OG 4:3:88

beginner's manual, bk rev MQ 45:3:161

beginner's booklet on geneal, bk rev GH 33:3:97

beginner's guide to tracing ancestors, bk rev GH 33:3:97

Burke method of recording fam hist GN 2:4:143

calendar dates changes FH 2:2:60

calendar explanations AGE 8:2:40 CI 13:1:4

cem inscr types CTN 11:2:187

cem searching tips ORB 18:3:52

census research notes GR 21:2:73 FR 2:4:114,124

certification of genealogists GH 33:4:5 LL 14:4:152 PGB 11:X:1

child's guide to geneal, bk rev BB 11:4:69

city directory as source FH 2:2:54

Col geneal res guide IL 11:4:201

communal soc as geneal source JCG 7:3:57

computer use in fam hist NER 133:3:194

correspondence NGI 3:1:20

court case as source JG 4:5:23

creating fam hist, bk rev QY 6:1:2 TB 6:4:27 CDS 16:6:44

definitions of words found in old documents STK 7:4:166

discover ancestors, bk rev GJ 8:1:51 AG 55:1:59

documenting your recs BGS 11:1:33

Draper collect, notes on AH 3:3:96

early Am handwriting & abbreviations ANC 14:3:95

early geneal, bk rev CTN 10:3:523

evaluating evidence CDS 16:3:13 16:6:3 SCS 14:2:57

everyone has roots, bk rev AG 55:1:59

fam heritage res guide, bk rev GH 33:1:81

fam hist handbook, bk rev GJ 8:4:216

fam hist for fun & profit, bk rev CTN 7:4:519

fam newsletter guide, bk rev AW 5:1:22

fam tree coloring bk, bk rev AG 55:2:128

find your roots, bk rev GJ 8:2:121

finding geneal bks in Eng TST 12:11:37

finding your ancestors, school ed, bk rev GH 33:4:109

finding your roots, bk rev OG 5:1:28 CTN 10:3:521 SCS 15:1:24

forming a fam assoc CTN 12:1:15

geneal & hist in Biblical work, bk rev GJ 8:2:122

geneal columns list BGS 11:3:94

geneal definitions TST 12:27:47

geneal dict KA 15:2:127

geneal documents abstracting SCR 2:3:10

geneal evidence, bk rev NER 133:4:311

geneal libs, guide & descr BGS 8:3:4 8:4:1 9:1:7 9:2:1

geneal merit badge (Boy Scouts) CTN 7:1:2

geneal my way, bk rev CTN 11:4:526

geneal periods CO 40:2:59

geneal pioneers FAM 18:4:146

geneal res at court house BGS 8:1:8

geneal res at home BGS 8:1:5

geneal res guide GH 33:2:11 TST 11:42:28 11:46:26 11:49:36 11:50:44 12:17:31 12:18:36 12:24:39 EWA 16:3:125 MD 20:2:137 20:3:178,224 20:4:289.190 GL 13:3:72 CTN 7:4:483

geneal res guide to midwest, bk rev TRI 19:3:38

geneal source handbook, bk rev BB 11:4:69 GH 33:6:76

geneal sources REF 21:2:20

getting started, bk rev TB 6:4:30

glossary of law terms ANC 14:1:14 14:2:70 14:3:99 14:4:136

gravestone rubbing SCS 14:3:100 PF 8:4:85

guide to geneal, bk rev YP 9:4:228

guide to LDS geneal res seminar, bk rev TB 6:4:33

guide to reference aids for genealogists, bk rev KN 2:4:26

handbk for geneal correspondence, bk rev OG 2:3:88

heraldry & hist for beginners, bk rev NYR 110:4:250

hiring a professional TST 12:12:37 HH 14:2:68

how to find fam roots, bk rev BCG 8:4:79

how to trace across the Atlantic Ocean BCG 5:1:12

how to trace fam hist, bk rev TST 11:50:45 NYR 110:3:184 NGI 3:1:34 BB 11:4:69 DWC 5:3:88 TB 6:1:4 6:3:24

how to trace your fam roots, bk rev CTN 12:1:178

imm geneal res guide, film rev GH 33:6:92

in search of fam tree, bk rev NGI 3:1:32

indexing TB 6:2:5

indexing vital statistics TST 12:33:37

introduction to geneal, bk rev ACL 4:1:6

know your ancestors (Williams), bk rev CTN 7:1:131 ACL 4:1:6 IR 11:1:71

land recs use in research IG 14:3:89 14:4:121 MN 10:3:132 SGS 29:2:103

LDS ch recs & res aids, bk rev TST 11:40:28 GJ 8:1:54 AG 55:2:124

LDS recs, descr & use TST 11:47:29 12:23:41 12:25:46 YV 11:2:81

letter inquiries guide, bk rev DG 2:2:58

lib res CO 40:3:93 40:4:147

maps, as source TST 11:52:44 BGS 8:4:3 DM 42:3:144 SCS 15:3:71 15:4:101

sources for purchase of THT 5:3:4

migration, reasons for HG 19:4:94 AH 1:2:5

mil recs, geneal res guide BGS 9:4:1

misc geneal sources KN 2:2:3 CDS 16:2:13 16:4:3 16:5:3 DCG 2:10:18

names AH 1:2:12

needlework samplers & mourning pictures as geneal source NGS 67:3:167

newspapers as a geneal & hist resource SCR 2:3:1

news geneal columns, bk rev DE 3:2:31

oral hist NGS 67:1:25 ORB
18:2:21 FH 2:2:50
oral hist manual, bk rev MHM
74:4:374
paper preservation CO 40:1:12
photographs, analysis, bk rev
CTN 11:2:341
 as source & preservation HH
14:2:65 MKT 2:1:6
 dating photos SCS 16:3:76
 guide to photographing old
photos TST 11:48:36 11:51:37
 heritage guide, bk rev GJ
8:4:216
 hist BGS 5:1:20a BCG 5:4:37
postcards as geneal source TST
11:44:28
preparing for a res visit TST
12:10:36
preserving fam photographs CHI
52:1:46
primer for basic geneal res, bk
rev IL 11:4:237
probate recs use GE 43:1
professional code for geneal
libs & librarians NGS 67:1:11
professional ethics in geneal
res NGS 67:1:3 67:4:243
Protestant Ch recs biblio &
sources NSN 4:6:56
publicizing your geneal bk, bk
rev GE 44:14 VAG 23:1:72 IG
15:1:8 KA 14:4:254 GGM 74:165
CI 14:4:151 CDS 16:5:45
publishing geneal BGS 3:1:1 PF
9:2:24 TST 12:22:39
publish it yourself, bk rev ACL
4:3:55
res aids for Col period, bk rev
BGS 9:2:35
res at a univ lib TB 6:1:7
researcher's guide to Am geneal
(Greenwood), bk rev CTN
7:1:131 TB 6:3:23
res alternate spellings, bk rev
CTN 12:1:182
search & res guide, bk rev SCS
15:2:46
search of fam tree, bk rev GJ
8:1:53
searching for your ancestors
(Doane), bk rev CTN 7:1:131
searching mil recs, bk rev GH

33:4:109
searching state, co & city recs
CTN 8:3:323
soundex coding system guide TST
12:8:44 12:10:37 12:13:38
speed indexing, bk rev VAG
23:1:72 IG 15:1:8 KA 14:4:254
GGM 73:165
sure guide to geneal res, bk
rev TB 6:3:25
systematic approach to geneal
res CDS 16:1:13
terms of relationship in Col
times AG 55:1:52
trace your roots notebk, bk rev
DM 42:4:185
tracing your ancestors, bk rev
OG 4:4:117
 guide for beginner, bk rev KCN
20:1:47 BGS 11:2:75
 today, bk rev KCG 20:2:91
using time line in geneal res
BB 11:3:49
US Govt Printing Office as
source TST 12:26:47
use of auto in fam hist
research FH 2:3:82 2:4:116
use of hist demography in fam
hist GJ 8:1:3
using printed genealogies FH
2:3:92 CTN 9:3:341
verifying of facts TST 12:21:54
where to write for, birth &
death recs, bk rev TB 6:3:26
 divorce recs, bk rev TB 6:3:26
 geneal information in a
foreign country SCS 14:4:97
 marr recs, bk rev TB 6:3:26
 war, pension & military recs,
bk rev TB 6:4:33
wills as geneal source BCG
6:3:3
writing auto & fam hist, bk rev
OG 4:3:88 HTR 22:1:5
writing fam hist GH 33:3:8 TST
11:51:36 BGS 6:2:26 TT 19:1:3
CTN 10:2:205 FG 21:475 STK
7:3:109
writing letters for geneal information MCH 7:1:16 TST
12:9:44 12:27:48 CTN 8:3:335
writing queries EWA 16:2:77
your fam hist, bk rev GJ

8:2:115

your fam hist handbk, bk rev GJ
8:2:121

METOYER, Nicholas Augustin
b1768, LA, biog notes FH
2:2:78

METZGER, Jacob b1747 w Mary, OH,
Bible rec MIS 11:4:56

MEXICAN-AMERICAN GENEALOGY,
geneal res guide, bk rev GH
33:5:69

MEYRING, Henry b1838 w Caroline
Sarah Sutton, Ger, NJ, CO,
geneal BGS 8:3:17

MEXICO, basic res in parish &
civil reg, part 2 SPG 31:582

preliminary survey of LDS recs,
bk rev SPG 31:589

MICHIGAN, Alger Co, courthouse
fire 1978, report on damage
DM 42:3:143

atlas 1873, bk rev GE 44:13

Berrien Co, Bertrand Twp, cem
inscr, bk rev GH 33:1:85

New Buffalo Twp, cem inscr, bk
rev GH 33:1:85

Niles Twp, Higbee cem inscr PF
8:3:65

Pearl Grange cem inscr PF
9:2:41

Berrien Springs, area scrapbk
index PF 9:2:26

Calhoun Co, Battle Creek,
Friends meeting & burial
ground recs MI 24:4:125

tax list 1838-1842 DM 42:4:169

cem compendium, bk rev TB
6:2:20

census 1840, index to, bk rev
CTN 12:1:181

Chippawa Co, Stalwart, hist MI
24:3:85

ch archives inv MI 24:1:14

Detroit, Burton lib hist
collect CTN 7:3:344

census 1860, index to, bk rev
CTN 12:1:182

Christ Ch marr recs 1849-1879
DM 42:3:115 42:4:161 43:1:35
43:2:81

church farm hist DM 42:3:107

hist (1926), bk rev TB 6:4:28

legends 1669-1815, bk rev OC

16:4:136

Dickinson Co, census 1894 DM
42:3:119 42:4:165

Emmet Co, Charlevoix Twp, census 1860 MI 24:2:52

Flint, Flint Cong Ch bapt list
1879 FG 21:1:6

photographers FG 21:3:70

geneal res index to periods, bk
rev GH 33:6:81

Genesee Co, Argentine school
pupils 1873 FG 21:4:91

death recs 1870-1871 FG 21:1:7
21:3:62 21:4:94

farmers acct bk 1886-1888 OC
16:2:57

Forest Twp, Otisville, hist &
map FG 21:3:55

geneal data in wills over 100
years old FG 21:1:15 21:2:35
21:3:64 21:4:96

marr recs 1857-1858 FG 21:1:10
21:2:41 21:3:60 21:4:92

Grand Rapids, carpenters &
joiners union 1884 MI 24:3:84

hist collects 1892, bk rev AW
5:2:60

hist notes BGS 1:1:6 1:2:4

imms from Can FAM 18:4:169

imms from RI RIR 5:2:17

index guide to sources in geneal periods, bk rev TST
12:21:56

Kent Co, Cedar Springs, news
extracts MI 24:2:48

centennial fams MI 24:3:82

inventory of recs MI 24:4:121

Lapeer, Turrill GAR Post 144
members 1883-1936, notes on
FG 21:1:16 21:3:66 21:4:98

Leelanau Co, death recs from
1867 DM 42:3:123 42:4:157
43:1:31 43:2:77

Lenawee Co, news death notices
1838-1865 DM 43:1:27 43:2:73

Livingston Co, Hartland Twp,
Hodges cem inscr DM 42:4:177

Lewis cem inscr DM 43:2:86

Manistee, Polish geneal sources PN 1:2:29

Montcalm Co, Greenville, Meth
Ch bapt 1855-1868 MI 24:2:88
24:4:123

Oakland Co, hist, bk rev BGS 9:4:35

Ogemaw Co, early plat maps, bk rev GH 33:1:86

Ora Labora, hist TST 12:21:54

Ottowa Co, Allendale Twp, direct 1876 MI 24:1:17

Olive Twp, direct 1876 MI 24:1:17

Talmadge Twp, direct 1876 MI 24:1:15

pioneer biogs DM 42:3:114 42:4:181 43:1:39 43:2:64

pioneers from OH, biog notes AH 3:2:48 3:3:84 3:4:122 4:1:13 4:2:54

Saginaw Co, Birch Run Twp, cem inscr TTL 7:1:7 7:2:35

Birch Run Twp, land recs TTL 7:4:114

Blumfield Twp, land recs TTL 7:2:41

Bridgeport Twp, land recs TTL 7:1:20

Chesaning Twp, Chesaning Twp mausoleum, Wildwood cem inscr TTL 7:3:78

Chesaning Twp, tax assessment 1882 TTL 7:2:54 7:3:82 7:4:99 emigs TTL 7:1:11

Frankenmuth Twp, land recs TTL 7:3:87

Kochville Meth Ch recs 1881-1891 TTL 7:3:76

map 1850 TTL 7:2:46

marrs 1860-1862 TTL 7:1:2 7:2:45 7:3:94 7:4:106

probate recs TTL 7:4:119

Saginaw Twp, census TTL 7:4:102

Saginaw Twp, Jefferson Ave Meth Ch marrs 1876-1880 TTL 7:1:14 7:2:36 7:3:72

Saginaw Twp, misc news abstr TTL 7:4:120,127

Saginaw Twp, Saints Peter & Paul Cath Ch birth recs TTL 7:1:13

Saginaw Twp, school reg 1879-1882 TTL 7:1:24

Tittabawassee Twp, census 1850 TTL 7:2:48 7:3:68

St Joseph Co, Hill Side cem

recs MI 24:1:18

Ives cem recs MI 24:1:20

Wood Side cem recs MI 24:1:20

Tawas City, "Herald" issues listed FG 21:1:6

Washtenaw Co, cem direct, bk rev GH 33:3:100 FAM 18:4:227

map direct, bk rev TST 12:14:39

Wayne Co, Brownstown Twp, Vreeland, cem inscr DM 43:1:60

census index 1860, bk rev NYR 110:3:186 GH 33:2:79 CTN 12:1:182

Detroit, census 1765 DM 43:1:19

Detroit, census index 1860, bk rev GH 33:2:79 NYR 110:3:186

Huron Twp, Nowland cem inscr DM 42:4:180

Nankin Twp, acct bk 1841-1843 of Harry Lewis DM 43:2:70

Plymouth Twp, Riverside cem inscr DM 43:2:65

MIDDLETON, Doc, biog, bk rev NA 2:2:46

fam of MD, geneal MD 20:2:126

MIDKIFF, John Rufus b1835 w Louisa Maria Cole, Bible rec THT 2:1:8

Thomas Oscar b1872 w Lillian Davenport, GA, TX, anc ch THT 7:1:12

auto THT 3:3:63

William b1833 w Elizabeth Frances Cole, Bible rec THT 2:1:8

MIESSLER, E G H b1826 w Johanna Pinkepank, Ger, MI, auto CHI 52:4:146

MILLARD, Samuel H b1820 w Maria L Blevins, TN, Bible rec BWG 8:1:41

MILLER, A D m1895 w Mary L McPheeters, IL, biog notes MCH 7:1:19

Abraham b1820 w Sallie A Bashore, OH, anc ch REP 19:1:35

Charles R m1895 w Mary Eliza Adamson, IL, geneal CI 15:4:125

Eri b1768 w Laura Perkins, Bible rec MI 24:4:120

Henry b1766 w Polly, NY,

geneal, bk rev NGI 3:1:31

Henry b1804 w Ellenor, Bible rec IG 15:1:6

Henry f1848 w Mary Goyer, PA, anc ch REP 19:3:127

Jesse f1840, OH, MO, biog notes BGS 2:1:7

John bc1604 w Lydia Coombs, Eng, MA, fam recs CTN 7:3:480

John b1817 w Ruth Ann (Franklin) Hunt, OH, OR, biog notes ORB 17:8:71

John b1819 w Katharina Stempel, Ger, OH, anc ch REP 19:3:125

John G m1882 w Martha Jane Bates, MA, MO, MN, Bible rec IL 11:3:129

John George b1862, MA, letter 1918 SGS 29:4:317

John Lowery b1858 w Sarah Elizabeth Lynch, IN, TX, anc ch HJA 6:3:49

Lafayette b1840 w Mary Elizabeth Foote, IL, CO, geneal BGS 11:2:53

Lloyd Francis w Helene Nansina Wrang Fischer, IL, anc ch FF 8:2:28

Marilyn b1898 (Mary Ellen Reynolds), IN, OH, biog notes TSP 3:1:14

Oliver Pierce b1888 w Jessie Ethel Steedley, AL, anc ch NAS 18:1:7

Robert (Rev) b1767 w Mary Highfield, Elizabeth Hanson, MD, KY, OH, biog notes TST 11:43:29 11:44:28 11:45:29

Tipton A b1842 w Mattie A Lassiter, KY, biog VQ 16:3:48

William bc1837 w Mary King, Sara Maia Green, NY, fam rec ANC 14:4:120

William Clyde b1880 w Maude Elsie Mason, IA, anc ch NGI 3:2:114

William Patterson b1885 w Lydia Ruth Freeman, TN, CA, anc ch RED 11:4:18

MILLERD, Jesse b1784 w Lucinda Loomis, VT, Bible rec SCS 16:2:46

MILLIKIN, James, homestead IL 1876 CI 12:2

MILLION, John J b1888, IL, anc ch RRS 12:1:75

MILLS, fam geneal, bk rev QY 6:1:2 KCG 20:2:94

John bc1660 w Sarah Harrold?, Eng, PA, geneal, bk rev GH 33:3:107

MINISH, Archie Ray b1894 w Elva Lorena Voorhees, IA, anc ch NW 2:3:90

MINNESOTA, Anoka Co, Blaine, poll list 1902 MN 10:3:145

archives guide descr TST 11:41:29

Big Stone Co, Artichoke Twp, Johnson fam cem inscr PR 3:1:16

Prior Twp, St Paul's Ch cem inscr PR 3:1:17

Blue Earth Co, abandoned cems inscr PR 3:1:14

Brown Co, Bashaw Twp, tax recs abstr 1878 PR 3:1:10

Chippewa Co, abandoned cems inscr PR 3:1:15

Louriston Twp, First Swedish Meth Epis cem inscr PR 3:1:16

Chisago Co, Sunrise cem inscr NGI 3:2:101 3:3:153

ch recs on microfilm PR 3:1:20

Cottonwood Co, Dale Twp, Epp cem, notes on PR 3:2:46

GAR recs PR 3:1:7

Midway Twp, Teichroew cem, notes on PR 3:2:46

Springfield Twp, soldiers cem inscr PR 3:1:18

Windom, old soldiers cem inscr PR 3:1:17

Windom camp, vets charter 1887 PR 3:2:28

Fillmore Co, Arendahl Norwegian Luth Ch cem inscr NGI 3:3:155

guide to the sources v1, bk rev MGR 14:2:62

Hennepin Co, Maple Grove Twp, Maple Knoll cem inscr MN 10:4:191

Kandiyohi Co, deeds index 1858-1870 PR 3:3:77

grantor index to bk A deeds 1857-1871 PR 3:3:53

Gennessee Twp, Atwater Norwegian Evan Luth Ch cem inscr PR 3:2:31

Fahlun Twp, Bethesda Evan cem inscr PR 3:2:33

Kandiyohi Twp, Old Bapt cem inscr PR 3:2:34

Lake Elizabeth Twp, Pioneer Union cem inscr PR 3:2:34

Pioneer cem inscr PR 3:1:3

LeSueur Co, marr recs 1854-1859 MN 10:4:158

Lincoln Co, Tyler, land office notices 1881-1884 PR 3:2:35

Lake Benton, land office notices 1879-1883 PR 3:2:40

Mankato, Hubbard Milling Co hist, bk rev GH 33:4:110

Mapleton, hist, bk rev GH 33:4:112

Martin Co, Manyaska Twp, Lone Cedar cem hist & inscr PR 3:2:29

Westford Twp, Horicon cem hist & burials PR 3:1:19

Pleasant Prairie Twp, Imogene, Rose Lake cem hist & recs PR 3:3:51

misc private burials recs PR 3:2:30

mort sched index 1860, bk rev GH 33:2:79 TB 6:2:17 KCG 20:1:46

Mower Co, cem recs v1, bk rev PR 3:1:2

New Ulm, hist 1853-1899, bk rev GH 33:1:86

news direct 1849-1860, bk rev OG 2:2:58

Nobles Co, Indian Lake Twp, Indian Lake Bapt Ch cem inscr MN 10:4:162

Ottertail Co, cem recs v5, bk rev PR 3:1:2

Pembina, half breeds memorial MN 10:3:111

Redwood Co, abandoned cems inscr PR 3:1:13

Redwood Falls, news abstr 1874 PR 3:4:76

Renville Co, Bird Island, news abstr 1879-1882 PR 3:4:69

Rice Co, Dundas, Ch of the Holy Cross (Epis) parish reg 1865-1886 PR 3:4:73

Traverse Co, Brown's Valley, St Luke's Epis Ch parish reg PR 3:2:32

US post offices, bk rev PR 3:1:2

Waseca Co, Vivan Twp, Mycue cem inscr PR 3:4:71

Washington Co, Guardian Angel's Cath Ch cem inscr MN 10:3:117

Newport cem inscr MN 10:4:179

Red Rock cem inscr MN 10:1:37

Salem Evan Luth Ch cem inscr MN 10:2:79

Winona Co, St Charles Grange accts 1873-1885 PR 3:2:24

Yellow Medicine Co, Lisbon, farmers alliance 1890-1891 PR 3:1:4

MINOR, John b1707 w Sarah Carr, VA, anc ch YP 9:3:127

Thomas bc1608, biog notes & fam assoc OC 16:4:115

MISSISSIPPI, battle of Brice's Cross Roads & misc Civil War hist, bk rev GH 33:5:74

cem & Bible recs v17, bk rev OK 24:2:74

Civil War, military hist, bk rev CDS 16:5:48

Columbus, Friendship cem inscr, bk rev GH 33:4:112

geneal & local hist guide v1, bk rev GH 33:2:71

Itawamba Co, cem inscr, bk rev GH 33:1:86 OC 16:2:67 CDS 16:5:44

census 1870, bk rev OC 16:2:68

Lafayette Co, cem inscr v1, bk rev GH 33:1:86

Lowndes Co, census 1850, bk rev GH 33:2:80

Natches, court recs 1767-1805 (1953), bk rev NGS 67:4:309 GH 33:6:81

pioneer hist, bk rev CDS 16:2:4

MISSOURI, Barton Co, Lamar, GAR muster bk KCG 20:4:182

Benton Co, Dr Skinner's acct bk KCG 20:3:128

Cape Girardeau Co, marrs 1829-1854 of IL natives IL 11:2:79

Carter Co, marrs bk A 1860-1881, bk rev BGS 9:2:35

Cass Co, Pleasant Hill Twp, cem inscr, bk rev KCG 20:4:209

Chariton Co, Fawks cem inscr THT 4:3:20

Glasgow, hist KCG 20:1:1

Gross cem inscr THT 7:2:110

misc recs from William C Thomasson's bk 1840-1848 KA 14:4:198,220,225

Tillotson fam cem inscr THT 7:2:114

Chillicothe, school reg 1881 BGS 5:3:32

Christian Co, IL natives in 1860 census IL 11:3:169

Company B 2nd MO Infantry Sp-Am War roster THT 1:2:21

Cooper Co, Booneville, hist KCG 20:2:54

misc recs 1831-1900 v7, bk rev GE 43:12

Edgerton, Winn fam cem inscr KCG 20:3:118

Gasconade Co, census 1864, bk rev KCG 20:4:209

geneal data from recs of legislature 1839-1841 GE 48:7

geneal res guide TS 21:4:131 bk rev GH 33:5:70

Grundy Co, misc recs 1804-1887 v6, bk rev GE 43:12

guide to tracing fam, bk rev TST 12:33:39 TB 6:3:24 STC 2:1:39 KCN 20:1:47

Hannibal, hist KCG 20:4:169

Hanson Co, Eagleville, hist, bk rev HH 14:3:162

Hermann, hist KCG 20:3:105

Hickory Co, misc cem inscr KCG 20:1:33

Jackson Co, common school graduations 1900-1907 KCG 20:3:113

teachers 1907-1908 KCG 20:3:119

Wayne City, map & hist notes KCG 20:1:13

Johnson Co, Lone Jack Bapt Ch hist & recs 1842-1916 KCG 20:1:19 20:2:60 20:3:121 20:4:174

Laclede Co, Bohannon fam cem inscr THT 2:1:33

Lafayette Co, Odessa cem inscr v4, bk rev GH 33:6:81

misc marrs from news 1812-1853, bk rev TST 12:14:39

MO Gazette death notices 1816-1822 NGS 67:3:193

Monroe Co, pioneer fam recs, bk rev GH 33:5:75

news abstr marrs 1812-1853, bk rev GH 33:3:100

Newton Co, hist v2, bk rev GH 33:2:80

hist v3, Neosho cem inscr, bk rev GH 33:5:76

hist v4, bk rev GH 33:6:82

hist v5, wills & admin, bk rev GH 33:6:82

Nodaway Co, hist 1910, bk rev OG 2:4:118

misc geneal news articles v1, bk rev GH 33:4:112

obits v1, bk rev YP 9:1:38 OC 16:1:33

obits v2, bk rev KCG 20:4:208

pioneer fams (1876), bk rev CI 14:1:30

pioneers v1-30, bk rev HH 14:3:161

Polk Co, Jackson Twp, cem inscr, bk rev GH 33:1:86

Madison Twp, cem inscr, bk rev GH 33:1:86

Union Twp, cem inscr, bk rev GH 33:1:86

Ray Co, Orrick, Brasher cem inscr KCG 20:2:70

St Charles Co, Dog Prairie, hist, bk rev GH 33:5:75

hist notes, bk rev KCG 20:4:209

settlers from VA, bk rev WCK 12:4:64

taxpayers 1819-1826, bk rev TST 12:32:38 KCG 20:4:208

Texas Co, atlas & plat map, bk rev BB 11:3:47

Vernon Co, cem direct, bk rev GH 33:6:82

Webster Co, Grant Twp, Bumgarner cem inscr KCG 20:1:33

Ozark Twp, Thomas fam cem inscr KCG 20:1:33

West Plains, Evergreen cem, misc inscr THT 5:2:19

Henry Fred b1874 w Mary Frances Morrison, AL, anc ch NAS 18:2:36

MITCHELL, John f1776, VA, geneal, bk rev CTN 9:2:309

Neil b1871 w Margaret Hayson, KS, MO, anc ch OG 5:4:96

William w Mary Wilcox, PA, KY, fam recs KA 14:3:152 15:1:32

William Frederick b1845, IL, 1863 letter IL 11:3:166

MIXON, fam of Am, geneal v3, bk rev GGM 71:9

MOBLEY, Lonnie L b1894 w Mary Blanche Marlowe, TN, anc ch THT 7:1:10

MOEHLMAN, Conrad Henry b1879, biog, bk rev CTN 11:4:702

MOHR, Jacob Luther b1798 w Eva C Reifel, Ger, PA, geneal, bk rev REP 19:1:42

MOLYNEAUX, J B b1840, OH, biog notes AH 2:2:66

MONK, Silas f1775, NC & GA, geneal, bk rev GGM 71:6

MONTANA, hist of Luth ch CHI 52:3:99

MONTGOMERY, Alexander b1800, Ir, geneal BGS 10:1:15

Donald Eugene b1928 w Marilyn Ruth Moellring, IA, IL, ND, anc ch BGS 11:3:128

James W b1863 w Mary Ellen Chapman, VA, TN, Bible rec BGS 9:4:31

William b1808 w Mary Elizabeth Dawson, MD, VA, IA, CO, geneal BGS 10:1:17

MOODY, Joseph m1873 w Mary Dix, MN, IN, Bible rec IG 15:2:58

MOOERS, Samuel, MA, 1814 letter from war prisoner DE 3:2:23

MOOLICK, James b1819 w Honorah Doyle, Ir, NY, PA, NE, letters BGS 10:3:20

MOON, John f1740 w Mary, Bible rec HG 19:4:93

MOONEY, Obadiah w Joanna Moore, Sarah, NH, notes on DM 43:2:71

MOOR, John b1793 w Pamelia Sanders, Bible rec HTR 22:3:84

MOORE, Barbara (Ebberts) d1904 h Cyrus S Moore, OH, Bible rec OC 16:1:19

Charles B, KY, letter bk 1855-1859 DG 25:1:46

Charles Bingley b1822 w Mary Ann Dodd, TN, TX, will & biog notes DG 25:1:34

fam of OH, KY, Bible recs BR 6:2:61

James C m1826 w Lucinda Hinds, Bible rec MIS 11:4:56

James Fuller bc1844 w Phylinda Arabell Lacey, OH, anc ch REP 19:2:84

John B b1828 w Elleanor Ann Graham, Bible rec CI 14:3:90

Sullivan b1852 w Maloda Wyckoff, NY, anc ch CPY 8:2:49

Thomas b1667 w Deborah Griswold, notes on CTN 8:3:477

Thomas b1745 w Mary Harrison, MD, PA, KY, fam rec BR 6:2:57

William f1852 w Catherine Walsh, Ir, NY, WI, geneal, bk rev GH 33:4:119

MOORMAN, John Thomas w Ann Eliza Davis, NC, TX,, Bible rec GR 21:4:160

MORATH, Karl b1828 w Maria Agatha Messmer, Ger, PA, Bible rec CPY 8:2:36

MORE, Richard, "Mayflower" desc, bk rev GH 33:4:112 GE 47:13 VAG 23:3:232 NYR 110:4:249 GN 2:7:216 CTN 12:2:365

MORFORD, Morford Historian, Rt 1 Box 43C, Shelley ID 83274

MORGAN, Albert G b1816 w Sarah M Classion, Sarah Richardson, IL, Bible rec & obit CI 15:2:9

Arthur Marion b1902 w Cena Lucille Brothers, IL, IN, anc ch BGS 11:3:133

fam of Co Limerick Ir, geneal IR 11:2:77

Herbert Harold b1922 w Ruby May Gray, TX, anc ch AGS 20:2:48

Shirley Warner b1892 w Ethel Josephine Palmer, NY, OH,

geneal, bk rev REP 19:4:169

Thomas b1765, Bible rec & letter TN QY 6:4:4

Thomas Richard Clinton b1876 w Minnie Louvenia Overall, CA, TN, anc ch NAS 17:3:65

William C b1838 w Nancy Watkins, Lucinda (Loyd) Allen, IL, biog CI 11:3:98

MORIN, Charles T b1878 w Viola B Hicks, KY, Bible rec KA 14:3:165

MORRILL, fam of MA & ME, geneal vl, bk rev NGS 67:4:303

MORRIS, Carnelius b1825 w Margaret E Cox, Mary J Vaughan, OH, IL, fam rec CI 14:3:96

fam of Eng & IN, Bible recKN 2:1:28

John P b1811 w Mary A Weach, OH, anc ch REP 19:3:116

Preston b1802 w Adaliza Miller, Salina Riggs, KY, IL, OR, biog notes ORB 17:7:63

Richard b1835 w Diannah Harris, IN, IA, NE, anc ch REP 19:1:33

S P b1850 w Rebecca E Pate, Bible rec CI 13:4:128

Sylvester Osmer b1898 w Jessie Leona Mickey, WA, anc ch OG 5:3:69

MORRISON, Jesse b1781 w Rebecca Vanmetre, Bible rec GR 21:4:157

MORRISSEY, Mary Mullins b1824 h Dennis Morrissey, Ir, Can, NY, biog GL 13:2:49

MORSE, Addison J b1846 w Suzette M Franch, WI, Bible rec WI 26:2:71

Austin b1800, NY, MI, Can, biog FAM 18:1:2

fam of IL, notes on GL 13:1:25

fam marrs ME DE 3:4:17

George L b1817 w Susan P Manly, ME, Bible rec DE 3:1:12

MORTIMER, Noah b1842 w Alzina Caroline Tubbs, Eng, KS, geneal KK 17:2:27

MORTON, fam of PA, geneal, bk rev REP 19:1:41

Silas d1871 w Elizabeth, IL,

fam rec BGS 8:2:5

MOSELY, R W, letters 1862 AK to TX THT 5:1:7

MOSELEY, Robert, VA, KY, geneal, bk rev WCK 12:3:49

MOSGROVE, John A b1818 w Elizabeth Miller, OH, anc ch DM 42:4:156

MOSS, John Gaston b1839 w Louisa E Betty, TX, Bible rec THT 5:1:29

MOSHER, fam geneal, bk rev CI 15:4:155

MOSIER, fam of PA, geneal AH 2:2:43

MOSSER, fam of VA & OH, geneal, bk rev REP 19:4:169

MOTLEY, fam assoc publ, bk rev CTN 10:3:521

MOTSINGER, Michael, IL letter 1861 CI 13:4:150

MOTT, Elisha b1801 w Esther A Bunce, Bible recs CTN 12:2:230

MOULIC, William m1890 w Emma Begemannum, IL, marr cert GL 13:3:71

MOULTON, Nathan Noyes f1839 w Mary Jane McKinney, MA, IL, geneal FF 8:2:52

MOWBRAY, Thomas b1365 w Lady Elizabeth Fitzalan, Eng, geneal CTN 10:1:3 10:2:187 10:3:393

MOWRY, Jacob b1819 w Catherine Crone, OH, anc ch REP 19:1:31

MOXEY, Cornelius b1774 w Hannah Curtis, fam rec BGS 5:4:9

MOYLAN, Charles Ellsworth Sr b1897 w Anna Mildred Wheeler, MD, anc ch PGB 11:8:85

MUDD, fam of Am, geneal vl,2, bk rev YP 9:2:107

Samuel A (Dr) f1865, biog notes TST 11:45:1 11:48:1

MUELLER, Johann f1770 w Katherine Schrag, Switz, Russ, SD, geneal, bk rev TB 6:2:23

Ralph b1877, OH, auto, bk rev REP 19:4:166

MUHLENBERG, Henry Melchior f1742, Ger, PA, biog CHI 52:2:50

MULHALL, D J B1847 W CATHERINE DOYLE, IR, WI, BIOG VQ 16:2:20

MULLEN, William Seabright b1835 w Mary Jane Ellicott, NY, IL, MO, fam rec MGR 14:4:166

MULLER, Jacob m1736 w Anna Catharina Stevens, Holland, Curacao, biog notes SGS 29:3:222

Johanna b1847, Holland, biog notes SGS 29:3:221

Johannos f1850, Bible rec WI 25:3:127

MULLINS, fam of KY, geneal, bk rev BR 6:3:96

MUNGER, Melvin S m1871 w Addie A Compo, Bible rec BGS 11:3:109

MUNN, Daniel Forest b1851 w Permelia E Root, Can, OH, obit AH 2:4:109

MUNROE, Alexander f1844 w Jane Dorkendorf, ME, fam notes DE 3:3:16

MUNSON, Albert b1844 w Josephine Bloomer, Bible rec AH 2:4:103

Albert b1881 w Elizabeth Bloomer, NY, Bible rec AH 2:4:103

MURRAY, Alexander b1836, Ir, Bible rec GFP 28:6:109

Robert b1834 w Jane, OH, anc ch REP 19:3:124

MUSGROVE, James Ratcliffe b1797 w Malinda Edwards, KY, Bible rec MIS 11:4:57

MUTTIE, Peter f1851 w Katharina, Switz, NY, OH, geneal, bk rev CTN 7:2:295

MYER, Thomas b1817 w Jane Morrison, CT, OH, anc ch REP 19:3:124

MYERS, Hardin f1866 w Eliza Jane Chronic, IL, biog notes MCH 7:4:96

Nelson bc1820, PA, TN, anc ch REP 19:1:29

MYLAR, Joseph m1929 w Alta Jane Scott, UT, marr cert TRI 17:2:34

NAFFZIGER, Peter b1789 w Barbara Beck, IL, biog MH 6:4:38

NALL, Martin bc1675, VA, geneal, bk rev KY 21:1:33

Mary d1845 h Nicholas Nall, NC, death notice NCJ 5:2:141

NALLE, Martin f1701, VA, geneal, bk rev VAG 23:3:229 EWA 16:1:I

NAMES, Dutch-English name equivalents SGS 29:2:125

nick names BR 6:2:48

girl's Christian names (1900), bk rev CDS 16:3:4

origin & comments BCG 7:3:63

surnames, notes on KN 2:3:17

NASH, William Perkins b1901 w Ota Lee Percifield, TX, anc ch STK 7:4:187

NASON, fam of VT, OH, MN MN 10:1:28

NAYLOR, Peter d1812 w Margaret Carmer, Bible rec CTN 11:2:215

William Addison b1867 w Alice Samantha Chappell, MA, Bible rec CTN 7:2:317

NEAL, fam of IL, geneal, bk rev YP 9:4:226

NEBRASKA, Adams Co, Verona Twp, Christ Luth Ch recs, Tooten reg 1891-1909 NA 2:2:28

Alliance, Fairview cem inscr NW 2:2:47

Antelope Co, marrs to 1880 NA 2:1:37

Blaine Co, misc residents NA 2:2:39

Box Butte Co, Alliance, Snake Creek cem inscr NW 2:3:89

Ball cem recs NW 2:2:38

Hemingford, Bohemia Pioneer cem inscr NW 2:4:135

Hemingford, Cong Ch hist NW 2:2:33

Hemingford, Nonpariel cem inscr NW 2:3:89

Hemingford, St John's Luth Ch (old Norwegian) cem inscr NW 2:4:113

hist notes NW 2:3:75

marrs bk A 1887-1888 NW 2:2:41 2:3:79 2:4:124

news abstr 1906 NA 2:2:13

patent rec bk I NW 2:2:43

2:3:77 2:4:120

tax list 1887 NW 2:2:39 2:3:85

Brown Co, hist notes NA 2:1:2

roster ex-soldiers & sailors 1887 NA 2:1:15

Buffalo Co, homestead claims to 1880 NA 2:2:21

Burt Co, Lyons, Luther fam cem inscr NA 2:2:43

Butler Co, Owls Club 1898 NA 2:1:25

Cass Co, misc cems inscr NA 2:1:24

misc women's clubs NA 2:1:29

census 1854, 1854, 1844, 1846, bk rev TRI 19:3:38

census 1870 v1, bk rev GH 33:4:112

Clay Co, Spring Ranch cem inscr NA 2:1:21

Colfax Co, school dist #18 & #43 notes NA 2:1:42

county boundary maps 1854-1925, bk rev CDS 16:3:4

Creighton, imms from IA HH 14:3:136

Custer Co, Comstock, hist notes NA 2:2:35

Dawes Co, Bethel Community early settlers NW 2:2:34

Chadron, land title abstract NW 2:2:50

Chadron, Shisler cem recs NW 2:3:87

Marsland, United Meth Ch recs NW 2:3:83

marrs bk A 1886-1887 NW 2:2:45 2:3:80 2:4:116

Dawson Co, Lexington, Meth Epis Ch recs 1897-1900 NA 2:2:14

Dixon Co, imms from IA HH 14:3:134

Douglas Co, Omaha, news abstr NA 2:2:30

early recs, bk rev TRI 19:3:38

Franklin Co, Franklin, Greenwood cem inscr TB 6:2:45

misc marrs NA 2:1:17

small cem inscr TB 6:2:44

Upland cem, Civil War vets burials NA 2:1:40

Gage Co, hist notes NA 2:1:9

geneal publ surname index NW

2:1:18

geneal res guide JG 4:4:15

bk rev GH 33:5:70

geneal soc list JG 4:4:4

Grand Island, Pres Ch recs 1869-1890 NW 2:4:122

Hamilton Co, first trading posts & post offices NA 2:1:43

Harlan Co, Scandinavia Twp, Immanuel Luth Ch hist NA 2:2:45

hist, bk rev CHI 52:3:139

hist soc JG 4:4:14,32

Jefferson Co, marr lics 1923 NA 2:1:5

Johnson Co, atlas excerpts 1917 NA 2:1:33

Prairie Glenn public school dist #75 booklist 1904 NA 2:2:19

Tecumseh, news abstr NA 2:2:38

Keya Paha Co, early settlers NA 2:2:44

Lancaster Co, Bethany, Bethany Christian Ch, hist 1889-1964 abstr NA 2:2:29

Lincoln, unclaimed letters 1874 NA 2:2:37

land entry & land patents NA 2:1:27

Madison Co, Meadow Grove high school graduates 1904-1920 NA 2:1:36

McPherson Co, early settlers NA 2:2:1

news abstr NA 2:1:1

misc Bible rec abstr NA 2:2:40

misc letters NA 2:1:16

misc marr recs & cem inscr, bk rev GH 33:2:80

misc news abstr NA 2:1:26

Nebraska Terr, Boulder Creek Settlement census 1860 BGS 6:3:9

pioneers' assoc 1913 NA 2:1:10 2:2:8

territ census 1860 index to heads of fams, bk rev GH 33:4:112 KCG 20:4:208

news abstr NA 2:2:13,16,20,30, 37

Nuckolls Co, Superior cem inscr

TB 6:2:45

Omaha, board of trade abstr 1877 NA 2:1:41

misc news abstr 1910 NA 2:1:44

Pawnee City, Plum Creek School honor roll 1878 NA 2:1:40

Pawnee Co, misc cems inscr NA 2:1:119

pioneer photographs & hist notes FH 2:1:4

pioneers from OH, biog notes OHR 20:2:73

Platte Co, Duncan, early residents NA 2:2:34

Polk Co, Stromsburg, Meth Epis Ch recs NA 2:2:4

Red Willow Co, cem rec, bk rev NA 2:2:46

Rock Co, news abstr 1908 NA 2:2:3

Saline Co, Brush Creek Precinct, cem inscr NA 2:1:8

Kasak cem notes NA 2:2:26

marr licenses 1909 NA 2:1:5

Sarpy Co, school census 1892, bk rev GH 33:3:100

Saunders Co, Chester Twp, Willow Creek cem inscr NA 2:1:8

misc residents, jurors & high school graduates NA 2:1:6

Scotts Bluff Co, news abstr 1912 NA 2:1:35

Seward Co, Beaver Crossing high school graduates 1909-1919 NA 2:2:31

Sheridan Co, Antioch cem inscr NW 2:4:111

hist notes NW 2:4:110

misc news abstr NA 2:1:26

Sherman Co, early settlers, notes on NA 2:1:7

Rosseter House, notes on NA 2:2:3

Sioux Co, hist notes NW 2:2:31 2:4:110

Thayer Co, Hebron, census 1870 NA 2:1:31

Washington Co, school dist #35 Rispin School census 1885 NA 2:2:17

Wayne Co, Sons of Herman cem inscr NA 2:1:7

Theophilus cem inscr NA 2:2:32

Webater Co, Five Star School dist #59, census 1898-9, 1903 NA 2:2:27

York Co, Gilmore cem inscr NA 2:1:1

NEELY, Abner Dale b1860 w Gladys Sarah Billick, PA, anc ch TB 6:4:21

fam geneal, bk rev CI 14:4:151

Samuel Leander b1880 w Minnie Alice Mathis, TX, anc ch GR 21:2:53

Samuel Leander b1880 w Minnie Azile Mathis, TX, anc ch GR 21:3:92

NELSON, Anthony bc1652 w Margareta, Sw, NJ, geneal, film rev GH 33:6:92

Lavonne Julana, geneal, bk rev CTN 11:3:526

Sarah Leon b1873 h John Scott Coleman, AL, TX, biog THT 5:4:23

Seth b1735 w Silence Cheney, ME, Bible rec CSB 14:1:28

Thomas f1638 w ___ , Joanna Dummer, anc ch DE 3:4:24

NETHERLANDS, Amsterdam, geneal res guide, bk rev GH 33:2:73

census of emig 1866 MI 24:2:56 24:3:92

geneal central bureau, bk rev BCG 8:2:34

geneal res guide OC 16:2:58 KCG 20:4:194

NETHERTON, Richard b1807 w Betsy Stevens, Eng, Can, anc ch TAK 9:2:31

NEUFANG, Balthaser f1727 w Anna Barbara, Elizabeth, PA, biog notes TST 12:2:45

NEUMANN, Gottlieb b1817 w Frederika von Knoll, Prussia, WI, geneal, bk rev GH 33:5:87

NEUSBAUM, Mary Ann b1856, IA, Bible rec KK 17:1:8

NEW ENGLAND, abstracting Col land & court recs CTN 7:4:492

Cath ch hist, bk rev CTN 10:4:702

dict of Eng emigs 1620-1650 (Banks), bk rev CTN 11:2:338

geneal advertiser quarterly

1898-1901, bk rev CTN 7:1:129
geneal dict (Savage) 1884, bk rev CTN 10:2:344 TB 6:3:25
geneal res guide TS 21:2:54
geneal source outline EWA 16:2:60
Indian Wars hist 1620-1677, bk rev BGS 10:4:33
land system of Col era CTN 11:4:556
migrations within N E CTN 9:4:536
New England Planters hist CTN 12:2:361
pioneers 1602-1628, hist (1929), bk rev CTN 7:3:363
pioneers of New France in N E, bk rev CLG 10:3:183
placenames biblio SCR 2:4:4
surname index SGS 29:1:45 29:2:135 29:3:251 29:4:345
NEW HAMPSHIRE, Barrington, marr recs 1813-1828 SCR 2:5:8 2:6:2 3:1:2
census 1800, notes on SCR 2:6:6
Cornish, hist 1911, bk rev CTN 9:2:308
Dover, hist Col era (1923), bk rev NGS 67:1:75
vr 1686-1850 (1894), bk rev NGS 67:1:75
Exeter, census & bus dire t 1908, bk rev GH 33:4:113 TST 12:27:48 CDS 16:5:48
hist 1888, bk rev GH 33:4:113 TST 12:23:48 CDS 16:5:48
geneal dict 1928-1939, bk rev CTN 9:2:315
geneal dict to 1699 (1928), bk rev TB 6:3:24
geneal res guide, bk rev CTN 7:1:159
Hampton, census & bus direct 1908, bk rev GH 33:4:113 TST 12:27:48 CDS 16:5:48
hist notes TST 12:1:52
Keene, hist 1904, bk rev CLG 10:3:184
Manchester, Parish of St Therese, marrs 1934-1976, bk rev CTN 10:4:702
place names guide SCR 2:4:2 2:5:1

Strafford, marr recs 1813-1828 SCR 2:5:8 2:6:2 3:1:2
vital recs policy SCR 2:5:6
Washington, hist 1876-1976, bk rev NER 133:4:312
Wentworth, hist, bk rev CTN 8:4:543
NEW JERSEY, Atlantic Co, census 1860, bk rev CTN 11:2:342
hist 1845, bk rev GJ 8:4:217
mort sched 1850 GNJ 54:2:65
Bergen Co, Bergen Twp, tax list 1784 GNJ 54:2:52
Burlington Co, marrs (1932), bk rev NYR 110:3:184 DM 43:2:90 CTN 10:3:526
Little Egg Harbor Twp, geneal hist incl marrs 1715-1859 (1880), bk rev TB 6:4:21
Upper Springfield Friends Burying Ground cem inscr GNJ 54:1:7 54:2:97
Camden Co, hist 1845, k rev GJ 8:4:217
Cape May Co, day bk of Nathaniel Holmes 1805-1808 GNJ 54:1:35 54:2:137
marrs (1931), bk rev GH 33:3:100 NYR 110:3:184 DM 43:2:90 CTN 12:1:184
mort sched 1850 GNJ 54:2:67
Col hist recs 1664-1704, bk rev OK 24:2:73
Cumberland Co, census 1800 GNJ 54:1:21
marrs (1932), bk rev GH 33:3:100 TST 12:8:45 NYR 110:3:184 DM 43:2:90 CTN 12:1:184
geneal res guide TST 12:2:44 CTN 8:4:483 9:3:352
geneal resources in southern NJ, bk rev GJ 8:4:217 NYR 110:4:247
geographic dict 1894, bk rev NYR 110:3:184 NGS 67:1:73
Gloucester Co, hist 1845, bk rev GJ 8:4:217
marrs (1930), bk rev NYR 110:3:184 CTN 11:3:517
Swedesboro, Trinity Epis Ch (old Swedes), recs 1785-1975, bk rev GJ 8:4:217 NYR

110:4:246

Hunterdon Co, Alexandria Twp, tax lists 1785-1786 GNJ 54:2:55

Grandin fulling mill bk 1774-1785 GNJ 54:1:41

recs 1701-1838, bk rev GJ 8:3:172 NYR 110:4:246

lineages to "Mayflower", bk rev CTN 7:4:517

Monmouth Co, militia women 1780 DAR 113:4:308

Stafford Twp, tax lists 1784, 1786 GNJ 54:2:59

natives in MD, FL, ME, NH mort sched 1850 GNJ 54:2:144

Passaic Valley, fam recs (1852), bk rev BGS 10:3:35

mort sched 1850 GNJ 54:2:70

pioneer fams of Northwestern NJ, bk rev GJ 8:4:218

Princeton, index to hist, bk rev CTN 9:2:312

Princeton Univ, biog dict 1748-1768, bk rev NER 133:3:223

Salem Co, loan office recs 1733-1751 GNJ 54:2:116

marrs (1928), bk rev NYR 110:3:184 CTN 11:2:342

ship pass lists 1600-1825, bk rev TST 12:16:40 CTN 11:4:704

Somerset Co, misc fams cem inscr GNJ 54:2:114

misc geneal, bk rev KN 2:1:39 2:2:36

tax list 1784-1786 GNJ 54:1:12

Sussex Co, abstr of estates 1789-1918, bk rev NYR 110:4:248

maps of divisions 1789-1918, bk rev NYR 110:4:248

slave births 1804-1833 GNJ 54:2:83

Wantage Twp, vendue 1774 GNJ 54:1:20

Warren Co, abstr of estates 1789-1918, bk rev NYR 110:4:248

Belvidere, Wesley Chapel cem inscr GNJ 54:2:135

Hardwick Friends Burying Ground cem inscr GNJ 54:2:133

maps of divisions 1789-1918,

bk rev NYR 110:4:248

slave births 1804-1833 GNJ 54:2:83

NEW MEXICO, Bernalillo Co, Chilili, Garland cem inscr NMG 18:1:21

Escabosa cem inscr NMG 18:1:20

Miera cem inscr NMG 18:1:20

Tijeras cem inscr NMG 18:1:19

cems list NMG 18:2:47

Chaves Co, tax assessment roll 1891 NMG 18:3:90 18:4:117

misc Spanish & Mex land recs SPG 31:577

Sierra Co, marrs NMG 18:1:3 18:2:35 18:3:67 18:4:99

Spanish enlistment papers 1732-1820 NGS 67:3:229 67:4:294

Taos Co, marrs NMG 18:1:11 18:2:41 18:3:84 18:4:105

Torrance Co, Abo, St Lawrence Ch cem NMG 18:3:73

Cedar Grove cem inscr NMG 18:2:57

Cedarvale cem inscr NMG 18:2:56

Duran, Old Duran Ch cem inscr NMG 18:4:116

Hindi cem inscr NMG 18:3:79

La Cienega Mission cem inscr NMG 18:4:115

Manzano Ch cem inscr NMG 18:1:21

Manzano Hills cem inscr NMG 18:1:23

Mt Calvary cem inscr supp NMG 18:4:114

Negra cem inscr NMG 18:3:79

Pinos Wells cem inscr NMG 18:3:78

Punta cem inscr NMG 18:4:112

Punta Ch cem inscr NMG 18:4:111

Tajique Cath Ch cem inscr NMG 18:4:113

Torreon Cath Ch cem inscr NMG 18:2:55

Torreon cem inscr NMG 18:2:54

will bk A1 NMG 18:4:118

Willard Cath cem inscr NMG 18:3:76

Valencia Co, Tome Cath Ch cem inscr NMG 18:2:59

Valencia Cath Ch cem inscr NMG 18:2:59

NEW YORK, Albany, Reformed Dutch Ch recs 1683-1809 (1904), bk rev TST 12:8:45 NYR 110:2:122 DM 42:4:185 NGS 67:1:73

Albany Co, Albany, First Meth Ch, marr recs 1806-1884 TT 19:1:21 19:2:85

  first settlers 1630-1800 (1872), bk rev CTN 9:4:610

alien residents 1825-1848, bk rev TST 11:48:44 NYR 110:1:57 DM 42:4:184 NGS 67:1:73 AG 55:1:64

anc ch bk I, bk rev CTN 9:3:471

appl for GAR membership TT 19:2:81

area key, bk rev IL 11:4:236 TB 6:2:17

Bedford, hist recs v9 geneal, bk rev NYR 110:4:248

Brooklyn, Old First Dutch Reformed Ch, hist notes SGS 29:2:123

Broome Co, will bk B TT 19:1:23 19:2:87

Brunswick, hist 1880, bk rev NYR 110:2:122 CDS 16:4:10

Carmel, Old Bapt Burial Ground hist BGS 11:1:32

Cayuga Co, Auburn news abstr TT 19:1:23 19:2:89 19:3:151

  biog review 1894 (1947), bk rev YP 9:2:108

census index 1800, bk rev TB 6:1:35

Chautaugua, Chautauqua Institutuion hist DAR 113:7:788

Chautauqua Co, Mayville, Mayville cem inscr TT 19:2:91 19:3:153

  misc marrs 1851-1890 by Rev Alfred J Wilcox SGS 29:1:9

Chemung Co, Big Flats, Kahler Road cem inscr TT 19:2:94 19:3:155

  Big Flats, Rural Home cem inscr TT 19:2:93

  Big Flats, Sing Sing cem inscr TT 19:2:93

  pioneer hist, bk rev CTN 7:2:294

census 1810 TT 19:4:i

East Guilford-Rockdale cem inscr TT 19:1:27

White's Store, Evergreen cem inscr TT 19:1:27 19:3:157

ch recs index (Vosburgh) MCR 10:2:35 10:3:50

Clinton Co, Peru Quaker Meeting, marr intentions 1799-1833 TT 19:2:95 19:3:159

Peru Quaker meeting, marrs 1799-1839 TT 19:3:159

Cortland Co, Cincinnatus, First Cong Ch membership from 1809 TT 19:1:29 19:2:97 19:3:14

wills bk I TT 19:3:161

county formation hist, bk rev GA 33:3:100 TST 12:11:37 GJ 8:2:116 NYR 110:3:181 CSB 14:1:23

Cumberland Co, census 1771, bk rev KN 2:4:22

Davenport, cem inscr, bk rev GH 33:3:101

Delaware Co, Walton, First Cong Ch recs TT 19:1:31 19:3:163

Dutchess Co, Eastman National Bus College class of 1866, 1882, 1883 DC 7:1:15 7:2:9

Milan, census 1865 DC 7:2:3

news abstr deaths 1826-1871 DC 7:1:3 7:2:11

Quaker recs CTN 12:4:555

will bk C DC 7:1:17 7:2:27

Elmira, Woodlawn National cem inscr NGI 3:1:45 3:2:123 3:3:186

emigs' land claims in OR TT 19:1:15 19:2:79

Erie Canal, hist, bk rev TB 6:3:20

Erie Co, Buffalo, hist v1 1884, film rev GH 33:6:92

Clarence, Beeman cem inscr TT 19:2:99

Eden, hist, bk rev CTN 8:1:38

Eden, hist v2, bk rev CTN 8:3:475

Eden, hist v3, bk rev CTN 10:4:701

Eden, index to hist v1-3, bk rev CTN 11:2:338

Evans Center cem inscr TT

19:3:165

Hamburg, Freewill Bapt Ch hist & recs 1827-1886, bk rev CDS 16:1:4

hist vl 1884, film rec GH 33:6:92

misc marrs 1851-1890 by Rev Alfred J Wilcox SGS 29:1:9

Essex Co, index to 1885 hist, bk rev GH 33:6:82

Jay, Jay Central cem inscr TT 19:2:101

Florida, hist notes ANC 14:4:128

Fulton Co, Mayfield, Mayfield Central Pres Ch roll 1857-1871 TT 19:2:104 19:3:167

geneal guide to Bureau of vr TT 19:3:148

geneal res guide OG 3:2:41 CTN 10:3:407 AG 5:2:40

geneal sources CTN 7:3:323

Genesee Co, Bergen, Barr/East Bergen cem inscr TT 19:1:33

Genesee Co pioneer soc recs TT 19:1:34

Herkimer Co, Manheim, Old Yellow Evan Ger Ch recs TT 19:1:35 19:3:169

hist mss: Dutch (Kingstow), bk rev GJ 8:2:118

Huntington, abstr & name index to highway bks 1671-1926, bk rev CDS 16:3:6

Jewish fam clubs, bk rev JJG 3:1:18

lists of inhabitants of Col NY (O´Callaghan 1851), bk rev NGS 67:4:309

lists of inhabitants of Col NY, index to Documentary Hist, bk rev GH 33:6:82

Jefferson Co, Clayton, Clayton Center cem inscr TT 19:1:37 19:3:171

Long Island, Bellmore, Southard fam cem inscr NYR 110:4:194

Flushing, St George´s Epis Ch, marrs 1782-1885 NYR 110:1:1 110:2:56 110:3:154 110:4:223

geneal 1895, bk rev OG 4:2:58

hist soc guide TST 12:4:36

Jamaica, First Reformed Dutch

Ch recs 1802-1851 NYR 110:1:43 110:2:78 110:3:141 110:4:198

Madison Co, Brookfield, vr 1847 TT 19:3:173

Hamilton, Rebecca Woodman cem inscr TT 19:1:39

Hamilton, Thompson/Madison Reservoir cem inscr TT 19:2:105

Peterboro, small cem TT 19:2:105 19:3:173

school rolls 1837-8 TT 19:1:39

Solsville, House fam cem inscr TT 19:2:105

manorial soc hist 1664-1775, bk rev NER 133:2:143

manumissions NYR 110:1:39 110:2:66

Marlborough, Friends marr cert 1809-1819 DC 7:2:31

marrs from "NY Weekly Tribune" 1843-1849, bk rev CTN 12:1:184

marrs to 1784 (1860, 1898), bk rev CTN 10:3:527 TB 6:1:35

migration study 1855 GH 33:2:5

misc Quaker recs 1814 THT 3:2:44

Mohawk Valley, first settlers 1720-1772 CLG 10:3:156

Rev War hist, bk rev YP 9:1:40

Monroe Co, birth recs 1821-1876 in Bradley diaries, bk rev CTN 9:3:466

canal hist, bk rev CTN 10:4:699

Henrietta, hist notes c1900, bk rev CTN 11:4:702

index to 1895 "landmarks", bk rev CTN 10:3:527

index to names in Bradley 1816-1880 diaries, bk rev CTN 9:3:466

misc wills to 1863 TT 19:1:41

name index to 1877 hist, bk rev CTN 10:3:520

Parma, Rev War patriots, bk rev CTN 10:4:700

Montgomery Co, aliens 1812 TT 19:2:77

Nassau Village, hist 1609-1830 & biogs, bk rev CTN 10:2:349

natives in NE deaths NYR

110:3:154

New Haven, Anderson fam cem inscr MI 24:3:99

New Paltz, hist & geneal 1678-1820, bk rev BGS 10:1:31 TB 6:1:35

Reformed Dutch Ch recs, bk rev TT 19:1:11

New York City, marrs by Mayor Gideon Lee 1833-1834 NYR 110:2:111

Quaker returns in tax assessment bks 1810-1819 NYR 110:3:164 110:4:216

"NY Magazine" marrs & deaths 1790-1797, bk rev DM 43:2:88

NY Public Lib res guide TST 11:48:36

"NY Weekly Tribune", marr abstr 1843-1849, bk rev NYR 110:3:182

misc infamous acts 1843-1864, bk rev CTN 12:2:366 NYR 110:4:247

news abstr 1862 THT 7:1:39

Niagara Co, letters of quard bk 2 TT 19:1:43

Onandaga Co, Manlius, Masonic Mil Lodge 1802-1829 TT 19:3:175

news abstr 1830-1831, 1842 TT 19:1:47 19:2:76,107 19:3:175

Oneida Co, Annsville, North Annsville, Miller cem inscr TT 19:1:45

Ara, Thornton cem inscr TT 19:1:45

Floyd, David fam cem inscr TT 19:1:46

Floyd, East Floyd cem inscr TT 19:1:46

Floyd, Moulton fam cem inscr TT 19:1:46

Floyd, Wilcox fam cem inscr TT 19:1:46

tax list 1792 NGS 67:3:175

Wood cem inscr TT 19:1:45

Ontario Co, aliens 1812 TT 19:2:78

Bristol, Coddington cem inscr TT 19:3:177

will bk A TT 19:3:177

Orange Co, Chester, cems inscr,

bk rev CTN 11:3:524

death notices "Whig Press" 8151-1865, bk rev OC 16:4:137

hist & index, bk rev CTN 10:4:703

Orleans Co, Albion, Pendry cem inscr TT 19:2:109

wills bk 1 TT 19:2:109

Oswego Co, Orwell Twp, Pekin cem inscr MI 24:2:65 24:3:98

Scriba Hills, East cem inscr TT 19:1:49 19:2:111 19:3:179

wills bk A TT 19:1:49

Otsego Co, Butternuts, Prentiss Burying Ground cem inscr TT 19:1:51 19:3:181

Palatine fams list CLG 10:3:138

Palatine immig 18th cent, hist, bk rev BGS 10:4:33

Philipsburg Manor rent roll 1760 NYR 110:2:102

Queens Co, hist 1775-1788 (1884), bk rev CTN 9:3:475

recs guide TST 12:13:38

Rensselaer Co, Brunswick, hist, bk rev TT 19:2:70

Lansingburgh, marr notices 1787-1850 TT 19:1:53

resident aliens enabled to hold land 1790-1825 NGS 67:1:42

Rev War, battleground hist, bk rev NYR 110:1:56

hist KN 2:1:7 2:2:22 2:3:41

Mohawk Valley recs, bk rev NYR 110:1:55

Richmond Co, Castleton, slave births after 1799 NYR 110:4:196

St Lawrence Co, Canton vr 1847-1849 TT 19:1:59 19:3:183

Saratoga Co, Ballston, Burnt Hills, Calvary Epis Ch cem inscr TT 19:2:113

death recs from "Charlton Epitaphs-Epis Cem" inscr TT 19:1:56

guardianship recs 1815-1825 TT 19:1:55

Saratoga Lake, fam cem inscr TT 19:1:56

Stafford Bridge, Bennett cem inscr TT 19:1:55

Schenectady, first settlers

1662-1800 (1873), bk rev CTN 9:4:611

Schoharie Co, Fulton, tax lists 1849 TT 19:2:115

Schuyler Co, dower bk I TT 19:1:57 19:3:185

hist, bk rev CTN 11:2:340

Seneca Co, Bayleytown cem inscr AG 55:1:37

ship pass lists 1600-1825, bk rev TST 12:16:40 CTN 11:4:704

six generation anc ch bk 1, bk rev CI 12:3:113

South Seneca Co, hist, bk rev TB 6:1:34

Stanfordville, United Ch of Christ recs from 1835 DC 7:1:21

Steuben Co, Bath, Buck Settlement cem inscr TT 19:1:61

Bath, Knight Settlement. cem inscr TT 19:3:187

Bath, old cems inscr TT 19:1:61

direct 1891, bk rev GH 33:5:76

guardians 1828 recs TT 19:3:187

hist gazetteer 1891, bk rev GH 33:5:76

natives who emig to MI MI 24:1:11

pioneer hist, bk rev CTN 7:1:130

Tioga Co, Candor, St Mark's Pres Ch bapt recs TT 19:3:189

hist, bk rev CTN 11:2:340

Owego, First Bapt Ch, funerals 1888-1895 TT 19:2:117 19:3:189

Tompkins Co, early probate proceedings TT 19:2:119

Tryon Co, Rev War minutes, bk rev DM 42:3:137

Ulster Co, Rochester, Dutch Reformed Ch, contributors 1741, 1743, 1767 NYR 110:2:85

vr use GE 48:9

Warren Co, will bk A TT 19:2:121

Wayne Co, Macedon, Johnson Farm cem inscr TT 19:2:124

will bk A TT 19:2:123

Westchester Co, Bedford, geneal

hist v9, bk rev CTN 12:2:367

Western NY, purchase by Holland Land Co TST 11:40:29

settlement by 1821 TST 11:41:29

Yates Co, Benton, census 1825 TT 19:2:125

NEW ZEALAND, geneal res guide, bk rev GH 33:2:74

NEWBROUGH, Joseph Samuel b1909 w Mary Gazell Hatch, Mexico, MS, LA, anc ch GR 21:3:95

NEWCOMB, Ernest b1915 w Emily Brophy, NY, anc ch BGS 10:1:34

Stanley Stowell b1912 w Miriam Eloise Nye, Phillipines, CT, NY, IL, anc ch BGS 11:3:130

Timothy J b1816 w Frinda Goodell, OH, Bible rec BGS 4:2:19

NEWELL, Joseph b1808, VA, OH, biog notes VQ 16:1:13

NEWHOUSE, fam of VA & OH, geneal 1967, bk rev REP 19:1:44

NEWLAND, Abraham b1795 w Anne G Cooke, Bible rec THT 2:2:15

Maggie & Art, letter to Edward Hamner, ID, CA, 1892 RED 12:2:17

NEWMAN, Walter f1683, Ir, NJ, geneal, bk rev HTR 22:2:41

NEWSOM, Macie Dee b1907 w Mary Katherine Keyser, TX, anc ch GR 21:3:95

NEWSOME, Joel Arthur b1888 w Ida May Hove, anc ch AGS 20:2:62

NEWSUM, B F d1890, obit VL 14:1:7

NEWTON, Abiathar V b1806 w Rachel Garlinghouse, MA, KY, OR, biog notes ORB 18:4:93

Richard mc1641 w Anna Loker, Eng, MA, biog notes AG 55:2:86

NICHOLLS, Richard d1775, Eng, NY, fam recs NGS 67:3:217

NICHOLS, Howard Gardner b1871, MA, AL, notes on NAS 17:3:i

Reuben f1745 w Elizabeth Stump, Ger, MD, geneal, bk rev GH 33:1:93

Stephen, IL, letter 1861 BGS 5:4:17

William b1784 w Mary Hall, GA, KY, IL, geneal CI 15:2:18

NICHOLSON, John m1776 w Lucy Edmunds, VA, Bible rec VA 17:1:28

NICKERSON, William b1604 w Anne Busby, MA, geneal vl,2, bk rev CTN 8:2:317 9:4:605

NIDIFFER, Freeman b1849 w Mary Rebecca Lunday, TN, OK, Bible rec TA 14:1:3

NIEBUHR, Clarence Faag b1914, TX, anc ch AGS 20:2:70

NILES, Robert bc1758 w Tacy Barber, NY, fam rec DM 42:4:191

NILSSON, Jonas b1813, Sweden, geneal MN 10:2:83

NITE, John E b1806 w Lucy Stepp, NC, geneal BGS 9:2:20

NIXON, David b1815 w Mary, Bible rec HH 14:3:159

Frederick Earl b1901 w Margaret Grace Sutherland, IL, anc ch FF 8:2:29

George w Mary, VA will 1797 & inv 1801 BGS 11:3:110

James Frank b1885 w Bertha Elizabeth Conder, AL, TX, anc ch THT 7:1:12

W C w Sarah E (Smyers) Nixon Rhoads, Bible rec THT 3:1:12

NOBLE, Guy Earl b1882 w Mary Belle Beadle, MI, CA, anc ch ORB 17:8:74

John Denison b1813 w Rebecca Moore, VA, IN, NE, anc ch REP 19:3:130

NOEL, fam of PA, geneal, bk rev LM 20:1:5

Joseph f1836, PA, geneal, bk rev REP 19:4:166

NOLAND, Robert Stanley b1879 w Edith Bell Creed, KY, anc ch RRS 12:1:117

NOLL, Frank Joseph b1851 w Mary Hampel, PA, AR, geneal, bk rev GH 33:3:106 KCG 20:2:88

NORMAN, George w Martha Milhiush, geneal, bk rev CTN 9:4:609

NORRIS, Patrick Henry b1821 w Georgia M (Bradley) Gray, AK, Bible rec YP 9:2:71

NORTH, Mary (Williams) f1856 h Stephen North, OH, letters BGS 1:1:7 8:1:17

Walter McCullough b1861 w Mettie Cortwright, NJ, MI, obit KK 17:3:69

NORTH CAROLINA, archives sources descr TST 11:39:36

Asheville, marrs & deaths in news 1840-1870, bk rev OC 16:3:108

Bertie Co, court minutes 1724-1739 bk 1, bk rev OC 16:2:70

court minutes 1763-1771 bk III, bk rev NCJ 5:2:137

tax list 1768 NCJ 5:4:221

Bladen Co, marr licenses 1789 NCJ 5:4:245

Brunswick Co, tax list 1769, 1772 NCJ 5:4:238

Burke Co, marr licenses 1787 NCJ 5:4:245

Bute Co, Committee of Safety minutes 1775-1776, bk rev GH 33:4:113 VAG 23:1:68

census index 1810, bk rev SCS 15:3:89

census index 1820, bk rev NGS 67:1:73

Charlotte, Sugaw Creek Pres Ch cem inscr CI 13:4:137

Chatham Co, court minutes abstr 1774-1778 NCJ 5:1:31

Col tax list NCJ 5:4:218

Craven Co, court minutes bk 1 1712-1715, bk rev NCJ 5:1:61 OC 16:1:32

wills abstr 1740-1800 LL 14:2:83 14:3:127 14:4:178 15:1:25 15:2:96 15:3:143 15:4:183

Cumberland Co, court minutes vl 1755-1779, bk rev GH 33:1:87

Davidson Co, will summaries vl 1823-1846, bk rev TST 12:1;37 NCJ 5:2:137

Duplin Co, cem inscr v7, bk rev NCJ 5:1:62

cem inscr v8, bk rev NCJ 5:1:62

cem inscr v9, bk rev NCJ 5:1:62

court minutes part 2 1788-

1791, bk rev NCJ 5:3:211

Edenton, tax list 1769 NCJ 5:4:235

emigs to GA GGM 73:219

Forsyth Co, cem inscr v1-4, bk rev YP 9:2:102
  cem inscr v5, bk rev GH 33:1:87 IL 11:1:57 GE 43:12 VAG 23:1:69 YP 9:2:102 OC 16:1:34 MN 10:1:42 TS 21:1:26 CDS 16:1:22 AG 55:2:123

Granville Co, court minutes 1746-1820, bk rev GGM 73:165
  deeds 1746-1765, bk rev GGM 73:164
  guardian accts 1810-1856, bk rev GGM 73:165
  misc recs 1765-1826, bk rev GGM 73:165
  wills & estate recs 1808-1833 v2, bk rev GGM 73:165

Guilford Co, fam cems & abandoned ch cems, bk rev GE 43:11
  will abstr 1771-1841, bk rev TST 12:10:38 NCJ 5:2:138

Halifax, black hist, bk rev NCJ 5:2:139

Halifax Co, Bible recs, bk rev NCJ 5:2:138

Harnett Co, Ferry cem inscr TST 3:2:26

Iredell Co, court minutes 1789-1800, bk rev GH 33:1:87 TST 12:6:46 YP 9:2:102
  deed abstr v1 1788-1797, bk rev GH 33:4:113 TST 11:51:37 YP 9:3:165
  hist, bk rev NCJ 5:3:211

Johnston Co, Bible rec, bk rev NCJ 5:4:257
  cem recs v3, bk rev NCJ 5:4:256
  court minutes 1759-1766 bk 1, bk rev OC 16:1:33
  court minutes 1819-1822 bk X1, bk rev NCJ 5:2:139

Lincoln Co, deed abstr 1769-1786, bk rev YP 9:2:107

Luth Ch recs survey NCJ 5:2:122 5:3:150

marr & death notices "Argus" 1848-1861 NCJ 5:2:105 5:3:184

migration as shown in powers of attorney NCJ 5:1:37 5:3:165

misc geneal resources, bk rev GE 46:8

misc wills abstr THT 5:2:8

New Hanover Co, St Phillip's Parish, tax list 1763 NCJ 5:4:238

Northampton Co, Bible recs, bk rev NCJ 5:2:138

Orange Co, Federal Direct Tax 1816 assessment NCJ 5:1:14 5:2:114 5:3:193
  waterways 1816 NCJ 5:2:115

Pamlico Co, hist, bk rev NCJ 5:1:62

Pee Dee, ances key, bk rev NCJ 5:1:63

Pender Co, Burgaw, hist, bk rev NCJ 5:2:139

pensioners reported 1835 CI 11:3:114

Person Co, Barnett place, slave reg births 1813-1864 NCI 5:4:254

Quakers, Soc of Friends early settlements TST 12:5:38 12:6:44

Raleigh, City Cem, blacks' cem inscr NCJ 5:3:173
  news abstr vr 1799-1819, bk rev NCJ 5:3:212

Rev War, acct of allowances 1792 THT 5:2:5
  claims abstr NCJ 5:1:24 5:2:100 5:3:158 5:4:248
  claims of British merchants NCJ 5:1:4 5:3:176
  hist, bk rev VAG 23:1:68
  loyalists, 1940, bk rev GH 33:3:101 VAG 23:2:149 NGS 67:4:307
  papers NCJ 5:1:44 5:2:89
  patriots at Moore's Creek 1776 THT 5:1:9
  prisoners of British Army 1781 NCJ 5:2:74
  recs of soldiers, sailors, patriots & descs v1, bk rev YP 9:4:228
  recs of soldiers, sailors, patriots & descs v2, bk rev YP 9:4:228

Rowan Co, court minutes 1763-1774 v2, bk rev NCJ 5:3:212

court of pleas abstr 1753-1760, bk rev KY 21:1:69

marr licenses 1785-1786 NCJ 5:2:127

misc inv & sales 1785-1787 NCJ 5:1:43

Rutherford Co, deed abstr 1769-1786, bk rev YP 9:2:107

surname list by counties THT 7:2:59

Surry Co, Hallows, early settlers hist NCJ 5:1:2

Tazewell, hist, bk rev NCJ 5:4:257

travel diary 1750 NCJ 5:3:146

Tryon Co. deed abstr 1769-1786, bk rev YP 9:2:107

Wade Co. court minutes 1787-1792 bk II, bk rev NCJ 5:4:257

Wake Co, court minutes 1771-1776 bk A1, bk rev NCJ 5:1:63 OC 16:2:70

deed abstr 1785-1802, bk rev NGS 67:1:66 GGM 73:164

Wayne Co, Goldsboro, misc deeds abstr VL 13:4:158

Washington Dist, hist QY 6:1:6

NORTH DAKOTA, Cass Co, hist & geneal v1-2, bk rev CTN 12:4:703

Cath emigs from Ger, bk rev TB 6:2:22

hist of imm Germans from Russ, bk rev TB 6:1:35 6:2:22

imms from Ger via Russ, bk rev GH 33:3:98

McIntosh Co, cems inscr OC 16:1:33

cems inscr, bk rev CDS 16:1:22

NORTHCUTT, fam of IL, letters c1862 CI 11:2:45

NORTHROP, Thomas Ledu b1881 w Maggie May Manion, IA, IL, CO, anc ch BGS 11:4:181

NORWAY, Bygdelag groups as geneal source TST 12:9:44

geneal res guide MN 10:1:3 10:2:53 GE 45:1 SCS 15:1:17 15:2:41 15:3:78

bk rev GH 33:2:74 33:5:69 TST 12:2:46 OG 5:4:116 MCR 10:3:67 NGI 3:1:34

guide to res on Ams from Norway AG 55:1:20

NORWOOD, Louis M b1876 w Nellie V Amis, AL, NM, fam rec NMG 18:2:53

NOTLEY, George Claire b1886 w Geraldine Stuart, OH, MI, anc ch TP 14:3:73

NOTTINGHAM, Luther b1817, VA, geneal, bk rev CLG 10:3:184

NOWLIN, fam of VA, AL, IL, notes on FF 8:2:35

NOYES, Matilda b1791 h John F Appleman, CT, biog notes AG 55:2:87

NUTT, fam of NH & Can, geneal, bk rev GH 33:4:118 GN 2:8:247 CSB 14:1:23 LL 15:4:182 KCN 20:3:150

OBER, Joseph f1775 w Hannah Munroe, MA, ME, fam rec DE 3:1:16

O'BRIEN, Paul L b1898 w Mary Rose Messel, IN, IL, TX, anc ch THT 7:1:17

William Henry b1800 w Sarah Teresa Slorach, Ir, NY, MI, geneal PF 8:3:61

O'BRYON, George W b1831 w Louisa Ealtha Kessler, MD, WV, OH, anc ch REP 19:3:116

O'CONNOR, William James b1901 w Carrie Loraine Birkhead, KY, CO, anc ch BGS 9:3:42

ODELL, Jonathan b1737, Can, loyalist, biog, bk rev GN 2:6:172

OFFICER, Harry Shepard Caircross b1882 w Mary Jane Campbell, TX, anc ch NGI 3:3:174

OGDEN, David, geneal, bk rev GR 21:4:125

William Riley b1816 w Mary Eliza Dickinson, geneal, bk rev OG 2"4"118

OGDIN, Sabert b1801 w Elizabeth Forrest, OH, anc ch REP 19:4:162

OGLE, Roy b1892 w Nora Marie

Taylor, NE, KS, anc ch TOP
9:2:46
OHIO, Adams Co, fams, notes on,
bk rev FH 2:4:98
Alger, hist 1975, bk rev REP
19:4:167
Allen Co,Bath Twp, hist 1976,
bk rev REP 19:4:167
Andover, hist corres collect,
bk rev AH 1:3:15
Ashland Co, Loudonville, news
abstr 1873-1892, bk rev TST
11:44:29
marrs v1 1846-1850, bk rev REP
19:1:40
marrs v2 1850-1860, bk rev REP
19:4:172
Ashtabula, births 1879-1891 AH
4:4:132
death recs 1880-1885 AH 5:3:72
5:4:114 6:1:25
hist AH 2:2:56 2:3:83 2:4:112
Masons of Rising Sun Lodge
1813-1910 AH 3:3:78 3:4:118
news extracts 1849-1850 AH
2:2:47 2:3:71 2:4:104 3:1:14
3:2:54 3:3:92 4:1:36 4:2:70
4:3:105 4:4:137 5:2:44 5:3:94
5:4:123
rec of births & deaths 1879 AH
3:1:25
Ashtabula Co, Andover Twp, biog
notes AH 5:2:48 6:1:9
cem inscr of misc vets AH
1:3:9 2:2:54 2:4:111 3:1:17
3:2:56
Civil War roll of honor, bk
rev AH 3:4:140
Conneaut, journal of Aaron
Wright 1813-1817 AH 2:3:91
2:4:117
Conneaut, news abstr AH
1:2:9,23 1:3:22 2:2:45 2:3:81
3:1:6 3:2:61 3:3:80 3:4:107
4:1:21 4:2:62 4:3:107 4:4:144
5:2:38 5:3:77 6:1:5,20
6:4:130
Conneaut, Post Office letters
unclaimed 1835 AH 6:1:32
Conneaut, South Ridge
Vigilanie Committee report
1884 AH 3:1:33 3:2:52
diaries of Alanson Millard

1848-1902 AH 3:3:82
Ducro & Son funeral recs
1884 AH 6:4:124
Durkee/Hale cem inscr AH 4:1:7
Grand Army of Republic posts
AH 4:2:49
misc death recs AH 3:4:131
Jefferson, War of 1812
soldiers petition for pension
in 1872 AH 2:4:128
mil pensioners 1840 AH 2:2:41
2:3:85
misc news abstr AH 3:4:109,116
4:1:12,14 4:2:58 4:4:142
5:4:104,122 6:1:17
misc marr returns 1825-1830 AH
3:1:21 3:2:53 3:3:77 4:1:4
4:2:72 4:3:79 4:4:123 5:2:37
5:4:103
Monroe Twp, Kellogsville, hist
notes AH 5:3:98
natural recs AH 5:2:32
pensioners list 1883 AH 4:2:56
4:3:78 5:2:52
probate court recs of deaths
1867-1871 AH 1:3:21 2:2:40
2:3:76 3:1:5 3:2:59 3:3:72
3:4:111 4:2:73 4:3:82 4:4:128
5:2:36 5:4:118 6:1:22 6:4:112
Wayne, hist AH 3:4:115 4:1:20
4:2:45 4:3:96 5:3:84 5:4:117
Windsor Mills, Pioneer cem inscr AH 1:3:8
voters 1813 AH 3:2:73 3:4:106
4:1:6
Assoc of Pioneers, deaths 1882
REP 19:2:79
Athens Co, atlas 1905, bk rev
TST 11:47:29
census 1850, bk rev GH 33:1:87
atlas 1868, bk rev REP 19:1:40
Auglaize Co, cem inscr, bk rev
REP 19:3:137
hist & biog rec 1892, bk rev
REP 19:1:39
misc biog sketches 1892, bk
rev TB 6:2:20
pioneer fams biog notes OHR
20:2:66
Austinburg, autograph bk 1879-
1889 AH 4:1:15
hist notes AH 2:4:120
autograph quilt c1880 AH 4:3:80

Belmont Co, early settlers REP
19:3:93

Benton Co, Dr Skinner's acct bk
KCG 20:3:128

Bible & fam recs at Western Reserve Hist Soc. bk rev AH
2:2:39

biblio of local & fam hist in
SE OH. bk rev IL 11:4:234 GH
33:6:82

Brown Co, fams, notes on, bk
rev FH 2:4:98

pioneers biog notes OHR
20:4:167

Butler Co, atlas 1895. bk rev
GH 33:6:83 TST 11:49:36

Carroll Co, hist atlas 1874. bk
rev CSB 14:1:22

Cath rec vl,2,3, bk rev REP
19:4:172

cemeteries, bk rev BGS 11:4:172
TB 6:2:20

Chesterville, hist 1976, bk rev
REP 19:4:177

Clermont Co, geneal res guide,
bk rev GH 33:2:80 REP
19:4:168

geneal soc descr TST 12:23:46

Cleveland, Ebenezer Church hist
& misc recs CPY 8:4:91

Mutual Protection Soc membs
1837 AH 2:3:76

news abstr deaths, marrs &
divorces 1837-1840 CPY 8:1:6
8:2:28 8:3:54 8:4:80

St Malachi bapt recs CPY
8:1:19

St Malachi Cath Ch marr recs
1865-1899. bk rev TST 12:2:40

Clinton Co, news abstr 1838-
1867. bk rev BGS 7:1:23

news death abstr 1838-1867, bk
rev CI 12:1:16 15:3:116

Colebrook, hist to 1876 AH
2:2:62 2:3:84 2:4:113 3:1:12
3:2:64 3:3:86 3:4:112 4:1:10
4:3:100 4:4:126

Columbiana Co, cem inscr v5, bk
rev REP 19:2:89

cem inscr v6, bk rev REP
19:2:89

hist 1803-1889. bk rev GE 49:9

Columbus, OH state univ annual

1894 LL 15:3:130

Coshocton Co, Pike Twp, Broomstick cem inscr, bk rev REP
19:2:92

county by county geneal guide,
bk rev PGB 11:10:118

Crawford, misc hist & biog
notes AH 2:3:89

Crawford Co, hist vl, bk rev
REP 19:3:136

Whetstone Twp, school reg
1849-1875 REP 19:3:101

Cuyahoga Co, Cleveland, location of recs CPY 8:1:16

Dover Twp, landowners 1874 CPY
8:4:7

location of recs CPY 8:1:16

Orange Twp, landowners 1874
CPY 8:3:64

old Rockport cem inscr CPY
8:3:62

Parma, land owners 1874 CPY
8:2:37

Darke Co, will abstr 1818-1857
vl, bk rev YP 9:3:164

Defiance Co, Riverside cem inscr, bk rev REP 19:3:137

Delaware Co, cem inscr, bk rev
REP 19:2:89

geneal index, bk rev REP
19:2:89

Houk Road (Bierce) Cem, geneal
recs of those buried here, bk
rev REP 19:4:171

residents 1800-1850, bk rev
REP 19:1:45

Scioto Twp, hist 1966, bk rev
REP 19:4:166

description for Welsh imm 1840,
bk rev REP 19:3:136

emig to IL 1830-1860, bk rev
REP 19:3:122

Erie Co, hist (1889), bk rev
CTN 11:3:527

Fairfield Co, hist 1883, bk rev
REP 19:2:90

Lancaster high school class of
1886 REP 19:3:103

First Fams of OH Soc SGS
29:1:52

Franklin Co, marr recs 1871-
1875 vl, bk rev CTN 12:1:179
REP 19:1:40

Worthington, St John's Ch communicants 1833 OHR 20:2:65

Fulton Co, marr bk 3 1864-1867 OHR 20:3:106

Galion, Fairview cem inscr, bk rev REP 19:4:175

Gallia Co, Gallipolis Twp, cem inscr, bk rev REP 19:1:44

tax list 1820, bk rev TST 12:33:39 NGI 3:4:208

Geauga Co, Hambden Twp, hist, bk rev REP 19:2:89

map 1910 AH 3:4:128

geneal period index by county 1979, bk rev GH 33:3:101 TST 12:7:46 OK 24:2:74 REP 19:4:176

geneal res guide TST 12:3:37 OG 3:2:45

Geneva, news extracts AH 2:2:49 2:3:73 2:4:100 3:1:10 3:2:50 3:3:90 3:4:135 4:1:32 4:3:98 4:4:140 5:2:47 5:3:78 6:1:19

Green Co, atlas 1855, bk rev GH 33:6:83

Guernsey Co, black hist, bk rev REP 19:4:169

Greenville, St Paul's Evang Luth Ch, hist 1850-1875, bk rev REP 19:4:166

Hamilton, hist 1896, film rev GH 33:6:92

Hamilton Co,, Anderson Twp, Clough Bapt cem inscr OHR 20:4:147

Anderson Twp, Salem cem inscr OHR 20:2:56

Cincinnati, Fulton cem inscr OHR 20:2:57

Laboyteaux cem inscr OHR 20:3:104

Mariemont, Ferris fam cem inscr OHR 20:4:147

marrs recs 1789-1817 v1, bk rev KY 21:1:33 TST 11:46:29 IL 11:3:148 SCS 16:1:24

Hancock Co, mort schel 1850 OHR 20:2:51

Hardin Co, mort sched 1850 OHR 20:2:54

Harrison Co, mort sched 1850 OHR 20:4:164

Henry Co, marr bk A 1847-1848

OHR 20:2:96

mort sched 1850 OHR 20:3:101

will abstr 1852-1855 OHR 20:4:184

will bk II index 1868-1875 OHR 20:2:96

Highland Co, mort sched 1850 OHR 20:3:108

hist 1873-1900 v5 (1943), bk rev REP 19:4:173

hist of Luth ch women, bk rev REP 19:4:173

Hocking Co, atlas 1876, bk rev REP 19:3:134

mort sched 1850 OHR 20:3:112

Holmes Co, Walnut Creek Valley, Amish pioneer hist, bk rev REP 19:1:43

will bk A index 1825-1852 OHR 20:3:137

will bk I index 1852-1869 OHR 20:3:138

Huroan Co, courthouse resources TST 11:42:30

news abstr 1822-1835, bk rev REP 19:1:44

photo hist 1896, bk rev REP 19:1:40

plat bk, bk rev REP 19:1:42

imm at NY going to OH REP 19:3:105

index to geneal period by co, bk rev YP 9:4:226

Jackson Co, census 1860, bk rev REP 19:4:176

tax list 1820, bk rev TST 12:33:39 NGI 3:4:208

Jefferson, deaths 1906 AH 5:4:127

news extracts 1901 AH 6:4:122

Kingsville, birthday bk 1920 AH 6:4:117

soldiers burials AH 3:4:130

Knox Co, rural direct 1915-1920, bk rev REP 19:3:136

Lake Co, landowners map 1840 (1978), bk rev REP 19:3:133

location of recs CPY 8:4:86

Painesville, location of recs CPY 8:4:86

Lawrence Co, US Postmasters REP 19:1:8

vets cem recs, bk rev REP

19:4:171
voters 1864 REP 19:1:9
Lima, First Ch of Christ Scientist 1913-1949, hist, bk rev REP 19:4:171
limited access to misc recs TST 12:12:37
Logan Co, hist & biog rec 1892, bk rev REP 19:1:39
ledges bk abstr REP 19:4:146
misc biog sketches 1892, bk rev TB 6:2:20
Lucas Co, Toledo, unclaimed letters 1837 OHR 20:3:129
Mahoning Co, Campbell, hist, bk rev REP 19:3:137
hist collect 1876, bk rev REP 19:4:177
misc marr lic 1879-1883 AH 4:2:4
Marion Co, probate court recs guide SGS 29:1:44
marrs 1898-1912, bk rev OK 24:2:73
Marysville, "Tribune" news abstr 1850-1859, bk rev REP 19:2:89
Medina Co, index to 1861 hist OHR 20:3:131
migration routes REP 19:2:61
misc place names AH 6:4:107,136
misc US post offices & town CPY 8:1:2
Monroe Co, Adams Twp, Pleasant Ridge cem inscr OHR 20:2:58
Malago Twp, Jerusalem area, small cem inscr OHR 20:2:59
Morgan Co, Manchester Twp, hist,bk rev REP 19:4:169
Morrow Co, atlas 1901, bk rev REP 19:4:170
hist 1880, bk rev REP 19:4:170
Muskingum Co, Zanesville, Woodlawn cem inscr, bk rev REP 19:1:45
New Lexington, misc ch rec 1816-1940, bk rev REP 19:2:92
Noble Co, cem inscr index, bk rev REP 19:3:135
hist 1887, bk rev REP 19:4:175
Oak Harbor, St Paul's Evan United Ch of Christ, bapt recs 1879-1883 GER 16:437

Oberlin College students 1833-1960, bk rev REP 19:2:92
OH Vol Free Homestead Colony KS 1873 AH 3:2:44 3:3:74 3:4:120
"Ohio Magazine" 1906, bk rev REP 19:4:169
Ostrander, Ostrander Pres Ch hist & recs, bk rev REP 19:1:45
pass list 1839 REP 19:3:104
Paulding Co, hist atlas 1892, bk rev REP 19:2:90
Perry Co, cem inscr, bk rev REP 19:1:44
hist 1883, bk rev REP 19:2:90
marr recs vl-11 1818-1904, bk rev REP 19:2:92
ministers, bk rev REP 19:2:92
name index to Martzolff 1902 hist, bk rev REP 19:3:136
New Lexington, Maplewood cem inscr, bk rev REP 19:2:92
wills vB, bk rev REP 19:2:92
Pickaway Co, Deer Creek Twp, misc fam cems inscr OHR 20:2:61 20:4:172
Pike Co, Waverly, Evergreen Union cem inscr OC 16:2:68
pioneers in IL IG 14:2:60
pioneers of first fams, 6th roster REP 19:2:68
Preble Co, Bank Spring cem inscr OHR 20:3:105
land grants (1968), bk rev YP 9:2:109
marr recs v2 1831-1840, bk rev YP 9:2:108
Rev War, descs of Rev War soldiers in OH OHR 20:2:93
Richland Co, biog hist 1901, bk rev REP 19:4:167
Jefferson Twp, school recs 1843-1862, bk rev REP 19:4:172
plat bk & city maps 1978, bk rev REP 19:3:136
wills abstr 1813-1873 vl, bk rev NGS 67:1:66
Ross Co, cem inscr, bk rev REP 19:1:46
Deerfield Twp, old Bapt cem/Ater fam cem inscr OHR 20:2:60

fam recs v2, bk rev GH 33:6:83 TST 12:27:48

roster of soldiers in war with Spain 1898-1899 (1916), bk rev REP 19:4:166

Sandusky Co, cem inscr v1, bk rev GH 33:5:96 TST 12:28:40 IL 11:4:238

school report 1893, bk rev REP 19:1:42

Scioto Co, Madison Twp, Squires cem inscr REP 19:1:20

Seventh Reg 1861-1865, biog notes, bk rev AH 3:3:88

Shelby Co, atlas map 1875, 1900, direc 1900, bk rev REP 19:1:39

hist & biog rec 1892, bk rev REP 19:1:39

memorial recs 1819-1975, bk rev REP 19:1:39

misc biog sketches 1892, bk rev TB 6:2:20

South Ridge, underground railway AH 4:1:18 4:2:47

southeastern OH local & fam hist sources in print, 1979, bk rev TSP 3:1:37 TST 12:31:40 GE 49:7 VAG 23:4:213 NGI 3:4:208

Stark Co, Alliance, Fox fam cem inscr REP 19:4:155

Sturgeonville, hist AH 1:3:25

Summit Co, Bath Twp, East Bath cem inscr OHR 20:2:63

Bath Twp, Stony Hill cem inscr OHR 20:2:63

cem inscr, bk rev TST 12:18:38 REP 19:4:171 CTN 12:2:364

Copley Twp, Stimson cem inscr OHR 20:2:64

Symmes Purchase recs 1787-1800, bk rev GE 47:14

township rec bks as source TST 12:33:38

Trumbull Co, Greene, misc residents c1900 AH 2:2:51

hist collect 1876, bk rev REP 19:4:177

hist notes AH 3:4:125

research notes AH 4:1:24

road tax recs 1887-1901 AH 4:4:131

Tuscarawas Co, marrs 1808-1844, bk rev TB 6:4:33

Twenty-ninth OH Vols 1861-1865, bk rev AH 3:2:40

Union Co, cem inscr, bk rev REP 19:2:89

census 1830, bk rev TB 6:3:24

Common Pleas court rec 1820-1850 abstr, bk rev REP 19:1:44

geneal index, bk rev REP 19:2:89

St John's Evang Luth Ch 1838 & 1843 members REP 19:1:19

univ lib recs of local govt, bk rev TST 11:39:35

Van Wert Co, roster 1891 46th OH Vols. REP 19:4:151

Vinton Co, atlas 1876, bk rev REP 19:2:90

Warren Co, hist TST 11:51:36

Washington Co, Coal Run, misc Sprague fam cems inscr OHR 20:4:148

Wayne Co, biog hist (1878), bk rev AH 3:4:124

census 1880, bk rev REP 19:4:175

Western Reserve, geneal data on women before 1840 index, microfilm rec REP 19:4:176

geneal data on women before 1840 (1850), microfilm rec REP 19:4:176

hist of achievements, bk rev TST 11:48:37

Whitewater, village of Shakers 1824-1916 hist, bk rev TSP 3:1:39 TST 12:26:47 GE 46:8

Wood Co, geneal res guide, bk rev REP 19:1:46

O'KELLEY, Thomas f1750 w Elizabeth Dean, Ir, VA, geneal, bk rev GH 33:3:107 VAG 23:2:147

O'KILL, Mary (Jay) f1822 h John O'Kill, NJ, biog notes GNJ 54:2:143

O'KILLEA, David d1697 w Jane Powell, Ir, Wales, MA, geneal, bk rev CTN 9:2:307

OKLAHOMA, Atoka Co, Seco-McGee fam cem inscr OK 24:1:22

Sexton fam cem inscr OK

24:1:22

Bryan Co, ledger 1850-1857 THT 4:2:10

marrs bk 1, bk rev DG 25:4:260

Caddo Co, Hinton, Cath cem inscr OK 24:3:139

Hinton, Hinton cem inscr OK 24:3:148 24:4:199

marrs bk 1 1901-1905 OK 24:3:121 24:4:192

Canadian Co, index to Terr marr recs bk 1 1890-1894, bk rev GH 33:4:113

Comanche Co, Lawton, Deyo cem inscr TA 14:2:31

co recs printed, index OK 24:1:32 24:2:85 24:3:143

Craig Co, marr licenses 1906-1907 TA 14:2:45

school teachers 1913 TA 14:1:18

Creek Co, Drumright, misc obits TA 14:1:10

Cushing, Cushing First Pres Ch SCS 14:1:4

Doaksville, unclaimed letters 1849 OK 24:4:180

Enid, Phillips Univ Student Army Training Corps 1918 TRI 19:3:50

Fort Gibson, Bean's Rangers roster 1832 OK 24:1:20

geneal res aids OK 24:3:146

Grady Co, marr bk 1 1908-1909 OK 24:1:8

marrs & obits 1892-1889 OK 24:3:135

hist sites, bk rev BGS 8:4:32

Hughes Co, Gum Springs, school census report 1913 OK 24:4:182

Indian Terr, Northeastern Area, US Court 1st Div Administrator Rec bk A 1891-1895 OK 24:1:23

Kay Co, cem inscr, bk rev GH 33:5:76

hist 1893-1968, bk rev TB 6:3:21

LeFlore Co, Friendship Bapt Ch recs OK 24:3:13

Logan Co, hist 1889-1977 v1, bk rev GH 33:5:77

Mayes Co, cem inscr TA 14:2:37

Muskogee, First Pres Ch recs 1875 TA 14:2:63

natives in Stickley Funeral Home TX reg bks 1910-1954 OK 24:2:65

natives in TX 1887-1889 OK 24:3:133

pioneer life from 1892 (1949), bk rev TB 6:3:22

Pittsburg Co, Carney cem inscr OK 24:4:179

Pond Creek, Odd Fellows hist OK 24:1:41

Pushmataha Co, Moyers cem inscr THT 7:2:112

Rocky Point cem inscr THT 7:2:112

Seminole Co, Konawa, news abstr 1904 OK 24:4:188

Texas Co, Hartville cem inscr OK 24:2:76

Tulsa, news vr 1912-1914 TA 14:1:21 14:2:53 14:3:87

Tulsa Co, probate recs abstr TA 14:3:79

Vinita, unclaimed letters 1884 OK 24:3:137

Wagoner, misc obits OK 24:2:91

OLIPHANT, Nancy b1826 h Andrew Martindale, IN, CO, fam letters BGS 8:4:14

William, NC, geneal, bk rev GE 46:9

OLIVE, Joseph Benjamin b1879 w Alma Elizabeth Posey, GA, TX, OK, anc ch THT 7:1:17

OLIVER, Achilles Kellis bc1780 w Martha Gill, VA, TN, anc ch YP 9:3:129

George K w Parthenia Burton, MS, MO, fam recs LL 15:3:136

Thomas H b1838 w Lydia J Marvin, NY, Bible rec TT 19:2:84

OLSEN, Gustave f1859 w Anna Olesdotter, Sw, IL, biog & fam notes IL 11:2:95

OLSON, August b1874 w Jennie Emelia Hed, MN, geneal, bk rev GH 33:4:119 MN 10:1:42

O'MEARA, fam of Ottawa Can FAM 18:3:121

O'NEAL, Samuel m1802 w Kiddy

Hinton, NC, anc ch AGS
20:2:66

O'NEIL, George Josepah b1906 w
Birchie Mary Lawson, MO, IL,
Bible rec GL 13:2:40

OOTHOUDT, Alexander b1787 w Belinda Sykes, NY, WI, MN,
geneal v3, bk rev GH 33:2:85
MN 10:1:40

ORDWAY, James f1635, MA, geneal,
bk rev CTN 9:2:311

OREGON, Applegate country, hist
& geneal, bk rev OC 16:2:67

donation land claims OG 1"2"38
1:3:74 3:2:36

adoption & name changes 1905-
1907 BB 11:1:5

Albany, Milton Hale/Syracuse
cem inscr ORB 18:1:10

Barlow Toll Road Foster-Petty
grove store lists 1846-1919,
bk rev TB 6:3:24

geneal resources 1980, bk rev
TRI 17:3:46 TB 6:4:29

Hillsborough, unclaimed letters
1851 BB 11:4:78

hist of OR terr, bk rev TB
6:4:33

Jackson Co, marrs v1 1853-1877,
v2 1877-1888, v3 1889-1896,
bk rev TB 6:2:19

mort recs 1904-1931, bk rev TB
6:4:30

Josephine Co, marrs 1857-1900,
bk rev TB 6:2:19

census 1880, bk rev TB 6:2:19

Lane Co, cem inscr & maps v1-3,
bk rev TB 6:4:30

marr recs index 1853-1873 ORB
18:3:55 18:4:79

marr recs 1870-1879 v2, bk rev
GH 33:5:77 BB 11:3:48

partial index of citizenship &
natural recs ORB 18:2:25

lawyers prior to 1910, biog
notes SGS 29:1:21 29:2:117
29:3:213 29:4:303

Lewis Co, census 1850 OG 2:1:15
2:2:43

Marion Co, Aumsville/Mill Creek
Ch of Christ, hist BB 11:4:73

Liberty School House honor
roll 1879 BB 11:4:78

marr recs v1-2 1849-1874, bk
rev TB 6:4:31

Turner, Hunsaker cem inscr BB
11:3:57

migration studies TB 6:4:5

misc memoirs, bk rev BB 11:4:70

Molalla, hist, bk rev GFP
29:3:47

Multnomah Co, marr recs bk 3
GFP 28:5:95 28:6:113 28:7:135
28:8:153 28:9:173 28:10:186

news death notices 1884-1885 BB
11:3:59 11:4:81

news marr notices 1851 BB
11:4:76

Oregon Terr hist notes SGS
29:4:289

pioneer cert list ORB 18:4:94

pioneer fams of OR Terr 1850,
bk rev TB 6:3:25 6:4:32

pioneer stories, bk rev CDS
16:3:4

Polk Co, Davidson cem inscr BB
11:1:9 11:2:31

Pleasant Hill Meth Ch, misc
marrs BB 11:2:32

Portland, Nineteenth St hist,
bk rev CDS 16:5:47

provisional land claims bk 7
GFP 28:5:91 28:6:111 28:7:131
28:8:149 28:9:169 28:10:193
29:1:13 29:2:37 29:3:55
29:4:75

Salem, unclaimed letters 1885
BB 11:1:2

Vancouver, St James Cath Ch
recs v1,2, bk rev BGS 9:4:34

wagon train travelers from MO
1844 NGS 67:2:141

West Linn, hist, bk rev TB
6:2:21

Wheeler Co, Caleb cem inscr BB
11:3:55

Waterman Flat/Mountain Creek,
Foppiano fam cem inscr BB
11:3:56

Willamette Valley, hist, bk rev
GH 33:3:101 GJ 8:4:215

ORENDUFF, Jesse William, VA,
Civil War letters 1863 DG
25:2:95

ORLANDINO, Vincent Arthur b1908
w Cira Marchese, NY, anc ch

BGS 11:3:135

ORMOND, William Jr b1769, NC, biog notes NCJ 5:4:263

William Thomas b1889 w Hattie Estelle Gale, VA, NC, anc ch THT 6:3:55

ORMSBEE, George Daniel b1882 w May Belle Luther, KS, CO, anc ch BGS 9:4:42

George Hubbard b1829 w Harriet Hosford, geneal, bk rev BGS 9:1:37 CTN 9:4:607

ORR, James w Janet McClement, Ir, geneal, bk rev IRA 13:280 AH 6:1:27 SCG 13:51

ORTEGO, Orise f1892 w Octavia DesHotel, LA, anc ch YP 9:2:66

ORTIZ, fam of Mexico, notes on KK 17:1:5

Piedad Maria b1890 h Librado Romeco, NM, fam rec NMG 18:3:83

ORWIG, Frederick f1800 w Elizabeth, PA, geneal, bk rev GH 33:2:86 KCG 20:2:89

OSBORN, Jeremiah f1775 w Miss Newman, VA, NC, fam notes LL 14:3:134

Peter Jr b1821 w Hannah Andrew, Louisa Sally, NC, MO, biog notes & anc ch SCC 16:3:69,71

OSBURN, Samuel b1760 w Mary Johnston, NY, biog notes AH 5:2:51

OSTRANDER, Charles f1823 w Elizabeth Hempstreet, Bible rec NYR 110:2:104

OSTWALD, Walter Alvin b1891 w Ila Minnie Forrest, CO, anc ch BGS 11:1:44

OVENDORF, William b1843 w Francis Viall, PA, OH, anc ch REP 19:3:122

OVERHOLSER, Overholser Fam Assoc Bulletin, Box 106, Oley PA 19547

OVERHOLT, Abraham b1765, PA, acct bk, bk rev GH 33:1:87

OVERLY, George b1819 w Hannah Elliot, OH, anc ch REP 19:3:119

OWEN, Frank C b1817 w Lucy W

Harris, AL, biog notes VL 13:4:171

Isaac N, AL, biog notes VL 13:4:170

Thomas bc1671, VA, geneal VAG 23:3:163 23:4:259

William bc1673, VA, geneal VAG 23:3:163 23:4:259

OWENS, Owen Pritchard b1823 w Elinor Morris, Wales, WI, geneal, bk rev CTN 8:1:39

OWINGS, Richard w Rachel, MD, geneal, bk rev CTN 9:2:316

OYER, Frederick f1764 w Elisabetha, Ger, NY, geneal, bk rev CTN 11:4:705

PABST, Heinrich bc1697 w Gertraut, Ger, PA, geneal, bk rev GH 33:1:93 NCJ 5:1:64

PACKARD, Harvey b1794 w Lucretia Chapman, MI, fam & Bible rec AGS 20:1:1

PADDOCK, Robert f1632, MA, geneal, bk rev MQ 45:1:27

PAGE, fam letters TX 1863 DG 25:1:32

Burt Wesley b1878 w Bernice Larkin, NY, anc ch NW 2:4:134

George, CT, geneal, bk rev DM 43:1:47 NGS 67:1:70

John H b1832 w Emily A Hamilton, ME, Bible rec DE 3:2:21

Rufus m1827 w Martha Howard, ME, fam rec DE 3:2:20

Rufus King m1819 w Caroline Hall, ME, fam rec DE 3:2:20

Samuel f1814 w Elisabeth, Bible rec PR 3:3:50

PAGELS, Adolph b1852 w Louise Bertram, Ger, TX, Bible rec STK 7:3:136

PAINE, William, reinterment 1929 IN TSP 3:1:35

PAINTER, John Aaron b1863 w Florence (Nibbett) Neilson Hoopes, Eng, UT, geneal, bk rev KCG 20:3:148

Lorenzo Sog b1817 w Elizabeth Bousman, Mrs Turner, OH, CA, biog RED 12:1:7

PALLETT, Stewart f1817 w Polly,

Bible rec TA 14:1:2

PALMER, fam of KY, fam recs KA 14:4:215

fam res notes OC 16:1:1

Frank b1872 w Minnie Darst, OH, anc ch REP 19:3:124

PANKONIN, Herman Louis b1895 w Margaret Emily Logan, NE, anc ch BGS 10:3:42

PAPINEAU, fam of Can, geneal, bk rev MN 10:1:40

PARK, Samuel w Anna Miller, NJ, MI, notes on FG 21:1:13

PARKE, Robert bc1580 w Martha Chaplin, Mrs Alice (Freeman) Thompson, Eng, CT, geneal notes CTN 9:1:12

William Demetrus b1895 w Susan Belle Davidson, WA, anc ch TB 6:4:26

PARKER, Daniel b1781 w Patsy Dixon, VA, IL, biog notes THT 7:2:102

Jerry B f1852 w Lucy D Baker, MA, Bible rec THT 4:2:9

Samuel d1862 w Maria Louisa Tyson, Bible rec CTN 11:2:214

PARKMAN, Ebenezer b1703, MA, diary, bk rev CTN 7:4:520

PARKS, Emily f1810, CT, notes on AH 3:4:108

PARMITER, Ralph Allen b1847 w Ellen, NY, Bible rec NGS 67:4:293

PARROTT, Benjamin bc1795, VA, NC, TN, geneal, bk rev FP 22:4:210 OK 24:2:73 VL 14:1:45

John b1792 w Rachel, MD, OH, geneal, bk rev REP 19:4:173

PARRY, Edward w Rebecca, PA will 1727 LL 15:2:102

PARSHALL, James b1630 w Catherine Nellis, NY, geneal, bk rev TS 21:4:174

PARSONS, Sarah E (Lee) m1890 h Orin H Parsons, OH, NE, obit AH 3:1:16

Thomas H m1862 w Mary M Birchum, Bible rec THT 3:1:10

PASLEY, Henry A bc1770 w Nancy, VA, KY, IL, fam rec CI 14:2:49

PASSMORE, Barbara Mary (Frey) f1918 h Luke Passmore, MI, corres AH 4:1:25

PATERSON, fam Bible rec NSN 4:5:43

PATIENCE, George, ME, Bible rec DE 2:5:7

PATRICK, Charles Edward b1833 w Elizabeth Marien, VA, NE, Bible rec THT 5:1:26

Richard bc1700, CT, NY, geneal, bk rev CTN 11:2:343 DM 43:2:90

PATTERSON, Andrew b1772 w Rachel Srvette, ME, Bible rec CTN 10:3:417

fam of Lincoln Co, Ontario, Can FAM 18:4:222

J W, VA, letter 186- THT 2:2:28

Nelson f1790, VA, TN, geneal, bk rev GH 33:1:94

William b1824 w Sarah Ann Megraw, Bible rec CI 15:3:85

PAUL, Ellen b1852 h John J Garlington, IA, biog notes BGS 8:2:23

PAULSEN, Gene Leroy b1929 w Euva Jo Crawford, OK, SD, NV, anc ch TRI 17:2:38

PAULUS, John Lewis b1860 w Beatrice Pearle Jenkins, IL, TX, anc ch GR 21:2:54

PAYNE, Elijah W f1840 w Mary J Bear, VA, IL, Bible rec GL 13:1:17

James f1873, WA, biog notes TB 6:2:14

James William b1871 w Nellis Josephine Crume, IN, NM, fam rec NMG 18:4:122

Martin b1817 w Mary Price, OH, IL, OR, biog notes ORB 17:7:64

PEAK, fam geneal, bk rev CTN 8:1:35

PEARSON, Karl Maurice b1905 w Ruth Alden Spooner Thayer, NH, MA, anc ch BGS 10:1:38

PEASE, John Sr bc1630 w Mary Goodell, Ann _ummings, Eng, MA, CT, geneal (1869), bk rev CTN 12:1:177 CDS 16:1:6

PECK, Arthur Francis Seaning

b1880 w Brenda Vance deVere Morrison, NY, PA, biog notes ANC 14:3:97

John Henry b1851 w Sarah Catherine Vannice, Bible rec BGS 7:3:1

Thomas b1798 w Lovisa Arnold, NY, VT, Bible rgc CTN 7:2:320

PECKHAM, Samuel b1759 w Hannah, CT, Bible rec CTN 7:1:160

PECOT, Charles Theodore b1814 w Claire Emilie Felicitie Sigur, LA, anc ch AGE 8:3:100

PEDEN, Alexander b1762 w Lydia Thomas, PA, anc ch REP 19:3:123

PEEBLES, William b1787 w Elizabeth Sheets, VA, TN, Bible rec BWG 8:1:44

PEEL, Jonathan m1839 w Ann Emoline Zachry, GA, AL, biog notes GR 21:4:151

PEERY, fam of Scot, VA, MO, geneal MGR 14:1:13

PEHRSSON, Pehr b1815, Sweden, anc ch OC 16:4:123

PEIRCE, Jesse d1847, OH, cem inscr AH 3:3:77

PELL, Jo C b1822 w Miss Curtis, KY, biog VQ 16:4:58

PEMBERTON, fam of Dublin Ir, geneal IA 11:1:14

PENCE, Raye E b1892 w M Lucile Ward, IN, CA, anc ch ACL 4:3:58

PENDERGRASS, Jasoan Calvin b1826 w Jane H Benson, SC, AK, anc ch HJA 6:2:41

PENDLETON, John Gilmore b1828 w Mary A, Sarah E Blanchard, ME, fam rec DE 3:1:28

PENN, Thomas d1818, Bible rec BCG 7:3:58

PENNINGTON, fam of SC, geneal, bk rev GH 33:6:88

John bc1820 w Sarah E, TN, MO, OR, biog notes GFP 29:2:9

PENNOYER, fam of Eng, N E & NY, geneal, bk rev NGS 67:1:72

PENNSYLVANIA, Adams Co, hist 1886, bk rev GE 42:11

hist of "Low Dutch" colony & Conowago Pres Ch, bk rev REP 19:1:43

Marsh Creek, Menn settlement hist 1769-1823 PM 2:4:2

Allegheny Co, court docket 1789 WPA 5:2:51 5:3:89

court docket 1791 WPA 5:4:134

Elizabeth Twp, hist, bk rev WPA 5:2:77

misc marrs 1851-1890 by Rev Alfred J Wilcox SGS 29:1:9

natural appl 1798-1840 v1, bk rev CTN 11:3:522 SCS 16:2:57

natural appl v2-3 1840-1869, bk rev SCS 16:2:57

Beaver Co, Fallston, letters held at Post Office 1830 WPA 5:4:133

Greersburgh, letters held at Post Office 1830 WPA 5:2:74 5:3:112

Ohio Twp, Oakgrove cem inscr WPA 5:1:23

Bedford Co, cem inscr, bk rev BCG 8:4:92

cem inscr v2, bk rev CDS 16:2:5 16:4:12

Everett, Steckman fam cem inscr NGS 67:4:286

Berks Co, Albany Twp, New Bethel Union Ch, recs from 1761, bk rev REP 19:4:174

hist sites, bk rev NGI 3:2:108

Reading, hist sites map, bk rev PM 2:3:25

Tulpehocken Settlement chs & recs sources TST 11:39:36

births 1675-1875, bk rev OG 4:4:117

Bucks Co, acc bk 1790-1833, bk rev GH 33:1:87

atlas 1876 & 1891, bk rev REP 19:2:91

Cameron Co, hist WPA 5:4:127

Centre Co, Boalsburg cem inscr, bk rev GH 33:2:80

geneal res guide, bk rev TB 6:3:25

Chester Co, geneal res guide, bk rev TB 6:3:22

Ch of the Brethren, hist, bk rev GE 42:12

Col & Rev War fams, 1911 v1-3, bk rev TST 12:10:38 NYR

110:1:54 CTN 11:4:699 NGS 67:1:67 AG 55:1:60

colonists killed, captured or missing WPA 5:1:8 5:2:57 5:3:106

county courthouse res guide, bk rev GH 33:5:70

county government & archives in (1947), bk rev TB 6:2:20

Crawford Co, Blooming Valley School, recs AH 4:4:124

Conneaut Twp, Steambaugh cem inscr AH 1:3:20 2:2:53

Dauphin Co, Derry Station, Ch of the Brethren (Dunkard) cem inscr GER 16:428

Derry Twp, Swatara Station, Huber farm cem inscr GER 16:429

Klinger Ch recs, bk rev GE 42:11

South Hanover Twp, Ebersole farm cem inscr GER 16:429

Delaware Co, Radnor Twp, hist, bk rev AG 55:2:121

Elk Co, hist WPA 5:3:85

emigs 1641-1819, ship pass lists (1934), bk rev CTN 11:3:518

Erie Co, Amity Twp, Williams farm cem inscr AH 2:4:118

Frances Corners, Frances cem notes AH 6:4:116

geneal res guide AH 3:4:129

Girard Twp, Henry Miller's acct bk 1840-1872,, names abstr AH 1:2:18 1:3:19 2:2:59

Girard Twp, news extracts AH 3:1:22,26 3:3:81 3:4:133 4:1:27,32 4:2:64 4:3:102 4:4:135 5:2:42 5:3:99 5:4:119

misc marrs 1851-1890 by Rev Alfred J Wilcox SGS 29:1:9

Pletea, Miller Corners cem inscr AH 1:2:13

Fayette Co, Old Uniontown Meth Epis cem inscr OHR 20:4:162

Springhill Twp, Mount Moriah Presb Ch cem inscr WPA 5:4:144

geneal guide to records TT 19:2:75

Ger cem inscr, bk rev GH

33:5:78

hist 1896, bk rev REP 19:4:173

hist of 41st US Vol Infantry 1899-1901, bk rev REP 19:3:137

Indiana Co, hist WPA 5:2:43

Jefferson Co, deaths 1852-1854 WPA 5:3:101

Juniata Valley, index to 1897 biog encyc, bk rev IL 11:4:236

Lancaster Co, Bart Twp, Bartville store recs 1842 SCS 16:4:103

New Holland, Trinity Evan Luth Ch recs 1730-1799, bk rev GH 33:1:88

land recs to 1732, bk rev CTN 9:3:473

Lawrence Co, Camp Run Covenater cem inscr WPA 5:2:70

Lebanon Co, acc bk 1794-1817, bk rev GH 33:1:87

Lehigh Co, Lynn Twp, Jacksonville, Jacob's Union Ch rec & hist, bk rev REP 19:3:135 TST 12:2:46

maps 1718-1920, bk rev YP 9:2:107 GH 33:1:88 TB 6:4:31

marrs to 1790 (1830), bk rev REP 19:4:173 CTN 9:3:475

marrs prior to 1790 (1742-1790), bk rev TB 6:4:32

marrs prior to 1810 v1-2, bk rev TB 6:4:31

Menn lib guide TST 12:1:52 12:24:39

Mercer Co, hist WPA 5:1:1

Mercer, "Western Press" death abstr 1836-1839 WPA 5:4:130

misc Col fams, bk rev DM 43:1:46

misc fam data in land patents 1760-1763 NGS 67:2:130

misc fams v4, bk rev REP 19:4:176

oral hist guide, bk rev MHM 74:4:371

PA Gazette, abstr 1775-1783, bk rev CTN 9:3:473

runaways 1775-1783 NGS 67:2:121

PA Ger hist 1898, bk rev CDS 16:3:4

Pitt Twp, tax lists 1795-1796 WPA 5:1:24

Pittsburgh, "Almanack" marrs & deaths 1827-1831 WPA 5:1:15 5:2:68 5:3:104 5:4:156

misc marrs 1870 AH 5:4:126

tax list 1818 WPA 5:1:30 5:2:62 5:3:97

Pittsburgh Co, tax list 1818 WPA 5:4:139

Radnor, hist, bk rev CTA 21:3:141

res guide to bks on PA, bk rev KCG 20:2:91

Rev War, Battle of Wyoming DAR 113:5:522

PA Ger hist 1765-1783 (1908), bk rev NGS 67:1:68

roster, Capt William Guthrie's Rangers, 1779 WPA 5:1:17

Scotch-Irish of Col PA 1944, bk rev GH 33:6:83

settlers from CT c1750 AG 55:2:72

Snyder Co, Menn hist PM 2:2:2

Somerset Co, Black Twp, Rhoads cem inscr LM 20:2:5

early marrs LM 20:1:6 20:2:3 20:3:6 20:4:3

hist notes LM 20:1:3

Hooversville, hist LM 20:3:1 20:4:1

Meyersdale, Hay-Boger house hist LM 20:1:1

misc estates 1818-1821 LM 20:1:4 20:2:7 20:3:5 20:4:4

Somerset Borough, notes on prominent men LM 20:4:5

state lib resources descr BR 6:2:33

Washington, tax list 1784-1785 MGR 14:2:82

Washington Co, Donegal Twp, Dutch Fork Settlement, geneal hist, bk rev NGS 67:3:222 TS 21:1:28

census 1850 v1,2, bk rev REP 19:1:44

early recs, bk rev GH 33:4:114

marrs before 1887 by Squires Isaac & Joseph F Mayes, bk

rev TST 12:9:45 GE 49:7 REP 19:4:171 GH 33:3:101 NGS 67:4:305

Welsh settlement, bk rev OG 5:4:116

Western Dist, fed courts list WPA 5:1:12

natural lists 1820-1840 WPA 5:1:12 5:2:59 5:3:113

Western PA pioneer settlers, bk rev SCS 14:2:53

Westmoreland Co, Bell (Washington) Twp, St James, Evang Luth Ch recs 1847-1875, bk rev REP 19:1:39

Ger Ch recs 1772-1791, bk rev GH 33:6:84 TST 12:19:39

marr & death notices 1818-1865, bk rev KN 2:1:40

natural recs 1802-1852, bk rev GH 33:4:114

Rostraver Twp, hist 1754-1894, bk rev CI 15:2:30

South Huntingdon Twp, tax lists 1820-1821 WPA 5:1:18 5:2:71

York Co, Yorktown, Quaker marr rec 1779 BGS 6:3:12

PENTECOST, Dorsey b1739 w Catherine Beeler, VA, biog, bk rev GH 33:5:87

PERKINS, Henry Platt b1830 w Lucy M Wallace, Can, MI, Bible rec MI 24:1:10

James b1757 w Martha, ME, Bible rec DE 3:3:16

Jenckes, letter 1784 BGS 2:2:11

John b1811 w Sarah Felix, NY, IN, OR, biog notes GFP 29:4:73

PERRIN, David m1638 w Jaque Blanc, Switz, geneal, bk rev GH 33:3:107

PERRY, Abraham d1839, NC, SC, biog notes NCJ 5:1:68

Benjamin f1860, KY, biog notes FH 2:2:50

Grover Cleveland b1892 w Ethelyn Lucile Roach, TX, anc ch THT 6:3:63

PERSON, Dorothy (Wooldridge), auto TB 6:3:7

PERSONETT, fam of MD, IN, geneal

MD 20:4:297

PESEK, Cyril Paul b1904 w Muriel Eleanor Fossum, SD, MN, anc ch BGS 10:2:42

PETERS, Ignatius G b1894 w Mary Ann Straub, TX, anc ch THT 6:3:60

Samuel b1735, CT, NY, biog, bk rev CTN 11:3:523

PETERSEN, Frederick b1837 w Katherine Marie Hansen, Kate Kramer Graeser, Denmark, NY, IA, geneal, bk rev GH 33:6:88 KCG 20:4:206

PETERSON, Malcolm McLeod b1792 w Sidney Curtis Walker, NC, geneal, bk rev GH 33:2:85

PETRY, Steffan b1729 w Anna Danner, Ger, OH, geneal, bk rev GH 33:2:86

PETTY, William A b1804 w Nancy Taulbee, GA, geneal FF 8:1:45

PEYTON, Valentine f1660, VA, biog notes NGS 67:1:60

PFEFFERLE, John b1842 w Margaret Walters, Ger, PA, IN, anc ch REP 19:2:85

PFOHL, William m1886 w Caroline Magel, MI, biog notes OC 16:2:57

PHELAN, Robert Joseph Sr b1911 w Opal Loveall (Rachel S Garrison), PA, CA, anc ch BGS 10:4:46

PHELLIS, Jacob b1805 w Marilda Brundage, NY, OH, anc ch REP 19:4:164

PHELPS, fam of NY & N E, geneal abstr, bk rev GH 33:5:88 CDS 16:3:3

Otto b1862, IL, NE, fam notes GL 13:1:25 13:2:55 13:3:85 13:4:109

PHILBRICK, George W b1815 w Julia A Flye, Bible rec KN 2:2:33

PHILLIPS, Luke b1789 w Cynthia, RI, fam rec RIR 5:3:10

PHIPPS, Porter f1856 w Sarah Jane Baird, PA, letters & diary, bk rev WPA 5:2:78

PIATT, Jacob b1747, NJ, KY, biog notes TST 12:35:36

PICKEL, John H b1824 w Sarah,TN, CO, biog notes BGS 5:1:8

PICKINS, Andrew d1817, notes on SGS 29:2:116

PIERCE, Elias D f1856, ID, auto, bk rev CDS 16:1:4

Maurice m1822 w Modeste St Germain, LA, biog notes PGB 11:5:53

PIERSON, Wyllys f1771 w Mary, NJ, PA, geneal DM 42:3:103 42:4:147

PIKE, Edgar Albert b1879 w Edith Pearl Rice, IL, anc ch BGS 11:1:38

PILLSBURY, Arnold Dexter b1911 w Marion Francis Fellows, ME, anc ch DE 3:2:11

PINNEY, Abner b1748 w Ruth Gillet, CT, anc ch OC 16:2:63

PITKIN, William f1659, CT, geneal, CT bicentennial series x1, bk rev CTN 9:1:127

PIXLEY, William d1689, MA, geneal, bk rev CTN 9:4:603

PLANTE, fam of MN, death recs Rice Co MN 10:1:73

PLESTED, Sophia Pamela (Lenton) f1832 h George Plested, James S Reed, Eng, NY, Can, photo & biog notes FAM 18:2:87

William b1842 w Alice Gordon, Can, NY,, CO, famphotos & biog notes FAM 18:2:87,88,91,92

POINDEXTER, fam of Fr, geneal, bk rev LL 15:2:82

POLAND, biblio for geneal res, bk rev PN 1:1:3

biblio of holdings of Enoch Pratt (MD) lib PN 1:2:16

emig study centers PN 1:1:15

emigs to Am MD 20:1:1

Galicia, geneal res guide PN 1:2:19 JJG 3:1:9

geneal res guide GH 33:6:9 BGS 8:3:1 NGI 3:3:171 PN 1:1:12

geneal res guide (Gnacinski), bk rev NGI 3:2:109

geneal res guide (Wellauer), bk rev TST 12:37:22 IL 11:4:234

geneal res guide to LDS lib recs GH 33:2:9

geneal res socities STC 2:1:39

heraldry & fams of nobility PN 1:1:1 1:2:17

map collect notes PN 1:2:27

names PN 1:1:11

Polish-Am geneal res guide, bk rev TST 12:25:48

Pomerania, geneal res notes PN 1:1:9

tracing Polish ancestry, bk rev GR 21:4:124

William Henry H b1855 w Paratine Pritchett, AL, Bible rec GR 21:4:147

POLCHOW, Catherine (Shannon) b1860, IL, obit IL 11:2:98

POLING, fam of N E, NY, NJ, geneal, bk rev NYR 110:3:180 110:4:216

POLK, Franz b1852 w Magdalena Haupmann, Austria, Czechoslovakis, TX, geneal, bk rev KCG 20:4:204 GH 33:6:88

Robert Bruce bc1620 w Magdalen Tasker, Ir, MD, biog notes CSB 14:1:20

POLLOCK, Samuel Sr d1812 w Jean, Scot, PA, will & fam recs CPY 8:3:74

POMMER, fam geneal, bk rev MN 10:1:43

POND, George M b1834 w Mary A, NY, MI, Bible rec MI 24:3:80

Silas b1798 w Angeline, Bible rec GL 13:2:44

PONS, Juan b1762 w Juana Catalina Andreu, FL, geneal ANC 14:4:139

POOL, Sanuel f1775, NC, GA & AL, geneal, bk rev GGM 71:6

William b1811 w Amy A Dodge, OH, anc ch REP 19:3:115

POOLE, Joe Williams b1902 w Lelia Newton Johnson, GA, TN, anc ch NAS 17:3:69

William James b1757 w Mary, MA, ME, Bible rec DE 3:2:10

POORMAN, George Warner b1838 w Eliza Jane Watson, OH, IL, fam rec FF 8:2:42

POPEJOY, William, Eng, Am, geneal, bk rev NYR 110:2:181

POPPLEWELL, John Flint b1828 w

Delphia Matilda Judd, KY, Bible rec GR 21:3:116

PORTER, William b1804 w Emeline McKnight, Bible rec GFP 28:10:191

William f1850 w Martha Coffey, OR, biog notes BB 11:4:74

PORTUGAL, Moors, hist, bk rev SPG 31:590

POSPISIL, Joe b1906 w Christina Bertha Brezny, OK, anc ch THT 6:3:88

POST, Stephen b1596 w Ellen Panton, Eng, CT, geneal NER 133:4:302

POTTER, Arnold b1758 w Poby, Bible rec BB 11:4:78

Edward b1793 w Lucy Austin, OH, Bible rec CTN 12:2:235

POTTS, Stacy Jr, diary 1798 KCG 20:4:189

POWDERLY, Terence V, biog, bk rev MHM 74:3:303

POWELL, Calvin b1792 w Clarrissa Richardson, VT, NY, biog notes ORB 17:5:47

POWERS, John Gilbert b1887 w Emma Ruth Joyce, WA, IA, OR, anc ch ORB 17:5:49

Robert Emmett b1910 w Mary Mozelle Aldis, TX, anc ch GR 21:4:135

PRATHER, John William, KY, anc chs, bk rev BR 6:3:96

PRATT, Lewis P m1854 w Joyce Ann Harper, Bible rec GFP 28:10:190

Nathaniel bc1660 w Sarah Beaumont, Sarah, Rebeccah, fam rec AH 2:4:115

Norman U b1903 w Marion R Burke, IL, CA, anc ch OG 5:1:17

Phineas bc1590 w Mary Priest, Eng, MA, geneal CLG 10:1:31

PRENTISS, Moses W b1827 w Chloe Boswell, IA, Bible rec HH 14:2:90

PRESCOTT, fam of Europe, geneal, bk rev AGS 20:2:36 OC 16:3:108 CTN 12:1:176

PRESTON, Ezekiel b1808 w Cornelia L Smith, NY, Bible

rec PR 3:4:72

Ezra L b1869 w Jennie E Aldrich, NY, Bible rec CDS 16:1:15

George, fam rec CDS 16:2:20

Roland b1799 w Clarissa F Snow, NY, Bible & fam rec CDS 16:1:15 16:2:20

Walter Boyd b1888 w Dorcas Ann Porter, TX, anc ch THT 6:3:67

William Tomlin b1826 w Margaret Ann Hatch, OR, Bible rec TB 6:4:16

PREUIT, fam of AL, biog notes & fam recs VL 14:2:67

PREWITT, Isham b1725 w Frances Maddox, VA, geneal, bk rev GH 33:5:88

marrs, bk rev GH 33:1:93

PRICE, C E b1825 w Catherine M Richey, Margaret J Richey, KY, biog VQ 16:4:58

Christian m1840 w Sallie Oswalt, GA, Bible rec DCG 2:10:11

David Wade b1845 w Nancy A Vansant, Mary Clementine Hartsfield, GA, fam rec DCG 2:10:10

Edmund m1757 w Jane Webb, NJ, Can, geneal, bk rev BCG 6:4:4

Thomas Stirling b1871 w Jennie Eliza McDonald, Eng, CO, anc ch BGS 9:4:44

William Clark b1792 w Elizabeth Younger Caplinger, VA, KY, MO, cem inscr NGI 3:1:35

PRIDGEON, Henry Edgar b1878 w Dora E Hartley, Bible rec THT 2:2:16

PRINCE, fam cem AL VL 14:1:42

fam of Am, misc biogs, bk rev CTN 12:4:697

fam of Eng, Can & Am, geneal, bk rev CTN 8:4:538

Hiram b1824 w Helen Mary Lindsay, AL, CO, geneal BGS 11:4:148

John Henry b1891 w Alice Edith Weaver, MO, NE, OR, anc ch ORB 17:5:48

PRINDLE, fam of OH, notes on AH 4:2:43

PRITCHETT, John b1757 w Elizabeth Whitehurst, NC, biog notes TSP 3:1:8

PROCTOR, John b1755, VA, IN, biog notes MIS 11:4:52

Lee Wilson b1882 w Murl Addie Powell, TX, anc ch THT 6:3:88

Robert f1635 w Jane Hildreth, MA, geneal, bk rev CTN 11:1:42

William b1760 w Elizabeth, VA, PA, KY, Bible rec KY 21:1:64

PROEPPERMANN, Henrich b1831 w Anna Katherine Hinnenkamp, Ger, OH, anc ch REP 19:1:34

PROETT, Elmer Marion b1903 w Patrice Fay North, MO, OK, CO, anc ch BGS 10:3:47

PROPST, Anthony b1810 w Lucinda Powell, VA, IL, biog notes ORB 17:6:55

PROVIN, Tyler W w Eugenia, MI, MO, letter 1869 MI 24:2:62

PRUETT, Jrhu Higgins b1820 w Elizabeth Ringo, MO, OR, biog notes ORB 18:4:86

PRUITT, Joanna f1895, CA, autograph bk KN 2:4:28

Thomas f1636, Eng, VA, geneal, bk rev GH 33:1:94

PRYOR, Andrew Jackson b1905 w Fabrice Nettles, LA, AR, anc ch GR 21:2:51

PURDIE, Andrew m1709 w Margaret Grieve, Scot, anc ch FAM 18:1:22

PURDY, Thomas Franklin b1824 w Margaret Plested, Can, photos & biog notes FAM 18:2:90

PURVINES, Carroll b1873 w Kate Blanche Irwin, IL, OK, TX, biog THT 6:2:45

PUTNAM, Israel b1718, CTa, biog, bk rev CTN 11:3:519

PYLE, Joseph Clinton b1890 w Ethel Mae Adcock, MO, IL, anc ch DWC 5:3:86

QUAKER, geneal biblio of WI hist soc lib, bk rev IL 11:3:178 GE 47:11

IN recs part 7, bk rev OK

24:3:138

NY City Quaker tax assessment bks 1810-1819 NYR 110:3:164 110:4:216

recs in Dutchess Co NY CTN 12:4:555

settlements in NC TST 12:5:38 12:6:44

QUICK, George b1828, NY, IL, geneal, bk rev IL 11:2:116 GH 33:4:119 KCG 20:3:153

QUIMBY, Charles b1803 w Susan T Fullerton, MA, Bible rec CTN 10:2:364

QUINN, Edward b1829 w Elizabeth Gaynor, Ir, OH, anc ch REP 19:3:120

RABEN, Walter Arnold b1916 w Etta Mae Piper, NE, anc ch BGS 10:3:44

RADCLIFF, Adam W b1827 w Martha Sefton, NY, IL, geneal FF 8:2:46

RADCLIFFE, Simon f1839 w Elizabeth Taulbee, IN, geneal FF 8:1:46

RADER, John M b1810 w Christiana Kennedy, OH, anc ch REP 19:1:34

RAGEL, John Martin b1883 w Mayne Nell Triplett, KS, fam recs FF 8:2:71

RAINES, James Harison b1888 w Ethel May Huber, AZ, OK, anc ch KG 16:1:16

William A b1840 w Elizabeth Fields, Bible Rec GFP 28:9:167

RAINEY, Rainey Times, Box 7, Walnut Ridge AR 72476

RALSTON, Robert b1780 w Susannah Windland, PA, geneal FF 8:3:65

Thomas b1812 w Catharine Rambo, IL, biog notes FF 8:1:55

RAMEY, James W d1953 w Amanda Glenn, KY, anc ch REP 19:4:164

RAMIREZ, JKesus b1852 w Urbana Ramos, TX, anc ch & biog notes AGS 20:2:58

RANCK, John Peter b1770 w Eva Christina Harper, PA, acc bk, bk rev GH 33:1:87

RAND, Clarence Kelton b1906 w Leah Lenora McGaughey, CO, anc ch RRS 12:1:99

RANDALL, Abraham b1778 w Elishaba Talbot, Elizabeth Merrihew, NH, OH, Bible rec AH 4:4:139

Joshua b1857 w Martha Ann Huntley, IN, biog & fam notes HJA 6:1:12

RANDLE, Samuel P b1792 w Sally Hyatt, Bible rec CTN 10:2:368

RANDOLPH, A F, marrs performed 1859-1885 IN, IA, NE, CO BGS 3:4:19 4:1:22

Abraham m1792 w Lydia Dill, NC, SC, AL, pension claim VL 14:2:73

fam of VA, geneal, bk rev KY 21:3:115

John bc1720 w Ann Osborn, VA, geneal, bk rev GH 33:5:88 VAG 23:3:229

RANIA, Daniel bc1849 w Elizabeth Reto, It, PA, anc ch ITG 2:35

RANSOM, fam of KY, geneal, bk rev NCJ 5:4:259

George Palmer b1762 w Elizabeth Lamareaux, PA, anc ch REP 19:1:33

RAPOPORT, fam of It, geneal (1861) bk rev CTN 12:4:700

RARICK, Conrad b1722, geneal, bk rev GE 49:7

Jonathan f1851 w Margaret Rugh, OH, anc ch REP 19:4:158

RATCLIFF, Gerald Clifford b1921 w Betty Jane Dunwoody, NE, anc ch ORB 17:6:56

Isaac b1808 w Mary Presnall, OH, IN, geneal, bk rev TST 12:28:40 GE 47:10 QY 6:4:6

RATHBUN, Rathbun-Rathbone-Rathburn Fam Historian, 11308 Popes Head Rd, Fairfax VA 22030

RAWN, George b1788 w Magdlana Hunsicker, fam rec WB 9:4:160

RAYMOND, Elisha b1832 w Mary E Blow, Bible rec MI 24:4:119

RAYNER, William Sr b1817 w Rachel Scudder Valentine, Catharine J Barrett, Eng, OH, geneal & biog notes BGS 11:4:162

REA, William d1793, NC, death notice NCJ 5:1:36

READ, Daniel b1774 w Alma Adams, CT, geneal CTN 11:4:736

READE, Andrew bc1555 w Alice Cooke, Eng, anc ch YP 9:3:126

REAMES, Augustus A b1887 w Amelia Francis Pray, TX, anc ch FF 8:2:30

REASON, George b1785 w Sarah Brown, Eng, NY, fam rec KN 2:3:27

REAVIS, Solomon f1817 w Mary Green, KY, IL, fam rec FF 8:2:34

RECKER, Nicholas Henry b1800 w Mary K Klappenberger, OH, anc ch REP 19:4:163

RECORD, George John b1839 w Mary Chapel, NY, OH, biog geneal AH 5:4:110

RECORD KEEPING, basic kit, bk rev TST 12:3:36
  birth order system for classifying fam roots, bk rev QY 6:1:3
  documenting res notes GH 33:5:7
  fam hist records bk, bk rev CLG 10:3:183
  guide for fam organizations, bk rev GH 33:1:81
  methods CTN 8:2:179,191
  organize your geneal recs, bk rev VAG 23:1:72 IG 15:1:8 CI 14:3:110 GGM 73:165
  organization for beginners in geneal res PF 9:1:6 9:2:22
  plastic sheet protectors PF 9:1:5
  preserving your past, bk rev CTN 11:2:338
  what to do with research, bk rev NGI 3:3:169
  what to do with roots, bk rev AGS 20:3:117

REED, Abner b1771 w Elizabeth Loring, CT, biog notes CTB 44:1:1

Andrew Jackson b1848 w Candace J Honeyman, Julia I Howell, IN, Bible rec HJA 6:4:38

John b1709 w Hannah Holcomb, CT, geneal CTN 11:4:734

John b1755 w Margaret Livingston, PA, Bible rec BGS 9:2:17

Quinton b1813 w Susanna West, Bible rec BGS 6:2:21

Wesley b1836 w Rebecca Murphy, Bible rec CI 15:3:84

William Roscoe b1885 w Pleasant Jessie McCormack, IA, MO, anc ch KG 16:1:18 16:2:42

REEP, Adolph m1753 w Christina Ruth Ruessel, PA, NC, geneal, bk rev GH 33:3:108

Elmer Leonard b1896 w Laura Viola Brown, KS, anc ch NGI 3:1:36

Reep Fam Assoc, 3511 55th Ave, Hyattsville MD 20784

REES, Morris m1718 w Sarah Butterfield, PA marr rec QY 6:4:5

William Clinton b1874 w Anna Araminta Howard, fam rec ORB 17:9:80

William Noah b1834 w Sarah Perin, Bible rec ORB 17:9:79

REEVE, Oscar b1844 w Hannah M, Bible rec LL 14:1:29

REEVES, Robert Ancil b1888 w Myrtle Ivia Rodgers, NE, IA, anc ch NW 2:4:129

REGULA, Peter b1815 w Catherine Metz, Ger, OH, anc ch REP 19:4:164

REID, fam of NC, geneal, bk rev KY 21:3:115

James f1812 w Hannah Kelley, OH, biog notes REP 19:1:25

Lenora J b1858 h Daniel E Reid, Albert D Mendenhall, Bible rec IG 15:2:57

Oliver Hazard b1844 w Mildred Texanna Allen, TN, TX, anc ch AGS 20:3:81

Victoria b1808 h Pablo Maria, Perfecto Hugo Reid, Mexico, CA, biog DAR 113:1:22

REINKING, Wendell b1919 w Wanda Herron, IL, anc ch BGS

10:4:40

RENICK, Samuel McKenney b1867 w Lota Campbell, fam rec AGS 20:3:82

REPASS, Gordon b1819 w Ann M Sharitz, VA, Bible rec RRS 12:2:223

REVENNAUGH, John R Sr b1785 w Jane Glass, PA, anc ch REP 19:3:120

REVERE, Paul, MA, will 1816 BGS 8:4:7

REVIS, fam of VA & IL, geneal FF 8:1:25

REVOLUTIONARY WAR, battles in 1779 ANC 14:1:8 14:2:48

collect of death notices of Rev War soldiers, bk rev AGS 20:3:118

deserters, dischargees & prisoners of war from British 7th Reg of Foot NGS 67:4:255

Ger allies in Am Rev, bk rev CI 14:1:29

Ger troops in Can, list QBC 2:1:11

guide to biog sources on soldiers & sailors, bk rev CTA 21:3:120

hist notes JMS 2:2:35

misc battles & geneals DAR 113:2:122

misc diaries & letters of military officers, bk rev CTN 12:2:366

misc graves of Rev soldiers DAR 113:1:28 113:7:792

misc soldiers, biog notes BGS 8:2:21 9:1:15 9:2:4 9:3:22 9:4:15 10:1:12 10:2:16 10:3:17 11:1:29

obits of misc patriots, bk rev GH 33:1:81

Pennsylvania-German hist, bk rev WCK 12:1:16

prisoners of British FL 1781 NCJ 5:3:157

recs of British Army in Am 1780-1785 MD 20:2:107

soldiers & patriots buried in IA, bk rev CTN 11:3:521

soldiers buried IL, bk rev CSB 14:1:23

vets buried Columbia Co NY, bk rev CTN 11:3:521

writings of officers of Cont army & navy, bk rev NYR 110:3:184

REYNARD, Adam d1842 w Catherine, OH, will QY 6:3:1

REYNOLDS, Abigail (Pennoyer) b1686, CT, biog notes CTN 7:2:308

fam in IL census 1900, bk rev GH 33:4:119

fam of TN & VA, annotated geneal, bk rev DM 43:1:45

George f1901 w Ida, KS, biog notes LL 14:2:64

Henry b1655 w Prudence Clayton, Eng, NJ, PA, geneal QY 6:1:7

RHEA, Lewis L b1797 w Martha Holloway, TN, SC, AL, Bible rec BWG 8:1:30

RHINEHAMMER, Daniel f1840 w Ann Syms, Holl, PA, geneal, bk rev KCG 20:4:204

RHOAD, fam of AL, Bible rec PT 21:4:129

RHOADES, Johannes Roth, VA, geneal, bk rev KCG 20:4:204

RHOADS, George b1755, PA, geneal LM 20:2:4

RHODE ISLAND, census 1782, bk rev GE 47:13 TST 12:31:40

East Providence, Newman cem inscr RIR 5:1:14 5:2:9

emig to MI RIR 5:2:17

Franco-Am hist JMS 2:2:19

freemen, census of reg noters 1747-1755, bk rev CTN 10:2:347

geneal reg publ, bk rev NYR 110:3:182

geographic dict 1894, bk rev NYR 110:3:184 NGS 67:1:73

hist, bk rev CDS 16:6:41

Little Compton, geneal hist, bk rev CTN 7:3:362

"Mayflower" descs RIR 5:3:5

misc fams geneal 1893, bk rev CTN 10:2:343

North Smithfield, Phillips farm cem recs RIR 5:3:10

Providence, hist of early settlers RIR 5:1:1

ward 8 annexation bus direct 1898 RIR 5:3:11 5:4:16

Quaker recs RIR 5:1:11 5:2:6 5:3:14 5:4:11

Rev War burials RIR 5:1:8 5:2:11 5:3:7 5:4:7

RI College class of 1854 RIR 5:2:19

South Kingston, cems inscr, bk rev CTN 12:4:702

town settlement dates RIR 5:2:20 5:4:i

Washington Co, births & marrs from cem inscr 1688-1850, bk rev TT 19:1:12 CTN 10:2:342

births from probate recs 1685-1860, bk rev GJ 8:2:120

misc marrs from probate recs 1692-1850, bk rev CTN 8:3:475

RHODES, William b1764/5 w Rebecca Wofford, NC, TN, anc ch THT 7:2:76

William b1796 w Sarah Hastings, SC, TN, Bible rec THT 3:1:10

RICE, fam of NC, misc recs, bk rev NCJ 5:1:64

George Dewey b1898 w Elizabeth Ann Eckes, WI, anc ch DC 16:2:64

John b1771 w Fannie Snelson, VA, Bible rec ACL 4:3:52

Samual J b1847 w Martha D Locke, Eliza Daniels, KY, IL, fam rec FF 8:1:56

William R b1825 w Sallie B Nowlin, Anne Booker Speece, Bettie F McGhee, Bible rec NGS 67:3:201

RICH, Jonathan b1771 w Ruth Slate, MA, biog notes AH 2:4:119

Orlando b1818 w Marietta B Rogers, Anna Maria (West) Cornwall, Orpha E Rich, Eliza, Mary Jane, OH, OR, Bible rec CTN 10:3:416

RICHARDS, Fay Alger b1892 w Winona Hazel Bayley, MT, WA, anc ch TB 6:1:23

RICHARDSON, Albert Edward b1908 w Ina Maude Kellums, NY, NE, anc ch NW 2:4:133

George Edward bc1892 w Eva Hor-

ner, MA, geneal, bk rev GH 33:5:89

John Milan b1880 w Ida Mae Lusher, MO, anc ch THT 7:2:66

Matthias Sr b1749 w Frances, SC, Bible rec THT 5:2:6

Samuel, MA, geneal, bk rev CTN 9:3:469

Washington b1816 w Mary Jane Wilson, KY, Bible rec KY 21:1:58

Wayne H b1917 w Joan Elizabeth Kercheval, CA, anc ch AG 55:2:115

RICHESON, James b1851 w Lucinda Shipp, KY, UT, biog notes BGS 2:2:4

Thomas bc1800< KY, geneal, bk rev GH 33:2:86

RICHMOND, William Julius b1873 w Martha Lou Carnes, AL, TX, anc ch THT 6:3:62

RICKARD, Caper b1822 w Catherine Kime, NC, IN, OR, biog notes ORB 17:8:71

RICKS, John H b1837 w Elizabeth Sparks, GA, AL, OK, fam recs OK 24:3:120

RIDENOOR, Nicholas b1695 w Rosina Kirshner, Fr, MD, geneal notes BGS 11:2:72

RIDGWAY, Rachel (Corlies) b1770 h Caleb Ridgway, John Butterworth, biog notes GNJ 54:2:49

RIEKE, fam of Ger & IL & IN, geneal, bk rev KCG 20:3:152

RIEKIN, Laut m1841 w Bemde B Siefken, Bible rec WB 10:1:22

RIGGS, John d1859 w Jane, TX Indian massacre descr THT 5:1:29

RIGHTER, John B b1823 w Emily Jane Atchison, PA, Bible rec CI 14:4:141

RILEY, William McCray b1835 w Marinda Chedrick Claytor, Rebecca Claytor, OH, IL, geneal FF 8:2:38

RINEHART, Jacob b1800 w Mary Messmore, MD, PA, anc ch REP 19:3:118

RINGER, Harvey Abraham b1859 w Mabel Jane Bright, MO, NM,

fam rec NMG 18:4:122

RINGO, Joseph b1806 w Mrs Mary (Ransdall) Clinton, KY, OR, biog notes ORB 17:9:83

RINGWALT, William b1844 w Maria Boger, IN, Bible rec ACL 4:2:28

RINKS, George William bc1820 w Avis, Mrs Susan A Wilbanks, TN, MO, geneal, bk rev GH 33:3:108

RIPLEY, fam of VT, misc letters, bk rev SCS 16:4:125

Nathaniel f1792 w Sibyl Huntington, CT, VT, geneal, bk rev CTN 12:4:698

RISH, Jacob b1809 w Mary Ann Dotts, OH, anc ch REP 19:1:28

RITCHEY, James b1741 w Eliza, VA, KY, geneal, bk rev TS 21:2:74 DWC 5:3:88

RITTER, George Kenneth b1901 w Rena Marie, LA, anc ch FF 8:2:29

William b1832, Ger, OH, mil & pension rec, bk rev REP 19:4:168

RIVARD, Nicholas f1646 w Catherine StPere, Fr, fam rec JMS 2:2:41

ROBB, Edward Livingston b1837, OH, diary & fam rec THT 5:3:30 5:4:33

ROBBINS, Jonathan C f1851, IN, Bible rec HJA 6:4:38

ROBERTS, Benjamin f1759< NH, biog notes SCS 16:4:112

George b1753 w Mary, NC, TN, Bible rec RRS 12:2:221

Jack Carl b1911 w Mary Elizabeth Boyd, TX, anc ch AG 55:2:114

John d1840 w Eunice Rogers, NC, TN, accts of sermons preached RRS 12:2:222

John Milton b1930, OH, baby bk REP 19:1:3

Lee Fermon Sr b1890 w Nona Ocy Tanner, TX, anc ch GR 21:2:49

ROBERTSON, Joseph b1833 w Drucilla Emaline McAtee, Scot, OR, biog notes ORB 17:6:55

ROBICHAUX, Philip b1860 w Georgina Falgout, LA, anc ch AGE 8:4:128

ROBINSON, Charles w Harriet Clark, TX, biog notes STK 7:1:31

John b1612, Eng, MA, geneal AG 55:1:16

Joseph B b1838 w Annie Russell, WV, MO, Bible rec GFP 28:6:109

Matthew b1836 w Mary Jane Burnside, Bible rec HJA 6:2:37

Moses, 1842 postal receipt VL 13:3:104

ROBISON, Robert bc1764 w Susanna Graham, PA, anc ch REP 19:3:118

ROCKEFELLER, Johann b1682, Ger, NJ, geneal, bk rev CTN 11:1:43 CDS 16:2:4

ROCKWELL, fam geneal supp, bk rev CTN 10:4:702

William f1630, geneal, bk rev CTN 10:4:701

ROE, Hugh f1642, MA, geneal suppl, bk rev CTN 11:3:526

ROGER, Gustave b1835 w Justilia Elfert, LA, anc ch AGE 8:2:64

ROGERS, Gilbert Earl b1912 w Sarah Perlena Stilley, IL, KS, anc ch TOP 9:1:13

Elwood C b1923 w Emogene Fout, VA, anc ch RRS 12:1:98

Ezekiel b1590, Eng, MA, geneal CLG 10:3:126

Hamilton b1758 w Mary Gibson, OH, anc ch REP 19:3:131

Henry Clay b1845 w Eliza Amanda Sisson, MI, Bible rec KK 17:2:28

Thomas, "Mayflower" descs, bk rev GH 33:4:112 GE 47:13 VAG 23:3:232 NYR 110:4:249 GN 2:7:216

ROHR, fam of Russia, NY, KS, geneal, bk rev BGS 9:1:38

ROHRBACH, Hans George bc1707, Ger, Am, geneal v2, bk rev NGS 67:1:69

ROHRER, David b1813 w Sarah Wibler, MD, IN, anc ch REP 19:1:28

ROHWER, Lucetta (Billingsley) m1887 h George Rohwer, CO, geneal, bk rev BGS 9:3:36

ROMANIA, geneal res guide GH 33:6:9 JJG 3:1:9

RONEY, James bc1775 w Mary Eakin, VA, KY, geneal, bk rev TB 6:2:16 CI 14:3:110

ROOSA, Cornelius b1830 w Catharine E Royce, NY, Bible rec CTN 12:2:233

ROOTE, John b1608 w Mary Kilbourne, Eng, CT, anc ch TTL 7:1:19

ROSBRUGH, William S Sr f1720, Scot, Ir, geneal, bk rev GH 33:5:89

ROSE, Robert, Scot, VA, diary 1746-1751, bk rev NCJ 5:4:258 DG 25:2:123 YP 9:2:101

ROSECRAMS, Almond Stark w Mary Breeden, KY, KS, MO, Bible rec GFP 29:3:59

ROSS, Abel b1800 w Celia Emmons, NY, OH, anc ch REP 19:3:123

ROSSMAN, Philip W b1875 w Ora Ellen Cobb, Ger, OH, anc ch REP 19:1:29

ROTHROCK, fam of PA, MD, VA, IN, geneal, bk rev YP 9:3:164

ROUTH, Joseph bc1747 w Mary Redfern, NC, geneal, bk rev GH 33:6:89

ROUTON, fam recs, bk rev GH 33:1:94 YP 9:2:106

ROWE, Charles Henry b1868 w Barbary Olive Reese, KS, OK, anc ch & geneal FF 8:2:27 8:3:68

Henry B, NC, will abstr 1924 NCJ 5:3:183

ROWLAND, Jeremiah b1758 w Elen, Bible recs CTN 10:3:415

John B b1825 w Priscilla (Stilwell) Rowland Kelty Larkins, biog notes GFP 29:3:53

ROWLEY, Charles b1812 w Eliza Voorhees, Bible rec HH 14:2:82

Joseph Venziles b1867 w Lacy Clark King, anc ch RRS 12:1:79

ROYSE, Carl Augustus b1898 w Lillie Bell George, AR, MS,

anc ch FF 8:2:28

RUBEL, Ulrich f1731, PA, VA, geneal, bk rev CTN 11:1:43 CDS 16:2:4

RUDD, Joseph b1740 w Mary, CT, biog notes CTN 7:2:310

RUE, Marthias d1777 w Nancy Perine, Elizabeth Gaston, NJ, biog notes GNJ 54:2:114

RUGG, Lovel b1812 w Mary Ann Bradley, MA, NH, Bible rec BGS 11:4:156

Merle Columbus b1893 w Clara Jessie Harpel, CO, anc ch BGS 11:4:182

RUSH, Jacob Sr b1780 w Catherine Dundore, VA, Bible rec VA 17:1:23 GER 16:431

RUSSELL, David Allison b1850 w Mary Wilson Neal, PA, Bible rec CPY 8:1:13

Ichabod d1871, MI, biog notes DM 43:1:18

Jefferson f1846 w Nancy Grimmett, MO, Bible rec GFP 28:6:109

John f1640, Eng, MA, biog NER 133:2:125

John S b1806 w Jane Simpson, PA, Bible rec CPY 8:1:11

RUSSIA, censuses as geneal res aid GJ 8:2:82

geneal res guide GH 33:6:9 NGI 3:2:117

RUTHERFORD, fam & related fams, geneal, bk rev NCJ 5:3:214 VAG 23:4:310 IL 11:2:113 AGS 20:3:119

William K w Anna Clay (Zimmerman), geneal v1,2, bk rev STK 7:2:78 AGS 20:3:119 NGS 67:2:154 GH 33:6:89 VAG 23:4:310 HTR 22:3:91 IL 11:2:113 AGS 20:3:119 HTR 22:3:91 BWG 8:1:91 SCG 13:51 PGB 11:3:28

RUTT, George f1881 w Daorothy Koch, Alice Schreiner, Russia, NE, biog notes NA 2:1:40

RYAN, Michael bc1780 w Margaret Gorman, IR, WI, geneal, bk rev GH 33:4:119

Patrick bc1800 w Honora Ryan,

IR, NY, WI, geneal, bk rev GH 33:4:119

Samuel Gee b1914 w Marion Roberta Ryan, WI, CA, anc ch WB 10:1:32

Sarah b1780 h Jacob Kern, MD, NC, biog notes PGB 11:8:90

SAGE, Hiram b1804 w Lucy Judd, CT, Bible rec CTN 10:3:417

Sarah Bishop h Charles Henry Sage, OH, geneal 1957, bk rev REP 19:4:168

Wayne Byron b1922 w Jane Ardis Failor, OR, IA, anc ch THT 6:3:74

SAGER, Oliver J b1886 w Laura M Sage, IN, anc ch ACL 4:4:82

ST CLAIR, James Alexander Jr b1900 w Hattie Ethel Kistler, CO, anc ch BGS 11:1:43

ST JAMES, John b1838 w Mary Louisa Beal, Bible rec TB 6:3:11

ST LAWRENCE, fam of Ir, notes on IRA 13:253

SAFFORD, Minnie Matilda b1867 h Olvah Thompson, William P Eyrich, NY, CO, obit BGS 8:2:8

SALTMAN, John b1784 w Martha Kerr, OH, anc ch REP 19:1:34

SALTS, Thomas, VA, geneal, bk rev IG 15:4:104

SAMS, Jonas b1750, biog notes KCG 20:4:196

Mrs (McCarthy) d1964 h Lee W Sams, NY, TN, obit BWG 8:1:65

SANBORN, Moses b1717 w Priscilla (Sherburn) James, Elizabeth Fuller, NH, geneal BGS 8:3:16

SANDEFUR, Julia Adell (Fassett) b1855 h George F Horton, William J Sandefur, WI, KS, auto MGR 14:4:170

SANDERS, Andrew J, NY, 1864 civil discharge AH 4:3:93

Elijah d1828 w Darkus Chandler, KY, geneal, bk rev GH 33:2:86

James b1800 w Mary Jane Wilson, SC, IL, biog CI 12:1:5

Joseph b1813, diary extracts

DAR 113:8:922

SANDERSON, John Finlay b1849 w Hannah Parker, Can, KS, geneal KK 17:3:45

SANFORD, Ezekiel b1648, CT, NY, geneal, bk rev CTN 8:4:537

George Oliver b1886 w Vera Mildred Edwards, MI, anc ch OC 16:3:97

William b1757 w Abigail Simmons, RI, NY, anc ch OC 16:3:98

SANDUSKY, Isaac Newton m1873 w Lucy Menefee, TX-KY letters STK 7:3:116

SAUNDERS, John, Eng, VA, N travel diary 1750 NCJ 5:3:146

John bc1755 w Hannah Sanders, Can, MA, Bible rec GN 2:6:170

John Jr b1782 w Jemima Wilson, Can, Bible rec GN 2:6:171

William d1887 w Ruth Patterson, ME, obit DE 3:3:11

SAUTER, fam of Switz, LDS Temple Ordinances bk B, film rev GH 33:6:92

SAVAGE, Asahel b1769 w Abigail Deming, Bible rec LL 15:1:21

Leven b1750, VA, Rev War affidavit TST 12:25:47

Raleigh Haynes b1886 w Willie Mae Minton, AL, anc ch NAS 18:1:5

Thomas f1851 w Mary, Wales, Bible rec REP 19:3:114

SAVOIE, Francois Zavier b1865 w Lee Nora Mauldin, Can, NC, MA, anc ch AGe 8:1:30

SAWYER, William b1799 w Lucy Meriam, NY, Bible rec REP 19:1:16

SAWYERS, Daniel S, letter c1863 MO to IN THT 5:1:8

SAYLOR, Elias b1843, Bible rec BGS 8:2:7

SCARETTI, fam of It, geneal notes ITG 2:48

SCHAFER, Richard F b1920 w Marijeanne Morrison, NE, anc ch NW 2:4:132

SCHANZ, John b1839 w Jaene Reid, Ger, Scot, NJ, Bible rec ANC 14:2:53

SCHAUBLIN, fam of Switz, bk rev
MD 20:4:362

SCHERLIE, Harn A m1891 w Bertha
C Schofield, MN, Bible rec PR
3:1:5

SCHIEFER, fam of Ger, PA, KY,
geneal MGR 14:3:119

SCHLEPPI, Hans Ulrich b1720 w
Anna Eva, Juliana, Ger, PA,
geneal, bk rev TS 21:1:26 CTN
12:1:181 SMV 11:1:2

SCHLOTT, fam of IL, notes on FF
8:2:52

SCHMIDT, Henrich bc1755, Ger, NC
biog notes NCJ 5:2:84
men from Ger 1777-1783 NCJ
5:2:88
William f1891, WI, complaint
MCR 10:4:92a

SCHMITZ, Joseph Christian b1887
w Wilhelmina Adeline Rose,
OH, anc ch CPY 8:2:47

SCHNEIDER, William Edward b1895
w Edith Ernestina Pulaski,
IL, MI, anc ch PF 9:1:7

SCHNURR, June N bc1915, IL, auto
notes SCS 16:4:100

SCHOELCH, David b1829 w Elizabeth, ME, Bible rec DE 3:3:16

SCHOLL, Septimus b1789 w Sallie
Miller, KY, MO, biog KCG
20:3:135

SCHONS, Nicholas John b1889 w
Mabel Ethel Falconer, NE, CO,
anc ch BGS 10:3:46

SCHOTT, Frederick Jr b1907 w
Leah Foos, WY, CO, anc ch NW
2:2:60

SCHROEDER, Joachim bc1806 w Margaretha Davids, Ger, IA, geneal, bk rev GH 33:1:94

SCHUH, Eberhard b1818 w Eveline
Koons, Ger, IL, WA, obit TB
6:4:18

SCHULTE, Mylen Elmer b1923 w
Eloris Harriet Kijak, MI, anc
ch PF 8:3:57

SCHULTZ, Frederick W b1873, CT,
auto SCC 16:4:91

SCHULUMBOHM, John Chris Fred
b1855 w Catherine Sophia Thi-
leman, Ger, OH, anc ch REP
19:3:119

SCHURMAN, William bc1743, Can,
loyalist, biog, bk rev GN
2:6:172

SCHUTT, William Jansen d1722,
Neth, NY, geneal, bk rev TS
21:4:173

SCHWALM, Johannes f1776, Ger,
OH, geneal, bk rev NER
133:1:60

SCHWAN, Emil L b1888, biog notes
CHI 52:4:175

SCOGGINS, Wallace Harper b1897 w
Gertrude Jeanette Friend, TX,
anc ch PGB 11:7:73

SCOTLAND, addresses for geneal
res BGS 11:2:74
emig to Am & Can pre 1783
(1900), bk rev NYR 110:1:58
geneal res guide GH 33:1:16 TST
12:16:40 TS 21:4:127
geneal recs sources, bk rev GH
33:2:74
heraldry, bk rev SCG 13:51
Highlanders settlements in Am
to 1783, bk rev NGS 67:1:68
in search of Scottish ancestry,
bk rev OG 3:3:88
introducing Scottish geneal
res, bk rev GN 2:7:217
origin of surnames, bk rev AH
6:4:123
recs of geneal value, guide, bk
rev TST 11:52:45
Reg of Deeds, geneal res guide
GJ 8:2:66

SCOTT, Buford, KY, cem inscr CI
13:3:107
Jesse Alvin b1898 w Zelma La-
Vada Aplet, OR, anc ch ORB
17:8:75
John, Chief, b1805, TX, cem in-
scr THT 4:1:28
John Winfield d1863 w Sarah
Fuller, NY, OH, WI, geneal,
bk rev CTN 9:3:470
Walter b1842 w Hannah S Howe,
PA, NE, Bible rec AH 3:3:79
William T b1828 w Melissa Mil-
ler, VA, KY, biog VQ 16:3:46

SCRIMSHIRE, William B f1830, GA,
geneal, bk rev FP 22:4:210

SCRUGGS, Forrest Stanley b1920 w
Bernice Marie Loewen, CO, KS,

anc ch BGS 10:3:39

SCUDDER, Elizabeth m1644 h Samuel Lothrop, Eng, MA, biog notes AG 55:2:107

Henry Joel f1876, speech excerpts ANC 14:4:123

SEAGER, Elizabeth f1663, CT, witchcraft trial, bk rev REP 19:4:177

fam of N E, geneal, bk rev GH 33:1:94 NYR 110:2:120 REP 19:4:174 CDS 16:4:12

SEARLE, John b1629 w Katherine Warner, Eng, MA, CT, biog notes CSB 14:1:19

SEARS, Clinton B, NY letter 1861 THT 2:2:31

SECHEVERELL, J H b1841, OH, biog notes AH 3:2:40

SEE, Isaac m1657 w Esther See, Ger, NY, fam rec NYR 110:2:100

SEED, Clarence Elmer b1912 w Gertrude Francis Robison, Can, ID, WAa, anc ch OG 5:1:19

SEELEY, Seeley Geneal Soc, Box 131, Allenspark CO 80510

SEELY, Josiah b1736, geneal notes CTA 21:3:125

SEFERT, Michael b1805 w Salome Wills, Fr, OH, anc ch REP 19:2:86

SEIBERT, Jacob d1761 w Mrs Susanna Schutz, PA, geneal, bk rev GH 33:3:108

SEITEL, Frank b1823, Bible rec BGS 5:2:14

SELF, John b1804 w Nancy Inbody, IN, Bible rec CO 40:4:186

Samuel C b1848 w Sarah J Devine, IN, Bible rec CO 40:4:185

SELLY, fam of Fr & It, geneal ITG 2:38

SERGEANT, Flora f1866, letters AH 3:4:117

SETH, Smith Hedderick b1859 w Ida Matilda Anderson, Scot, Nor, NM, fam rec NMG 18:2:50

SEVERY, Glenn Leon b1888 w Minnie Marguerite Galster, WI, MI, anc ch BGS 9:4:46

SEVERY, Myron b1816 w Altha M Wilson, Alice A Burley, VT, Bible rec BGS 9:4:30

SEWALL, Samuel, diary 1674-1729, bk rev SGS 29:2:157

SEXTON, Manford Etehel b1899 w Wilda Baker, TN, biog & fam notes HJA 6:2:22

SEYBERT, Henry b1856 w Eliza Hickman, OH, geneal, bk rev CI 12:4:155

SEYMOUR, Ebenezer f1775 w Dorcas, VT, geneal NER 133:1:20

SHAFFER, William b1775 w Sophia Blocher, Ger, Fr, anc ch REP 19:2:82

William b1800, KY, IN, biog notes HJA 6:1:22

SHANNON, James Q b1844 w Susan Miranda Darrough, Bible rec GL 13:2:41

SHARP, Henry b1737 w Lydia Morgan, NJ, PA, geneal, bk rev KCG 20:4:207

Henry b1737 w Lydia Morgan, NJ, PA, geneal supp, bk rev OC 16:1:32 KCG 20:4:207

Henry b1819 w Margaret Jane Mills, Bible rec SCS 14:4:111

Solomon Zook b1835 w Salome Zook, PA, KS, biog PM 2:1:8

SHATTUCK, fam geneal #2, bk rev NYR 110:1:55

SHAW,, Kenneth Ralph b1898 w Margaret Jessie McIntosh, IA, CO, anc ch BGS 10:2:43

Robert dc1839, KY heirs KA 15:2:97

Samuel T d1843, NH, cem inscr OC 16:4:130

William f1777, VA, NC, biog notes NCJ 5:3:216

SHAYLOR, Thomas f1660 w Marah (Spencer) Brooks, Eng, CT, geneal CTN 12:4:705

SHEARCH, Isaac m1891 w Martha Deusler, NY, marr cert AH 3:4:108

SHEARER, Jacob b1744 w Elizabeth Deal, PA, OH, geneal, bk rev REP 19:4:167

William b1780 w Mary Hozier, NY, Bible rec NGS 67:3:228

SHED, Sally b1811 h William H
Barton, ME, biog notes OC
16:3:94

Thomas b1745 w Eleanor Spurr,
Hepzibah Winship, MA, geneal
OC 16:1:17

SHEETS, Jacob S b1827 w Nancy J
Smith, IN, anc ch HJA 6:4:37

SHELDON, David b1818 w Charlotte
Bell, PA, IN, OH, anc ch REP
19:4:161

Elisha m1759 w Sarah Bellows,
CT, geneal, CT bicentennial
series XIII, bk rev CTN
9:1:128

Thomas J b1789 w Hulda Tharp,
NJ, OH, IA, anc ch REP
19:4:158

SHEPARD, Elizabeth K, IL,
letters BGS 11:4:166

fams of N E, geneal v2, 1972,
bk rev OG 2:3:88

Stephen b1750 w Prudence Adams,
MA, Bible rec NGS 67:4:252

SHEPHARD, Justin J b1848 w Ellen
G Brydle, NY, Bible rec AH
3:1:21

SHEPPERSON, Nathaniel b1761, VA,
Bible rec VA 17:1:25

SHERIDAN, John w Ellen, NE,
geneal, bk rev BGS 8:2:30

SHERK, Peter b1780, Can, loyalist, biog, bk rev GN 2:6:172

SHERMAN, Henry bc1511, Eng, MA,
geneal CLG 10:1:4

SHIP PASSENGER LISTS, biblio HG
19:3:53

for New England BGS 3:1:22
3:3:21 3:4:22 4:1:28 4:2:27
4:3:26 4:4:36 5:1:25 5:2:23
5:3:35 5:4:30 6:1:28

"Fulda" It to NY 1893 ITG 2:41

"Helene" 1849 CI 14:4:130

imms to middle colonies, bk rev
CTN 11:2:339

misc excerpts WI 25:3:123
25:4:173 26:1:9

misc lists 1618-1878 v1,2, bk
rev GH 33:5:70 NYR 110:4:245
MQ 45:3:162 CTN 12:3:533 TB
6:4:33 NGS 67:4:307

Morton Allen direct of pass
arrivals NY 1890-1930 & NY,

PA, MA & MD 1904-1926 (1931),
bk rev NYR 110:3:184 GH
33:2:72

NY & NJ 1600-1825, bk rev TST
12:16:40 DM 43:1:45 KN 2:1:39
AG 55:1:64

national & N E 1600-1825, bk
rev DM 43:1:45 TST 11:44:29
CTN 10:4:703

publ pass lists GJ 8:4:177

"Republik" Bremen to NY, imms
to WI 1856 WI 25:4:174

"San Francisco" from Glasgow to
NY 1854 TB 6:4:7

ship pass lists in period literature, bk rev DM 43:2:88

South (MD to LA), bk rev CDS
16:4:11

use & value REP 19:3:105

SHIPP, fam of MS, CO, notes on
BGS 4:2:6

John Wesley b1859 w Laura
Dulin, IA, NE, SD, anc ch BGS
10:4:44

William f1637, VA, geneal, bk
rev BGS 8:1:26

SHIPPEE, Mercy E (Card) b1822 h
William W Shippee, RI, biog
notes RIR 5:4:9

Welcome Allen f1834, RI ledger
& fam recs FH 2:3:68

SHIRA, John b1854 w Mary Cox,
MO, KS, Bible rec TS 21:2:71

SHIRLEY, Abraham Laurence b1846
w America Idella Snively, IN,
anc ch REP 19:3:121

James bc1820 w Frances Mary
Anderson, OH, anc ch REP
19:4:163

SHIVELY, David b1803 w Hannah
Clapp, OH, anc ch REP 19:1:29

SHOAF, Jacob Jr m1833 w Elizabeth Berrier, Sarah Mayab,
NC, Bible rec DG 25:3:163

SHOEMAKER, Abraham b1804 w Mary
Dever, OH, anc ch REP
19:3:115

Alice, NE, letter 1883 BGS
3:4:17

Edmund b1803 w Clarissa Morris,
NY, Bible rec FG 21:3:69

Peter, PA letter 1830 BGS 4:3:7

SHORES, Jonathan Jr bc1770 w

Charlotte Cobb, MA, Bible rec DM 42:4:190

SHORTER, Henry d1849, NY, notes on DM 43:2:54

SHREVE, Harold b1911 w Virginia L McDaniel, KS, MI, anc ch TOP 9:2:44

SHUMAKER, James b1827 w Mary Anne, fam reg CI 13:4:129

SHUMATE, William Riley b1777 w Martha Ellen Acord, WV, geneal, bk rev YP 9:3:166 OC 16:4:136 AGE 8:4:109

SHURTS, Arthur Hall b1882 w Olive Whittemore Fengar, CT, anc ch AG 55:2:117

SHUVORT, Andras C b1792 w Luwanna Howes, NY, Bible rec MI 24:1:9

SIEG, Jacob b1784 w Lydia Haines, VA, anc ch REP 19:1:28

SIEGEL, Anthony b1855 w Anna, Bible rec KCG 20:1:31

SILK, Thomas b1889, LA, Bible rec GGM 74:302

SILLS, Donald Keith b1929 w Helen Bernice Tipton, OK, anc ch RRS 12:1:81

SILVER, Gershom b1725 w Millicent Archer, NJ, geneal, bk rev CTN 11:2:337

SILVERS, Jacob bc1814 w Charlotte Southern, VA, IL, geneal DWC 5:4:113

SIMMONS, Edward b1823 w Betsy E Weed, Bible rec MI 24:2:46

SIMON, Ignatz (Joseph) f1893 w Roza Schlesinger, Hungary, photo & biog notes JJG 3:4:28

SIMPKINS, James Henry b1847 w Mary Jane Lahmon, OH, IN, IL, fam rec FF 8:2:51

SIMMONS, Julia E b1812, Bible rec CTN 11:3:405

Philip bc1912, SC, biog notes FH 2:1:14

SIMPSON, Ambrose Niver b1832 w Hannah Christina Williams, NY, Bible rec CTN 11:3:406

Jefferson D d1882, OR death notice BB 11:2:31

Joseph f1780, NC, biog notes

NCJ 5:2:144

Wesley Ernest b1894 w Estelle Dulaney, MI, anc ch NAS 18:2:38

SIMS, Ira Lucian b1885 w Flora May Davis, TX, anc ch GR 21:4:142

SINCLAIR, Dohrman J w Mary Donaldson, geneal, bk rev CTN 9:4:604

SIPE, Paul f1752, Ger, geneal, bk rev HH 14:3:162

SISCHO, Luther b1827 w Almina Brown, WI, Bible rec BB 11:2:30

SKEEN, Robert m1817 w Polly Hart, VA, fam rec VAG 23:3:199

SKIDMORE, Mabery w Elizabeth Jane Evans, Naoma, Bible rec HH 14:1:39

SKINNER, Charles Denison b1846 w Ella Jane Perkins, NY, WI, anc ch BGS 10:1:36

Daniel b1733, CT, biog notes ANC 14:2:57

John f1636, Eng, CT, geneal, bk rev BGS 9:2:34

Uriah b1866 w Ella Shultz, PA, Bible rec AH 2:3:75

SLADE, Philip b1804 w Eliza, Eng, NY, OH, Bible rec BGS 4:4:9

SLAGLEY, Jane, IL letter 1868 CI 15:2:10

SLAUGHTER, Orlando V b1854 w Elizabeth Havron, MO, geneal, bk rev GH 33:3:108 VAG 23:1:70 KCG 20:3:154

SLOAN, Edcar H b1859 w Ida E Bright, Bible rec NAS 17:4:106

SLOANE, Oliver b1829, OH, OR, letters KCG 20:1:26 20:2:67

SLOMINSKI, Michael b1869 w Joanna Szczodrowska, anc ch PN 1:2:27

SLONAKER, Conrad Leroy bc1926 w Coralie Mildred Mark, OH, IL, AZ, anc ch KG 16:2:47

SLOSS, James Long b1791 w Letitia Van Dyke Campbell, Ir, VA, letters & biog notes

THT 6:1:15

SMALL, Andrew Buchanan, TX letter 1892 THT 2:1:22

SMALLWOOD, fam of MD & VA, geneal, bk rev TB 6:2:21

SMELTZER, Adam b1807 w Margaret Smith, OH, anc ch REP 19:2:85

SMITH, Adam m1811 w Maria Yates Town Root, NY, Bible rec NSN 4:2:12

Bartlett m1837 w Eliza Cheney, OH, Bible rec AH 4:2:52

Basil Gaither b1806 w Nancy Nuckols, KY, Bible rec TA 14:1:4

Carl J f1940, WA, notes on SGS 29:2:158

Charlie J b1901 w Virginia Belle Duke, MS, LA, anc ch GR 21:4:134

Cole Fro b1884 w Ada Christine Cecil, IL, TX, anc ch RRS 12:1:105

Daniel b1765 w Mary Keeler, CT, anc ch REP 19:3:132

David b1742 w Elizabeth Godfrey, Mrs M Tinkham, MA, ME, Can, Bible rec NER 133:4:303

David Floyd b1893 w Georgia Hazel Scott, TX, anc ch GR 21:1:7

Edgar Oscar b1830 w Joanna Eliza Hatheway, Bible rec CTN 11:4:593

Floyd Monroe b1899 w Velma Elnora Mitchell, AR, anc ch FF 8:2:26

Henry b1619 w Elizabeth, MA, geneal, bk rev CTN 11:4:705 BGS 8:2:30

Howard H b1904 w Helen Sharp, anc ch ACL 4:3:59

Ignatius b1726 w Susannah Howland, MA, notes on MQ 45:3:144

Jacob b1806 w Sally Ginn Tyler, Eliza Kendall, ME, Bible rec DE 2:5:23

James b1834 w Emma McWhorter, NC, TX, letters 1862 THT 3:2:19

Jamie b1846, NC, letter 1865

THT 3:1:15

John, OH, letter MD 1838 BGS 4:1:4

John m1828 w Eliza Makimson, Bible rec LL 14:1:26

John R b1869 w Ida E Cox, IL, anc ch FF 8:4:43

John W b1824 w Mary Elizabeth Mason, OH, CA, WA, Bible rec TB 6:1:20

Joseph m1799 w Sarah Blake, GA, marr rec NCJ 5:4:263

Laura G d1901 h Edward J Delaney, CA, fam rec SCC 16:2:25

Lindley M b1881 w Grace Selby, biog, bk rev GH 33:5:90

Miles m1797 w Betty Marshall, NC, marr rec NCJ 5:4:263

Miriam b1777 h Jonathan Smith, NY, photo & biog naotes FAM 18:2:86

Ozro Jackson b1841 w Miranda Brimmer, MI, Bible rec DM 42:4:156

Perry Edward b1891 w Herminea Ruth Myers, IN, biog notes ACL 4:3:45

Peter bc1794 w Martha, OR, biog notes GFP 29:1:10

Robert bc1626 w Mary French, Eng, MA, biog notes, will GJ 8:4:201

Robert b1782, NC, IL, geneal CI 14:3:87

Roxanna (Griggs) b1813 h Daniel Haskins Smith, OH, obit AH 4:3:94

Silas f1846 w Lurinda Smith, TX, deposition giving fam recs YP 9:3:149

Stirling m1857 w Grace Bossance, Ir, Bible rec IA 11:1:3

Thomas b1792 w Sarah Strong, CT, OH, Bible rec AH 3:1:18

Thomas b1799 w Elizabeth, CT, fam rec AH 3:1:18

Thomas b1832 w Elizabeth, KY, IN, Civil War letters LL 14:4:174

William b1768, VA, CA, biog DAR 113:3:258

William H b1813 w Sarah A Martin, Martha J Watkins, NY, IL, Bible rec IL 11:2:112

William "Tangier" d1705 w Martha Tunstall, NY, geneal, bk rev DM 43:2:88 GJ 8:3:170 VAG 23:1:71 NYR 110:1:53 SCS 16:1:21 AG 55:2:122

SMITHERS, Edward Charles b1916 w Mildred Mary Dumatrait, LA, anc ch AGE 8:4:125

SMOLA, Martin b1801 w Ludmila Benda, Ger, NY, IL, geneal, bk rev GH 33:4:119 KCG 20:3:149

SMYTH, James Morris m1887 w Kate Wright Bensan, KS, Bible rec KK 17:1:8

Thomas b1837 w Eliza Jane Baxter, Ir, IA, anc ch REP 19:3:121

William Isaac b1892 w Vivien Coates White, CA, IL, NE, anc ch BGS 11:4:183

SNIDER, Abraham b1802 w Elizabeth Myers, OH, anc ch REP 19:4:158

Charles Leo b1907 w Mary Martha Brown, MO, anc ch BGS 11:3:137

SNOEK, William Karel b1884 w Flora Bell Freeman, Hol, TX, anc ch YP 9:4:204

SNOKE, Adam Jonas b1839, OH, auto, bk rev REP 19:1:40

SNOW, Edward b1745 w Betsey Myrick, MA, ME, anc ch OC 16:3:97

Ross B b1912 w Vera M Harrison, VT, anc ch THT 6:3:81

SNYDER, David Lee b1943 w Linda Maureen Burns, OR, CA, anc ch THT 7:1:8

William Henry b1858 w Belle Righter, IL, fam rec CI 14:4:140

SOCIETIES, Adoptees Liberty Movement Assoc CTN 11:4:571 TST 12:14:37

Am Antiquarian Soc OC 16:1:23 CTN 8:2:163

Am Fam Recs Assoc JG 4:1:28

Am Hist Soc of Germans from Russia JG 4:4:31 KCG 20:2:81

Assoc for Geneal Educ JG 4:1:21

Ch of Latter-Day Saints, geneal lib descr TST 12:23:46

Clan MacLennan Assoc BCG 7:1:8

CT hist soc CTN 9:3:323

Desc of Washington's Army at Valley Forge LL 15:4:186 CI 13:1:13

fam assoc list GH 33:3:21 ORB 18:4:98 AW 5:2:45 5:3:71 5:4:104

fam hist soc in Britain OC 16:3:87

Federation of Fam Hist Socs, publ bk rev EG 12:294

Federation of Geneal Socs ORB 18:3:45 JG 4:1:24 CTN 8:4:524

geneal soc guide bk, bk rev TSP 3:2:25

German-Texan Heritage Soc AGS 20:1:23

International Soc for British Geneal & Fam Hist JG 4:3:7 GE 43:13 EG 12:295

Kansas City (MO) Adult Adoptees Organization KCG 20:1:24

LDS, finding aid, bk rev AGS 20:4:143

guide to geneal lib & ch hist dept 1973, bk rev TB 6:4:29

lib Salt Lake City UT REF 21:1:3

Maine Hist Soc DE 3:1:32

Missouri State Geneal Assoc TS 21:3:120

Natl Soc of Daughters of the Am Rev, lib guide TST 12:4:36

patriot index & supp 1,3, bk rev TB 6:3:22

Natl Geneal Soc GE 49:11

New Eng Hist Geneal Soc TST 12:9:46 GE 49:11

NY Geneal & Biog Soc TST 11:48:36

NH Soc of Genealogists SCR 2:3:11

organizing fam assoc EWA 16:1:19

Palatines to Am CTN 10:1:182 STC 2:1:23

PA Ger Soc GE 43:14

publishing a fam newsletter SCS 16:4:106

RI Hist Soc CTN 8:1:3

Richland Co IL Geneal Soc CI 14:1:31

Soc of Genealogists EG 12:295

Sons of the Am Rev, KS roster 1892-1977, bk rev CTN 10:2:341

Natl Reg 1902, bk rev TB 6:4:28

surname publ list TB 6:3:27 6:4:11 GH 33:3:33

Swedish Council of Am KCG 20:3:145

Thomas ap Catesby Jones Soc BB 11:1:4

War of 1812 Socs MI 24:2:64

Western Reserve Hist Soc SGS 29:4:323

SOLANDER, Mary fl1871, CO, biog notes BGS 5:4:10

SONNER, John Ferdinand b1889 w Rose Vincent, LA, anc ch AGE 8:4:130

SORENSON, Hans Wilhelm b1822 w Anna Peterson, Norway, Sw, MI, bible rec GFP 28:7:129

SORREL, G Moxley, CSA, Civil War recollections, bk rev CDS 16:1:22

SOUCH, William bc1795 w Emelyn Dennis, Eng, Can, geneal EG 12:287

SOULE, George bc1600 w Mary Bucket, Eng, MA, geneal MQ 45:4:189

SOUTH CAROLINA, Abbeville, Upper Long Cane cem inscr GGM 73:205

abstr recs of Secretary of Province 1692-1721, bk rev GGM 71:10

Charleston Com geneal res guide, bk rev GH 33:2:80 CDS 16:3:3

Chester Co, Fishing Creek Pres Ch cem inscr THT 3:2:25

Fishing Creek Pres Ch visitation bk 1774-1775 THT 7:2:98

Dorchester Co, cem inscr vl, bk rev GH 33:1:88

Edgefield Co, probate recs vl, bk rev NCJ 5:3:211 GGM 71:7

geneal period, bk rev NCJ

5:1:66

jury lists 1718-1783, bk rev NGS 67:4:304

Mecklenburg Co, Bethesda Pres Ch cem, Rev War soldiers cem inscr THT 3:1:24

natives in TN 1850 GGM 74:287

Pee Dee, ancestral key, bk rev OC 16:3:108 CTN 12:1:176

Pendleton Co, deed bk B GGM 73:225

pensioners census 1840 THT 3:2:37

Pickens Co, misc recs GGM 71:105

recs 1692-1721, bk rev VAG 23:2:149

Rev War, muster roll of Capt Harman Dairs 1777-1778 THT 7:2:121

prisoner court of inquiry GGM 73:209

women in Rev DAR 113:4:356

St Stephen, St Stephen's Epis Ch recs 1754-1873, bk rev NCJ 5:4:257

Spartanburg Co, Nazareth Ch cem GGM 74:305

Union Co, cem inscr, bk rev YP 9:2:102

deed bk B GGM 71:113

hist, bk rev GGM 71:7

York Co, Lesslie, Neely's Creek Associated Reformed Pres Ch cem inscr SCS 15:1:15 15:2:38

SOUTH DAKOTA, Aberdeen, early settlers, notes on BGS 8:3:8

Dolton, hist, bk rev TB 6:2:24

Freeman, Hutterthal cem inscr TB 6:4:35

imms from Ger via Russ, bk rev GH 33:3:98

Marion, hist, bk rev TB 6:2:24

Menno, hist, bk rev TB 6:2:23

hist 1879-1979, bk rev TB 6:2:19

misc Black Hills area cems vl,2, bk rev TB 6:2:21

Monroe, hist, bk rev TB 6:2:24

Pennington Co, early marr recs vl 1887-1904 v2 1904-1919, bk rev TB 6:2:20

SOUTHERN STATES, Col fams geneal

1911, bk rev CTN 10:1:156

Confederate pension recs sources NSN 4:4:32

hist southern fams, geneal v22, bk rev CTN 11:4:701 NGS 67:1:68

Knights of Labor hist, bk rev MHM 74:3:303

misc fam geneal, bk rev NGI 3:1:32

misc fam geneal v22, bk rev NYR 110:1:58

SOWELL, Joe Lawson b1906 w Mabel Williams, TX, anc ch THT 6:3:61

SPADI, Henry b1887 w Elizabeth Kreiger, Rus, CO, anc ch BGS 10:3:48

SPAHR, Ben f1842 w Sarah Peterman, OH, anc ch REP 19:1:37

SPAIN, guide to archives & libs part 3 SPG 31:569

heraldry, bk rev SPG 31:588

ancient hist, bk rev SPG 31:590

Moors, hist, bk rev SPG 31:590

SPALDING, Daniel b1757 w Mercy Hewitt, CT, NY, Bible rec NGS 67:3:201

SPARKS, The Sparks Quarterly, 1709 Cherokee Rd, Ann Arbor MI 48104

William Pleas b1900 w Cora Lou Pettiet, TX, anc ch GR 21:3:93

SPEARMAN, David Bowden b1903 w Mary Helen Elizabeth Ham, TX, anc ch GR 21:3:96

SPECHT, Edward John b1895 w Lana Helen Clapps, WI, anc ch NGI 3:3:176

SPEECE, Frederic b1785 w Nancy Booker Morton, VA, Bible rec NGS 67:3:201

SPENCER, James Marion b1876 w Nora Estella Wallace, TX, OK, anc ch THT 6:3:92

SPERRY, Anson f1861 w Thryza Garrison, NY, TX, MN, geneal, bk rev MN 10:1:41

SPICER, Arthur d1700, Eng, VA, notes on NGS 67:3:212

Hiram b1818 w Abigail L Hartshorn, Lydia Ann Scott, OH,

Bible rec MIS 11:4:63

Nathan b1735, NY, geneal, bk rev CTN 12:3:697

SPITLER, David W b1838 w Mary Shuman, OH, anc ch REP 19:2:84

SPONSLER, James Oscar b1836 w Mary Ellen Babb, PA, Bible rec HH 14:2:85

SPRAGUE, Charles Enos b1881 w Luella May Cain, MO, OR, anc ch ORB 17:8:73

SPRIGG, Sarah f1680 h John Pearce, MD, geneal notes PGB 11:10:113

SPRING, John bc1787 w Elinor, Eng, MA, geneal AG 55:2:65

SPRINGER, Charles b1658, DE, Sw ancestry, bk rev NYR 110:1:53 AG 55:2:121

Matthias b1758 w Athalial Barnes, NJ, PA, anc ch REP 19:3:118

fam of DE & Sw, geneal, bk rev NGS 67:2:152

SPROULL, Robert b1777 w Anna Montgomery, Ir, VA, OH, anc ch REP 19:4:157

SQUIBB, Charles Leonard b1894 w Bertha Edna Rickell, NE, anc ch NW 2:2:57

SQUIRES, Frederick A b1819 w Miranda Wade, MA, CT, RI, IL, CO, geneal BGS 9:1:12

STACKHOUSE, Frederick b1837 w Sarah J, LA, Bible rec CI 15:3:86

John f1860 w America Ann Davidson, Bible rec CI 15:3:85

letter IL 1862 CI 15:3:96

STACY, Moses f1793, Bible rec NER 133:4:300

Simon b1592 w Elizabeth Clerke, Eng, MA, geneal, bk rev GH 33:2:86 KCG 20:3:151

STADING, John b1867 w Elise Krause, Rus, ND, anc ch NW 2:2:61

STAFFORD, George bc1758 w Nancy Huff, PA, NC, geneal CLG 10:1:13

STANDERFER, fam Bible rec CI 14:4:122

STANHOPE, Everrett Leo b1930 w
Anne Irene Beard, OR, WA, anc
ch OG 4:4:100

STANLEY, Archie Mercer b1880 w
Nina Alma Hamner, AL, TX, anc
ch THT 7:1:14

STANNAH, Richard M b1811 w Sarah
M Meloy, OH, anc ch REP
19:3:116

STANSBURY, Andrew H b1842 w
Lydia Marie Morton, Catherine
Wats, IL, KS, Bible rec BGS
8:2:4

fam of PA, MD, VA, geneal, bk
rev NGS 67:2:149 DM 42:3:136

STANTON, Thomas b1696 w Mary,
NC, geneal BGS 9:2:7

STAPLE, fam of MA, geneal, bk
rev GH 33:2:86 NGS 67:3:227

STARR, Samuel Clifton b1895 w
Zelma Simmonds, TX, anc ch
THT 6:3:78

STAUFFER, fam of Switz, geneal,
bk rev PM 2:1:23

Lowell M b1885 w Ruby Eva
Myers, OH, MT, anc ch NW
2:4:126

Ulrich f1760 w Frainey, VA, PA,
geneal CLG 10:1:47

STECKMAN, George d1853 w Elizabeth, PA, fam cem inscr NGS
67:4:286

STEEL, Nathaniel b1824 w Mary
Smith, anc ch REP 19:2:84

STEELE, William Jackson b1857 w
Mary Susan Little, VA, MO,
AZ, anc ch GR 21:2:51

STEIN, fam of IL, geneal FF
8:1:51

STEINER, Jacob b1844 w Mary
Moser, Switz, OH, Bible rec
DM 42:4:174

STEPHEN, Zachariah b1805 w Mary
Crawford, OH, anc ch REP
19:4:165

STEPHENS, Stephens-Stevens-
Stephenson-Stevenson Quarterly, 1356 Elderberry Dr, Concord CA 94521

STEPHENSON, Floyd Earnest b1894
w Capitola Eugene Jones, TX,
OK, anc ch RRS 12:1:103

Jeremiah bc1790 w Malinda Dunn,

WV, geneal, bk rev GH
33:4:119

Thomas b1735, Bible rec WPA
5:1:34

William Jefferson b1804 w
Celina Roberts Crawford, NC,
KY, IL, Bible rec CI 15:3:99

STERCHI, Peter b1764 w Elizabeth
Zingrich, Switz, anc ch REP
19:2:82

STERRETT, Guy b1900 w Helen
Lucille Brelsford, KS, AZ,
anc ch TOP 9:2:48 KK 17:4:76

STETSON, Orrin R b1820 w Lydia M
Ames, ME, Bible rec DE 3:4:22

STEVENS, fam of N S, geneal, bk
rev GH 33:5:90 GN 2:8:248

Joseph b1808 w Mary Dillard
Warnick, Margaret (Stentenay)
Cunningham, IL, Bible rec &
biog CI 14:2:63 14:3:98

STEVENSON, Enoch G b1820 w Mrs
Ann (Rader) Harshbarger, VA,
OH, anc ch REP 19:2:87

fam of NJ, geneal, bk rev LL
15:2:82

Henry H w A M, TX, 1863 letter
THT 6:3:105

Samuel Jr b1742, NJ, geneal, bk
rev CTN 10:3:522

STEWARD, Daniel d1802 w Mary
Ireland, ME, fam rec DE
2:5:28

STEWART, Alexander b1817 w Agnes
Moreland, Scot, NJ, WI, geneal, bk rev GH 33:5:90

Jean Willard b1912 w Bonita
Belle Dabner, MO, OK, KS, anc
ch TOP 9:1:14

Jefferson Milford b1883 w Olive
May, AR, CO, anc ch BGS
11:1:45

STIENS, Gerd Heinrich f1807 w
Katharina Maria Redemacher,
Ger, anc ch REP 19:1:34

STIGALL, William bc1770, NC, IL,
fam rec FF 8:4:44

STILES, Hermon f1863 w Ellen,
NY, letter BGS 8:1:19

Howard Thompson b1878 w Grace
Helen Barnes, KS, anc ch BGS
10:4:42

STILWELL, David b1755 w _____,

Mourning Brogden, IN, biog notes TSP 3:1:9

STINHAUER, fam of IL, geneal FF 8:4:31

STITH, Jordan f1839, KY, IL, fam rec CI 14:2:48

STIVERS, fam of east TN, geneal, bk rev CTN 9:4:606

STOCKBRIDGE, John bc1607 w Ann, Mrs Elizabeth (Hatch) Soan, Mary, Eng, MA, geneal NER 133:2:93 133:3:187 133:4:286

STOCKER, Ephraim f1693, Eng, VA, notes on NGS 67:3:212

STOKES, Joseph Green b1867 w Navada Harris, anc ch FF 8:2:25

STOLTZFUS, Henry U f1901 w Melinda Stoltzfus, fam photo PM 2:3:i

John b1805 w Catharine Holly, PA, biog PM 2:3:17

STONE, Alban M b1807 w Mary Adams Morse, RI, Bible rec NGS 67:4:266

Ezra b1768 w Lucina White, Bible rec CTN 7:2:315

Joel C, KY letter 1863 FF 8:3:41

Susanna f1620 h Richard Cutting, Henry Kimball, Thomas Low, Eng, MA, notes on AG 55:1:26

Theodore A b1873 w Grace Reed, IL, KY, CO, anc ch BGS 11:2:87

STONECIPHER, Raymond b1899 w Estella Emrich, IN, anc ch ACL 4:3:57

STONEHOUSE, Joseph b1776 w Martha Jane Rushforth, Eng, Can, biog notes FAM 18:3:127

STORM, Orville b1898 w Dorothy M Stirewalt, IL, anc ch MCH 7:3:81

STOUFFER, Matthias bc1700, Ger, PA, geneal, bk rev HH 14:3:162

STOVALL, Bartholomew b1665 w Ann Burton, Eng, VA, geneal, bk rev GH 33:4:120

Joel b1797 w Rebecca Rickman, VA, TN, KY, Bible rec & cem

inscr KFR 7:95

STOVER, Lewis b1781, TN, geneal, bk rev OK 24:2:73 FP 22:4:210 VL 14:1:45

STOWE, Noah dc1939, AZ, notes on FH 2:4:123

STRAMLER, Robert Weston b1894 w LaRue Hawkins, TX, anc ch THT 6:3:71

STRANDSKOV, Lars f1872 w Ane Marie Andersdatter, Denmark, MN, geneal, bk rev BGS 10:4:34

STRANGE, John Wade Morgan b1861 w Corinna Almanza Conner, Mrs Sarah Jane (Ferguson) Uber, MO, Bible rec GR 21:4:148

STRAUB, Andreas f1742, Neth, PA, gengal FF 8:2:56

STRAW, Jonathan Soloman b1814 w Rebecca Long, PA, Bible rec HH 14:2:87

STRAYER, David b1855 w Lucinda Stull, OH, anc ch REP 19:2:88

STREY, William J b1865 w Lena Mather, Ger, WA, anc ch OG 4:2:40

STRICKLAND, fam of IL, geneal CI 14:4:137

STRICKLER, fams of VA & WV, geneal, bk rev CDS 16:1:5

STROHM, David, IL oath of office 1860 CI 14:1:10

STRONG, Daniel b1780 w Prudence Wells, NY, OH, anc ch REP 19:4:156

John f1630 w _____, Abigail Ford, MA, geneal CTN 8:1:36

John b1899, Bible rec MI 24:2:47

STRUBLE, William b1768 w Catharine DeWitt, OH, Bible rec REP 19:3:112

STRYKER, fam of Am, geneal, bk rev NYR 110:4:251

STUBBLEFIELD, Jefferson L bc1803 w S Nancy, TN, TX, fam rec THT 7:1:34

Robert d1870 w Sarah Funk, Dorothy Funk, VA, biog GL 13:3:81 13:4:101

STUBBS, T B f1860 w Catherine Louise Kauffman, PA, TX, geneal, bk rev GH 33:6:87

STUCKI, fam of Switz, LDS Temple Ordinances bk B, film rev GH 33:6:92

STURDYVIN, James D b1868 w Kathryn Delaney, IL, CO, anc ch BGS 10:2:44

STURGEON, Samuel Dickson b1780 w Nancy Rowen, PA, anc ch REP 19:1:30

STURGIS, Andrew f1775, GA, geneal, bk rev CTN 9:2:309

SUBLETT, William bc1760 w Ruth Ford, VA, KY, anc ch REP 19:3:132

SULLIVAN, Herbert Joseph b1887 w Adele Virginia Overbeck, MO, CO, anc ch BGS 9:4:37

Neil Carmichael b1877, OH, letter, biog notes BGS 5:3:25

SUMPTER, Miranda b1835, cem inscr TB 6:2:45

SURNAME INDEX, British Columbia geneal soc BCG 1973, 1977, 1979

British index of geneal interests by surnames, bk rev NSN 4:5:43

East TX Geneal Soc 1977, bk rev AGS 20:4:146

Elkhart Co IL Geneal Soc MIS 11:2:1 11:4:52

Eng surnames EG 12:306

IA Geneal Soc surname index 1972, bk rev CTN 7:2:295

IA Geneal Soc surname index 1975, bk rev CTN 9:2:309

Irish names & notes, bk rev ACL 4:4:75

KS Geneal Soc 1978 TS 21:1:39

NC by county THT 7:2:59

NC Geneal Soc v5, bk rev AGS 20:4:153

Peoria IL Geneal Soc 1979, bk rev CDS 16:4:13 TST 12:10:38 GH 33:3:97 IL 11:2:114

Sacramento CA v2 1980, bk rev TB 6:4:33

St Louis MO Geneal Soc 1968-1977, bk rev KCG 20:4:211

Scottish Am Geneal v1-12 SCG 13:7

Tulsa OK Geneal Soc (several years), bk rev KCG 20:4:209 SGS 29:4:340

SURRATT, Marshall England b1923 w Margaret Irma Nash, TX, AR, anc ch THT 7:2:70

SURRIAGE, Agnes b1726 h Sir Charles Harry Frankland, John Drew, MA, Eng, biog DAR 113:1:14

SUSOR, Joseph b1840 w Sarah Jane Gaffney, Bible rec GFP 28:8:148

SUTPHIN, Samuel f1776, NJ, biog notes BGS 8:3:11

SUTTON, Millard Oliver b1916 w Virginia Oma Cromlich, IN, anc ch RRS 12:1:107

SVENSSON, Sven, geneal, bk rev NGI 3:2:108

SWAFFORD, Johnnie Noel b1918 w Pauline Glouser, TX, KS, CA, anc ch BGS 11:2:88

SWALLOW, Jacob b1795 w Keturah Perryman, IL, Bible & fam rec CI 14:3:91

SWAN, George d1798 w Abigail Randall, CT, Bible rec CTA 21:3:122

SWANSON, Ralph A b1905 w Myrtle Louise Pfundt, WA, anc ch OG 4:3:67

SWEARINGEN, Thomas H b1824 w Sarilda J Clay, Sophi J Richardson, MO, Bible rec TA 14:1:6

SWEDEN, ch recs guide, bk rev GH 33:2:74 TST 11:52:45

Emig Institute GJ 8:4:192

geneal res guide MN 10:4:188

emigs to MN, notes on TST 12:10:36

Sw-Am geneal res guide, bk rev IL 11:2:113

SWEET, Hannah (Mrs) b1817 h David F Sweet, CT, RI, biog notes RIR 5:4:9

SWENSON, Carl Allen b1895 w Mamie Edna Dugan, KS, anc ch TOP 9:2:47

Lars b1845, Bible rec PR 3:1:6

Swen b1817 w Sara Maria Ohrn, Sw, IA, IL, geneal, bk rev IG 15:4:103

SWIFFORD, John H m1903, IL, biog notes MCH 7:3:88

SWIFT, Oliver Cromwell b1797 w Eliza Robinson Jenkins, MA, anc ch ANC 14:3:91

SWITZERLAND, Amish emig to Am, bk rev REP 19:1:43

geneal res guide GH 33:5:11 JG 4:3:12

geneal res guide, bk rev GH 33:5:69 TST 12:19:39 IL 11:3:182 GJ 8:4:214 NGI 3:3:170

Palatine guide, bk rev CTN 8:4:543

Thurgall, misc parish reg abstr, film rev GH 33:6:92

SYLVESTER, Arnold Elmer b1909 w Merle Olive Bartos, NE, anc ch NW 2:2:59

TABOR, Phillip f1784, PA, loan cert KA 14:4:197

TACKETT, Jeremiah bc1810, KY, IN, IL, geneal, bk rev CI 14:4:151

TAFT, Robert f1680 w Sarah, MA, geneal (1874), bk rev MQ 45:4:230

TALBEE, Samuel bc1715 w Elizabeth Hitchcock, MD, geneal FF 8:1:40

TALBOT, John bc1384, Eng, biog EG 12:268

TALBOTT, Richard J m1865 w Celiann Ryan, NE, IA, anc ch NW 2:3:91

TANNER, John Logan Jr b1893 w Laura Estep, VA, KY, TX, anc ch THT 6:3:62

TATOR, James Henry b1835 w Margaret Ann Fraleigh, NY, Bible rec CTN 11:3:404,405

TATRO, John f1832, Can, CT, notes on LL 14:3:136

TAYLOR, see also FOX TAYLOR

Berriman Z f1877 w Louisa Bennett, IL, fam rec FF 8:3:78

Charles E b1843 w Lucy Ann Hitchcock, IL, MO, anc ch CPY 8:1:24

Clarence Curtis b1906 w Hilda

Irene Harbin, MT, ID, anc ch OG 4:4:102

David Frederick b1919 w Joanne Dorine, MT, SD, anc ch TRI 19:1:6

Eber b1811, PA, OH, biog notes BB 11:3:50

fam of NY, Bible rec SCC 16:3:78

Frazier Jr b1799 w Lucy Remley, PA, OH, anc ch REP 19:3:115

Henry f1878 w Susan Caroline Claytor, fam rec FF 8:2:37

Josiah b1814 w Catherine Koger, MO, KY, Bible rec FP 22:1:34

Marion Estes b1898 w Bertha Grissom, MO, TN, anc ch EWA 16:2:76

Mary Elizabeth (Smith) d1894 h O P Taylor, OR, obit BB 11:4:75

Nancy b1823 h Sherman A Kellogg, Lucius T Wilmot, CT, OH, Bible rec & biog notes AH 1:3:17

Washington b1818 w Martha Morehead, PA, OH, biog notes VQ 16:1:13

William Edgar b1886 w Nancy Jane McHugh, AR, AL, OK, anc ch NAS 18:1:6

William H b1841 w Mary McFarland, OH, Bible rec CI 15:2:15

TEAKELL, John D b1883 w Exer Bell Harrison, AL, TX, CA, anc ch NAS 17:3:72

TEARS, John B b1823 w Catharine E (Royce) Roosa, NY, Bible rec CTN 12:2:233

TEDBALL, Burke Abraham b1875 w Emma Rose Drow, MO, MI, anc ch AGE 8:4:129

TEGAR, William F d1926 w Lucy Belle Watson, IL, fam rec FF 8:2:43

TEMPLE, William f1687, VA, geneal, bk rev NGS 67:3:219

TEMPLETON, John Rufus b1879 w Amanda White, TN, MO, TX, anc ch THT 7:1:21

Rufus Lee b1883 w Cleopatra Small, TN, AL, TX, anc ch THT

6:3:54

William T, geneal, bk rev GFP 29:1:5

TENISON, John R m1829 w Nancy Ann, Bible rec LL 15:1:19

TENNESSEE, Benton Co, cem inscr, bk rev GH 33:4:114

census 1850, bk rev GH 33:1:88

Carroll Co, census 1850, bk rev GH 33:3:102

marrs vl 1838-1859, bk rev GH 33:2:81

Carter Co, tax list 1834 BWG 8:1:79

Cheatham Co, Kingston Springs, hist notes THT 5:1:31

Chester Co, misc small cem inscr THT 6:3:109

Civil War, battles & sketches, bk rev CDS 16:6:44

vets questionnaire 1914, 1915, 1920 SCS 16:1:8 16:3:85

Claiborne Co, Tazewell, hist 1825-1899, bk rev WCK 12:3:47 TST 12:21:56 VAG 23:4:312

Cumberland Co, hist 1956, bk rev TST 11:43:29

hist vl-4, bk wev KK 17:2:39

Davidson Co, pioneer hist 1965, bk rev GH 33:4:114 VAG 23:2:150

geneal res guide YP 9:3:165 SCS 15:4:112

geneal res guide, bk rev TSP 3:2:4 WCK 12:4:63

governors' biog collect, bk rev YP 9:1:41

Henderson Co, misc small cem inscr THT 6:3:109

Hickman Co, Blue Spring Hollow, Brown fam cem inscr MGR 14:1:20

Humphreys Co, Bakersville news abstr vl 1896-1897, bk rev GH 33:1:88

Knox Co, marr recs 1792-1900, bk rev CTN 7:2:295

Lawrence Co, marr recs 1818-1923, bk rev GH 33:5:78 VL 14:2:96

Lewis Co, cem inscr, bk rev GH 33:4:114

Lincoln Co, office holders

1878 THT 4:2:13

Lynchburg, Arbor Grove Bapt Ch charter 1831 THT 4:1:28

Maury Co, misc fam recs vl, 1967, bk rev GH 33:1:89

Rev War vets recs, bk rev GH 33:1:89

Moore Co, Walker cem inscr THT 5:3:3

Morgan Co, hist, bk rev GGM 71:9

news list, bk rev TB 6:1:34

Obion Co, marr recs 1824-1877, bk rev CDS 16:1:5

Overton Co, geneal recs 1967, bk rev GH 33:4:114 VAG 23:2:150

Rev War pensioners 1840 census GR 21:1:24

Roane Co, tax lists 1814-1821, bk rev OK 24:2:74

Sullivan Co, Rock Springs, Hite cem inscr BWG 8:1:51

Kingsport, Rock Springs United Meth Ch, Lower cem inscr BWG 8:1:56

Kingsport, Rock Springs United Meth Ch, Upper cem inscr BWG 8:1:52

Sumner Co, will bk 1,2 1788-1842, bk rev GH 33:4:115 VAG 23:2:150

Unicoi Co, Beals cem inscr BWG 8:1:76

Blankenship cem inscr BWG 8:1:73

Divide cem inscr BWG 8:1:72

Marbleton, McInturff/Peoples cem inscr BWG 8:1:68

Rice Creek cem inscr BWG 8:1:66

Sams fam cem inscr BWG 8:1:63

Washington Co, Boone's Creek Ch cem inscr SCS 14:3:64

land entry rec bk vl 1826-1845 BWG 8:1:45

Maple Grove, Friend's Ch, hist BWG 8:1:33

Williamson Co, marr recs 1804-1850, bk rev WCK 12:3:48

TENZER, fam of Poland & Am, geneal, bk rev NGS 67:2:153

TERRILL, Thomas F b1892 w Truie

H Herrick, IA, anc ch ACL 4:1:12

TERRY, James Y b1805 w Mary Ann Stoddard, Bible rec CTN 11:2:215

TEVEBAUGH, Edwin Elmore b1857 w Margaret King, IN, MO, CO, anc ch BGS 9:4:43

TEXAS, Albany, Meth Ch ministers THT 2:2:43

Anderson Co, Antioch cem inscr DG 25:1:57

marrs 1846-1869 FP 22:2:55 22:3:119 22:4:177

Archer Co, misc small cem inscr THT 5:4:22,32

Armstrong Co, Goodmight College, misc pupils THT 3:2:61

Austin, agents for "Gazette" 1830 YP 9:1:47

banks & bankers hist 1835-1875, bk rev YP 9:4:227

Beaumont, French fam cem inscr YP 9:2:64

Bell Co, Bapt Ch cem inscr THT 3:1:28

census 1860, cont HTR 22:1:26 22:2:59

probate recs 1850-1930 HTR 22:3:93

Bevil Precinct, census 1835 FP 22:1:39 22:2:87

Bexar Co, census 1850, bk rev TRI 19:1:4

Bexar Dist, Ft McKavett, mort sched 1870 STK 7:3:133

biblio of TX education hist, bk rev STK 7:1:30

Bosque Co, marr recs bk D 1875-1885 FP 22:1:11

marr recs bk E 1885-1889 FP 22:1:13

marr rec bk F 1889-1897 FP 22:1:19 22:2:97 22:3:149

Brazoria Co, census 1860, bk rev YP 9:2:107

Burnet Co, Crownover Chapel cem inscr THT 5:4:5

Hoover's Valley cem notes THT 6:1:11

Calhoun Co, census 1870, bk rev NGI 3:4:212

Callahan Co, Zion Hill cem

inscr DG 25:3:167

Castro, hist, bk rev CDS 16:3:4

Chambers Co, census 1880 YP 9:1:50

Cherokee Com Killough Massacre Site cem inscr THT 5:1:12

Childress Co, Arlie cem inscr THT 5:4:6

Buck Creek cem inscr THT 7:1:37

Civil War vets burials THT 5:1:10 5:2:5 5:3:23 5:4:32

Coke Co, marrs bk 1 1890-1900 STK 7:2:63 7:3:129 7:4:157

Mule Creek cem inscr STK 7:4:161

Robert Lee Meth Epis Ch recs STK 7:1:14

tax list 1889 STK 7:1:28

Coleman Co, Rough Creek, school souvenir 1898 STK 7:2:62

Vale, Spring Creek Bapt Ch of Christ minute bk 1894-1905 STK 7:3:137

Collin Co, cem inscr vl, bk rev OC 16:2:71

cem inscr v2, bk rev DG 25:2:123

census & mort sched 1850, bk rev GH 33:6:84 DG 25:3:188

marrs 1846-1858 vl, bk rev NGI 3:4:211

Collingsworth Co, cem inscr of vets THT 5:3:24

census 1880 THT 4:1:28

Dozier cem, hist & inscr REF 21:3:9

Fresno School, pupils 1927 THT 3:2:61

Indian Creek school recs 1892, 1919 THT 3:1:33

Mill Iron Ranch, Hay Camp cem inscr THT 5:3:3

misc marrs 1896-1957 THT 5:3:6

Rocking Chaire Ranch hist THT 5:1:34

school hist THT 6:1:10

Concho Co, tax recs 1864-1865 STK 7:4:186

Confederate vets, notes on THT 2:1:27

Cooke Co, marr rec, bk rev NGI 3:4:210

Coryell Co, Ater cem inscr HTR 22:3:101

Fort Gates cem inscr HTR 22:1:4

Hope cem inscr HTR 22:1:4

Pearl cem inscr HTR 22:2:51

probate minutes 1854-1866 HTR 22:4:151

Warren cem inscr HTR 22:1:3

Crosby Co, Emma cem inscr THT 6:2:30

Dallam Co, hist, bk rev OC 16:2:68 CDS 16:3:4

Dallas, lib hist & geneal collect DG 25:1:1 25:3:150

probate rec index 1846-1900 v1, bk rev GE 43:11

Dallas Co, animal sales 1867-1871 DG 25:4:215

criminal dockets 1848-1852 DG 25:1:21 25:2:73

civil dockets 1850-1852 DG 25:1:14 25:2:64

Dallas, Oak Cliff cem recs bk 1,2 DG 25:4:226

Dallas, city direct 1881-1882 DG 25:4:193

Dallas, Dallas Female College hist & recs DG 25:4:224

inventory bk A 1847-1852 DG 25:4:238

direct 1881-1882 DG 25:4:193

index to bonds 1854-1878 DG 25:2:85

marrs bk F DG 25:2:76 25:3:139 25:4:248

marrs bk G DG 25:4:252

declaration of independence signers 1836 REF 2:1:7

Denton Co, marr recs, bk rev NGI 3:4:210

tax rolls 1867-1868 FP 22:1:37

east TX geneal soc surname index v1,2, bk rev FP 22:4:212

Erath Co, Patilo, hist, bk rev FP 22:4:209

Falls Co, Travis, Phillips cem inscr HTR 22:4:132

Fannin Co, Bonham, road pet 1859 THT 3:1:43

census 1870, bk rev NGI 3:4:211

marr rec, bk rev NGI 3:4:210

marrs 1838-1852, bk rev GH 33:3:102

Fort Bend Co, Hodge's Bend cem inscr THT 2:1:35

Fort Worth, "Texas Wesleyan Banner" abstr 1850-1851 FP 22:1:1 22:2:69 22:3:113

Galveston, flood, personal letter 1900 DG 25:2:93

rec of interments 1859-1872, bk rev TSP 3:1:37

"Texas Christian Advocate" abstr 1857 FP 22:4:169

geneal res guide HTR 22:1:37

George's Creek, hist, bk rev GH 33:6:84

Ger imm 1847-1861, bk rev TB 6:2:18

Grayson Co, landowner biogs 1836-1869, bk rev HTR 22:2:41 NGI 3:4:210

marr rec, bk rev NGI 3:4:210

pioneer index 1836-1869, bk rev CSB 14:1:24

Hamilton Co, hist THT 7:2:95

handbook & res guide v1-3, bk rev BGS 10:4:32

Hardin Co, Gore cem inscr YP 9:1:42

marrs 1888-1896 YP 9:2:80 9:3:146 9:4:199

poll tax assessment 1866 YP 9:4:202

Harris Co, Alief cem inscr GR 21:4:145

Bible rec v1, bk rev NGI 3:4:209

commissioners court minutes bk B 1861-1865 GR 21:1:16

deeds bk A GR 21:1:12 21:2:55 21:3:98 21:4:130

geneal res guide GR 21:3:105

McDougle cem inscr YP 9:1:16

natural recs GR 21:4:126

Harrisburg Co, legal division 1839 GR 21:1:29

Hartley Co, hist, bk rev OC 16:2:68 CDS 16:3:4

Henderson Co, Athens, city direct 1904 DG 25:1:24

marr bk 1 1860-1870, bk rev GH 33:2:81

hist (1874), bk rev NGI 3:4:211

hist 1519-1834, bk rev GR 21:1:4

hist & geneal res guide NGI 3:4:219

hist notes THT 4:2:17

Hockley Co, hist, bk rev OC 16:2:71

Hopkins Co, marr rec, bk rev NGI 3:4:210

Houston, Glenwood cem inscr GR 21:1:40

Howard Co, census 1880 THT 7:2:94

marr licenses 1918 THT 3:1:40 3:2:8

Hunt Co, archives & prioneers v1, bk rev NGI 3:4:211

census, mort & slave sched 1860, bk rev GH 33:6:84

census 1870, bk rev NGI 3:4:211

Confederate soldiers, bk rev NGI 3:4:212

marr rec, bk rev NGI 3:4:210

occupational tax reg 1895-1908, bk rev NGI 3:4:211

Indianola, cem inscr, bk rev GH 33:5:78 NGI 3:4:212

Irion Co, Mertzon cem inscr STK 7:1:36

Jack Co, misc cem inscr THT 5:4:35

Jasper Co, cem inscr, bk rev OC 16:3:107

probate index bk A 1849-1851 YP 9:1:36

Jefferson Co, cattlebrands to 1877 YP 9:4:241

chief justices, justices of the peace, sheriffs, officers of police court 1837-1900 YP 9:4:193

courthouse hist YP 9:4:183

deed bk B 1834-1838 YP 9:1:12

pioneers hist YP 9:1:44 9:2:77 9:3:158

slave owners 1860 YP 9:4:210

tax roll 1837 YP 9:4:208

Willie Denton College pupils 1899 THT 3:2:62

Lampasas Co, Kempner School pupils 1897 THT 4:2:8

land titles 1831-1878 10 vol by

county, bk rev NGI 3:4:209

legislative abstr 1829-1836 FP 22:3:129 22:4:187

Liberty Co, destruction of recs 1874, affadavit 1942 YP 9:3:144

hist YP 9:3:134,143

marr bk B 1886-1888 YP 9:3:140 9:4:206

officers 1937, 1939 YP 9:4:145

Llano Co, Castell Trinity cem inscr THT 7:2:116

Castell, Trinity Meth Ch cem inscr GR 21:1:18

Cold Springs cem inscr THT 7:2:120

St John's Luth Ch cem inscr THT 7:2:116

Madison Co, Confederate vets THT 3:2:38

Martin Co, census 1900 THT 7:2:85

Stanton, St Joseph cem inscr THT 3:1:33 3:2:27

McGregor, Federal & Confecerate burials HTR 22:2:45

McLennan Co, index to wills & survivorships 1850-1918 HTR 22:4:152

probate recs 1854-1887 HTR 22:1:22 22:2:42 22:3:95

Waco, Oakwood cem inscr v3, bk rev GH 33:4:115 HTR 22:1:6

Menard Co, marrs in deed bk C 1876-1878 STK 7:4:176

Mexican War, First Mounted Vols AGS 20:4:127

First TX Mounted Rifles AGS 20:1:9 20:2:27 20:3:91 20:4:127

Hays' TX Cavalry AGS 20:4:127

Midland, Fairview cem vets inscr THT 3:2:9

First Bapt Ch minutes 1886 THT 3:1:30

Newnie Ellis Funeral Home recs THT 4:3:2 5:1:14

school boards 1907-1975 THT 3:2:10

Midland Co, cattlebrands reg 1885-1887 THT 6:2:23 7:1:28 7:2:82

Fairview cem vets, inscr THT

2:2:6

Greenwood cem inscr THT 2:2:5

hist THT 2:1:6 5:2:2 5:3:1 5:4:1 7:2:84

jurors 1885 THT 1:1:3

misc letters THT 6:1:8

natural recs THT 2:1:7

office holders THT 3:1:6

place names THT 7:1:29

Porter fam cem hist THT 7:1:36

probate recs THT 4:1:22

school census 1885 THT 1:2:4

school hist THT 6:2:25 6:3:94

tax list 1887 THT 2:2:4

tax list 1888 THT 1:2:6

vets memorial THT 5:2:5

Milam Co, Pin Oak cem inscr HTR 22:3:87

Mineral Wells, hist notes THT 2:2:45

misc landowners, bk rev NGI 3:4:213

misc mil recs THT 3:1:29 3:2:42

Montgomery Co, cems v1, bk rev GH 33:6:84

muster roll SCA, Capt Samuel Mains' Co FP 22:3:157

Nacogdoches Co, anc ch 1977, bk rev GH 33:3:103 TST 12:11:37

census 1860 annotated, bk rev TST 11:45:29 OC 16:2:69

marr recs, bk rev NGI 3:4:210

misc recs 1870, bk rev GGM 71:9

Navarro Co, Battle Creek Burial Ground cem inscr THT 7:2:115

newspapers 1867 GR 21:2:62

news obits & marrs THT 3:2:45

Newton Co, ferries hist YP 9:1:9 9:3:169

Salem, hist notes YP 9:3:169

North Harris Co, hist, bk rev NGI 3:4:210

Oldham Co, Tascosa, Boot Hill cem THT 5:1:13

Palo Pinto Co, hist notes THT 4:2:14

poll tax descr AGS 20:3:105

pre-emption (homestead) claims 1852-1854 HTR 22:1:7

Rev War soldiers plaque THT 5:1:25

Robertson Co, Easterly, A Corn

& additional sections cem inscr GR 21:3:108

Rockwall Co, cem inscr, bk rev GH 33:3:103 OK 24:1:44 OC 16:3:110 GGM 73:164 RRS 12:X:2

Runge, fifth grade class 1912 photo DG 25:1:39

Runnels Co, Ballinger news extracts 1897 STK 7:4:179

roll of ex-confederate soldiers 1896 STK 7:4:169

Winters, First Meth Ch hist STK 7:2:74

Rusk Co, marr rec, bk rev NGI 3:4:210

Sabine Co, census 1850 annotated, bk rev FP 22:4:212 YP 9:4:227

San Augustine, Cora Roberts fam cem inscr STK 7:3:111

Shamrock, First United Meth Ch, ministers' service rec THT 2:1:31

Smith Co, Bell fam cem inscr THT 6:1:11

census 1870, bk rev GH 33:1:89 YP 9:3:167

Jamestown, Old Jamestown cem inscr FP 22:4:196

marrs 1846-1899, bk rev YP 9:3:167

South Austin, Little Texas Lane cem inscr AGS 20:3:115

state troops 21st brigade muster roll 1862 FP 22:3:160

Stephens Co, misc fam recs, bk rev GH 33:4:115 GE 49:7

Sterling Co, Divide School census 1924 STK 7:1:3

Foster cem inscr STK 7:2:68

names in co death recs not abstracted in cems STK 7:2:73

Swedish colony hist DG 25:1:22

Tarrant Co, Arlington, Johnson Station cem inscr FP 22:3:135 22:4:197

Henderson fam cem FP 22:3:118

muster roll of mounted vols or rangers 1861 FP 22:4:192

natural rec 1878-1886 FP 22:2:79

Thorp Spring, Add-Ran College

hist THT 1:1:6
Tom Green Co, Knickerbocker cem (east) cem inscr STK 7:3:134
San Angelo, city direct 1909 STK 7:1:11 7:2:80 7:3:112 7:4:172
San Angelo, Fairmount cem search for legal heirs STK 7:2:79
San Angelo, fire hist 1904 STK 7:3:125
San Angelo, Masons 1882 STK 7:2:66
San Angelo, news abstr 1884 STK 7:1:17 7:2:75 7:3:121
Travis Co, early recs, bk rev AGS 20:2:37
Trinity Co, Apple Springs, Burke cem inscr FP 22:1:35
Glendale cem inscr THT 7:2:115
Zion Hill cem inscr THT 7:2:114
The Grove, Grove School graduates 1926 HTR 22:3:83
Tyler Co, Smith fam cem inscr THT 3:2:22
Upshur Co, misc Civil War vets THT 3:2:40
vets burials THT 2:2:33
Waco, hist HTR 22:2:74
registered deaths 1887 HTR 22:2:43
registered deaths 1888-9 HTR 22:3:78 22:4:121
Walker Co, marr rec 1846-1880, bk rev YP 9:3:164
War of 1812 vets hist, bk rev TST 12:34:38 IL 11:4:235 VAG 23:4:308 DG 25:4:260 NCJ 5:4:258 KY 21:4:158
Ward Co, Barstow School pupils 1908 THT 3:2:62
Wellington, First Bapt Ch, hist THT 3:2:55
First Christian Ch, notes on THT 3:2:54
First United Meth Ch, hist THT 3:2:56
hist notes THT 5:1:32
West TX bank direct 1936 STK 7:1:8
Williamson Co, Donahue cem inscr THT 3:1:25

Wood Co, census index 1880, bk rev GE 49:9
THAYER, C A bc1808, OH, biog notes AH 1:2:7
THERIAULT, Olive m1886 w Joseph-Eugene April, MA, anc ch AGE 8:2:61
THIBODEAUX, Emile b1912 w Nolia Broussard, LA, anc ch AGE 8:2:60
THOMAS, Evan b1757 w Hannah Nixon, VA, IN, Bible rec HJA 6:1:46 6:3:43
fam of CA, Bible rec RED 12:2:10
James f1776 w Mary Standley, NC, KY, biog KA 15:2:93
James b1838 w Rebecca Jane Allen Sammons, KY, geneal, bk rev TSP 3:1:37
John f1622, VA, geneal, bk rev NCJ 5:1:65
Ronalo Blaine b1934 w Mary Ada Scofield, OH, IL, CO, anc ch BGS 11:4:178
Samuel b1762 w Phebe Holiday, Bible rec CTN 12:2:238
THOMPSON, Alexander R bc1838 w Mary Evelyn Highland, IN, OR, biog notes ORB 18:2:30
Floyd W b1917 w Fredda E Carlisle, TX, anc ch THT 7:2:81
George Washington b1851 w Arabelle Randolph, MO, Bible rec BGS 3:4:8
John f1842, auto FF 8:3:35
John A b1828, VA, cem inscr VA 17:2:50
John B b1830 w Mary Plant, Bible rec REP 19:1:15
Lida J b1873, Bible rec REP 19:1:15
Young b1828 w Catherine Megie, OH, IN, anc ch REP 19:3:128
THOROUGHMAN, Aaron Lewman b1822 w Hannah Mariah Davis, OH, IN, geneal MGR 14:1:43
THORPE, Abbie (Lincoln) b1868, IL, obit MCH 7:4:95
THORVALDR, surname variations & origin FAM 18:2:50
THRASHER, fam of VA, geneal, bk rev CTN 9:2:309

THURMAN, John w Neelfje Quik, NY bill of sale 1755 NYR 110:4:193

TIBBETTS, Levi f1861 w Lorinda Withee, ME, biog notes TB 6:1:32

TILDEN, Joseph w Sarah Parker, MA, biog notes MQ 45:1:5

TILLOTSON, Luther b1788 w Priscilla Buell, NY, IN, Bible rec TOP 9:2:35

Luther Rudolph b1884 w Eva Gertrude Kinley, KS, anc ch TOP 9:2:38

TILSON, fam supp to 1911 geneal, bk rev GH 33:5:91 MQ 45:3:160

TINKER, John Braddock b1816 w Mary Ann Benson, NY, Bible rec CTN 10:2:366

TINKHAM, Joseph b1753 w Mercy Waterman, MA, Can, Bible rec NER 133:4:305

TIPPETT, Clyde Vernon b1907 w Kenneth Louella Thurston, OH, anc ch PGB 11:9:96

TODD, Daniel d1824 w Jane, MA, fam rec NSN 4:5:42

fam of Ir & PA, geneal, bk rev REP 19:1:41

William f1861 w Eliza, Eng, NY, CO, Bible rec BGS 7:2:14

TOFFELMIRE, Charles bc1829 w Eliza Replogle, Can, MI, AR, geneal PF 9:2:35

Emily A bc1840 h James Marion Olmsted, Can, MI, geneal PF 9:2:37

TOLLE, Armon Thornton b1908 w Oretha May Jonas, CA, NE, anc ch NGI 3:1:37

TOLSON, Francis b1686 w Mary Clark, MD, geneal MD 20:2:123

Thomas, Eng, geneal, bk rev CI 13:4:153

TOMLIN, Aaron f1834 w Sarah Baldwin, TN, anc ch HJA 6:3:48

TOMPKINS, James dc1848 w Nancy Mills, Mahala Brooks, NC, VA, IL, biog notes IL 11:4:204

John b1863 w Wealthy Jane James, Bible rec VL 13:3:108

TOOL, Pearl Dayton b1875 w Lutie A Keller, IL, anc ch GL 13:3:70

TOOLEY, Frederick W b1833 w Florence V Holdridge, IL, Bible & fam recs CI 15:3:86

TOOZE, fam of MI & OH, geneal, bk rev CTN 11:1:45

James b1831 w Anna A Rich, Bible rec CTN 10:3:416

TOTTEN, Thomas b1859 w Harriet B Cohoe, Can, anc ch BCG 7:1:25

TOURTELLOT, Jonathan A b1812 w Maria Wade, RI, CT, IL, CO, geneal BGS 9:1:14

TOWNE, About Towne, Towne Family Association, 38 Sayles Rd, Asheville NC 28803

TRACEY, Basil b1836 w Hannah Reed, IA, Bible rec BGS 6:2:22

TRAFTON, William b1793 w Rhoda Wadlia, MA, Bible rec BGS 10:3:24

TRAMMELL, Thomas f1776, TX, AL, geneal, bk rev FP 22:4:209

TRAPHAGEN, fam of MI, geneal FG 21:4:80

TRASK, Elbridge b1815 w Hannah Abell, MA, OR, biog notes ORB 18:4:96

TRAVER, William H b1825 w Philenia Worden, NY, Bible rec CTN 11:3:404

TREBER, John d1827 w Mary Campbell, PA, KY, OH, anc ch REP 19:4:157

TREES, John bc1753 w Hannah, KY, OH, geneal OHR 20:4:182

TREHEARNE, William b1847 w Barbara Sarah, Bible rec BCG 7:3:58

TRESSELT, Albert b1880 w Annie Irene Hyland, NY, IL, anc ch CHG 11:1:12

TREUSDELL, Thomas b1759 w Hannah Collin, Bible rec NYR 110:2:75

TREXLER, W W m1864, IL, marr cert BB 11:4:75

TRIPLETT, Reuben d1780, VA, fam rec VA 17:2:58

TRUE, William H b1854 w Ella L Angle, IN, KS, obit KK

17:3:62

TRUEHEART, Aaron bc1710, SC, anc ch YP 9:3:127

TRUMBULL, David b1819, CT, Chile, biog & fam notes CTB 44:3:80

Jonathan Jr f1759, CT, biog, bk rev CTN 11:3:520

TRUSSELL, Bible rec THT 1:1:5

Jane, Bible rec 1810-1831 THT 1:1:5

TUCK, John bc1730 w Mary Powell, VA, geneal, bk rev KCG 20:2:92 GGM 71:7

TUCKER, Guy Earl b1888 w Minrie Marie Traher, OH, anc ch GR 21:3:92

Jesse b1803 w Sophrona, SC, AL, fam rec NAS 17:3:73

John Gorcealus b1879 w Ethel Venice Wilkie, AL, GA, anc ch NAS 18:1:5

Joseph A b1835 w Ellen L Osgood, ME, anc ch REP 19:3:122

Lewis Albert b1905 w Cora Bell Davis, AR, MO, anc ch FF 8:4:43

TUFTS, Tufts Kinsmen, Box 571, Dedham MA 02026

William b1840, MA, IN, biog notes MIS 11:4:51

TULL, Nathan Forrest b1853 w Nancy Ann Hilsabeck, IL, obit MCH 7:3:86

TUNNELL, John b1755, VA, biog notes BGS 4:1:20

TURFIS, Luke bc1851, CT, biog notes GFP 29:3:51

TURNBAUGH, Franklin Edward b1895 w Hazel May Schwone, IL, NY, OK, anc ch THT 6:3:56

TURNER, Earl b1913 w Lila Inez Guthrie, OK, anc ch NGI 3:2:111

fam of GA, Bible recs DCG 2:10:6

fam of MD, geneal, bk rev AGS 20:4:145

George R b1836 w Mary A Cantrell, GA, fam rec DCG 2:10:5

Hugh C bc1832 w Mary Ann Burkett, NC, anc ch RRS 12:1:111

James b1758, MD, GA, SC, geneal, bk rev GGM 73:163

John Welsey b1875 w Lola Montez Franks, TX, NM, fam rec NMG 18:3:80

TUSTIN, Charles Samuel b1818 w Mary Jarvis/Chaplin, MD, PA, OR, biog notes GFP 29:1:9

TUTTLE, John d1825 w Lois, Bible rec CTN 11:4:594

Levi b1811 w Dolly Earls, Lucinda Wright, NY, Bible rec WB 10:1:29

TYLER, Augustus C f1825 w Clarissa Smith/Wheeler, OH, marr lic appl AH 2:4:108

Clinton Monroe b1834 w Sarah Emma Smith, NY, MI, CO, biog BGS 2:3:22

Royal b1756, MA, biog notes CDS 16:2:20

Royall b1757, MA, auto, bk rev CDS 16:1:33

Thaddeus W f1844 w Elizabeth N Reed, NH, MA, biog notes BGS 6:4:14

TYREE, John Claiborne f1774 w Hannah Clay, VA, geneal, bk rev VL 13:3:148

UGGERBY, fam of Den & Am, geneal, bk rev IL 11:2:115 CSB 14:1:22 CTN 12:1:173

ULIN, Benjamin f1792, KY, biog notes TST 12:25:49

ULOTH, Ludwig Warner b1895 w Rosa Mina Fenn, TX, anc ch GR 21:2:51

ULRICH, Jacob d1821 w Susannah Lear, PA, fam notes GE 44:1

Ralph Lewis b1917 w Kathryn Dorothy Oltman, NE, anc ch FF 8:3:61

UNDERWOOD, David b1815 w Mary Ann, OH, geneal 1973, bk rev REP 19:4:170

Myranda Pike, WI letter 1847 THT 2:2:24

UNITED STATES, Alamo heroes & their Rev War ancestors, bk rev GFP 28:8:147

Am fams with british ancestry

(Burke), bk rev OG 4:2:58

Am ch recs survey, bk rev GJ 8:3:169

Am marr recs to 1699 (1926), bk rev OG 4:2:58

Am state papers, "claims" index JG 4:6:22 4:7:27 4:8:19 4:9:6

Archives CTN 10:3:371

Archives, regional branches descr TST 12:18:36
res guide, bk rev GH 33:2:71
Soundex system SCS 14:3:70 IL 11:4:231

Bible recs, in Natl Archives, index DG 25:3:183
list TB published TB 6:4:13
misc fam recs index CI 13:1:7 13:4:147

cem rec compendium, bk rev TB 6:4:28

census 1850, index to city, co, town & twp, bk rev GH 33:5:70 33:6:76 IL 11:4:233 GE 47:14 VAG 23:3:235 NYR 110:4:246 NGI 3:3:167

census 1870, notes on NGI 3:1:21 3:2:95 3:3:142

census 1890, notes TST 11:46:29

census 1900, notes on ANC 14:2:64 IL 11:4:223 SMV 11:1:4

census 1910 & later, information restrictions TST 12:8:44

census direct 1973, bk rev OG 2:1:28

census, hist notes on LL 15:2:44

circular letters of Congressmen 1789-1829, bk rev MHM 74:3:305

cities, geneal res guide 1974, bk rev OG 2:1:28

city, co, town & twp index to 1850 federal census scheds, bk rev BB 11:3:47 KN 2:2:32 CDS 16:5:45

Civil War, burials NGI 3:1:45 3:2:121 3:3:184
cems locations BGS 6:4:15
Confederate Army of TN hist 1861-1865, 1906, bk rev GH

33:4:114

Confederate Mil memoirs of Bennett Young, 1914, bk rev GH 33:4:110

CSA MI Inf medical log TA 14:2:39

Gettysburg papers vl,2, bk rev CDS 16:1:5

hist of Army life SCC 16:3:55 16:4:81

official recs collect in KS TS 21:2:69

pension recs BB 11:2:19

recs of Confederate prisoners, guide TST 12:8:44

searching for recs TB 6:3:4

tracing your Civil War ancestors, bk rev OG 2:2:58 NGI 3:4:207

Col almanacs hist, bk rev CTN 11:1:42

Congressional private relief & related actions index JG 4:10:17 4:11:5 4:12:19

copyright law JG 4:5:25

emancipation & equal rights, bk rev MHM 74:3:303

fam recs received by Geneal Soc of NJ 1978, list GNJ 54:2:95

Fed mil prnsions (1918) JG 4:6:5 4:7:3 4:8:5 4:9:5 4:10:5 4:11:29 4:12:5

founders of Col Am (1926), bk rev CTN 9:2:306

founders of early Am fams 1975, bk rev CTN 8:4:538

geneal source recs, bk rev TST 11:39:35 NGS 67:4:306 CDS 16:3:6 ACL 4:1:6

geneal sources CTN 10:1:19

geneal sources in DC MH 6:2:13

Ger, Swiss & French Col settlements GER 16:412

guide to fam recs, bk rev GE 43:11

heraldry, roll of arms, Ninth Part NER 133:2:83 133:3:180 133:4:271

historical boundary data file JG 4:5:15

historical recs survey program GR 21:4:125

hist of western mining wars, bk

rev CDS 16:2:5

hist to 1877, bk rev TB 6:4:27

Huguenot influence in Am DAR 113:9:1030

imm 1600-1800 v1,2, bk rev TST 12:18:38

imm & ethnicity, bk rev ITG 2:55

Indian Wars campaign medals, hist & recipients, bk rev KCG 20:3:146 GH 33:4:110 TST 12:16:40

list of pre-1840 Fed Dist & Circuit Court recs, bk rev GR 21:1:4

major geneal collect TS 21:2:51

marr notices from "Massachusetts Centinel" & "Columbian Centinel" 1785-1794, bk rev FAM 18:3:138

medal of honor, hist & recipients for Indian wars, bk rev TST 12:36:23 KCG 20:3:146

migration 1850, bk rev CTN 11:1:42 ACL 4:2:25

migration patterns & reasons STK 7:2:59 7:3:117 7:4:153 MD 20:1:18

migration studies in 1850, bk rev ANC 14:1:11 ACL 4:2:25

military reserves map & descr CO 40:1:3

misc Col fam geneal, bk rev GH 33:2:87 TST 11:47:29

misc fams of MA, VA, OK, geneal, bk rev GH 33:6:85

misc news in Univ of IL news lib CI 11:1:12

misc vr LL 15:2:56 15:3:110 15:4:159

misc wills in TX file THT 3:2:7

mort sched as geneal source GH 33:6:5

national genealogists' reg 1978, bk rev TST 12:8:45

natural recs TST 12:36:22 SCS 16:3:72

natural recs guide, bk rev OG 3:3:88

offices of immig & natural CI 15:4:129

Oregon Trail hist 1963, bk rev REP 19:4:175

Pacific Northwest hist, bk rev TB 6:4:30

Pacific Northwest, index to people & places in bks, bk rev SGS 29:4:328

pension list 1883 v2, bk rev TB 6:4:28

pre-statehood, territ & state censuses BCG 5:2:25

Presidents, biblio of ancestry of US Presidents AG 55:1:46

descendants of US Presidents, bk rev AG 55:1:61

probate court recs OG 3:2:47

recs of geneal value, bk rev GJ 8:1:53

religious hist DAR 113:9:980

Puritan Sabbath, bk rev NER 133:2:141

Protestant patterns of childrearing c1776, bk rev NER 133:3:221

Roman Cath bishops 1513-1974, bk rev NYR 110:1:56

roads survey 1789, bk rev BGS 8:3:31

Scotch-Irish pioneers (1910), bk rev ACL 4:4:75

Spanish borderlands frontier 1513-1821, bk rev TB 6:4:27

statewide civil vital registration GJ 8:3:135

survey of Am ch recs, bk rev TB 6:4:30

twp atlas, bk rev BB 11:3:48 NGS 67:1:67

transportation hist 1865-1890, bk rev TB 6:4:33

vital recs laws update JG 4:1:24 4:5:8 4:6:3 4:8:3 4:9:3 4:10:3 4:11:3 4:12:3

vital recs, use & restrictions CSB 14:4:153

wars & mil engagements to 1900 STC 2:2:78

wills, custodians by state NGI 3:3:183

UPCHURCH, fam of Eng, VA, NC, geneal, bk rev BGS 5:2:19

UPTON, James Newton b1850 w Elizabeth C Rabb, TX, NM, fam rec NMG 18:3:80

URE, William b1828 w Marian M

Clymonth, Bible rec THT 4:1:30

UTAH, Woods Cross, hist, bk rev CTN 11:2:341

VADEN, John b1793 w Martha Uhles, VA, TN, geneal, bk rev GH 33:6:89

Joseph B m1839 w Virginia Eliza Martin Banks, NC, Bible rec VA 17:3:91

VALENTINE, Edward Pleasants, VA geneal recs v1-4 1927, bk rev GH 33:4:120

VAN ALSTYNE, Jan Martense bc1623 w Dirckje Harmense, NY, geneal, bk rev BGS (;4:34

VANASSE, Simon w Alvina Germain, WI, MI, Can, geneal, bk rev AGE 8:4:110 MN 10:1:41

VAN BLARICOM, Helen Neva (McGraw) b1871, NY, MI, Bible rec MI 24:1:8

VAN BURAN, Catherine b1784 h William Burwell, John Butler, NY, Bible rec MI 24:4:117

VAN CLEEF, fam of NY, geneal, bk rev MD 20:2:134 DM 43:1:44

VAN CORTLANDT, fam papers v3 1800-1814, bk rev CDS 16:3:5

VAN CURLER, Arent f1644 w Antonia Slaghboom, NY, children NYR 110:2:82

VAN DEN UYTHOF, Wouter w Elizabeth (Hendricks) Lansingh, NY wills 1678 LL 15:3:122

VAN DER GRIFT, fam of PA, geneal, bk rev OC 16:1:34

VANDERPOOL, Elmer H b1891 w Clara Alice Roads, MO, anc ch RRS 12:2:219

VAN EPPS, John V b1813 w Catharine Smith, IA, Bible rec NSN 4:2:11

VAN HORN, fam of PA, geneal, bk rev OC 16:1:34

VAN HORNE, Nancy bc1792 h Daniel Cramton, Nathan A Townsend, NJ, VT, NY, geneal FG 21:2:26

VAN HOUSE, Kenneth John b1890 w Selma Pauline Nelson, WA, anc ch TB 6:1:27

VANIER, Henry James b1907 w Elizabeth Marshall Ryan, NY, OR, WA, anc ch OG 4:4:100

VAN LIEW, Henry C b1825 w Hannah Jane Foster, NJ, TN, bible rec OC 16:1:20

VANNATTA, James b1811 w Martha Watson, Jerusha (Clardy) Nash, Bible rec CPY 8:4:88

VAN PATTEN, George Wesley b1890 w Mildred Charlotta Israelson, NE, anc ch NW 2:2:53

Nicholas b1745 w Margareta Ecker, NY, anc ch NW 2:2:54

VAN TREESE, Van Treese Family Newsletter, 9350 Vandergriff Rd, Indianapolis IN 46239

VAN WESTERVELT, James Jacobus b1737 w Maria Demaree, Holl, NJ, anc ch RRS 12:1:116

VAN WIE, Garrett b1810 w Louisa Spalding, NY, Bible rec NGS 67:2:142

VANWOAT, Bible rec PR 3:3:50

VAN ZANDT, Elijah b1825 w Susan Radliff, NY, IL, fam rec FF 8:2:50

VAN ZANDT, fam of PA, geneal, bk rev OC 16:1:34

VARD, fam of Nor & Am, geneal, bk rev GH 33:1:92

VAUGHAN, Daniel b1746 w Dinah, Bible rec WB 10:2:63

VAUGHAN, Jesse Lee Sr b1923 w Oralee Frances Kelley, TX, anc ch GR 21:2:50

Samuel d1864 w Anna, NY admin papers LL 15:3:153

Zebulon, soldiers journal 1777-1780 DAR 113:2:100 113:3:256 113:4:320 113:5:478

VAUGHN, Martin f1846 w Adelaide, IN, WA, biog notes GFP 29:1:12 29:2:33

William R b1861 w Emma C Dillon, WA, Bible rec TB 6:3:12

VAUGHT, fam of PA, geneal, bk rev KY 21:3:115

VEATCH, Joseph Guy Sr b1877 w Harriet Grace Lyons, IL, anc ch GL 13:3:69

Sylvester Ewing b1831 w Mariah Elizabeth Knox, IL, OR, biog

notes ORB 17:9:82

VERMONT, Bridgewater hist, bk rev CTN 10:1:158

geneal res guide CPY 8:3:61 QBC 2:1:8

hist of migration NER 133:1:3

marrs, vl 1789-1876, bk rev TB 6:1:34

misc biogs c1770, bk rev TB 6:3:24

misc geneal notes, bk rev CTN 9:2:311

Montpelier, Rev War soldiers hist, bk rev CTN 9:2:312

Pittsford, hist 1872, bk rev CTN 9:1:124

place names, bk rev CTN 10:2:342

Poultney, hist (1875), bk rev CDS 16:4:12 KCG 20:L3:147 GH 33:4:115

Stowe, school dist #11 1828-1973, bk rev CDS 16:1:3

Windham Co, surname guide in 1870, bk rev CDS 16:1:22

Windsor Co, biog sketches 1891, bk rev SCS 15:4:118 CTN 11:4:703

VERWIEBE, J F W m1895 w Josephine Boehmer, AR, Bible rec VQ 16:1:9

VEST, Jesse Earvin b1863 w Esther Annie Lourash, IL, Bible rec CI 12:3:90

VESTAL, Alfred b1804 w Winney, Bible rec MIS 11:4:64

VETTER, Andreas, TX, letter to Ger 1851 GR 21:1:33

VICKREY, fam of AL, bk rev CI 13:3:115

VINCENT, fam in Can census 1851 & U S census 1850 v2, bk rev GH 33:5:91 NYR 110:4:249

VINSON, Charles Energy b1870 w Fannie Shaw, Bible rec VL 13:4:156

James Glardon b1918 w Mary Carlisle Sheegog, KY, anc ch AGS 20:2:47

VIRDIN, fam of DE, geneal, bk rev BR 6:3:96 CI 13:4:153

VIRGIN, Richard m1696 w Frances Sparks, MA, geneal NGS

67:2:107

VIRGINIA, Albemarle Co, co road hist, bk rev VAG 23:3:235

deeds 1748-1763, bk rev VAG 23:3:228

Fredericksville Epis parish hist 1742-1787, bk rev GGM 71:9

hist 1902, bk rev CDS 16:1:33

hist 1937, bk rev VAG 23:4:305

Alleghany Co, census 1830, 1840, 1850, bk rev YP 9:1:39

Amelia Co, marrs 1735-1815, bk rev GH 33:3:103 VAG 23:2:146

will bk 1 1735-1761, bk rev VAG 23:4:305 KY 21:3:115

will bk 2X 1761-1771, bk rev VAG 23:4:305

Amherst, deeds 1761-1807, bk rev VAG 23:3:228

Arlington, hist, bk rev BGS 9:3:38

Augusta Co, court martial recs 1756-1783 VA 17:1:10 17:3:96 17:4:124

hist 1937, bk rev VAG 23:4:305

Pilson cem inscr MGR 14:1:23

Bath Co, marr bonds 1791-1853, bk rev GH 33:2:81 VAG 23:2:140

Bear-Lithia Spring, Bear Lithia cem inscr GER 16:433

Bedford Co, geneal hist, bk rev CTN 10:2:344

Blue Ridge fams geneal, bk rev TSP 3:1:37

border settlers 1768-1795 (1915), bk rev RES 11:1:3

Botetourt Co, misc fam recs, bk rev GH 33:4:115

British mercantile claims 1775-1803 VAG 23:1:59 23:2:120 23:3:183 23:4:271

Brunswick Co, soldiers in French & Indian War 1757 VAG 23:3:193

Campbell Co, hist & biog notes 1782-1926, bk rev WCK 12:1:17

Caroline Co, hist 1937, bk rev VAG 23:4:305

census 1810 supp, bk rev YP 9:1:40

Charles City Co, autographs

1701/2, bk rev GH 33:5:78
deed & bond bks, notes on BGS 7:4:22
early settlers geneal v2, bk rev CTN 11:4:703
will & deed bk 1692-1694 VA 17:2:43 17:3:103 17:4:128
Charlotte Co, marr bonds res notes VAG 23:1:3
Charlottesville, Ch of Our Saviour parish reg, bapt & burials 1896-1911 VAG 23:2:83 23:3:175
Chesterfield Co, wills 1749-1774, bk rev VAG 23:2:139
Culpeper Co, deeds v3 1762-1765, bk rev VAG 23:4:313
deeds v4 1765-1769, bk rev VAG 23:4:313
hist 18th cent, bk rev OC 16:3:108,109 YP 9:2:106
delinq taxpayers 1787-1790 VAG 23:1:31 23:2:113 23:3:195
emig to AL VA 17:3:89
Essex Co, hist 1937, bk rev VAG 23:4:305
Fauquier Co, public claims 1782-1783 VAG 23:1:25 23:1:88
Rev War hist, bk rev RRS 12:X:2
first fams descs, bk rev KCG 20:2:91
Franklin Co, hist 1785-1979, bk rev TB 6:4:29
Frederick Co, early fams hist, bk rev GH 33:1:89
tax list 1800 VAG 23:1:8 23:2:97 23:3:168 23:4:266
Fredericksburg, Civil War burials, bk rev KN 2:3:44
geneal res guide TST 12:16:39 OG 3:2:43 JG 4:2:23
geneal sources 1971, bk rev REP 19:4:171
Gloucester Co, hist 1937, bk rev VAG 23:4:305
Kingston Parish Reg 1749-1827, bk rev VAG 23:2:146 GH 32:2:81
Goochland Co, hist 1937, bk rev VAG 23:4:305
James River fams & hist v1 1974, bk rev GH 33:6:85 VAG

23:4:308 CTN 7:4:519 NGS 67:4:309
marrs 1733-1815, bk rev GH 33:3:102 VAG 23:2:146
Hampshire Co, early fams hist, bk rev GH 33:1:89
Hanover Co, court recs 1733-1735, bk rev SCS 16:3:86 GH 33:4:115 VAG 23:3:227
Day fam cem inscr VA 17:4:132
hist 1937, bk rev VAG 23:4:305
headrights 1667 & 1672 VAG 23:1:44
Henrico Co, citizenship appl 1783-1794 VA 17:1:18
James River fams & hist v1 1974, bk rev GH 33:6:85 VAG 23:4:308 CTN 7:4:519 VGS 67:4:309
Henrico Parish, St John's P E ch hist & recs 1904, bk rev VAG 23:2:146 GH 33:2:81 NYR 110:3:185 DM 43:2:90 NGS 67:3:225
hist of industrial slavery 1715-1865, bk rev MHM 74:4:368
holdings of VA state archives BGS 8:4:11
index to Hayden's genealogies, bk rev CTN 10:3:527
James f1853 w Hulda, VA, geneal NGS 67:2:104
James City Co, index to wills from 1608, bk rev CTN 11:1:44
recs 1634-1904, bk rev VAG 23:2:145
Kanawha Co, personal property tax lists 1806 & 1809, bk rev KN 2:4:26
King & Queen Co, hist 1937, bk rev VAG 23:4:305
King George Co, cem inscr, bk rev GH 33:5:79 VAG 23:4:306 NGS 67:3:309
will bk A-I 1721-1752, bk rev VAG 23:1:65 KY 21:3:114 KA 14:3:190
King William Co, hist 1937, bk rev VAG 23:4:305
Lancaster Co, Col women & men they married CLG 10:3:143
court orders & deeds 1656-

return of recruits 1781 VAG
23:3:173
land patents & grants 1623-1666
v1, bk rev TRI 17:2:32
Louisa Co, Fredericksville Epis
Parish hist 1742-1787, bk rev
GGM 71:9
hist 1937, bk rev VAG 23:4:305
marrs 1766-1815, bk rev CDS
16:1:3
Low Moor, Mt Carmel cem of St
Joseph's Ch cem inscr VA
17:2:67
Lower Norfolk Co, recs bk B
1646-1651, bk rev VAG 23:1:65
GH 33:5:79
Lunenburg Co, marrs 1746-1853,
bk rev GH 33:2:82 VAG
23:2:147
Mathews Co, Kingston Parish,
Reg 1749-1827, bk rev GH
33:2:81 VAG 23:2:141
Mecklenburg Co, War of 1812
officers VA 17:3:84
Middle New River Settlement
hist, bk rev OC 16:4:136
misc abstr from MD Gazette VA
17:1:34
misc early fams, bk rev GH
33:3:103
misc fams geneal, bk rev CI
15:3:116
misc fams hist v3,4 1922, bk
rev REP 19:4:166
misc geneal recs in Valentine
papers v1-4, bk rev VAG
23:3:227
misc imms, bk rev TB 6:4:29
misc marrs 1826-1850 v1,2, bk
rev REP 19:4:171
Montgomery Co, "entitled-free
papers" 1823-1863 VA 17:4:133
Nansemond Co, misc fam recs VAG
23:1:39 23:2:109
New Kent Co, hist 1937, bk rev
VAG 23:4:305
New River Co, geneal collect
descr GJ 8:4:197
Norfolk Co, court recs bk B
1646-1652, bk rev NGS
67:4:312
tithables 1730-1750, bk rev GH
33:4:116 VAG 23:2:139

Northumberland Co, recs 1678-
1713, bk rev VAG 23:2:145
Orange Co, cem inscr, bk rev GH
33:5:79 VAG 23:4:306 NGS
67:4:307
hist 1937, bk rev VAG 23:4:305
importation oaths 1739-1741 VA
17:2:51 17:3:100 17:4:121
Page Co, Bear-Lithia cem inscr
VA 17:2:66
Pendleton Co, census 1810 &
marr bonds 1791-1853, bk rev
GH 33:5:80 VAG 23:3:228
Pittsylvania Co, hist 1929, bk
rev OG 4:3:88
militia officers 1775 VA
23:3:225
Prince George, autographs
1701/2, bk rev GH 33:5:78
Prince George Co, early
settlers geneal v2, bk rev
CTN 11:4:703
recs 1666-1719, bk rev VAG
23:2:145
Prince William Co, Dettingen
Parish, vestry bk & recs
1745-1785, bk rev NGS
67:4:306
order bk 1759-1761 VAG 23:1:47
23:2:130 23:3:201 23:4:292
Princess Anne Co, deed & minute
bks 6 & 7 abstr 1740-1762, bk
rev GH 33:5:80
Rev War, pens appl v32, bk rev
VAG 23:4:314
pens appl v33, bk rev VAG
23:4:314
state marines in Rev DAR
113:4:368
Rockbridge Co, Alone cem inscr
OC 16:1:24
marr bonds 1778-1805 VAG
23:1:19 23:2:104 23:3:178
23:4:249
executor, admin & guardian
bonds abstr 1778-1864, bk rev
YP 9:2:106
Russell Co, hist & geneal v2,
bk rev YP 9:2:101
Shenandoah Valley, misc fams
recs of Pastor Braun 1799-
1813, bk rev GH 33:1:89
geneal hist & Civil War hist,

bk rev CDS 16:1:6
Ger pioneers hist (1907), bk
rev CDS 16:1:3
source recs abstr (Valentine),
bk rev NGS 67:3:225
southwest VA, fams, geneal v2,
bk rev YP 9:2:75
historic homes & biog notes,
bk rev CDS 16:1:6
Stafford Co, geneal res guide
VAG 23:1:55
Summers Co, geneal res guide
VAG 23:1:57
Surry Co, autographs 1701/2, bk
rev GH 33:5:78
colonists 1678-1705 VAG
23:4:255
geneal res guide VAG 23:2:125
Sussex Co, geneal res guide VAG
23:2:127
misc marr bonds 1754-1843 VA
17:2:53
Palestine, misc cem inscr VA
17:2:50
Taylor Co, geneal res guide VAG
23:3:217
tax payers 1782-87 (1940), bk
rev OG 4:3:88
Tazewell Co, geneal res guide
VAG 23:3:218
Tucker Co, geneal res guide VAG
23:3:221
Tyler Co, geneal res guide VAG
23:4:281
Upshur Co, geneal res guide VAG
23:4:283
Virginia Company of London
1607-1624, bk rev VAG
23:2:145
Virginia State Lib, geneal res
guide SGS 29:1:33
War of 1812 recs VA 17:1:6
17:2:72 17:3:80 17:4:115
Warren Co, geneal res guide VAG
23:4:284
Westmoreland Co, misc wills CDS
16:1:32
York Co, deeds, wills #10 1694-
1697, part 1, bk rev VAG
23:4:313
index to wills from 1608, bk
rev CTN 11:1:44
wills, deeds, orders 1657-

1659, bk rev VAG 23:2:145
VIZIER, Jefferson Monroe b1837 w
Naomi Priscilla Bryan, TX,
anc ch YP 9:1:5
VLIET, Frances d1776 h Jacob
Wyckoff, John Pratt, NJ, biog
notes TST 12:35:36
VOGEL, William b1839 w Sybilla
Katherine Otto, Ger, OH, biog
notes REP 19:1:10
VON ROEDER, Louis A b1908 w
Ethel Schlenk, TX, anc ch GR
21:4:137
VON WOMMEL, Franz f1841, Ger,
TX, notes on NMG 18:2:50
VOORHEES, Abraham b1765 w Char-
lotte Worth, NJ, Bible rec
GNJ 54:2:80
Jesse David b1942 w Judith
Irene Moffet, OR, WA, anc ch
TB 6:2:32
VORCE, Frank b1885 w Eliza Mae
Hyman, IL, anc ch FF 8:2:30

WACASER, Anderson b1836 w Emma A
Ross, NC, IL, auto & fam recs
MCH 7:4:99
Paul T b1908 w Helen M Keyes,
IL, anc ch MCH 7:4:99
WADDILL, Elijah Witt bc1852 w
Mary Nan Carter, VA, FL,
geneal ANC 14:3:85
Samuel James b1880 w Frances
Elizabeth Shearer, VA, FL,
anc ch ANC 14:1:12
WADLEIGH, Mary Jane (Morey)
b1828 h Joseph Wadleigh, OH,
IL, fam letters, bk rev GH
33:5:71 REP 19:4:172
WADSWORTH, William b1595 w Sarah
Talcott, Elizabeth Stone,
Eng, MA, geneal, bk rev GH
33:1:94
WAGGONER, Christian F f1819,
Ger, NC, biog notes NCJ
5:2:144
WAHL, Christian w Anna Kliber,
Ger, IA, letter 1867 HH
14:3:121
Frederick E b1861, IN, Bible
rec KK 17:1:8
John Ernest b1859 w Anna Maria

Bosch, Ger, IA, CT, biog notes KCG 20:1:30
WAKEFIELD, Orin b1808, NY, IL, auto DWC 5:2:31
WALDRON, Charles P, NY, Civil War rec BGS 10:4:22
Chalres P m1869 w Louisa McMinn, MI, CO, Bible rec & biog notes BGS 7:1:9 8:1:16
WALDROP, Gilbert Coleman b1889 w Camilla Maree Butler, TN, TX, anc ch THT 6:3:82
WALES, geneal res guide BGS 9:3:1
geneal res guide v2,3, bk rev OG 2:3:88 2:4:118
National Lib recs, descr & use TST 12:29:47
Peter Thatcher b1777 w Lucinda Stanton, RI, NY, Bible rec CTN 11:4:592
bk rev CTN 7:3:362
WALKER, Adam L, IL, Civil War diary CI 12:2:57
Albert Ward b1853 w Olive Jane Lord, ME, anc ch OC 16:4:124
Angeline C (Mrs) d1883, KS obit MGR 14:1:11
Buckner dc1882, AL probate rec VL 13:4:172
Clyde William Richard b1888 w Laura Belle Clark, OR, anc ch FF 8:4:43
Eugene A f1877 w Mattie P, IA, ID, WA, journal of bapt, funerals YV 11:2:85 11:3:138
fam of VA, notes on AW 5:1:7 5:2:37
fam of MA, 1861 geneal, bk rev CDS 16:5:45
fam recs in KY courthouse KA 14:3:142
Horace Tracy b1869 w Cora May Lathrop, geneal, bk rev GFP 28:7:127
James b1752 w Christina Smith, Scot, Eng, anc ch THT 6:3:53
James b1812 w Elisa Ann Jones, Eng, TN, MS, Bible rec THT 2:2:20
Jesse b1766, VA, biog, bk rev CI 15:3:116
John b1792 w Nancy Owen, AL,

Bible rec VL 13:4:188
John Brown b1815, PA, biog notes TST 12:27:1
Matthew Jr m1849 w Elizabeth Halliday McKnight, OH, letters THT 6:2:37
Nathan Davis b1801 w Susannah, IN, fam cem inscr NGS 67:2:97
Richard b1784 w Drusilla, IN, fam cem inscr NGS 67:2:129
Robert b1783 w Dorcas, NC, IN, fam recs BGS 10:2:19
William m1811 w Nancy Ann Cornell, GA, marr rec OK 24:1:38
WALLACE, Edward b1837 w Barbara A Billman, Ir, OH, anc ch REP 19:3:125
John Thomas b1897 w Eleanor Madeline Ewing, PA, anc ch MD 20:4:333
Leonard b1811 w Sarah Wright, VT, geneal, bk rev GH 33:6:70
Paul Bennett b1904 w Eleanor Margaret Kirk, NB, anc ch AW 5:3:75
William, TX estate sale 1877 STK 7:1:26
William d1839 w Mary Hamilton, OH, anc ch REP 19:1:33
William Alexander Anderson, VA, biog notes OC 16:2:55
WALLER, Phebe b1856 h John Hardenbrook, IN, MI, biog notes MI 24:3:106
WALLIN, Elisha m1854 w Angalona Carson, OH, Bible rec TSP 2:3:14
WALLS, Goldsberry b1853, fam rec NA 2:2:40
WALRATH, John J b1815 w Marietta St John, Bible rec AB 7:3:57
WALTER, Thomas Ustick b1804, PA, biog notes DAR 113:5:506
WALTER-WALTERS, fam of NJ, notes on SGS 29:1:29
WALTERS, John b1814 w Penelope Woodruff, VA, KY, OH, biog notes VQ 16:1:12
Moses bc1770 w Elizabeth Cauthon, VA, TX, anc ch AGS 20:2:64
Nathaniel T bc1813 w Belinda

Barker, Bible rec REP 19:1:14

WALTHER, Henry b1852 w Emma Augusta Pratt, geneal, bk rev AGS 20:1:8

WALTON, George b1749 w Dorothy, VA, GA, biog DAR 113:9:1016

Iverson b1824 w Delphia Ann Matthews, GA, fam rec DCG 2:10:4

John m1822 w Sarah Durkee, NY, Can, VT, Bible rec SCS 14:2:33

WAKEMAN, fam of CT, geneal 1900, bk rev CTN 10:3:524

WAMEL, William Julius b1850 w Martha Elizabeth Hinyard, TX, NM, fam rec NMG 18:2:50

WARD, Elisha m1803 w Zelima Denslow, CT, Bible rec CTN 10:3:420

John b1790 w Tamer Masterson, KY, IN, anc ch REP 19:2:83

William b1797 w Mary Williams, OH, Bible rec AH 5:4:120

WARDELL, Robert Fowler b1759, NJ, VA, IN, biog notes HJA 6:1:18

WARDER, John B b1841 w Mary F Hardman, Andrea Arguello, MO, NM, fam rec NMG 18:3:82

WARDERS, William Joy b1941 w Phyllis Jean Sperry, KS, anc ch TOP 9:2:45

WARDWELL, fam of MA, geneal CTN 11:1:19

Meribah m1742 h William Eaton, ME, parentage AG 55:2:83

WARNER, Gilbert b1802 w Polly Custin, Bible rec CTN 12:2:236

Harriet Elizabeth b1851 h Lewis M Goodwill, OH, auto AH 3:1:20 3:2:65 3:3:85

WARNER, John bc1615 w Margaret, Eng, CT, geneal CTN 9:1:3

WARREN, James A, geneal, bk rev MGR 14:4:159

Peter P b1827 w Amanda P Hyland, IN, geneal MCH 7:3:74

Phineas b1718 w Grace Hastings, MA, biog notes DE 3:3:12

WARRINER, Loren bc1795 w Hester G VanNess, MA, NY, anc ch REP

19:2:88

WASHBURNE, Henry G b1813 w Anna Maria Benschoten, NY, OH, Bible rec KK 17:3:48

WASHINGTON, Adams Co, cem inscr, bk rev OC 16:3:107

Bellevue Pioneer cem inscr SGS 29:4:300

Benton Co, hist notes & museum TRI 17:1:3

Prosser, school recs 1902-1909 TRI 17:1:4 17:2:39 17:3:49 17:4:66

vr 1905-1907, bk rev TB 6:1:34

Centralia, hist 1845-1900, bk rev TB 6:4:32

Chelan Co, Malaga, schoolhouse cem inscr AB 7:3:46

marr recs 1900-1930 AB 7:3:49 7:4:65 8:1:7 8:2:27

Wenatchee City cem inscr AB 7:3:47 7:4:67 8:1:5 8:2:23

Clallam Co, Port Crescent Pioneer cem inscr SGS 29:3:210

Clark Co, Dublin cem inscr TB 6:1:12

hist, bk rev TB 6:3:22

land recs, bk rev TB 6:1:33

misc marr recs TB 6:2:24 6:4:12

personal property tax roll 1894 TB 6:1:40 6:2:35 6:3:37 6:4:40

small cem inscr TB 6:2:44

Venersborg cem inscr TB 6:1:10

Cowlitz Co, post offices & postmasters, bk rev TRI 19:1:3 GH 33:1:90

donation land claims OG 1:2:38 1:3:74 3:2:36

Douglas Co, school dist #1 1900 AB 8:1:15

early US Senators & Representatives TB 6:2:13

Edwin Bradford Peter b1906 w Lola Gussie Bates, DC, VA, anc ch PGB 11:10:108

fam anc ch to royalty, bk rev GH 33:6:90

Fern Prairie cem inscr TB 6:2:39 6:3:32

Fort Konewock, hist notes YW 11:4:195

Garfield Co, rural cem inscr & index EWA 16:1:1

geneal resources 1980, bk rev TB 6:4:29

Grand Coulee Dam area, hist, bk rev GH 33:3:102

Grays Harbor Co, hist sites, bk rev OG 5:1:28

King Co, Newcastle cem inscr SGS 29:4:293

Klackitat Co, Bickleton, hist YV 11:3:109

Bickleton, land recs YV 11:3:125

death & birth recs, bk rev TRI 17:2:32

misc pioneers YV 11:2:92

Lewis Co, news abstr v3 1890-1893, bk rev GH 33:1:90

post offices hist, bk rev GH 33:1:90

list of governors TB 6:1:6

Mason Co, Tornow fam cem inscr SGS 29:2:113

misc cem inscr, bk rev NGI 3:2:108

mort sched 1975 AB 7:3:55 7:4:73 8:1:9 8:2:31

Naselle, area cems inscr GH 33:4:116

North Cove, North Cove Pioneer cem inscr SGS 29:3:211

North Kitsap, area hist, bk rev OG 1:4:118

Okanogan Co, direct 1914-1915 AB 7:3:53 7:4:71 8:1:11 8:2:33

oral hist index 1974-1977, bk rev TB 6:4:32

Pacific Co, cem inscr, bk rev TST 12:15:31

Pend Oreille Co, cem inscr, bk rev OC 16:3:107

Pierce Co, census 1892 RES 11:3:137

death recs 1902-1907 RES 11:2:59 11:3:111 11:4:165

Piper funeral home recs 1925-1928 RES 11:1:5 11:2:49 11:3:85 11:4:150

pioneer fams index, descr YV 11:2:77

pioneer marr AB 8:1:16

postal system hist, bk rev CDS 16:2:4

St Martin´s College, hist OG 2:3:76

San Juan Co, births & deaths from news 1931 WB 10:1:37

census 1880 WB 9:3:93 9:4:131 10:1:18

Lopez Island, Lopez Union cem inscr WB 10:2:74

Seattle, news abstr 1865 SGS 29:2:124,128 29:3:208,220 29:4:292,313,318

Seattle Public Lib geneal collect SGS 29:1:5

Skagit Co, Bow cem inscr WB 9:3:85

Guemes Island, Edens cem inscr WB 9:4:163

marr lic 1884-1908 WB 10:2:47

Skamania Co, births 1893-1926, bk rev TB 6:3:26

cems inscr, bk rev TB 6:3:26

census 1860, 1870 & 1880; terr census 1885-1887; index of misc deeds & recs, bk rev TB 6:3:26

marr recs index 1854-1931, bk rev GFP 29:4:67 TB 6:3:26

Snohomish Co, hist SGS 29:3:199

WW I hist, bk rev TB 6:4:31

Snoqualmie Valley, hist, bk rev OG 1:4:118

Spokane, Westminster Cong Ch roster EWA 16:2:54

Spokane Co, hist 1900, bk rev TB 6:4:29

State Lib, geneal holdings TRI 19:1:9

Stemilt cem assn recs AB 8:1:14

terr & state censuses GJ 8:1:20

Toledo, hist & biogs, bk rev OG 3:3:88

Thurston Co, Bush Prairie/Union cem inscr OG 1:3:84 1:4:115

cem map OG 1:1:24

cednsus 1870 OG 4:2:41 4:3:71

marr lic 1878-1893 OG 5:2:42 5:3:74 5:4:103

marr rec 1853-1878 OG 1:4:98 2:1:6 2:2:36 2:3:70 2:4:100

Mima Prairie Pioneer cem inscr OG 1:1:25

Olympia, area chs direct 1975
OG 1:4:116

Olympia, census 1860 OG 1:1:15
1:2:41 1:3:76 1:4:101

Olympia, census 1870 OG
2:4:106 3:1:14 3:2:49 3:3:73

Olympia, excerpts from Gazetteer 1907-8 OG 1:1:13 1:2:36
1:3:67

Olympia, Forest Memorial Gar-
dens cem inscr OG 2:2:52
2:3:81 2:4:12 3:1:20 3:3:80

Olympia, St Michael's School
Providence Academy, 1881 pu-
pil list OG 1:4:100

Pioneer/Ruddell cem inscr OG
1:4:109 2:1:22

receipt bk 1887-1888 OG 2:1:10
2:2:39 2:3:66

Tumwater, Olympia Masonic Memorial Park cem inscr OG
4:2:46 4:3:78 4:4:110 5:1:20
5:2:47 5:3:79 5:4:109

Univ of WA Suzzallo Lib hist &
geneal biblio, bk rev SGS
29:4:329

Vancouver, hist notes 1881 AB
8:2:19

St James Parish (Our Lady of
Lourdes Ch), direct 1980, bk
rev TB 6:4:31

Wahkiakum Co, cem inscr, bk rev
TST 12:15:31

Western Pacific RR hist, bk rev
CDS 16:5:46

Whatcom Co, agricultural census
1893 WB 9:3:109 9:4:137
10:1:6

Bellingham, abstr of title WB
10:1:3

land ownership map 1912 WB
9:3:124

Lynden cem soldier burials WB
10:1:5

peddlers & liquor lic 1887-
1916 WB 9:4:153

pioneers WB 9:3:101 9:4:155
10:1:23 10:2:55

Whatcom, high school roll
1915-1917 WB 9:3:105

Whatcom, Trinity Meth Epis Ch
roll 1890-1902 WB 9:4:127

Yakima, Capitol Theatre hist YV
11:2:55

high school football players
1906 YV 11:4:165

misc res YV 11:3:143

Yakima Co, census totals 1910
YV 11:1:33

land recs YV 11:2:93 11:4:189

Outlook School recs 1894-1898
TRI 19:2:25

Outlook School recs 1904-1918
TRI 19:3:40 19:4:62

Prosser, school recs 1902-1909
TRI 17:1:4 17:2:39 17:3:49
17:4:66

vr 1869-1907, bk rev TB 6:1:34

WASSER, John f1868 w Anna Margaretha Miller, Ger, IL, geneal FF 8:4:39

WASSON, John W, TN, IL, geneal,
bk rev CI 15:4:155

WATERBURY, Epenetus b1758 w
Elizabeth Bates, CT, notes on
CTA 21:3:117

Epenetus b1762, CT, notes on
CTA 21:3:117

WATERMAN, geneal corr AG 55:1:

WATERS, fam of VA & MD, geneal,
bk rev WCK 12:2:34 AGS
20:4:145

Shelah b1768 w Nancy Turner,
MD, VA, TN, geneal, bk rev FP
22:4:210

WATKINS, John M, TX citizenship
document 1836 GR 21:2:64

WATROUS, Leland Rice b1926 w
Marta Marga Goeb, Can, anc ch
TTL 7:4:121

WATSON, Alfred b1817 w Christin-
ia Dial, OH, IL, geneal FF
8:2:40

fam of MD, notes on PGB 11:5:52

WATT, Thomas, Ir, PA, biog notes
IG 14:2:41

WATTS, Ridley b1901, geneal, bk
rev CTN 8:2:317

WEAR, Hamilton Bradford b1829 w
Nancy Ann Townsend, TN, AR,
anc ch NAS 17:4:96

WEATHERBEE, Paul b1797 w Elizabeth Smith, OH, anc ch REP
19:1:28

WEATHERLY, Job bc1761 w Mary
Polly Watter, Susanna Carson,

MD, NC, TN, Bible rec & geneal YP 9:4:196

WEAVER, Jacob J, geneal, bk rev REP 19:1:45

WEBB, Achillais b1816 w Cornelia Ann Barnett, KY, Bible rec KA 14:4:229

Laura b1852, IL cem inscr CI 15:3:110

WEBBER, fam of IN & IL, geneal, bk rev NGS 67:2:154

fam of ME & MA, geneal, bk rev NYR 110:4:250

Thomas bc1629, Eng, ME, MA, biog notes CTN 12:4:704

WEBRE, Richmond Joseph b1896 w Leslie Caro, LA, anc ch AGE 8:2:65

WEBSTER, Henrietta E d1854, MD, biog notes PGB 11:4:37

WEED, Charles m1784 w Mary Platt, NY, fam rec CTA 22:1:25

Charles A b1840, OH, biog notes AH 3:1:13

Jonas f1630 w Mary, Eng, MA, geneal, bk rev REP 19:1:40

WEEDMAN, Weedman Newsletter, 4106 N 27th St, Tacoma WA 98407

WEESETH, fam Bible PR 3:1:7

WEGENER, August F b1882 w Gertrude C Meyer, MO, anc ch BGS 11:1:41

WEGMAN, John, letter 1867 KCG 20:1:29

WEGNER, George Eugene b1912 w Clellie Mae Foreman, OK, anc ch THT 6:3:65

WEICH, Robert Henry Sr b1919 w Vivian Ann Hayes, OR, anc ch AW 5:1:23

WEIK, Jacob M b1756 w Susannah Moir, PA, NC, geneal, bk rev KCG 20:2:93

WEILAND, Berend Ubben b1856 w Francis J Holscher, Ger, NM, Bible rec CI 14:2:51

WEISEL, Levi O b1830 w Nancy Hoover, PA, OH, anc ch REP 19:1:37

WELCH, Ransom Frank w Susan Curtin, geneal, bk rev BGS 7:1:23

William C b1804 w Betsey Goodenough, NY, VT, Bible rec FG 21:1:11

WELDON, Joseph f1809 w Elizabeth Green, KY, fam rec FF 8:2:32

WELLES, Thomas bc1585 w Alice Tomes, Mrs Elizabeth (Deming) Foote, Eng, CT, geneal CTN 7:1:32

WELLING, fam of NY, geneal notes CTA 21:3:127

WELLS, Elmer Elsworth b1870 w Minnie May Coats, OR, anc ch ORB 17:5:50

Howard Clezelle w Jenny Lucille Thrasher, IL, anc ch FF 8:2:30

Ida May f1905 h Fred Kutz, Westray Johnson, NE, Bible rec NA 2:2:40

WENGER, Christian bc1698 w Eve Graybill, Switz, PA, geneal, bk rev PM 2:4:31

Martin b1749 w Amali Giurich, Bible rec TB 6:2:8

WENRICH, Maltheis f1709 w Judith, PA, geneal, bk rev REP 19:3:138

WENTWORTH, Clifford m1917 w Lucy Schroeder, IL, geneal CI 13:3:108

WERNER, Henry bc1715, Fr, PA, geneal, bk rev GH 33:6:91

WERTS, George Peter d1885 w Susannah Huff, OH, geneal, bk rev REP 19:4:177

WERTZ, Hans Jacob f1731 w Anna Barbara Hoff, Ger, PA, geneal, bk rev GH 33:1:95

WESCOTT, Roy Russell b1883 w Geneva Evageline Moolick, IA, NE, anc ch BGS 11:1:47

WEST, Alexander b1825 w Martha, WV, MO, Bible rec TB 6:4:15

fam of Eng, VA & Can, geneal, bk rev GN 2:6:174

Hiram d1858 w Sodema, Bible rec CTN 10:3:415

Joseph b1793 w Joanna Smith, NY, IN, Bible rec ACL 4:1:8

Warren b1798 w Silvia Tallman, VT, MI, Bible rec DM 43:1:12

WEST VIRGINIA, Boone Co, misc
fams rec v4, bk rev GH
33:1:90
misc fam rec v5, bk rev GH
33:4:116
geneal res guide AG 2:3:79
geneal sources 1971, bk rev REP
19:4:171
Monongalia Co, hist vl, bk rev
WPA 5:1:38 YP 9:2:104
hist v2, bk rev CLG 10:1:59
New River Co, geneal collect
descr GJ 8:4:197
Nicholas Co, fams lists, census
1820, 1830, 1840, bk rev BR
6:2:55 IL 11:4:238 GH
33:4:116 TST 12:14:39 VAG
23:3:230 NGI 3:2:108 KCG
20:1:47
Pendleton, marrs 1781-1853 &
census 1810, bk rev OK
24:3:138
Upper Monongahela Valley, hist
& geneal 1912, bk rev VAG
23:1:66 NYR 110:1:58 NGS
67:3:225 AG 55:1:61
Wyoming Co, index & gazetteer
for Bowman's hist, bk rev GH
33:3:103
WESTALL, Billy d1898, CO, biog
notes BGS 11:4:174
WESTBROOK, William Jr, VA indenture 1818 BGS 6:1:15
WESTBY, Thorwald O b1860 w
Johannille Larson, Norway,
MN, Bible rec PR 3:3:49
WESTON, Samuel b1783 w Margaret,
Eng, VA, KY, MO, biog KCG
20:4:179
WETHEE, James d1796 w Sarah Parker, NH, geneal, bk rev REP
19:1:42 CI 14:4:151
WETHERBY, fam of NY, geneal, bk
rev CTN 8:1:39
WEYMOUTH, Robert f1650, Eng, ME,
geneal LL 14:3:135
WHEATCRAFT, Samuel b1789 w
Chloey A Potter, MD, PA, OH,
anc ch REP 19:2:82
WHEATON, Jonathan b1755 w Penel-
ope Lacy, NY, OH, anc ch REP
19:3:129
WHEELER, Charles b1812 w Ruth

Ann Nichols, Bible rec OC
16:1:22
Christian b1800 w Catherine
Sibley, NY, anc ch REP
19:1:33
John b1630 w Mary, MD, geneal,
bk rev PGB 11:9:101
Martin Ward b1805 w Caroline
Kemper, Bible rec CTN
12:3:415
Stephen H b1812 w Harriet N
Williams, Bible rec LL
15:1:29
WHERRY, Edward Robinson b1869 w
Clara Valentine Roevekamp,
PA, MO, TX, anc ch THT 6:3:70
WHIPPLE, William b1730, ME, biog
notes DE 3:4:25
WHITACRE, Seth T b1874, MO obit
MCH 7:2:45
WHITAKER, LeRoy b1885 w Anna
Estella Eldred, KS, MO, anc
ch NGI 3:3:179
WHITCOMB, John b1861, IN,
geneal, bk rev IG 15:4:104 OC
16:4:135
WHITE, Amon Haward b1875 w Viola
Ovela Garner, AL, TX, anc ch
ORB 17:6:57
Elijah b1777 w Sarah Rush, PA,
OH, Bible rec LM 20:2:5
fam of Ir, PA, KY, LA, geneal,
bk rev CTN 11:1:43 CDS 16:2:4
James E m1885 w Ellen Campbell,
TX marr rec THT 1:2:3
James Early b1837 w Carrie H
Jackson, VA, MO, Civil War
diary DG 25:2:108
James Lewis b1865 w Nellie E
Reid, Bible rec IG 15:2:58
Jesse Cleveland b1832 w Avalena
Weatherford, AK, anc ch YP
9:2:68
Joseph Culbertson b1811 w Jane
Lynas, Bible rec CI 15:1:12
Linzy Cecil b1885 w Gertrude
Mattie Douglas, anc ch NGI
3:3:175
Lloyd B b1859 w Maria
Wilhelmina Schumann, Ger, WI,
NE, anc ch AW 5:4:107
Otto Fredrick b1895, anc ch FF
8:2:29

Robert Marley b1781 w Nancy Echols Banton, AL, Bible rec VL 13:4:152

Samuel f1829 w Mary Ann Ross, KY, OH, IN, anc ch HJA 6:3:49

Tabitha d1802 h John White, NY will ANC 14:1:30

The White Papers, 19 Crinkleroot Ct, The Woodlands TX 77380

Thomas Wells b1739 w Naomi, MA, VT, biog notes BGS 10:4:19

William b1837 w Martha A Myers, IL, Bible rec MCH 7:4:106

WHITECOTTON, Bert Thomas b1883 w Mabel Myrtle Powell, IL, CO, anc ch BGS 10:1:40

WHITEHEAD, Willie Hayne b1930 w Melva Ray Yates, TX, anc ch RRS 12:1:109

WHITEHURST, Richard dc1654, VA, geneal, bk rev NCJ 5:2:140

WHITEFIELD, fam of VA, biog notes, bk rev GH 33:5:92 CTN 10:3:526

Henry b1591 w Dorothy Sheaffe, Eng, CT, biog notes BGS 10:1:29

WHITFORD, Adelbert Edward b12919 w Wanda LaVonne Peterson, NJ, NE, anc ch FF 8:3:60

Maria Langworthy h Samuel Whitford, NY, diary 1857-1861, bk rev CTN 9:4:610

WHITING, Hiram S b1811 w Sarah A Holt, CT, Bible rec CTN 10:2:364

William b1776 w Elizabeth S Coates, Ann Hufflett, Bible rec SCS 15:1:22

WHITLEY, Thomas Rice b1855 w Mary Francis Holcomb, GA, fam rec DCG 2:10:12

WHITMER, fam of KY, geneal, bk rev WCK 12:2:35

Michael m1838 w Volumnia Ann Knox, PA, Bible rec MI 24:2:45

WHITNEY, Benjamin f1815 w Abigail, NY, name change pet TS 21:3:89

fam recs CPY 8:1:18

WHITON, Joseph b1776 w Betsey

Otis, CT, anc ch REP 19:3:131

WHITSON, Edmond Pendleton b1879 w Lonia Margaret Stanley, AL, TX, anc ch THT 6:3:86

WHITTEN, Charles L b1919 w Lorraine Glasgow, WY, anc ch FF 8:3:61

Reuben b1771 w Salley Sawyer, NH, cem inscr RES 11:1:4

WICK, Randall Bruce b1937 w Susan Jean Knight, WA, anc ch WB 10:1:33

WIESE A F Carl, Ger, TX, geneal, bk rev HTR 22:1:6

WIGLEY, Oliver Lawson b1899 w Eva Shows, LA, anc ch THT 6:3:75

WIKE, Jacob M b1756 w Susannah Moir, PA, NC, geneal, bk rev NCJ 5:1:65 GH 33:2:86 KCG 20:2:93

WILCOX, Calvin b1833 w Sarah Jane Randall, MN, geneal MN 10:4:153

WILCOXON, John d1716 w Magdalen, MD, geneal PGB 11:6:59

WILEY, James Brooks b1836 w Amoretta Laura Dunham, ME, IL, KS, OK, fam rec MGR 14:1:43

John Alexander Jr b1892 w Mary Mildred Schmitz, OH, TN, anc ch PGB 11:2:12

Owen W b1837 w Martha McGannon, IN, fam rec MGR 14:3:132

William Thomas b1859 w Florence Emmeretta Hickinbotham, IN, KS, biog MGR 14:3:134

WILKIN, Archibald bc1737 w Ann Duncan, Ir, PA, anc ch IRA 13:277

WILKINSON, alias, see John Herbert

Cora, 1889 KS teacher's cert TS 21:2:73

fam of AL, geneal, bk rev CDS 16:2:5

Joseph b1848 w Lucendie Findley, Martha Elizabeth (Massengill) Dodds, TN, NM, geneal NMG 18:1:28

WILKS, George Washington b1858 w Frances Ellen Fields, TX,

biog THT 5:4:20

WILLARD, Amrose b1807 w Olive Davis, Bible rec ORB 17:5:43

WILLET, Rolant E b1883 w Ina M, Bible rec MI 24:3:81

WILLETT, Benjamin Garland Winfred b1880 w Lena Cherry Pendergrass, OK, TX, anc ch KG 16:2:42 RRS 12:1:112

WILLIAMS, Albred Evans b1873 w Fannie Mae Sprouse, IL, anc ch FF 8:3:59

Almon m1837 w Harriet Maria Hurlbut, NY, OH, Bible rec AH 1:2:15

Edmond b1799 w Ann Ellis, TN, Bible rec BWG 8:1:37

Eleazer f1712, MA, CT, geneal, bk rev CTN 7:4:517

Ennion b1752, PA, letter 1811 BGS 3:3:3

fam of KY & IL, notes on CI 13:4:146

fam of MO, notes on SMV 11:1:6

Jacob L b1897 w Opal Stephenson, IA, anc ch THT 6:3:59

Paschal K b1819 w Joanna Garvin, Bible rec THT 6:3:98

Robert Moore b1907 w Margaret Porter Jelley, MO, PA, AZ, anc ch RRS 12:2:211

Samuel b1831, NY, PA, KY, auto & fam recs, bk rev NYR 110:3:186

Samuel W H b1838 w Edna Victoria Miller, TN, fam rec BWG 8:1:36

William b1731 w Mary Trumbull, CT, CT bicentennial series XII, bk rev CTN 9:1:128

Zophar b1810 w Cynthia Pumphrey, NJ, OH, anc ch REP 19:4:161

WILLIAMSON, Micajah f1776, fam rec THT 7:2:101

Paul Bernard b1891 w Edna Marie Talley, TX, anc ch GR 21:4:136

WILLIS, Pierson d1872, KY funeral notice KA 14:3:168

WILLSON, John b1810 w Jane Elizabeth Weir, Mary Jane Snider, VA, TX, Bible rec &

geneal DG 25:3:165

WILMOT, Lucius T b1824 w Nancy Taylor, OH, Bible rec AH 1:3:17

WILLOUGHBY, Thomas b1601, Eng, Barbados, VA, geneal, bk rev VAG 23:1:142

WILPER, Margaret b1838 h Joseph Juenemann, Bernard Wilper, Ger, WI, IA, MN, obit MGR 14:2:91

WILSHUSEN, Carl Emil b1902 w Ruth Patterson, Eng, CO, anc ch BGS 10:1:39

WILSON, Alexander Dromgoole b1817 w Rebecca McNair Riley, OK, Bible rec TA 14:1:1

fam of MD, geneal, bk rev AGS 20:4:145

Frederick DePeyster f1885 w Mary Eleanor Wodruff, IL, SD, biog notes BGS 8:3:8

Henry Bannon b1824 w Mary Elizabeth (Godbey) Cowan, Bible rec THT 6:3:96

Henry Bannon b1861 w Dinella Adelaide Sandlin, AL, TX, anc ch THT 7:2:68

Homer B b1881 w Irma Bernice Miller, OH, KS, anc ch TOP 9:1:12

James b1810, VA, OH, diary extracts 1834-1837 REP 19:1:4

James VanBuren b1865 w Rachel Elmanzie Walker, AL, anc ch NAS 18:1:2

Josepah m1850 w Catherine Potter, OH, Bible rec CTN 12:2:236

Stephen b1765 w Hannah Pope, Bible rec PR 3:4:70

Thomas b1825 w Margaret A Dodson, IL, TN, OR, biog notes GFP 29:4:72

Thomas Neil b1876 w Sallie Durah Hipp, TX, biog THT 4:2:1

William Robert Lee b1862 w Allie F Robinson, TN, Bible rec GR 21:4:156

Wilson Warehouse, 19 Crinkleroot Ct, The Woodlands TX 77380

WILT, Theophilus m1856 w Eliza-
beth Miller, MD, anc ch REP
19:1:27
WIMSEY, fam of Eng, bk rev AG
55:2:127
WINCHELL, fam geneal, bk rev CDS
16:4:10
WINCHESTER, Jonathan, CSA
receipt & oath of amnesty
1865 VL 13:3:107
WINEY, Jacob bc1768, PA, biog
notes PM 2:2:5
WINGFIELD, John fc1330 w Anne
Peche, Eng, Geneal EG 12:284
WININGS, John b1728 w Elizabeth
Grider, PA, IN, geneal MCH
7:1:10
WINNEY, John b1838 w Matilda
Britton Watters, MI, AL, TX,
geneal THT 5:3:16
WINSTON, William m1860 w Ellen D
Moore, KY, Bible rec BR
6:2:61
WISCONSIN, archives guide descr
TST 11:41:29
Barron Co, map WI 25:3
marr, births, deaths 1876-1879
WI 25:3:129
mort sched 1870 WI 25:3:129
Bayfield Co, Butternut Colony
1877 WI 26:1:13
deaths WI 26:1:13
jurors 1879 WI 26:1:14
marrs WI 26:1:14
misc recs WI 26:1:14
school honor rolls 1878 WI
26:1:13
biblio of Quaker recs in WI
lib, bk rev GH 33:5:80
Brown Co, natural papers index
WI 25:3:37 25:4:185 26:2:75
Buffalo Co, Nelson Lipter Luth
Churchyard cem inscr WI
25:3:133 25:4:187
Calumet Co, Brillion Bluffs
cem inscr WI 25:4:189 26:1:15
misc recs WI 26:1:16
Rantoul Twp, Rantoul E U B cem
inscr WI 26:1:15
Dane Co, Albion Twp, fam heads
census 1847 WI 26:2:78
Albion Twp, Primitive Meth Ch
cem inscr WI 25:4:191 26:1:17

26:2:77
Madison, hist (1877), bk rev
CI 15:4:155
McFarland cem inscr WI
25:3:135
probate court 1882 WI 26:2:78
Dodge Co, Horicon direct 1858
WI 25:3:137 25:4:193
Hubbard, St Michael's/Hubbard
cem inscr WI 26:2:79
marrs & deaths WI 25:4:194
Door Co, Carnot, Forest Luth
cem inscr WI 25:4:195 26:1:19
26:2:81
homestead entries abstr WI
26:2:81
Eau Claire Co, marrs WI
25:3:139
Fond du Lac Co, Calumet, Roth-
mann cem inscr WI 26:2:83
Eden, Eden Central/Baumhardt-
Odekirk cem inscr WI 26:1:21
26:2:83
Eden, Rohlf cem inscr WI
26:1:22 26:2:83
Forest, Union/Twohig cem inscr
WI 26:1:22 26:2:83
Friendship, Lakeview cem inscr
WI 25:4:198 26:1:21
Marshfield, St Joseph cem inscr WI 25:3:141 25:4:197
Metomen, Round Prairie cem inscr WI 25:4:53
Forest Co, births, deaths &
marrs WI 25:4:200
Crandon Twp, Gibson fam cem
inscr WI 25:4:199
Wabeno Twp, Lakeview cem inscr
WI 25:4:199
geneal res guide GH 33:2:7
geneal res guide to hist soc
resources, bk rev GH 33:6:85
Grant Co, Bloomington high
school alumni direct WI
25:3:143 25:4:39 26:1:23
farm & ranch direct 1966 WI
26:1:24
Green Co, Exeter, East Dayton
cem inscr WI 26:2:86
Exeter, West Dayton cem inscr
WI 26:2:85
guide to geneal res in WI libs,
bk rev GH 33:3:103 NGI

3:3:169

hist soc as geneal resource, bk rev NGI 3:4:208

Hudson, hist 1932, bk rev GH 33:5:81

index to pioneer fams, bk rev TST 12:29:49 OG 4:3:88

Iowa Co, Bryn Zion cem inscr WI 25:4:203

Dover cem inscr WI 17:3:107 25:4:204

Mifflin Twp, Penniel cem inscr WI 26:2:87

natives who went to CA 1849-1852 WI 25:4:204

Iron Co, marrs, deaths & legal notices WI 26:2:89

Jackson Co, marrs WI 26:1:25

Millston Twp, St Andrew's Cath cem inscr WI 26:1:25

Jeffersoan Co, Aztalan Twp, Aztalan-Milford cem inscr WI 25:4:205 26:1:27 26:2:91

Lake Mills Twp, St John's Luth Ch cem ainscr WI 26:2:91

Kewaunu Co, death notices WI 25:3:145

Forest View cem inscr WI 25:3:146

Wiesner cem inscr WI 25:3:145

LaCrosse Co, Shelby, Old Settler's Mormon Coulee cem inscr WI 26:1:29

Lafayette Co, Argyle, Old Argyle cem inscr WI 26:1:32 26:2:93

marrs WI 25:3:147 25:4:207 26:1:31

Shullsburg, St Matthew's cem inscr WI 25:3:147

Langlade Co, Neva Twp, Star Neva Town cem inscr WI 26:2:95

Rolling Twp, Hall Pioneer cem inscr WI 26:2:96

Lee Co, pet 1838 KN 2:4:20

Manitowoc Co, Manitowoc, Evergreen public cem inscr WI 25:3:149 25:4:209 26:1:33 26:2:97

map WI 26:2

Marathon Co, Eau Pleine, Emmanuel Luth Ch cem inscr WI

26:2:99

Frankfort, Peace Luth Ch cem inscr WI 26:1:36

Johnson cem inscr WI 26:2:100

marrs WI 26:2:100

Wien, St John's Luth Ch cem inscr WI 26:1:35

Marinette Co, Pound, Old Pound cem inscr MCR 10:2:45

Marquette Co, Crystal Lake Twp, Matz-Tagatz cem inscr WI 26:2:102

Newton Twp, Krentz cem inscr WI 26:2:102

Westfield Twp, Oak Hill cem inscr WI 26:1:37 26:2:101

Milwaukee, Epis Ch hist MCR 10:6:134

Hanover St Cong Ch hist MCR 10:3:67

hist notes 1895 MCR 10:3:71

index to "Milwaukee Sentinel" news 1837-1841 MCR 10:1:3 10:2:31 10:3:56 10:4:84 10:6:126

indigent servicemen & dependents 1900 MCR 10:4:110

Spring St Cong Ch hist MCR 10:2:41

Welsh Cong Ch hist MCR 10:4:92

Milwaukee Co, geneal soc surname index 1978, bk rev NGI 3:1:32

Monroe Co, marrs & deaths WI 25:3:151

Wellington Twp, Day cem inscr WI 25:3:151

Outagamie Co, Grand Chute cem inscr WI 26:1:39

marrs WI 26:1:39

Ozaukee Co, mort shced 1860 WI 26:1:42

Woodworth fam cem hist & inscr WI 26:1:41

persons to whom bounty paid on wild animals 1881-1882 MCR 10:1:26 10:2:34 10:3:70 10:4:93 10:6:135

Pierce Co, imm & natural papers index WI 26:1:43 26:2:103

Portage Co, census index project PN 1:2:23

Post Offices 1821-1917 WI

25:3:125 25:4:183 26:1:11
26:2:69
Racine Co, Heg Memorial Park
hist (1940), bk rev NGI
3:3:168
Rock Co, Janeville, deaths 1878
WI 25:3:153
Lima Center cem inscr WI
26:2:106
Magnolia Twp, East Magnolia
cem inscr WI 26:1:45 26:2:105
Magnolia Twp, West Magnolia
cem inscr WI 25:4:211 26:1:45
Porter Twp, St Michael cem inscr WI 25:3:154 25:4:211
Rusk Co, Atlanta Twp, Nathaniel
Luth Ch, Blue Hills cem inscr
WI 25:4:214
Atlanta Twp, Nathaniel Luth
Ch, Maple Valley cem inscr WI
25:4:214
deaths & births WI 26:2:108
Island Lake cem inscr WI
25:3:155 25:4:213
list of officers of co cems WI
26:2:107
map WI 25:4
marrs WI 25:4:213
Mud Lake Indian cem inscr WI
26:2:107
Wilson Twp, Holy Hill cem in-
scr WI 26:2:107
St Croix Co, Hudson, hist 1932,
bk rev TST 12:15:31
misc recs WI 26:2:110
mort shced 1850 WI 26:2:110
Somerset Twp, census 1870 WI
26:1:47 26:2:109
Sauk Co, Ironton Twp, plat map
index 1893 WI 26:1:49
Lower/Webster Prairie/Dell
Prairie cem inscr WI 25:3:157
marrs WI 25:3:158
Woodland Twp, Friendswood
(Quaker) cem inscr WI 26:1:50
Woodland Twp, Oaks cem inscr
WI 25:4:215 26:1:49
Sawyer Co, marrs WI 25:3:159
Shawano Co, Almon Twp, St
Paulus German Evan Luth Ch
cem inscr WI 26:1:52
Wittenberg Twp, Native Am Ch
cem inscr WI 26:1:51

Sheboygan Co, misc marr lic WI
25:3:162
Wilson, Fladers Rest cem inscr
WI 25:3:161
Van Buren Co, pet 1838 KN
2:4:20
Vernon Co, Genoa, res born in
Switz from 1850 census WI
25:4:217
marrs WI 25:4:217
vr res guide TST 11:51:37
vr use restrictions SGS 29:1:52
Walworth Co, Darien cem inscr
WI 25:3:163
deaths WI 25:3:163
Heart Prairie, Norwegian Evan
Luth cem plot & cem inscr WI
25:3:164 25:4:219
Washburn Co, Springbrook, Earl
cem inscr WI 26:1:53 26:2:111
Waupaca Co, hist 1890, bk rev
TB 6:2:21
Little Wolf Twp, Poor Farm cem
inscr WI 25:3:166
Scandinavia Luth cem inscr WI
25:3:165
Waupun, state prison expenses
1852 MCR 10:4:102 10:6:128
state prison inmates 1860-1863
MCR 10:6:130
Winnebago Co, Oshkosh, school
program 1898 WI 25:4:221
26:1:55 26:2:113
Wood Co, Hansen, Vesper, St
James Cath Ch cem inscr WI
26:1:57
Hansen, Vesper, Trinity Luth
cem inscr WI 26:1:58
map WI 26:1
marrs bk 1 1867-1888 WI
26:2:115
WITHERELL, fam of N E, geneal,
bk rev CTN 10:2:351
WITHINGTON, Robert b1807, NH,
IA, geneal, bk rev HH
14:2:104
WOLCOTT, fam of CT, geneal CTN
11:1:3
Walter b1791 w Abigail Cornwell, Bible rec CTN 10:3:419
WOLF, Gottlieb August b1819 w
Johana Louise Heinze, fam rec
AGS 20:3:78,79

WOLFE, William Oliver b1851 w
Hattie Watson, Cynthia Hill,
Julia Elizabeth Westall, PA,
biog, bk rev GH 33:1:95
WOMACK, Carl Abbott b1894 w Ila
Nelson, OK, TX, anc ch THT
6:3:69
Green b1788 w Polly, Agnes
(Galleon) Cunningham, fam rec
SGS 29:4:314
WOOD, Warren K b1887 w Maude
Lanyon, IL, KS, anc ch TOP
9:3:77
WOODARD, Charles Anges b1847 w
Elizabeth Hughes, IL, Bible
rec GL 13:2:42
James B b1793, biog notes NCJ
5:1:23
WOODS, Edward Melven b1874 w
Lottie Louise Jeffrey, MA,
biog notes & anc ch AW 5:2:54
5:4:109
WOODSON, Charles D d1890, AL,
GA, obit VL 13:3:102
WOODWARD, James d1836 w Jane
Hyden, VA, fam rec DWC
5:2:59,60
WOODWORTH, Ralph Newkirk b1877 w
Edna I Howell, Gertrude A
Muhl, IL, Bible rec GL
13:2:41
WOODY, Albert Parish b1893 w
Phoebe A Noel, IL, Bible rec
CI 15:2:16
WOOLISCROFT, William Bentley
f1930, auto & geneal KN
2:1:30
WOOLSTON, William m1839 w Hannah
Tanner, Eng, NY, OH, MI,
Bible rec TTL 7:4:123
WOODWARD, Amanda M m1850 h
Orimal H Drake, Bible rec CTA
22:1:27
WOOSTER, William b1757 w Hannah
Bragdon, ME, fam rec DE
3:1:16
WORDEN, Samuel M b1794 w Cather-
ine Southard, NY, Bible rec
CTN 11:3:404
WOTRING, fam of PA, geneal, bk
rev TS 21:1:28
WRIGHT, Caleb b1760 w Deborah H
Morgan, MD, geneal, bk rev

PGB 11:1:4 MD 20:4:362
Cecil Myron b1909 w Vivian Dail
Hamilton, MI, anc ch OC
16:1:31
Elizur b1762 w Rhoda Hanover,
Clarissa Richards, CT, OH,
biog notes CTB 44:4:117
fam geneal, bk rev YP 9:3:164
fam of VA, geneal, bk rev VAG
23:2:143
Milton b1828 w Catharine Koer-
ner, IN, OH, misc letters THT
2:1:11
Moses b1767 w Ann Gurnsey, fam
rec AH 3:3:76
Russell B f1873 w Martha Ellen
Watson, IL, fam rec FF 8:2:42
Solomon b1779 w Hepzibah Russ-
ell, fam rec AH 2:2:48
William Victor b1892 w Mary
Grace Martindale, KS, MO, anc
ch BGS 10:2:39
WULLENJOHN, Christopher b1857 w
Anna Maria Hansville, Ger,
AR, geneal, bk rev GH
33:3:106 KCG 20:2:88
WYATT, Peyton S, TX headright
cert 1838 VL 14:1:32
WYNNE, Martha bc1745 h Henry
Dixon Jr, VA, geneal, bk rev
YP 9:2:105
WYOMING, Masons 1874-1924 KN
2:3:28
Platte Co,, Iowa Flats Meth
Epis Ch hist, bk rev HH
14:3:162
WYSS, Samuel, geneal, bk rev LL
15:3:142
WYTHE, Nicholas bc1600 w Margar-
et Clark, Rebecca (Parks)
Andrews, Eng, MA, geneal FG
21:1:3

YARBROUGH, James b1785 w Eliza-
beth P Harris, SC, GA, Bible
rec NAS 18:1:14
John C b1837 w Elizabeth
(Pyatt) Pitchford, Bible rec
GFP 28:9:168
YATES, Bartholomew b1676 w Sarah
Staniard, VA, anc ch CLG
10:1:54

Kipling Edward b1899 w Velma
Juanita Adams, TX, anc ch THT
7:2:73
YOE, Justinian f1614, VA bapt
rec of child DG 25:1:23
YORK, Elisha Lee b1893 w Martha
Jane McConnell, MS, PA, anc
ch ANC 14:3:87
YOUEL, William b1734 w Elizabeth
Nelson, Scot, VA, biog, bk
rev GH 33:2:87
YOUND, Bennet H, CSA, Civil War
memoirs, bk rev CDS 16:6:41
YOUNG, Augusta d1867 h Anton
Young, WA, obit TB 6:2:9
David b1804 w Susannah Beery,
OH, anc ch REP 19:2:85
Henry b1872 w Mary Ellen Rich-
ardson, MO, IL, CO, anc ch
BGS 9:4:49
Mary Elizabeth (Vincent) b1824,
VA, MO, MN, Bible rec ORB
17:9:79
YUGOSLAVIA, geneal res guide GH
33:6:9

1860 ANC 14:1:18
ZIRKLE, Ludwig f1725, Ger, PA,
VA, geneal, bk rev GH 33:1:95
YP 9:1:39
ZIRKLE, Luther f1725, Ger, Am,
geneal, bk rev TS 21:1:26
ZOOK, David, PA, geneal, bk rev
PM 2:4:29
ZUG, Moritz bc1718 w Maria,
Switz, PA, geneal, bk rev GH
33:3:108 TST 12:6:46 PM 2:1:2
KCG 20:2:89
ZUMWALD, Balthasar d1800 w Maria
Clara Linn, PA, geneal, bk
rev GH 33:5:92
ZUMWALT, Donald William b1897 w
Violet Mary Hufft, CA, anc ch
RED 12:2:7

ZACHRY, Jesse b1789 w Elizabeth
L Cooper, Bible rec GR
21:4:149
ZAHL, fam of Poland & Am,
geneal, bk rev NGS 67:2:153
ZEIGLER, fam of IL, notes on FF
8:2:52
George bc1845 w Barbara Wasser,
IL, fam rec FF 8:4:42
ZELLER, Charles Frederick b1894
w Inez Irene Hoevet, NE, MO,
anc ch NW 2:2:58
ZEMAN, Joseph d1906 w Cornelia
Johnson, ME, Bible rec DE
2:5:7
ZERANGUE, Michael f1720 w Ursula
Spaet, Barbara (Haertel) Al-
bert Bailiff, Ger, LA, ge-
neal, bk rev GH 33:5:92
ZIEGLER, Abraham, PA, geneal, bk
rev WPA 5:3:118 GJ 8:1:55
Jacob Sr b1740 w Mrs Judith
Saurer, PA, OH, biog notes IG
14:2:41
ZIMMERMAN, Charles Frazier b1825
w Susan Bard Johnston, diary